UNSPOKEN WORLDS

Other Titles of Related Interest in Religious Studies

Biblical Studies

David Barr, *New Testament Story*
Edwin D. Freed, *The New Testament: A Critical Introduction*
Benton White, *From Adam to Armageddon: A Survey of the Bible*
Denise and John Carmody, *Jesus: An Introduction*

Ethics

Ethal Albert et al., *Great Traditions in Ethics*, 5th Edition
Robert Kruschwitz / Robert Roberts, *The Virtues: Contemporary Essays on Moral Character*
Richard Purtill, *Moral Dilemmas: Readings in Ethics and Social Philosophy*
James Sterba, *Ethics of War and Nuclear Deterrence*
Marilyn Pearsall, *Women and Values: Readings in Recent Feminist Philosophy*
Donald VanDeVeer / Christine Pierce, *People, Penquins, and Plastic Trees: Basic Issues in Environmental Ethics*
Christine Pierce / Donald VanDeVeer, *AIDS: Ethics and Public Policy*
Denise and John Carmody, *How to Live Well: Ethics in the World Religions*
David Chidester, *Patterns of Action: Religion and Ethics in a Comparative Perspective*

Selected Titles in the World Religious Traditions

Catherine Albanese, *America: Religions and Religion*
Kenneth Cragg / Marston Speight, *House of Islam*, 3d Edition
Byron Earhart, *Japanese Religion*, 3d Edition
Sam Gill, *Native American Religions*
Thomas Hopkins, *The Hindu Religious Tradition*
Noel King, *African Cosmos*
Jacob Neusner, *The Way of Torah*, 4th Edition
Stephen Reynolds, *The Christian Religious Tradition*
Laurence Thompson, *Chinese Religion*, 4th Edition
Mary Jo Weaver, *Introduction to Christianity*
Denise and John Carmody, *Christianity: An Introduction*, 2d Edition
Denise and John Carmody, *Ways to the Center: An Introduction to World Religions*, 3d Edition

Introduction to Religion

Roger Schmidt, *Exploring Religion*, 2d Edition
Frederick Streng, *Understanding Religious Life*, 3d Edition

UNSPOKEN WORLDS

Women's Religious Lives

NANCY AUER FALK
Western Michigan University

RITA M. GROSS
University of Wisconsin—Eau Claire

WADSWORTH PUBLISHING COMPANY
Belmont, California
A Division of Wadsworth, Inc.

Religion Editor: Sheryl Fullerton

Editorial Assistant: Marla Nowick

Production Editor: Harold Humphrey

Managing Designer: Carolyn Deacy

Print Buyer: Karen Hunt

Compositor: DEKR Corporation

Interior & Cover Designer: Christy Butterfield

Signing Representative: Cathy Twiss

Cover: The illustration is a *triquetra*, an ancient religious symbol of the female trinity, regarded as protective. As here, the design was sometimes further interlaced with a surrounding circle. Despite its basic female shapes, the symbol was exploited by Christian mystics as a sign of the male trinity. (Information from Barbara G. Walker, *Women's Dictionary of Symbols and Sacred Objects*, Harper & Row, 1989; and Clarence P. Hornung, *Hornung's Handbook of Designs and Devises*, Dover, 1959.)

Printed in the United States of America   49

1 2 3 4 5 6 7 8 9 10——93 92 91 90 89

Library of Congress Cataloging-in-Publication Data
Unspoken worlds : women's religious lives / Nancy Auer Falk, Rita M. Gross.
    p.   cm.
  Bibliography: p.
  ISBN 0-534-09852-5
  1. Women—Religious life.   I. Falk, Nancy Auer.   II. Gross, Rita M.
BL458.U57 1989   88-14394
291′.088042—dc19   CIP

In memory of our teacher, Mircea Eliade, and in gratitude also to Joseph M. Kitagawa and Charles H. Long. They may not have always agreed with what we said, but they gave us the training and, at crucial times, the latitude to say it.

Contents

Acknowledgments

S everal sources of support were crucial to the appearance of this book. First of all, we must thank each other for encouragement and critical thinking. Each of us spent hundreds of hours editing and checking the other's work. The final product is a blend of the thinking and literary style of each of us, now so closely woven that they cannot be disentangled. Next, we want to acknowledge our contributors, who submitted so many diverse and interesting articles and displayed extreme patience with the long gestation period this book went through, as well as with our rather extensive editorial work on their manuscripts. Our respective institutions supported us well in various ways. We are especially grateful to our patient secretaries: Elizabeth Searing and Delores Condic, who did much typing for the first edition, and Gwen West, who entered volume after volume to our computerized bibliography for the second. Nancy Falk's former graduate assistant, Juleen Eichinger Samuels, mined Western Michigan University's library to assemble the first phase of our bibliography; Nancy's colleagues Byron Earhart and David Ede, and Mary Schneider of Michigan State University, furnished many valued subsequent entries. Byron Earhart also very generously furnished lists of "Further Readings" for our chapters by Youngsook Kim Harvey and Kyoko Motomochi Nakamura, as well as much prized early commentary and advice; Mary Hegland helped us with an early version of Erika Friedl's list. We cannot praise any of these friends enough. Our thanks, too, to the reviewers of this edition, who provided helpful advice and criticism: Alan Anderson, Western Kentucky University; Linell Cady, Arizona State University; Christine Downing, San Diego State University; Mary Jo Meadow, Mankato State University; and Marla Selvidge, Converse College. Last but not least, we must thank our households, who lived with us while we lived with our book.

A User's Preface: Editors' Guidelines

A lthough this book is written by many authors, it is not an anthology. It has been painstakingly forged into a coherent whole, which evolves from simple vivid portraits of individual women to analyses of complex systems. It contains a single, unified discussion of the manifold possibilities of women's religious lives in the world's varied religious traditions. This book is best read from beginning to end, rather than randomly. Furthermore, the various introductions—both to the book as a whole and to its various sections—are integral parts of the text, essential to full understanding of the book's contents.

Our approach is conscious and deliberate: we illustrate cross-cultural patterns in women's religious lives. Because no single person as yet has enough expertise to document such patterns through individual research, we have assembled a kind of collage, drawing on the fieldwork or historical research of numerous scholars. Our desire to keep our materials vivid and sharply focused—to draw readers into women's worlds—has led us to prefer case studies as our medium of illustration. Our desire to illumine patterns that cross cultural and religious boundaries—to stress commonalities in women's experiences rather than differences—has also led us to reject several simpler methods of organizing our materials. We have chosen not to cluster materials by tradition, or region, or historical period, because such an approach would blur and scatter patterns, rather than drawing them out and emphasizing them. However, the teacher who prefers to work with such more conventional groupings can readily do so while using this book. We have identified the time, tradition, and place of each study in each of our chapter titles in order to facilitate such regroupings. Teachers who prefer to use this book in this way may wish to use it as "reader" for one of the more general, survey-style texts now on the market, such as Arvind Sharma's *Women in World Religions* (SUNY Press, 1987).

Our own classifications and the patterns that we seek to illumine are discussed in detail in the introduction to our first edition, which is reprinted on the following pages. Introductions to the book's several sections further specify these patterns and point out each separate chapter's relationship to them. Also important to the organization of the book is the increasing complexity of each pattern, as well as the increasing complexity of each section's level of analysis. The book begins with simple but arresting portraits of strong women who have served as religious leaders. It then documents two very basic patterns: the often-explosive transformations of women who move into such extraordinary roles, and the household and family-based concerns of women who combine religious practice with more "ordinary" lives. The book's last three sections explore more complex patterns as women's concerns and movements are set into a variety of religious and cultural contexts. To understand these latter chapters, it is helpful first to understand the more basic patterns discussed earlier in the book; therefore, if teachers rearrange our readings into a "world religions" or historical format, they should first read the book through from beginning to end themselves so that they can fill in this basic understanding for their students.

No teacher or student could possibly have enough background to cover all the cultures and historical epochs cited in this book. We have therefore taken several steps to aid those who use our book, whether as students or as teachers. Most importantly, the book is designed to be self-sufficient; that is, each chapter contains enough information about its setting to make it understandable without forcing the reader to seek information outside of the volume. Realizing that many of our readers will be students with little previous knowledge of our authors' various fields of study, we have also minimized the use of technical jargon. We have further eliminated most foreign terms, keeping only the original names of very central practices and concepts. Each foreign term is used in simplified form; it is also defined and explained at the time of its first occurrence in the text. If readers wish to explore further, we offer two options. For this new edition, each of our writers has listed additional readings that aid further exploration of the topic discussed. Editors Falk and Gross have also compiled a much longer bibliography of books and articles covering additional aspects of women's religious lives. Many of these have appeared since the original publication of *Unspoken Worlds*; we hope that some, at least, drew part of their inspiration and challenge from its appearance.

Introduction to the First Edition: Patterns in Women's Religious Lives

As graduate students in the same program (not at the same time) in the cross-cultural, comparative study of religion, we were taught that we were seeking to understand *homo religiosus*, "religious man." Intended as a parallel to "political man," "economic man," and so on, the phrase "religious man" asserted that religion is as basic and spontaneous a form of human expression as working in communities, pursuing wealth, or any of the other aspects of human activity that had been accorded the distinction of their own academic disciplines. We were preparing for a life work that would be studying "religious man's" various and fascinating practices and statements and that would be trying to capture the patterns of human experience and intent that had given rise to them.

We were supposed to infer (the issue was never directly discussed) that, of course, "religious man" was used generically to include all humans. In practice, however (although the realization came to us slowly), it was clear that our discipline focused quite literally on religious *man*—that is, on the males of the religious community. In our field whole volumes and courses were devoted to minute analyses of men's interpretations and practices; when women entered the descriptions at all, they entered them peripherally, as bearers of children or as singers on the sidelines. Rita, while still a graduate student, became extremely unhappy with the prospect of spending her life studying essentially the religious male. While working at the doctoral level during the late sixties, she began to call for a study of "religious woman" as well as religious man and to suggest that the failure to take into account women's religious expressions indicated a serious flaw in our discipline's approach.

This volume is, in large part, an outgrowth of that insight and that call. Despite an initial and, to some extent, continuing resistance, Rita's critique has proved accurate time and again in every facet of religious studies. More specifically, the book grows out of conversations between the two of us that started at professional meetings some years later, when we had developed some expertise in the roles of women in particular religious traditions and we both were trying to teach courses that compared women's roles in various religious traditions of the world. The lack of adequate sources made such courses a frustrating enterprise; there were no books surveying women's religious roles cross-culturally and precious few detailed studies of any aspect of women's religious lives in any culture. So we asked ourselves, "Why not search for people who are also trying to understand religious woman and pool our findings to create a volume that our students and theirs can use?"

Assembling such a book involved three tasks. The first, carried out largely outside this volume and prerequisite to it, essentially involved fleshing out the critique of our field by trying to discover just why our discipline had left us such a skewed and incomplete picture of women's religious lives and roles. More conservative scholars in religion tend to say that the discipline's inattention to women is an inevitable consequence of women's lesser degree of involvement—especially as priests or theologians—in the world's religions. In other words, they seem to be claiming that religion actually *is* a predominantly male enterprise and that the neglect of women only reflects the fact that women are genuinely less important. There are two problems with this argument. In the first place, women have always been conspicuous in some arenas of religious life, such as the shamanic practices described in several places in this volume, in domestic rituals such as the ones that we have grouped in Part III, and in many varieties of "new" religious movements. Yet, even in the arenas in which women are conspicuous, their activities still receive scant attention. In the second place, although many religious systems are quite male-dominated, very few have had only male membership. Thus women inevitably have some kind of religious lives, even if these consist only in responding to male-defined ideals and expectations (see Part IV). If we are making a genuine effort to recall the whole human experience in religion, it stands to reason that women's experiences must still be a significant part of the picture.

The attempt to justify our discipline's neglect of women's experience and practice on the basis of women's lesser prominence in religion is, however, largely a hasty rationalization. Most scholars who would make such an argument have spent little time in trying to determine whether or not women's roles are actually significant. The source of distortion is far more subtle, and is found in the habitual assumptions of scholarship itself. These are more readily traced through a second excuse that is commonly offered for our discipline's scant attention to women. As some of Rita's own mentors told her when she first voiced her critique, the generic masculine is said to "cover" and "include" the feminine; that is to say, when we have understood religious man, we will *de facto* understand religious woman as well. Thus the charge that our discipline ignores women is called irrelevant and the challenge to study women separately is said to be superfluous. This argument is made despite the fact that there are few, if any, religious systems in which men's and women's religious lives are indistinguishable. What such assertions in fact reveal is that, like practically every other discipline focusing on "human studies," the study of religions has unconsciously operated with an "androcentric," or male-centered, model of humanity. That is to say, it has assumed that central and significant humans are male and has investigated the world from the male point of view. When such a perspective is taken, women, like any other segment of religious life, will be seen only as they appear to men. All too often this has meant that we don't really see women as human beings at all, but as objects, symbols, appendages to someone else's enterprise, as problematic others to be assigned a neat "place."

Clearly our volume had to find a very different kind of vision. It could not be a book about how religions view women. Too many times in our experience people had written about various religions' views of women without the slightest awareness that they had failed to tell us anything about women as human beings. We were not told about the texture of their lives, and we had no way of knowing for sure whether the views portrayed corresponded in any way to women's self-concepts. Since most religions' views of women have been recorded and shaped by men, the study of these views all too easily becomes an extension of andro-centrism.

To offer a new vision, our volume had to take up women's lives; it had to place women in center stage—as men had been placed so often in the past—and meet them as subjects, not objects, with their own experiences and aspirations. We had to create an understanding of women's own enterprises, whether the world around them defined these as "in" or "out," respectable or shocking. We had to show that women have their own perspectives and claims on religion, even in systems in which men have traditionally done most of the acting and talking. If our authors did discuss men's ideas about women, they needed to show how such ideas actually affected women's efforts and religious options. Most impor-tantly, our readers needed to come to see women of other traditions as real human beings, who know pain and release, frustration and fulfillment, just as other humans do. In short, like our teachers and many respected colleagues, we pro-posed to help our readers discover new and meaningful religious worlds. But we would explore the so-far unspoken religious worlds of women rather than the much more familiar religious worlds of men.

Once we had a clear idea of what kind of book we wanted to achieve, we could begin our second task, that of "recovering the data" that would let religious woman appear. The study of religion has so persistently ignored women that we were overwhelmed by the task's enormity. What kinds of examples should we search for and how? First, we opted for an anthology, because at this point in the study of religious woman no two people have enough expertise to recover the variety of activities and cultural and religious contexts that we hoped to bring together. Second, we chose to search for case studies rather than survey articles, because case studies would allow the closer view of the human experience that we hoped to capture. We wanted new rather than old materials; since resources of any kind on women's religious lives are still hard enough to find, it seemed inappropriate to duplicate what was already available. Following much the same reasoning, we limited our scope to those traditions customarily defined as "non-Western," because excellent studies have appeared elsewhere on women in Judaism and Christianity. Within this boundary, we tried to provide at least one sample from every major non-Western religious tradition and/or cultural region of the world.

As we began our search for contributors, we swiftly learned that our fellow historians of religion could not command materials on women's religious lives in enough different areas of specialization to give us a volume with the range that we had hoped to achieve. So we turned to cultural anthropologists and area specialists who had gathered such materials through their own field research. Inevitably this meant that a large part of our volume would focus on contemporary forms. But, since we thought it important to show that religious woman has a history, we included four studies on women of the more distant past.

Originally we had intended simply to reveal the rich variety of women's religious lives. Here we succeeded beyond our best hopes. The papers that came to us showed women in their own religious arenas and in the religious worlds of men. We met young women and old, urban and rural, in public and in private, as leaders and as followers. But, as we worked through the separate studies, we discovered that our authors had also revealed significant unities. This allowed us to complete our third major task, that of trying to put in order the materials that we had gathered.

Two interlocking themes predominate in all the sections of the book. The more important theme is the contrast between extraordinary callings and everyday concerns in women's religious lives. The ordinary calling of women in traditional societies around the world has been that of mother and housewife. Women's religion can either call women away from that ordinary venture to enterprises that are usual for both women and men, or it can validate and support women in their ordinary roles as mothers and housewives. Religious systems vary quite dramatically in their accommodation of or hostility to both extraordinary women and women called to fulfill ordinary roles. Thus a second theme—running through the entire book and especially noticeable in its latter half—explores the level of support women find, whether they are called to extraordinary ventures or bound up in everyday concerns.

The book's first section explores the discontinuity, as well as continuity, between everyday concerns and extraordinary callings. By far the more dramatic pattern is that of discontinuity, in which women who follow an extraordinary calling break out of, or somehow transform, the usual role. Some leave it behind altogether, as does Jnanananda, the Hindu guru described in the second chapter of our volume; others continue to be wives and mothers but effect reversals in former and often oppressive family structures. Good examples are Julia, the first woman we encounter in the book (Chapter 1), the Korean shamans of our fourth chapter, and probably also the women of ancient Greece, called to the ecstatic cult of the god Dionysus (Chapter 5).

But the religious impulse does not have to bring so explosive a rupture; thus we find also a pattern of continuity, where women's religious life supports and validates women's everyday concerns. This pattern is best seen in our section on housewives' rituals (Part III), which explores a variety of ways in which women have integrated religious practice into their own domestic worlds. Here they preside over life and death and continue on a religious level the modest but essential work for the well-being of their families that has always been a hallmark of women's everyday life.

The distinction between ordinary concerns and extraordinary callings remains an important motif of our book's second half as well. Most of its chapters either take a longer historical view of the extraordinary venture or describe situations in which the interplay between the two types of careers can be seen more clearly. But the second half of the book emphasizes more explicitly the other significant theme that runs through our volume—the greatly varying degree of support that women's religious enterprises receive within differing types of religious and cultural systems.

In one way or another, whether or not they operate within a religious context that is overtly male dominated (as do the Hindu and Muslim women of Chapters 6, 7, 8, and 10), the women studied in the first half of the book seem to find or make for themselves sufficient accommodation to their needs and aspirations. But in some situations in which men dominate religious institutions and ideologies, women's options can be far more limited. Our fourth section explores two variants of this pattern: first, the relatively rare cases, such as the Muslim tribal women studied in Chapter 12, in which women are confined to the ordinary domestic round and their ordinary callings are not supported by religion and ritual; second, those cases of extraordinary women who may be successful in making a new kind of place for themselves only to find their efforts eventually undercut and frustrated by the system (Chapters 13, 14, and 15).

Students in the West who know only the great male-dominated "World

Religions" are less accustomed to religious systems in which women and men share a balanced measure of opportunity and power. Our authors have explored women's roles and activities in three such systems in Part V. The balance is achieved quite differently in each: in two—the Longhouse religion of the North American Iroquois and the ancient Qollahuaya tradition of the Bolivian Andes—women and men have separate spheres that are essentially equal; in the third—the Tantric Buddhist tradition of India and Tibet—gender is irrelevant to attaining the tradition's highest goal.

The final section does double duty: it returns to the opening critique concerning our discipline's failure to study religious woman in her own right, and it also explores a complex pattern in which—despite a seeming male dominance in religion—women's bodies, which menstruate and give birth, become a major focus of both women's and men's religious lives. A male-dominated religion focused on a female function may be confusing, but only if one holds to an androcentric view. Who's really in charge here anyway? The answer may be neither men nor women, or perhaps both women and men. One conclusion to be drawn is that the data on women's religious lives and, consequently, the interaction of women and men in religious systems as well are much richer and far more complex than anyone imagined when people were content to study "religious man" alone. In fact, it seems clear that, to study religion properly, we must also begin attending to the women who have constituted and do constitute at least one-half of almost all of the world's religious communities.

RITA M. GROSS
University of Wisconsin—Eau Claire

NANCY AUER FALK
Western Michigan University

On Transliteration

Of necessity, our volume includes a number of names and terms from the languages and dialects of the regions that our authors have studied. For the sake of consistency, and because most of our readers will not be familiar with scholarly systems of transliteration for these areas, we have romanized these terms in the simplest way possible, omitting diacritical marks wherever this is feasible.

Introduction to the Second Edition

Almost a decade has passed since we issued the first edition of *Unspoken Worlds*. We are pleased that so many students have had the opportunity to meet the many fascinating women whose religious worlds were articulated in that volume.

Thanks to Wadsworth Publishing Company, we are now able to reissue our volume and to expand it with seven additional articles. This expansion makes the volume more comprehensive. Because we have never liked the artificial distinction between "Western" and "non-Western" religions, we are including materials from the so-called Western traditions in this edition. Six articles new to this volume explore North American materials, including new works on Haitian and Native American women. In addition, we have included an article on women's practice in a Sunni Muslim region to complement previously included studies of Shi'a Muslim women.

Most major themes and categories of our first edition are retained. In Part I of our new edition, another extraordinary woman, Roman Catholic social activist Dorothy Day, joins Julia and Jnanananda to greet the reader. A portrayal of Moroccan Muslim women receiving comfort at the shrines of saints expands our sampling, in Part III, of the many ways in which women find support for their ordinary roles as wives and mothers. Two new articles in Part IV extend our explorations of how women fare in male-dominated religious systems. Examples from nineteenth-century Protestantism and twentieth-century Judaism show how women may reshape and reappropriate such systems. Our Part V now includes an example of how a major tradition that normally subordinates women to men can sometimes inspire a move to establish balance and equality. Our new article in this section studies the surprisingly egalitarian Shaker tradition, a utopian movement within Christianity. Finally, our Part VI now includes two new articles, each of which focuses on the crucial feminist issue of women's response to female images of the Sacred. The first examines the intricate relationship between a Haitian Vodou priestess, her daughter, and two female Vodou spirits whom they serve. The second shares Native American Apache perceptions of a powerful Earth Mother goddess.

We have been pleased to see that much new material about the unspoken worlds of women's religious lives has appeared since we first assembled our volume. To help our readers locate and mine this new material, we have included two kinds of bibliographical material in our new edition. A short list of "Further Readings" has been added to each chapter; most of these have been prepared by our contributors themselves. At the end of our book, readers will also find a list of additional cross-cultural studies and collections, assembled by co-editors Falk and Gross. We hope that this volume, with its added materials, will continue to enhance our readers' awareness of women as religious subjects and creators of their own universes of religious meaning.

NANCY AUER FALK   RITA M. GROSS
Western Michigan University   *University of Wisconsin—Eau Claire*

I

ENCOUNTER

Extraordinary Women

Encounters with three women of extraordinary callings and personality initiate us into the complex fabric of women's religious lives.

Julia, a village woman of Mozambique, East Africa, and Satguru Jnanananda Saraswati of Madras, South India both follow pursuits unfamiliar to many American teachers and students. Once Julia was a Christian laywoman, and a wife and mother like most other women in this volume. Now she has become a traditional African medium and diviner. On many nights, she seeks possession by the old African gods, and, through those gods, messages and help for her people. Unlike Satguru Jnanananda, Julia has not completely broken with her old life, for she continues to run a household and work in the fields. But her new role has greatly changed her relationships to her family and community. The woman *guru*, or spiritual guide, Jnanananda is quite unusual in India, for she has received the vows of religious renunciation and has completely left behind the husband and family with which she lived for most of her life. Now, like many of the other women of extraordinary callings, she sometimes prefers not to think of herself as a woman at all. Nor do her devotees primarily perceive her as a woman. She is the guru.

The late American Catholic activisit Dorothy Day forged a role for herself that was both less and more "traditional" than those of either Julia or Jnanananda. As founder and leader of the independent lay Catholic Workers movement, she broke away from all roles for women that were usually accepted by her own Roman Catholic Church. She was neither a nun, nor a sister, nor a conventional wife and mother. Yet in her "new" role she nurtured and sheltered the helpless and the poor—activities so typically "female" that the author has labeled her a "Catholic Earth Mother."

Though Day seems in many ways to be quite different from the other extraordinary women who precede her in this section, common threads run through their stories. Each showed uncommon intelligence and sensitivity during her early life. Each then underwent a period of tension between her adopted life-style and a sense of "spiritual calling." Each finally and dramatically redirected her life to accept that calling and devote her energies towards service to others. And each emerged as an enormously compelling and charismatic personality. We shall see this pattern again in our next section's chapter on women shamans in Korea and in later descriptions of the lives of religious founders Ann Lee and Sayo Kitamura.

1

Julia: An East African Diviner

MARTHA B. BINFORD

I met Julia by accident. Lamanga, a friend from a Rjonga village in Mozambique, East Africa, where I was doing my fieldwork, dropped by my hut and announced that we were going for a walk. After an hour on the narrow paths, tripping over vines and roots, I stopped lamenting the fact that I had left my notebook at home. Lamanga was giving me nonstop information of the sort dear to an anthropologist's heart, but I couldn't have written it down anyway, since every inanimate object seemed bent on attacking me. I appreciated Lamanga's visits and the whirlwind tours he took me on, but I never knew what to expect next. Suddenly, we emerged from deep bush into a clearing with two paths leading into a rather large, well-kept homestead of several huts. Three of the huts faced east, as was customary, but the fourth, set apart from the rest, faced west. Lamanga hesitated a moment, then took the public, or eastern, path and walked slowly toward the homestead. I looked curiously at Lamanga; he was usually quite uninhibited and barged right into people's homes at any time of the day or night. This time he stayed on the front walk and called out a greeting, asking permission to enter.

MARTHA B. BINFORD   received her Ph.D. in Anthropology from Michigan State University in 1971 after two years of fieldwork in Mozambique. She was formerly Associate Professor of Anthropology at the University of Michigan–Dearborn and is currently living in Washington, D.C. Her major research interests are the study of religion, symbolism, and cultural dynamics.

Author's Note   The research on which this paper is based was made possible by a National Institute of Mental Health Research and Training Grant, 1968–1971.

A woman walked slowly out of one of the huts and stood looking at us, her hands on her hips. I was immediately struck by her poise and dignity and the feeling of power that exuded from her. She was in complete control of the situation. Here was none of the obsequious eagerness to greet me that I had already learned to distrust, since it seemed to hide fear and suspicion of me, the only white person in this village of almost two thousand tribal people. She was looking us over very carefully.

"My gods don't hate whites. Come in." Laughing, she moved slowly forward to greet us. Her husband came out of one of the huts and stood slightly behind her while she initiated the ritual exchange of news. This, too, was most unusual, since it was typically the men who exchanged the news while their womenfolk stood respectfully behind them listening. She asked how I was. I responded, "I am well, mother, thank you." She nodded and began her part of the ritual exchange.

"I am well, my husband is well"—this with a flick of her hand to indicate whom she meant. "And my children are well." She paused to study my face. "My goats are well, my chickens are well, my pigs are well, and my oxen are well." She was looking intently at me, and when I began to smile she laughed with delight. I had understood what she was saying and knew that it was peculiar to detail the health of one's livestock. She was testing me.

"I had heard that this one is different. She is not a mission woman. All they know how to say is 'good morning' and 'good evening.' They don't know our language." She had used bad grammar and pitched her voice in a high falsetto to mimic a missionary, venom in her tone. The other villagers had seemed anxious to convince me that they were good Christians, and those who were pagans had been avoiding me. Since I had begun to despair of convincing the villagers that I wanted to learn about all their customs, not just those they had adopted from the whites, I found Julia's attitude a refreshing change. I was also most thankful for the tor-

tuous hours spent studying the Rjonga language with my assistant, Valente.

After being introduced to Rolando, Julia's husband, Lamanga asked if we could return later when Julia played her drums and her gods "came out" (possessed her). I finally realized who she was. This was Julia, the famous diviner and healer whose drums I had heard beating in the bush almost every evening since my arrival in the village. I looked more closely at her, understanding why I had felt power in her. For a Rjonga woman, she had a fantastic self-assurance, standing with her head slightly thrown back, looking down her nose at us. One foot was forward of the other so that one hip jutted out, and her hands were crossed over her breast. No other Rjonga woman stood like that, in such a deliberately arrogant pose. I was quite taken by her. She was dressed like other village women—a short-sleeved blouse, a long cloth wrapped around the waist dropping to her ankles, and a dark scarf tied around her head so that no hair showed. But her jewelry was uncommon. She wore a bracelet of red and black beads on her left wrist and, on the second and third fingers of her left hand, rings an inch thick, made of the same red and black beads that were on her wrist.

Julia responded, "This is a good night, a special night, because my gods have asked me to play the drums. I played the drums yesterday a little, out of habit, to keep in practice. I must play even if they don't want to come, but tonight they will." She gestured toward the hut behind us, whose doorway faced west. "I go to the gods' house every morning, where I keep my medicines and bones. I throw the bones to know if it is a special night for the gods or not."

Lamanga stuttered a little with excitement. "What should Marta bring as a gift to the gods?" Julia looked at him somewhat scornfully. Lamanga was a nominal Christian who had stopped attending church years before, but she enjoyed needling him about it still. "You have walked in the church too long. You should not need to ask, you should know. How can I tell what the gods want? But it must be metallic—coins, pins, needles."

She told Rolando to escort us out of the homestead on the western path. He stayed with us, but behind us, until we reached the main path. He was an attractive middle-aged man, not without his own dignity, but he paid deference to Julia because of the power of her gods. We shook hands at the fork in the path, and, as we walked back to my hut, Lamanga told me a little of Julia's story and explained the meaning of the eastern and western paths and of the red and black beads.

Everyone in the village was surprised when Julia became a diviner, because she had been a staunch member of the Swiss Mission church. Her daughters were married, her husband and two grown sons had good jobs in Lourenço Marques (as the capital was called in 1968), and the family was upwardly mobile. Lamanga hinted that it had annoyed Rolando considerably that his wife had reverted to pagan ways just when the family was doing so well. Nonetheless, about three years ago, Julia had suddenly gone as an apprentice to a diviner and less than a year later had returned to Mitini and "sealed" many of the paths into her homestead. Christian households typically have many paths leading into them, but Julia had blocked all but the traditional eastern and western paths to protect her homestead from the witchcraft or sorcery of people envious of her newly acquired power. Lamanga explained that the east is associated with the living; paths into homesteads are from the east and must be used by all visitors, especially nonrelatives. The west is associated with the dead. Corpses are carried out of homesteads on the western path, which is regularly used only by members of the family or by non-kin who have permission from the family. Anyone using the western path without permission would be accused of witchcraft or sorcery.

Lamanga went on to explain the three major categories of gods in the Rjonga pantheon.

Ancestor gods are particular to each family. They may visit an occasional illness on their living relatives if they feel neglected or if they think that their relatives have been misbehaving. The color white is associated with the ancestors and only white cloths, livestock or wine are offered to them. The Rjonga are quite emphatic that their "own" gods never kill people as do the other two kinds of gods. These other two kinds are "foreign" gods believed to belong to the Nguni (Zulu) and Ndjao tribes. The "foreign" gods possess people, so that they are forced to become diviners or be killed by the rejected gods. I knew that these two tribes had actually conquered the Rjonga in battle in the past. Now, it seemed, their gods continued to conquer them in the present. The color black is associated with the Nguni gods, who are male, while red is associated with the Ndjao gods, who are female and less powerful. This explained the meaning of Julia's red and black beads. Most diviners have two possessing gods. The colors of her jewelry let villagers know who her gods are.

People consult diviners for different reasons. Some may want to know the future—for example, if a certain plan or journey is a good idea. The majority, however, have been visited by some sort of misfortune and want to know its cause and remedy. Most people who went to Julia were ill. Her gods would possess her and speak through her in an arcane language, divining the cause of the illness. Sometimes the god would also prescribe a cure; other times it would send the patient to another healer for a cure.

THE GODS SPEAK

I could not return that evening because of a crisis in my homestead, but I made arrangements to go another time. About ten days later a messenger summoned me. Lamanga, who was visiting again, my servant, Carlos, and another guest went with me through the night to Julia's homestead. When we arrived, the small circular hut was very crowded, and the light was so dim that it was difficult to see. Chairs were brought in for us, and we sat down just inside the door. An oilcan was upended in the entrance with a kerosene lantern set on it, the wick turned very low. The still red coals of a dying fire could be seen behind the central beam, which served as an upright.

A woman, one of Julia's apprentices, was seated in front of the beam in a trance. Another apprentice, a man, was seated to her right. They both lived with Julia. Lamanga whispered that they were in trance tonight so that they might be purified. Angelica—the female apprentice—had four strings of shells around her otherwise bare head. Around her naked torso a string of beads crossed under her breasts and over her back. Over her shoulders, tied loosely under her chin, was a white cloth. She was sitting cross-legged, knees high, her hands on her knees, with a red cloth draped over her legs. A third cloth, wrapped around her waist, appeared to be her normal clothing. During her possession, Shanda—the male apprentice—often retied the white cloth or wiped Angelica's brow with a corner of it. I noticed a miniature mattock on the ground by Angelica's right hand. She was shivering and trembling; occasionally she jerked and twitched convulsively. The drums were beating loudly. The people chanted with the drums while Angelica continued to shiver; sometimes she stretched her hands out rigidly at her sides, just beside her knees, and shook all over. She made horrible groaning sounds like a person being punched in the stomach. Her head twisted spasmodically, jerking high over one shoulder, held there tautly while the rest of her body shivered and trembled, caught by her god. I could see Julia beating the large drum while other people shook metal carraca-like instruments that rattled. Angelica picked up the little mattock and began shaking it in rhythm with the drum, a smile on her face. When she

put it down again, the music and singing immediately ceased, and she began to talk in a small, baby-like voice. The people laughed as someone told me that her god was afraid of whites and would not stay. The drums began beating again, and this time she picked up a knife, which she flourished as if in a fight. When she put it down, all was quiet, and Julia leaned forward, asking her questions.

During her trance Angelica had divined the cause of a person's illness and specified certain measures to be taken. She groaned and grunted as she came out of the trance, and people greeted her by telling her which god had possessed her, since diviners can remember nothing of what happened during the trance. Julia helped her out of her ceremonial regalia, and Angelica dressed in her normal clothes. The people relaxed and exchanged greetings with me and my friends; there was much laughter and talking while Angelica was told what happened when she was in trance. Hardly had she settled back against the upright, apparently exhausted, when Shanda, the male apprentice, began to jerk and twitch and be torn by those awful guttural groans. He was possessed but came out of trance relatively quickly.

Then, within minutes, Julia's god seized her. She began to grunt and tremble, as the other two had, while a young boy helped her take off her clothes and put on the ceremonial attire. Lamanga whispered that her "spirit helper," who is chosen by the god, must be pure, someone who has never had sexual relations. While Julia was dressing and grunting, the rest of the people chatted and laughed as if nothing unusual were happening.

I watched the young boy dress Julia. She wore a band around her head to which was attached a brush made of ostrich feathers. The Zulu used to wear these devices in battle to confuse the enemy. Julia was dressing as a warrior because her god had been one in life. A gazelle skin fit over her head and extended down over her chest and back, worn like an armor. On her right wrist was a ring made of hyena hide. Beads crossed over her breast and back, and a small trumpet made of ivory or bone hung on her chest. Also on her chest was a pouch with medicines; Lamanga speculated that they probably included the nose of a hyena and maybe part of an elephant's trunk. A black cloth was tied around her shoulders, and shells were strung around her head. The boy handed her a small shield made of cowhide, which she put on her arm. In one hand she held a *tchoba*, a sort of whisk used to brush the head and shoulders, and in the other a long root from which the shield was slung. She continued to wear her ordinary bronze bracelets—circles whose ends didn't meet so as not to "tie up the power of the god." A small knife was laid on the ground near her.

When she was fully dressed, Julia placed the various objects on the ground and began to dance toward the back of the hut. I craned my head to see. A huge forked limb was planted in the back of the hut, with a red and a black cloth draped over it; Lamanga said that the limb was like an altar. Julia stayed on her knees there for about ten minutes. Then she came forward and picked up the knife, shield, and root and began to mimic a warrior in battle. She thrust and feinted with the knife in what seemed an expert manner, then began to come toward me on her knees, the knife flickering and darting in front of her. She came closer and closer, sometimes throwing the shield up in front of her face as if to protect herself. She arrived in front of me, still on her knees, and we stared each other in the eye. I felt that she was very much "there" and was testing me again, as she had done the day we met for the first time. The drums were beating loudly, the people near me drawing away. My guest gripped my arm in obvious fear, but I shook him off and smiled at Julia, who smiled faintly in return. I was amazed by her enormous power and by the force of her personality. She danced at my feet, always on her knees, the knife weaving in front of her. Then, suddenly, she placed the knife, shield, and root

on the ground at my feet. I could feel the knife blade across the toe of one of my shoes. She danced back a little, looking at me, then picked up her paraphernalia and retreated to the front of the hut, where she did a long pantomime of a warrior in battle. She subsided momentarily, then began to tremble and make horrible grunting sounds. Her throat was wracked by the cries torn from her and by occasional fits of coughing. The others were talking to each other, watching Julia from time to time. Obviously all of this was preliminary, and no one would pay serious attention until the god arrived. The grunting, groaning, and trembling continued for some time. Suddenly Julia spoke in a deep, guttural voice totally unlike her own: "I will see all of you, tell everything, destroy all of your secrets." The people fell quiet.

"Kakulu, kakulu, kakulu. Kakulu, white woman." The others replied "kakulu." Then she began to chant. She sang a phrase, and the people repeated part of it.

"What house is this which is preferred by men?"

"It is preferred by men," the people chorused.

"What village is this in which I am so adored by boys?"

"You are adored by boys."

The chanting continued until the drums stopped playing. Julia settled down in a corner by the drums and signaled her young helper to start playing again.

Then her god began to speak in earnest, and the people present sang a refrain after each utterance.

"I want to get out. I want to speak with the gods. I want to speak with my wife. I want you to play the drums. My father showed me everything. I want to come out. I want to tell you everything. I want to come out and meet the white. I want to come out with my woman. Let me play the drums. With my gods. My father made me see with my eyes. I want to get out to cooperate with the white. I want to tell you everything. In the middle of this land

I want to make myself happy with my own spirit. To be happy with the white grandparents. To tell secrets of your grandsons. To cooperate. I want to tell all of you, the whites also. Good, good, good, good, good."

Julia grunted and coughed, then began to sing again. The drumming and singing continued for some time, then she spoke again, addressing Lamanga directly.

"I want to speak to my grandson only" [that is, "to the young man"].

"Yes," Lamanga replied.

"And he will tell his white friend."

"I am here."

"I don't want to leave him. He arrived with his white friend. I come to speak to my grandson only. I want to speak to him only, I want to please him—and his white friend who came here to my homestead. I want to cooperate with the white grandparents. What is it that the white woman wants in my house? Play the drums so that I can come out boiling! I want to live well in the midst of my family. We will visit each other every day. I speak only with the white woman. I will speak with my grandchildren only. Sit down and play the drums; I want to hear them with my ears."

She spoke in this vein for some time, her utterances constantly punctuated by a chorus from the people. When the session was over, Rolando translated the entire episode for us. He also told me that for several nights Julia's god had been visited by my own ancestors, who had "come across the seas" with me to take care of me in the village. My grandfather had gone to Julia's homestead in the night to visit with her god and to learn about his "work." Julia's god had explained that Julia had not wanted to "have the materials of the gods" but that she had inherited her gods from her family and had no choice. My ancestor and Julia's god spoke for a long time. The former Zulu warrior told my grandfather how he had come many years ago, when there was a war, and how he was killed in battle. His spirit,

wanting to be hidden, sought refuge and found it in Julia, in whom he was now sheltered. Occasionally he would "come out" to treat someone who was sick or to help someone about to die. He also helped people who had problems with their family or neighbors. Sometimes he helped good people who came from far away. My ancestor had assured Julia's god that I was a good person with no evil intent. Julia's god was curious about my purpose in the village, so my grandfather had explained that I simply wanted to learn about the people's life and customs. The god was satisfied that I was to be trusted. I was stunned by my good fortune in acquiring unsolicited endorsement by one of the most powerful diviners in the kingdom. I would not fully comprehend the reasons for it until some time later.

Several days later Julia requested to hear the tape I had made of her possession. My assistant Valente and I went to her house in the early afternoon, and Julia, with her two apprentices and her spirit helper, gathered around to listen. There were many exclamations of wonder from the listeners—especially Julia, who reacted to herself grunting and groaning with loud "ohs!" After listening, we chatted and I asked permission to come another day to learn about Julia's conversion, her medicines, and everything else she could tell me. She agreed readily and began a long explanation of what had led up to the god's revelations during her possession. It was essentially what Rolando had already told me but richer in texture and details.

After my first visit to Julia, she wanted to sleep in the spirit house. Her husband was afraid to sleep alone in the other hut, so he went with Julia. Rolando fell asleep immediately, but Julia lay awake for a long time. Then she fell asleep, and one of her gods, the Zulu warrior, came to her. When he arrived, he shook Julia awake and asked her if she could see the two white spirits, my grandparents, who were just coming into her homestead.

Julia couldn't see them. The white spirits arrived at the doorway and asked permission to come in. Julia's god asked the white spirits, "What do you want in Julia's homestead?" They said they had come to visit and to see all the materials (meaning the bones, clothes, medicines, etc.) of the gods. The god said that they couldn't enter because, once in, they might not want to leave again. He didn't want white spirits in his house because "the races don't understand each other." The whites answered, "We haven't come to do harm," but Julia's god wouldn't let them come in. He said, "Perhaps you want to take these materials outside and burn them or throw them away." Then the white spirits asked for a place to rest outside. They stayed on the verandah, where they sat down on their own chairs, which they had brought with them. They also had some papers in their hands. They stayed there a long time, resting. Finally they got up, said goodby, and went to the homestead where I lived. After they left, Julia woke up and began to think about what had happened. She looked at the door and saw that it was closed. Then she understood that she had not been dreaming and that the spirits had really come, because when she had gone to sleep the door had been open. She woke Rolando and told him what had happened. He demurred saying, "Perhaps you dreamed all this because Marta was here in the afternoon." Julia insisted, "No, they really came."

Two nights later the same thing happened again, except that Rolando wasn't there. When the white spirits returned, Julia's god asked again, "What do you want here?" They replied, "Nothing; we came only to see." Then the white spirits explained that they had come to Africa because they knew that their granddaughter had been sent there and they wanted to take care of her. They were now living in my homestead. Julia's god still wouldn't allow them to enter the spirit house, and this time they didn't stay to rest but returned instead to

my hut. On other nights Julia's god went to my homestead to visit with my grandparents, and long conversations ensued. As before, Julia told Rolando what had happened.

I was enchanted by this story and assured Julia that, if my ancestors were indeed with me, it was as they had said. All of us were interested only in learning and meant no harm. She said she knew that. She also said that her god had told her people that I was good and should be helped. I was also quite interested in her husband's reaction, so "Western" in nature. He apparently did not believe in Julia's spirits, and I remembered Lamanga's telling me that Rolando and his sons wanted to become *assimilados*, Portuguese citizens. *Assimilados* were "civilized" people, and I could clearly see that having a "witchdoctor" in the family might be an embarrassment to his ambitions.

Different members of the family came on several occasions to hear the tape of Julia's possession. Her elder daughter told me that she had never believed in her mother's gods until she heard my tape. It was clear to her now that her mother truly "had gods," because she spoke ancient Zulu and in a man's voice. She knew that Julia could not speak or understand Zulu. The daughter also said that she was pleased that her mother was a diviner; she had been very lonely, with her husband, sons, and daughters living in the capital city while she stayed in the bush. Now, said the daughter, her mother had company. This was an intriguing comment. I wanted to hear more about the events that led up to Julia's becoming a diviner, so I made arrangements to speak with her again.

My assistant Valente and I arrived in Julia's homestead around five in the afternoon and found no one at home. Valente, a Christian, showed none of the nervousness that had beset Lamanga. He led me into the homestead, and we waited for Julia, who finally appeared. She left us soon afterward to go clean up after a day of working in the fields. Being a diviner was a part-time job, and she, like all the other villagers, had to tend her crops in order to eat. A few minutes later she joined us, and we exchanged news and pleasantries. Finally I asked whether she could tell me how the gods had come to her. She gave me a sharp look.

"What will you do when you have that knowledge?"

"I will learn." She laughed and said that it was all right. As she started speaking, her apprentice Angelica joined us.

JULIA'S STORY

"Before I was born, my mother was often sick. She went to the hospital many times, but they could do nothing that helped her. Finally her family consulted a diviner who threw the bones, which directed that she go to the family altar and stay here. She would become pregnant, and she should give the child the name of the god who sent the sickness. So my mother bought the 'clothes of the gods'—cloth of various colors—and went to pray at the family altar. Then she became pregnant. The time came when I was born, and my parents went again to the diviner, who said to call me Musengele because that was the name of the god who had sent my mother's sickness.

"When I grew up, I became sick, and they sent me to the hospital, but they couldn't cure me there. So they went to the bones, and the bones said to send me to my mother's mother's home to live. When I arrived at the entrance of my grandmother's homestead, even before I had a chance to speak, I was cured.

"I have two kinds of gods. The female comes from my mother's house. The male comes from my father's. The god tells me his name is Mahlabazimuke. He is the chief one. The female is called Nyankwabe."

While listening, I watched Angelica, who

was obviously taking vicarious pride in this tale. Occasionally she would look contemptuously at Valente, as if to remind him of the traditional power he, a Christian, had forsaken.

Julia continued her story, saying that she had not begun her apprenticeship until many years after she married and after her parents and grandparents had died. Since I knew that possessing gods become hereditary once they are established in a family, this reference to the death of her parents and grandparents was very meaningful. Julia became the heir to the family gods who, in native belief, sought among the living the descendants of their dead hosts until they found a new host. Refusal to become a living host for the gods could lead to the death of the person the gods sought. The "chosen" person could not automatically become a diviner, however, just by being sought out by the gods. He or she then has to enter into an apprenticeship with an established diviner that might last anywhere from a few months to several years.

Julia went on to say that, after her children were born, she became sick and went to the hospital. She had a pain in her lower right side, but they couldn't cure her. She spent a long time seeking a cure from the European doctors and from native healers, without success. She went to the hospital several times, and finally the doctors at the Swiss Mission hospital decided to operate on her. When Julia arrived at the hospital for her operation, she was told to lie down so that blood could be drawn from the vein in her arm. Her vein collapsed, and she interpreted this event as a sign that the gods didn't like her being there. She indicated that she didn't want to go through with the operation. The European doctor, apparently in disgust at her native "superstitious" belief, told her to go home and seek a cure. By this time Julia was becoming desperately ill, and, though her husband preferred to continue trying European medicine, he finally consented to consult the bones. The bones said that the gods were causing her illness, so the unhappy couple sought a diviner. The diviner gave Julia three kinds of medicines. As soon as she started taking them, the gods "came out" because they had been so long repressed. They possessed her and spoke through her mouth: "We want you to go far away to be treated, so we can work." It is believed that the possessing gods have themselves been diviners and healers in life and that they seek hosts so that they can continue their work after death. Julia didn't like the first diviner she had consulted and insisted that she go far north to a diviner there.

Her husband and sons took her north to this diviner so that she could begin her apprenticeship and learn the "things of the gods." When she arrived, her god asked to be treated as fast as possible so that they could return home quickly. All this was three years ago, Julia told me. She observed that the god was strange in that he liked everything to be done in a hurry. Since he had been well fed and well treated in the north country, Julia was never seriously sick now. Occasionally she might feel unwell, and, if her husband was home, he still tried to get her to go to the European hospital. But her god would immediately come out and say, "I don't like hospitals," and within a few days she would be well again.

I reflected on what her daughter had told me about the loneliness of Julia's life before she became a diviner. Her two sons were unmarried, so she had no daughters-in-law to live with her; her sons and her husband lived in the city where they worked. They came home to the village only occasionally for holidays or weekends. Julia had lived completely alone in her homestead, tending the family fields unaided. Her only companionship came from the other members of the Swiss Mission church in the village, which she attended regularly. Sometimes she would go to the city to visit her family, but she could rarely stay long because

of the necessity of caring for the crops. She was an attractive middle-aged woman, perhaps in her forties, quite intelligent and intense, and it must have been difficult for her to accept a life of drudgery and boredom. Now, instead, her home was full of people. She had two apprentices who lived with her and helped her in the fields. She had the young boy who was her spirit helper and who tended her cattle. The cattle themselves were a sign of her success. Diviners charge their patients fees, and apprentices pay princely sums for their tutelage. She had converted this wealth into cattle, still the most prestigious symbol of affluence to the Rjonga. People sought her out continuously. Her life was now full, and she had achieved an importance rare for a man and almost unheard of for a Rjonga woman.

I asked if I could come back sometime and ask her more questions. After thinking a while, she agreed: "I can't refuse to help you, since you came to learn the life of the people. The country has received you, and I have no right to refuse my help. But the story of the gods is very difficult." Suddenly she began to speak again, telling me in much greater detail how her husband had been convinced to let her become a diviner.

She had gone to the capital city to visit her family and had just finished making dinner when her gods saw that it was almost time for her daughters to return from school. I started, since I had been unaware that her young daughters had also lived in the city. Yes, she assured me impatiently, they had lived in the city when they were children; now they were married and still remained there. It was most unusual for unmarried daughters not to live with their mothers in the village, helping with the daily chores. This put Rolando's upward mobility in a new light. He had been determined, indeed, to surpass the limitations of village traditional life, and Julia had borne the brunt of his ambition, being forced to live alone without the comfort of her daughters.

Village women had told me often that one of the few consolations of married life was having daughters who shared one's burdens and eased the loneliness of a woman's lot somewhat.

Julia continued her story by telling how her gods came out and paralyzed her hands. Her ankles were also paralyzed, so that she was forced to lie down on the bed. When her family came home, she could hardly breathe, nor could she speak. When they touched her, she felt like a corpse, as if the blood had stopped running. After a while her gods began to speak through her: "We want you to send Julia far away so we can be treated. If you don't do it, someday you will find her dead. And we want you to arrange now for all the money for the diviner who will treat us. We don't want to spend a lot of time there in our apprenticeship."

Then the gods disappeared. Julia's husband and daughters were frightened for a while and encouraged her to follow her gods' demands, but, when after a few days she started feeling better, Rolando changed his mind. She became sick several more times with paralysis and convulsions, but again her husband did nothing, although she felt that her life was threatened. Finally a son, Rafael, came home from the north where he was working. He said that his mother should leave the church and seek relief from the diviners. And so, finally, the family planned for the trip to the north. Rolando and Rafael got together the prepayment that would guarantee a speedy treatment. Rafael went ahead and arranged for a diviner to take Julia as an apprentice.

After Julia's arrival, the diviner began to treat her with the special medicines demanded by her gods. After three months Julia became sick for three days, vomiting bile and having difficulty breathing. On the fourth day her gods came out and said, "Why are you making Julia delay? We have already paid the fees, and we said we wanted to go home quickly. But you still send her to do your work in the fields

and around the homestead. If you continue, we will kill her and you will be to blame." The next day Julia was all right again and could sit up. The diviner, convinced of the power of Julia's gods, began treating her with the last of the medicines, then arranged for a big feast. At this feast the power of Julia's gods would be tested to see if they were authentic. People from all over the area would attend this feast and examination, and Julia's family would come north to see if she "graduated."

On the day of the final rituals, many people came to the diviner's homestead bringing drums to play for the gods. This public validation of a diviner's power was very important. Without it, a diviner would be accused of being a quack and would have no patients. Before beginning the tests, Julia was taken out of the homestead into the bush so that she could not see what tests were being prepared. The people in the homestead took the "gods' clothes"— the cloths of special colors in which diviners dressed—and wrapped them in a bundle. They took Julia's gold ring and gave it to a man to hide; he put it in his pocket. The ring symbolized Julia's marriage to the gods and was called "money." Julia removed her head scarf to show me the gold ring tied to a lock of hair over her forehead, which was normally hidden from view. A goat had been killed for the feast; its gallbladder was removed and given to another person to hide. All these hidden objects were tests for Julia's gods. If the gods were "authentic," she would have no trouble finding the hidden objects. One of the primary duties of a diviner is to discover hidden things, be they material items or secrets or knowledge of the future.

Julia was brought back from her seclusion in the bush and given medicines so that her gods would come out. Quickly they possessed her, and she fell to the ground. Then she got up and began to sing and dance. The people called out: "If you are a real god, find the house where your clothes are hidden." Still possessed, she began to search and found the house and the clothes wrapped in a bundle. She came out of the house dressed as a diviner, her breasts bare and covered with beads, a black cloth wrapped around her waist. She carried the small shield in one hand, a knife in the other. Again the gods began to dance through her body. The people called: "Now find your money," referring to the gold ring. Julia danced and sang a new song. Then her gods told the people to be quiet, and she sat down on the ground to think. The gods began to sing again, and the drums picked up the song and beat out a rhythm that lifted Julia off the ground into another dance. She danced directly to the person who had the ring and sat down in front of him. "You have the money. Put it here," she said, holding both hands cupped in front of him. The man asked where he had put the ring, and her gods pointed to his pocket. He took it out and gave it to her while the people laughed and clapped. Then her gods were told to find the goat's gallbladder; they found the person who had it right away. The people clapped more, the gods danced a while longer, then left. Julia was herself again. This ended her tests; she had passed with flying colors, and the people ate and drank, feasting far into the night. Julia stayed in the north for three more days, finishing the medicines for her gods, then came back to Mitini and started curing. By the time I arrived, she was a famous and powerful diviner.

CONCLUSION

After hearing this story I finally understood why Julia had so unexpectedly endorsed me through her god. She had lived a life of loneliness in the village while her family lived in the city. Other women had a similar lot, but Julia was clearly more intense, vibrant, and intelligent than the majority of village women.

She chafed against living out her life as the family drudge, tending the fields alone day after day. Furthermore, she had a history of spirits in her family. This provided the mechanism by which her life could be changed. After the original hosts of the family spirits—her parents and grandparents—had died, it was natural that the family spirits should seek her out. She had originally been named by a spirit; this in itself would attract the spirits to her. The only obstacle in her way was her husband's ambition, which had led to her lonely state in the first place. Despite Julia's repeated illnesses, convulsions, and paralysis, her husband refused to believe that she "had gods." I have no doubt that she was truly on the verge of death, since she was fighting for her own social survival. The intervention of their son had convinced Rolando to let her go as an apprentice and set up practice.

But it was clear that her family was still quite ambivalent about her power and authenticity. Her daughters said that they had not believed in her spirits until they heard my tape, and Rolando believed that she had dreamed about my ancestors simply because she had met me. Although Rolando was traditional enough to be afraid of her gods and to defer to her power, which was clearly accepted by others as real, he still did not accord her full belief. My journey to their homestead to meet Julia, my attendance at her possession, the questions I asked, and my sincere admiration of her had finally impressed her family to a degree that she had been unable to achieve herself. Being white, I validated her power and eased her family's anxiety about their being accepted as "civilized" people. Each of us was marginal to village life, each was suspected by others of unknown schemes. But Julia had been quick to see what I had not. I had inadvertently helped her gain respect in her own family; her public endorsement of me through her god made villagers relax and be less afraid to speak to me about their lives. Julia had responded to my interest by utilizing a very important principle in Rjonga life: reciprocity. Thus each of us had helped the other find acceptance and tolerance in the social spheres important to us. I had made a good and powerful friend.

Further Readings

Junod, Henri Alexandre. *The Life of a South African Tribe*. 2 vols. New Hyde Park, N.Y.: University Books, 1962.

*Morris, Martha B. "A Rjonga Curing Ritual: A Functional and Motivational Analysis." *The Realm of the Extra-Human: Ideas and Actions*, edited by Agehananda Bharati. Vol. 3, *World Anthropology*. The Hague: Mouton, 1976.

——————. "Rjonga Settlement Patterns: Meanings and Implications." *Anthropological Quarterly* 45, no. 4 (October 1972).

Turner, Victor Witter. *The Drums of Affliction: A Study of Religious Processes among the Ndembu of Zambia*. Oxford, England: Clarendon Press, 1968.

——————. *Forest of Symbols: Aspects of Ndembu Ritual*. Ithaca, N.Y.: Cornell University Press, 1967.

---

* Former name of Martha B. Binford.

2

Mother Guru: Jnanananda of Madras, India

CHARLES S.J. WHITE

I first met Her Holiness Sat-guru Swami Shri Jnanan-anda Saraswati in the summer of 1976. An American who had traveled around India for several years as a Hindu monk took me to have her *darshan* [literally, "to look at her" but also "to share her spiritual presence"]. At that time I was trying to gather material for a lecture on women's leadership roles in Hinduism. Jnanananda was very cooperative in telling me about herself, and I looked forward to a time when I might talk with her again. In the fall of 1978 I returned to Madras, hoping to meet with her for a longer time, but I was able to speak with her only once. She was absorbed in almost constant *samadhi*, or mystical trance, and was not giving interviews. Finally, in March of 1979, I returned to Madras once again and was able to speak with Jnanananda several times during a six-week period. During these interviews I learned much about her life and experiences, as well as her attitudes towards many things, both worldly and spiritual. I also watched her give advice to many of her

CHARLES S.J. WHITE holds a Ph.D. in History of Religions from the University of Chicago and is currently Professor of Religion at American University in Washington, D.C. He has travelled in India many times, studying contemporary Indian gurus. He is the author of the monograph *The Caurasi Pad of Sri Hit Harivams* (Honolulu: University of Hawaii Press, 1977), as well as of *Ramakrishna's Americans: A Report on Inter-Cultural Monasticism* (Delhi: Yugantar Prakashan, Ltd., 1979).

Author's Note I wish to express my sincere appreciation to The American Institute of Indian Studies for financial support during the time that this research was being completed.

devotees, who come to her with a variety of questions and problems.

Ma [a familiar form of "mother"], or Sat-guru [a title meaning "true guru"], is quite unusual among Indian women, for she is both a guru and a *sannyasi*. In order to appreciate Ma and her interviews, it is necessary to know something about these two important religious roles. The guru is perhaps the most influential religious specialist in Indian culture. As religious teachers, gurus usually have no official positions at local temples and may conduct no ceremonies at all. Instead they counsel their disciples and teach meditation and spiritual understanding. The bond between a disciple and his or her guru is very strong; when the disciple finds the proper guru, complete commitment should follow. A *sannyasi* is one who has taken a formal vow renouncing all worldly life, including family ties and possessions. Such a vow, in effect, means death to one's former life. This renunciation allows full-time pursuit of spiritual goals and fosters spiritual development. Such vows have been common in India from ancient times to the present.

In India, not all gurus are *sannyasis*, nor are all *sannyasis* gurus. However, though notable exceptions have occurred throughout Indian history, usually women do not take on either role. In fact, Jnanananda is the only woman ever allowed to take *sannyasa* vows by the present Shankaracharya of Kanchipuram who, as a chief teacher of classical *Advaita* Hinduism, is one of the most authoritative and important religious figures in South India today.[1] This exception was granted because the Shankaracharya recognized her as a fully realized *jnani*—one who knows experientially through mystical states of consciousness the deepest truths of Advaita Hinduism. She had attained this state while in her worldly life, during which she had been married and had raised five children. It is to be expected that one whose realization of truth is so deep will be a guru and teach spiritual discipline. In fact, Jnanananda already had students in her worldly life before she took the *sannyasa* vow.

I had arranged to attend Ma's *darshan*, at which she would see her devotees, on Friday, March 9, 1979. The *darshan* was to begin at 5:30 P.M. We parked our cycles inside the gate and were greeted by one of several young men devotees who were to help during the evening *darshan*. The spark of religious fervor in their eyes, their expectant attitude, and a kind of nervousness signaled the familiar feeling of being in the proximity of a saint. Toward the rear of the compound was a low shed that had been converted into a reception area and prayer hall. A large photograph of Satguru was suspended on the back wall, with a red light, covered with flowers, hanging above it. In this room we waited with others to see Ma. When our turn came, we ascended the outside staircase of the bungalow and went through a door directly into the room where Ma was sitting on a mat covered by a small orange carpet.

One of the first impressions one has of Jnanananda is of her wide, frank smile. Many of her photographs depict her this way. Now, as part of her *sannyasa* vow, she has given up symbols of human vanity, such as long, well-groomed hair, jewelry, and saris. She wears instead an ochre cloth around her body and a thick paste of ashes on her forehead and on her arms, where the paste forms horizontal stripes. She has cut her hair short. Her pictures show that, before she put on the ascetic habit, she was a beautiful woman. The beauty is still there, but it impresses one as being more a reflection of her spiritual state. A lilting chuckle sometimes ripples behind her comments. One feels a radiant, peaceful joy in her presence.

As she greeted me, she asked where I had been since the previous November. Then she asked me what I would like to discuss with her now and made reference to the twelve questions I had left with her at our previous meeting. She said she would set up an appointment to go over them. Almost without interruption from these preliminaries, she began speaking from a spiritual viewpoint. She uses vigorous, idiomatic English with a clear accent. Her manner is completely natural, homey, motherly. Her hands make sweeping graceful gestures. She appreciates her listener's catching on to what she says and will throw back her head and laugh heartily when others show that they find her comments amusing.

She said near the beginning of the conversation, "My work is growing slowly, but it will become very big. The world is ready for it—needs it before chaos encompasses everything. I teach the path of surrender, whatever your walk of life is and whatever you are doing. I followed that path and underwent terrible *tapas* [austerity] for many years. But the Divine spoke to me constantly. I never had a guru. Everything came from within. For years I had this most terrible burning sensation, *mahabhava*, all over my body. I tried every kind of medication—ayurvedic,[2] homeopathic, and allopathic. Can you imagine it? Some doctors even gave me injections for it!

"The Divine Command would come to me: 'From today onward, you fast.' It never said 'until next Tuesday'! It went on indefinitely. Eventually the starvation turned to dysentery, and blood came out.

"You know I had disciples twenty-five years ago in my worldly life. So that is nothing new. I directed them even when I was in the householder stage. You may wonder why I stayed so long in that stage. Partly it was for the children. The Divine spoke to me and said that my children were to be extraordinary. Two of them have been working closely with me. Eventually they will become *sannyasis*. My youngest daughter, when she was only five, observed voluntarily the full day's fast of *Shivaratri*—not even taking water.

"Really, I didn't require initiation by the Shankaracharya. It came as a Divine Command. He was touring and came to the city where I was living then. I went to the place where he was staying. You know they never receive women. But he did receive me. Then the impulse came to me. I asked him if he would come to my house. (They never go to private houses.) He smiled and said, 'You want

me to come to your house? Where do you live?' I gave him my address, and we fixed the day. About two hundred people had gathered there on the appointed day. But I was unconcerned. I have no need of a guru, I was only following instructions. When he arrived at my house, I was upstairs. Up to that time I had been talking to people around me but when he arrived, I fell into *samadhi*. There was no one to receive him at the gate. So he simply walked into the drawing room and sat down. Then I 'woke up' and came downstairs. He stayed for a short while and then went away. But, I repeat, I did not feel the need to call upon him to become my guru although he did give me *mantra-diksha* [initiation into a sacred Sanskrit phrase used in meditation], which is something they normally never do for women. This was on the previous occasion.

"It was the Divine Command that led me to ask for *sannyasa*. It was not a necessary thing for me, since my *tapas* and spiritual training were already complete. In fact many people did not like the ambiguity of a woman being initiated by the Shankaracharya. But now that they see what I am like and what my tendencies are, there is less resistance."

I asked, "Will these young men you are initiating into *sannyasa* work with you?"

"Yes, to some extent. I may call them for some work. The first one I have had initiated, Sadashva Giri [a former Indian air force officer], I have sent to an *ashram* [religious community] some 180 kilometers from here. He still has a great deal of *tapas* [austerity] and *sadhana* [spiritual practice] to complete."

"Do you plan to train any women for *sannyasa*?"

"It is not a question of men and women. I am looking for the best material, and so far these young men have been most suitable."

At another interview—in fact nearly the last I had with her—Ma Satguru talked more about the trance state of *samadhi*, which was such an important ingredient in her role as guru. When I came to see her on April 4, 1979, her elder son told me that she had been in *samadhi* more or less continuously for the past few days. He said that I might find she was having difficulty answering questions. When I sat down in front of her for *darshan*, I could sense the difference, so to speak, in her level of consciousness. With a kind of sympathetic response, I even felt myself carried away by her self-absorption and did not much want to pursue a conversation. But we both made an effort, and I was able to gather a few comments.

She said that she had experienced this deep absorption many times ever since she was a child. She added that when one is finally fixed in it, there is no more ego. Now that absorption is always the background of her consciousness. *Samadhi* is an experience without content and yet is not empty. It is complete fullness. "In that state I used to ask myself, 'Where am I?' Then I would try to think of myself at some point, but I immediately felt myself to be at the opposite point. In short, it is a feeling of being simultaneously everywhere. But there is no perception of the physical world. The physical world is dissolved in the unity."

She said that in a way she had been different from others from childhood. She had never been distracted by the things that trouble most people—problems of self-control, for example. Even as a young girl she had entered a *samadhi*-like state. "I knew that I was standing by a sea. At first there were others with me, then I was alone. The waves rose up, and I felt they would wash me away. I was afraid, but later I fearlessly experienced complete immersion in the waves. In my early journeys into *samadhi* I sometimes saw the moon shining on a completely darkened ocean. This, the Shankara-charya told me, is one of the signs of the true *jnani*. I also experienced, and still experience, a blinding white light in this state.

"At one point many years ago, when I was attaining what I did not know then was the highest level of classical yoga, I thought I was going mad. In fact, they were ready to take me to a mental hospital. But the Divine Voice told me to go to a nearby book stall. There, on a particular shelf and in a particular book, was the writing on the page that directed me to consult a description of the advanced yogic realization I was experiencing."

At present, teaching seems to be Ma's major occupation. She stays mainly at home and performs no religious ceremonies. Congregational meetings, a part of her routine in the past, have been temporarily suspended. For the time being, Ma seems to be concentrating on her personal relationships with disciples and on the counseling of those who seek to come within her circle.

In several other interviews I was able to ask her questions that I thought would help bring out more clearly her teaching, life experience and special slant as a woman. On other occasions I was permitted to listen as she gave interviews and advice to some of her students or to others who sought her counsel. Many of her comments during these interviews are typical of any contemporary Indian guru, female or male. Only on some questions specifically about women does any special "woman's slant" come through.

On March 15, 1979, I had a two-hour private interview with Ma Satguru. I report my questions and her answers.

Q *"Do you find the public life of the spiritual teacher distracting?"*

A "There is no distraction for one who is completely realized. [*Realized* is a term employed in discussions of Indian spirituality to refer to one who is identified entirely with God.] But premature publicity is very dangerous. It can increase conceit and arrogance and also egoism. Without the Divine Command one should not teach."

Q *"Can the guru communicate directly with the hearts and minds of the disciples?"*

A "Quite a lot depends on the state of mind, or consciousness, of the disciple. Through faith, complete surrender, and openness on the part of the disciple I am fully accessible. One thought from such a disciple penetrates my own consciousness, and the response is instantaneous. I may be anywhere. The disciple may have difficulty in seeing me physically, but that doesn't mean that help and communication are not available."

Q *"What form has your* sadhana *taken since your vow of* sannyasa *in May 1975?"*

A "I do no special meditation or *puja* [worship]. I am always lost in God. There is no need for anything else."

Q *"Does the Satguru perform miracles?"*

A "The question of miracles is a fascinating one to the general public. All I can say is that 'miracles'—if that is the right word—have happened to my devotees. For example, there was a young *sannyasi* who came to see me. I was giving him instruction in meditation and the theory of *advaita*. One night he was on his way here, arguing with himself whether he should think of me without form or with form as the Goddess Rajarajeshwari. His mind was so absorbed in the question that he didn't see the motorcycle bearing down on him on the dark road. Just then the answer overcame his hesitation. 'Think of her as the Goddess Rajarajeshwari!' At that very moment the motorcycle struck him, but he put up his arm defensively, and the vehicle was 'miraculously' deflected to one side. He arrived here more or less in a state of shock and with some scratches on his arm but otherwise unhurt."

Q *"How can we know who is the true guru? How do we choose when different gurus teach different paths?"*

A "Very few of the so-called gurus are fully realized. Some may have achieved partial realization. Generally speaking, when the *chela* [disciple] is ready for the guru, the guru comes. No true guru will promise in-

stantaneous enlightenment. When one finds the true guru, one should surrender completely. Think of it as schools and universities. There are classes and classes and classes and teachers for all of them. They are also subjects that certain individuals should not enter into."

Q *"It has been the tradition, especially among orthodox Hindus in South India, to regard women as unsuitable candidates for spiritual initiation or leadership while they are menstruating. After all, there are strong objections to menstruating women here; they have to sleep in a separate room and cannot even do the cooking. What is your view about this?"*

A "I think such ideas are foolish and wrong. It shouldn't make any difference. Of course there are emotional differences between men and women, but these do not relate to self-realization. Yet, this tradition has its good points, too. It really gives the woman a needed rest. And I think that was its main purpose."

Q *"What should be the spiritual goal of modern Indian and Western women?"*

A "My teaching is the same for everyone. It is summed up in the principles of absolute *truth, purity, dharma,* and *ahimsa*. Truth contains them all, but purity emphasizes moral perfection or morality, while *dharma*, or righteousness, has more to do with responsibility to duty. Of course, *ahimsa* means nonviolence. All who wish to practice complete self-surrender—my way of *nishkama karma* [action without desire]—must adopt these principles."

Q *"Are men and women exactly equal in spiritual characteristics?"*

A "Have you ever seen the statue of Shiva Ardanari [a Hindu god]? He is depicted in two sexes but one body. It is primarily at the gross physical level that we must perceive precise distinctions. When the male and female elements are completely developed and complement each other in the same individual, the soul is fully realized. It is certainly true that men and women have different characteristics. The woman tends to be more emotional, also motherly and loving; whereas the man is more intellectual, perhaps braver. But we cannot rely absolutely on these distinctions. For myself I no longer feel that I inhabit a body of particular sexual gender. In fact, I sometimes refer to myself with the masculine pronouns."

Q *"Your younger married daughter mentioned that you are from the Nayar caste in Kerala. This caste has practiced inheritance through the female line. Hence women have great status in your caste. Do you think this background gave you more confidence to pursue your spiritual path independently?"*

A "Well, you must remember that I hardly lived in Kerala. My father was the deputy general manager of the Southern Railway—during British times, the highest office that an Indian had ever held in the Southern Railway. We lived luxuriously in Madras, with a large house, many servants, and so on. I was educated in Catholic convents and did very well in certain subjects. I was always very good in English; it was even predicted in my natal horoscope. As a child I adopted a strict code of behavior for myself, although I could also be mischievous. My motto came to be—I preferred the German form—*Ich dien*, 'I serve.' When I was a young married woman, I became quite good at music, photography, and gardening. I played the *vina* [a string instrument] and once performed on All India Radio. But God stopped everything. For a long period of my life—even in the midst of my householder duties—He required complete seclusion of me. That whole time I was being trained by the Divine Voice. I had visions,

including one of Jesus with a dazzling sacred heart that shot rays of power throughout my body. I just mention these facts by way of background. It may be that the great dignity generally accorded women in Kerala influenced me, if indirectly. Also, the literacy rate among the people of Kerala is the highest in India. Even the servants are always reading books and newspapers. So we are accustomed to the pursuit of knowledge.

"It may also be true that women find it a little easier to come to me than to a man. They can talk over their personal problems with me without shyness. In fact, the Shankaracharya has sent a number of women to me in this regard, since he himself does not advise women disciples."

On March 29, 1979, Satguru granted me a great privilege in allowing me to sit with her on the first of two evenings while she gave *darshan* to her Indian disciples individually or in small, mainly family, groups. In all, I saw and listened to about forty persons during those exchanges. At least for now Ma is able to see personally most of the people who approach her. What an experience of relief this intimate discussion of problems must be to hard-pressed individuals who discover Ma, the loving mother, in the torturing crosscurrents of Indian life! Nevertheless, she does not always say what one would prefer to hear. For Satguru may also be regarded by her disciples as the incarnate goddess, Rajarajeshwari. Westerners could probably identify with this approach more fully if they thought of her as an incarnation of the Blessed Virgin Mary. I don't believe Ma would consider it wrong to do so. Her motherliness, therefore, is in a different category altogether from ordinary human motherliness.

The first person to come in was a young man, about college age, whom I had seen waiting outside. To me nothing seemed to be wrong with him. After prostrating before Ma, he knelt and with a fervent, pleading smile asked her for help in getting a job. "With your grace, mother, I will get it. Please help me. Please."

Jnanananda replied, "But how many jobs can I help you get? After three months you always quit. You have to learn to stick to one job. Are you still taking your medicine?"

"Yes, mother. With your grace, I know I can get the job."

When he had left, she said, "You know, he is a mental case. He cannot keep a job. He is heavily medicated with tranquilizers. It is too bad."

A pretty young woman knelt before Ma. She spoke in a very low voice, so that I could not hear all of the conversation. At one point Ma said, "You must continue to pray at all costs, even when you feel that you cannot. Pray mechanically, if nothing else. This ultimately will help you to overcome your depression and despair."

By the end of the interview the woman was sobbing quietly and saying, "Please help me, mother. Please help me." Jnanananda smiled and closed her eyes with an expression of deep peace. When she opened her eyes again, she gave a handful of *vibhuti* [sacred ash] on a banana leaf to the young woman, who prostrated and then left. (Ma gave some kind of *prasad*, a sacramental substance—water, for example—that has been blessed by the god or the guru, at nearly every *darshan* that I came to. Besides *vibhuti* she gave rock candies or toffees. Once she gave me a small bunch of bananas. It is also the custom for those coming to have *darshan* to give a gift to the guru— things such as fruit, coconut, flowers, incense sticks, or money. Trays were placed in front of Ma to receive these offerings.)

An elderly white-haired Brahman lady, dressed in the elegant dark-colored sari of her class, spoke to Ma for some time. At one point Ma sat back, smiled broadly, and said in a loud voice, "How can he go wrong or fail as long as I am here? There is nothing to worry about." The woman, I learned later, had been asking about her son, who was undergoing intense *sadhana* [spiritual discipline] under Ma's guidance. The woman had with her a large, rectangular envelope whose contents she seemed to be discussing with Ma before she placed it on one of the brass trays for the reception of offerings. Ma told me afterward that the woman had brought her a deed of gift for a house but that she didn't know whether she would accept it.

A girl of about twelve came with her mother. Ma chatted pleasantly with them in Tamil. The emotional ambience had become relaxed and domestic. At one point the girl took out her pen and placed it on the tray in front of Satguru, who smiled indulgently, picked up the pen, and handed it back to the girl. Afterward she laughed and said that the girl wanted a special blessing for the pen, which she was going to use to write her examinations.

A plumpish middle-aged woman with several teeth missing came and sat in front of Ma. She spoke enthusiastically, smiling, frowning, and using gestures. Ma said afterward that the woman complained of her family life. She was a widow with three sons and three daughters, but she couldn't get along with her children. She lamented that her daughters-in-law had thrown her out of the house. She wanted to come to live with Ma and take the vows of a *sannyasi*, but Ma had to tell her no. She was not ready for that life and would not be in this incarnation.

An athletic looking man in his late twenties or early thirties came in and prostrated full length on the floor (as do most of the male devotees) before Satguru. Then he stood and beamed at her for a few minutes as they talked quietly. He was one of her close disciples, Satguru revealed after he had left. He worked for the Defense Department and now rose daily at 4:00 A.M. to practice an hour of meditation before going to work. She said that the after-effects of the meditation gave him a feeling of happiness throughout the day.

A middle-aged father and mother and their grown daughter came shyly forward. Most of the discussion after the preliminary bows and prostrations had to do with the man's job prospects. He had been offered a new job. Ma told him not to take it unless he received an appointment letter and by no means to resign from his present job until he received such a letter. His aged mother, who was blind, lived about 200 kilometers away and would not leave her house. Satguru told him that they must do something to look after her welfare—either their daughter could go to stay with her grandmother or the wife should. They reverted to the question of the job. The man said he didn't think he should change jobs until he had collected the annual bonus, which was due to be paid at the end of March. Ma agreed with him. He mentioned that negotiations had begun to marry his daughter to someone. Horoscopes had been exchanged, and they were harmonious, but there was nothing definite yet. They left, with the father making elaborate and prolonged, full-length prostrations. When they were gone, Ma said that the man was very naive about his employment and had lost several jobs because of this. The daughter had no push and wouldn't go out to work even though she had graduated.

The next man, short, his face twisted with emotion, prostrated and squatted on his heels before Ma. He tried to smile, but there was a bitterness in his words. "I did everything you told me to." Ma had a stern look on her face and said nothing. He opened his mouth crookedly. Satguru said, "I have told you many times that nothing can happen without complete surrender. You haven't surrendered completely." The man clenched his teeth in a last attempt at a smile and went away.

Satguru commented, "That man is very well read in Indian spirituality—he knows the philosophies by heart—but doesn't know how to practice a line of it. He is very stubborn. He and his wife are separated legally, and the wife has custody of the child. He wants my help to

regain custody of his son, but nothing can happen without complete surrender to God."

A young society lady swept in, an air of hurry about herself. She was wearing a pair of glasses with fashionably owlish frames and a sari with a large pattern in the current mode. When she was seated in front of Ma, she began immediately to talk. "I have just come from a journey of two-thousand-plus miles," she said. "I hurried here as fast as I could, and then last night you wouldn't admit me."

"We have changed the schedule now," Satguru said. "*Darshan* is only on Tuesdays and Fridays—otherwise I wouldn't have any time at all to myself."

"But tonight," the woman interrupted, "after so many delays, they have made me wait until nearly the end of the *darshan* time. Ma, I think you are trying to cut me off!" She looked the part of a petulant ingenue in a Hindi film.

Ma smiled—wanly, I thought. "But it's the same sort of thing. Don't you see? If we don't take people in order, there can be great trouble. As it is, the volunteers have a difficult time restraining some of the people who come here to see me. There have been rows. I have to be perfectly fair—it's only right, anyway—first come, first served! You must have arrived after the others. And what about your plans?"

"We are supposed to go to the States. I don't want to go, but he [her husband] wants me to go. I don't know what to do. Who will look after the dog?"

"If he wants you to go," Ma said, "you should go—to please him. When do you leave Madras?"

"Tomorrow morning, for Hyderabad. There is another wedding. Then back north." The woman, somewhat subdued, departed after placing an offering of money in one of the trays.

On other occasions I went to Ma with Westerners who wanted spiritual guidance. Although the questions are someone else's they could be mine or those of any seeker, Indian or foreign. Her answers reveal many of her religious teachings. After I had introduced my twenty-four-year-old friend from South America, Satguru began to speak without waiting for the first question.

"One must surrender completely to God. There is no alternative. In the morning one should spend some time in prayer and meditation in whatever form is suitable to one's chosen deity. Then one should turn one's attention to the day's work or activity. No one can be without activities, but they should be done in such a manner that the mind's attention may still be focused on God. The object is always to surrender completely to God. I suggest various paths, depending on temperament. Not everyone is ready for self-inquiry or for the practice of deep religious teachings. If one has not achieved a good deal of self-control at the lower level and doesn't have some degree of mental discipline, then such attempts are mere mockery. They can lead us into delusion. If we are not ready for them, they may affect our health and cause high blood pressure. I'll tell you a story. An old *sannyasi* came to see me. He claimed to have developed a good deal of realization. I had a question about that. I asked him whether he usually ate polished rice or unpolished rice. He said he usually ate polished rice. I told him to switch to unpolished rice and come to see me after a week. When he returned, I asked him how he had been. 'Very sick,' was the reply. You see, his body still had such a hold on him that even such a simple change in diet was enough to throw him off. I went for years with only about one hour of sleep a night, engaged in terrible fasts; now I don't even know whether the next day I shall eat anything. For days now I have been on a liquid diet.

"So, use your simple prayer and try to purify your mind. When certain thoughts, distracting thoughts, enter the mind—they should not be entertained there—remember that they can be managed and controlled by substituting prayer, a *mantra*, or thoughts of God. God realization should be one's entire goal in life, and everything else should be secondary. All else in the world pales alongside God realization. As you come closer to it, the valuable things of the world will draw you less because they will be less attractive. You should become aware of the passage of life from childhood on to old age. Nothing lasts—the joys, the sorrows. So much is fated—the result of past *karma*. We cannot avoid anything. But the attitude toward events, the type of attention we give to them, these are within our control. That is where we exercise our freedom. Do you understand?"

"Yes," my friend said. "I think I do understand what you say. It is difficult, but I agree with it. I have a couple of questions, though."

"Yes."

"First of all, I was wondering about studies. Should we continue our studies? What relation do these have to God realization?"

"As I said," Ma replied, "you have to do something. You should continue your studies in the normal course of things but turn your mind as much as possible toward God. As with all outward activity, you may reach a point at which you are no longer capable of continuing in the old way. That is the time to stop—when the things of themselves automatically fall away."

"I have another question," the young man went on. "It is about the sex side of life. It doesn't bother me too much, but I wonder how I can completely control my sexual desires."

She answered, "The first thing to remember is that your case is nothing rare. Most people are in the same situation. They choose between being married and being single. On the whole, from the point of view of a religious life, it is better to be single. Marriage inevitably draws you toward the world and its problems. The way toward divine love eventually cancels out the loves of the lower nature. You must love God and desire divine union to such an extent that you want to shed tears of longing. We all have a higher and lower nature. The higher nature, when it becomes more developed, tends to triumph over the lower nature. Marriage for some people is necessary—as the Bible says, 'It is better to marry than to burn.' But married life is difficult, it is like a three-legged race!" (She laughs.) "You can't go very fast. Those who have purified their lives can rise very rapidly toward God realization. There is another thing, too. I rarely answer direct questions about sex. These answers generally come from within. Sex is an intensely personal matter."

EPILOGUE

Over the weeks, months, and years that I have been meeting Ma, I have felt increasingly attracted to her. What part of my attraction has to do with her being a woman? I think most people would like to have a mother like her—without apparent inner conflicts, dignified, wisely admonitory, and, at the same time, completely accepting. But beyond that, as far as I can tell, her spiritual knowledge stems from a profound inner life that seems to illuminate general human experience, a man's as well as a woman's. True, she has a powerful personality, and this is especially meaningful at a time when women are seeking leading roles in all areas of human endeavor. But Shri Jnanananda Saraswati, the guru-goddess, will be most attractive to anyone, female or male, who wants to know about the depth of the spiritual reality from one who is amazingly articulate in stating her perception of it.

Notes

1. *Advaita* Hinduism teaches the essential oneness of the soul (*atman*) and the Absolute (*brahman*). The material world in relation to that oneness is a mere slide show.
2. *Ayurvedic* medicine, using primarily herbal potions and ointments, is the traditional Indian medical practice; its origins lie in ancient, even prehistoric times.

Further Readings

Nikhilananda, Swami. *Holy Mother: Being the Life of Sarada Devi, Wife of Sri Ramakrishna and Helpmate in His Mission.* London: George Allen and Unwin, 1963.

White, Charles S. J. "The Hindu Holy Person." *Abingdon Dictionary of Living Religions.* Nashville, Tenn.: Abingdon Press, 1981.

——————. "The Indian Situation: The Saints and Holy Ones." *Sainthood: Its Manifestation in World Religions,* ed. by Richard Kieckhefer and George Bond. Berkeley, Calif.: University of California Press, 1988.

——————. "Jidda Krishnamurti." *The Encyclopedia of Religion.* New York: Macmillan, 1987.

——————. *Ramakrishna's Americans: A Report on Intercultural Monasticism.* Delhi: Yugantar Prakashan Ltd., 1979.

——————. "The Sai Baba Movement: Approaches to the Study of Indian Saints." *Journal of Asian Studies,* 1972.

"Swami Muktananda and the Enlightenment Through Shakti Pat." *History of Religion* 13, no. 4 (1974).

3

The Catholic Earth Mother: Dorothy Day and Women's Power in the Church

DEBRA CAMPBELL

Roman Catholic women's struggle for equal access to the ordained priesthood is a relatively recent development. The hierarchical power structure of the Catholic Church, a closed system in which decisions trickle down from the pope through the ranks of the (male) bishops and priests to "the people" below, has precluded the possibility of women's full participation in the church's ministry, not to mention women's power within the institutional church. In the 1980s small advances have been made. A delegation of Catholic women met with members of the American hierarchy in Washington, D.C. in November 1983 to discuss matters of mutual concern, and a bishops' pastoral on the role of women in the American Catholic Church has been in the planning stages for several years. After two centuries of not-so-benign neglect, the American bishops have officially expressed an interest in listening to the women in the church.[1]

This dialogue between the American bishops and Catholic women, as well as the growing involvement of lay women and sisters in the unordained ministries of the church, raise important questions concerning the kind of power women can or should have in the

DEBRA CAMPBELL is Dana Faculty Fellow and Assistant Professor of Religion at Colby College in Waterville, Maine. She received her Ph.D. in Church History from Boston University in 1982. She is currently working on a history of lay Catholic evangelism in England and America and a history of lay ministries in the American Catholic community.

Editors' Note This article is reprinted, with some alterations, from *Cross Currents* (Fall 1984): 270–82, by permission of the author and the publisher, *Cross Currents*, Mercy College, Dobbs Ferry, NY 10522.

church. The issue of whether women should be able to join the existing ecclesiastical power structure almost inevitably raises related questions. Might women point the way to an alternative vision of power and leadership within the American Catholic Church? What form might Catholic women's power or leadership assume? Can women improve upon the male patterns of authority and find ways to function efficiently without falling into the all too familiar power trap? Most feminists would agree that it would be a major mistake to emulate male hierarchical power structures, but we have few models of specifically female alternative forms of power at our disposal. This is especially true in the ecclesiastical realm. Traditional works in American religious history contain few exemplars of women's power or leadership. Nevertheless, upon closer inspection, we find some instances in which women have wielded *a kind of power*.

This essay explores one such instance and focuses upon the contribution of Dorothy Day to the debate on how women's power has actually functioned in the recent past in the American Catholic Church. It does not recommend Day as a "role model" for today's women. Instead it suggests that we examine Dorothy Day's experience as an illuminating example of how one twentieth-century Catholic woman achieved a unique kind of authority which paradoxically challenged and acknowledged the male hierarchical authority structure of the Roman Catholic Church. Day was a lay woman, a convert, who developed her own personal model of a Christian life of total commitment in the world, a model which allowed her to sidestep traditional constraints and to exercise an alternative form of leadership within the American Catholic Church. In the process Day became a celebrity. Long before her death in December 1980 Day's name and story graced the pages of the secular and religious press with surprising frequency. Articles in *The New Yorker* and *The New Republic* as well as in *Commonweal* and *America* examined Day's lifestyle and her unique Christian witness.[2] Day's vision and power were not derivative; they sprang from her own personal experiences. Therefore in order to understand the nature of Day's power we must first turn to her life.[3]

The daughter of a sportswriter, Dorothy Day moved during her childhood from Brooklyn to Oakland to Chicago as her father went from newspaper to newspaper. The San Francisco earthquake of 1906 had a profound effect upon young Dorothy Day. She relived it in a recurring childhood dream:

As soon as I closed my eyes at night the blackness of death surrounded me. I believed and yet was afraid of nothingness. What would it be like to sink into that immensity? If I fell asleep God became in my ears a great noise that became louder and louder, and approached nearer and nearer to me until I woke up sweating with fear and shrieking for my mother. I fell asleep with her hand in mine, her warm presence by my bed.[4]

Even as a child Dorothy Day grappled with the supernatural. It is poignant to note that only her mother could save her from the menacing God she apparently connected with the natural calamity of the earthquake. Ironically Dorothy's memories of the earthquake are intermingled with those of another disturbing event which had transpired only a few days before; she had seen her mother faint suddenly and crash to the bedroom floor. Both events combined to give young Dorothy a sense of overarching natural tragedy and to impress upon her the fragility of her mother and of the earth itself. The aftermath of the earthquake also taught her a lesson which she would teach others in later life, "the joy of doing good, of sharing whatever we had with others."[5]

Meanwhile the Day family suffered another loss. After the paper plant in San Francisco was destroyed in the earthquake Dorothy's father had to move the family to Chicago. The contrast between their California home, "a bungalow surrounded by trees and flowers," and their six-room flat on the South Side of Chicago which overlooked a "cement paved yard with neither tree nor blade of grass," deeply moved young Dorothy.[6] She began to identify closely with the poor. Even after another move to a house in a nicer neighborhood, she continued to haunt the poorer sections on the West Side pushing her baby brother in a carriage "through interminable gray streets, fascinating in their dreary sameness, past tavern after tavern." Even in these grim surroundings young Dorothy found signs of hope in the tiny gardens tucked into odd corners of the ghetto and in the homey odors wafting by. In her autobiography she recalled it all in delicious detail:

> The odor of geranium leaves, tomato plants, marigolds; the smell of lumber, of tar, of roasting coffee; the smell of good bread and rolls and coffee cake coming from the small German bakeries. Here was enough beauty to satisfy me.[7]

In this adolescent attraction to the poverty of Chicago's West Side and to its multifarious smells we see Dorothy Day's social conscience and her nascent sensuality awakening simultaneously. Both came to fruition during the next decade. At sixteen Day entered the University of Illinois at Urbana. She read Dostoyevsky, Gorky and Tolstoy. She mingled with the literary crowd and began to write. She joined the Socialist Party. Then in 1916 she moved with her family to New York City.

Soon Dorothy Day was a "radical" journalist writing for *The Masses* and *Call* and living among the bohemians in Greenwich Village on the eve of the First World War.[8] Malcolm Cowley writes about Day's legendary drinking abilities in *The Exile's Return*.[9] Day gained this reputation in a Village bar called the Hell Hole where she had sat "in a sort of trance" while her good friend Eugene O'Neill recited Francis Thompson's "Hound of Heaven" from memory.[10] There were other even more intimate scenes with O'Neill in the Village during the winter of 1917–18. Often, after the Hell Hole closed at three or four in the morning Day and O'Neill

> would venture out into the cold, making their way down to the East Side, stopping off frequently at taverns on the way. . . . Dorothy had a room on the East Side, and when they got there, she would put the shaking and exhausted O'Neill to bed and then lie beside him under the covers and hold him close to her trying to keep him warm. During such moments, Dorothy said, O'Neill would ask her, "Dorothy, do you want to surrender your virginity?" In O'Neill's usual sodden condition, this question would have been pointless. Even so, said Dorothy, she always turned the question aside. Early in the afternoon, when O'Neill awakened, he would call Dorothy, wherever she happened to be working then, and have her meet him at the Hell Hole to begin the cycle again.[11]

During the decade between 1917 and 1927 Day worked as a freelance journalist in New York, Chicago and New Orleans and remained politically active. She went to prison twice, first in 1917 with other participants in the Washington march for women's suffrage[12] and later in 1923 when she was caught in a raid on the Wobblies headquarters in Chicago. A turning point in Day's life arrived in 1924 when a Hollywood studio paid her five thousand dollars for the movie rights to her autobiographical novel, *The Eleventh Virgin*.[13] Day used the money to buy a cottage on Staten Island which she shared with Forster Batterham, a biologist with anarchist sympathies. In 1927 Day gave birth to Batterham's child, a daughter named Tamar. In December of the same year Day was baptized a Roman Catholic, a step which alienated Batterham and ended their relationship.

Day had long been engaged in a protracted spiritual quest. Even in her Greenwich Village days she had puzzled her friends by her intermittent visits to Catholic Churches.[14] Day's deepening relationship with Batterham and the love of nature they both shared intensified her religious feelings. "How can there be no God and all these beautiful things?" she continued to ask.[15] Finally, after the birth of her daughter, Day entered the Catholic Church. She explained her reasons in her autobiography:

I knew that I was going to have my child baptized, cost what it may. I knew that I was not going to have her floundering through many years as I had done, doubting and hesitating, undisciplined and amoral. I felt that it was the greatest thing I could do for my child.[16]

Then, in order to be able to raise her Catholic Child properly, Dorothy overcame her own hesitation and followed her infant daughter into the Catholic Church.

The rest of the story has become a familiar chapter in American religious history. For several years Day sought a way to combine her new religious commitments with her old political convictions. She dutifully submitted to the Roman Catholic Church's official condemnation of socialism and thus found herself sitting on the sidelines, watching her former comrades engage in actions which, in her heart, she still considered right. In December 1932 when she covered a communist hunger march in Washington, D.C., for a Catholic journal Day felt herself torn apart by conflicting loyalties and conflicting emotions. As she later recalled:

I stood on the curb and watched them, joy and pride in the courage of this band of men and women mounting in my heart, and with it a bitterness too that since I was now a Catholic with fundamental philosophical differences, I could not be out there with them. I could write, I could protest, to arouse the conscience, but where was the Catholic leadership in the gathering of the bands of men and women together, for the actual works of mercy that the comrades had always made a part of their technique in reaching the workers?

How little, how puny my work has been since becoming a Catholic, I thought. How self-centered, how ingrown, how lacking in a sense of community.[17]

Shortly after this difficult episode Day returned from Washington to New York and met Peter Maurin, once aptly described as "a cross between a bum and a twentieth-century Isaias."[18] Together Day and Maurin founded the Catholic Worker movement, launched in May 1933, with its three-fold plan to spread Catholic social teachings in a penny paper called *The Catholic Worker*, to settle in urban outposts called Houses of Hospitality where volunteers would live lives of poverty and service to the poor, and to establish experimental farming communes, models of non-capitalist Christian communal living.

The Catholic Worker movement has become synonymous with the name Dorothy Day. It has had its ups and downs, but has remained dedicated to the original ideals of voluntary poverty, social justice, peace and solidarity with workers and the poor. It has also expanded geographically and in the size of its membership. Judged by the standards of longevity and growth, the movement is a success. In 1980, the year Dorothy Day died, *The Catholic Worker* had between 85,000 and 100,000 subscribers.[19]

The Catholic Workers, an organic, decentralized movement in a hierarchical church, remains a monument to Dorothy Day's vision and her leadership. Clearly it was Day and not Maurin who kept the movement together and mobilized its members when the occasion demanded it. Maurin played a crucial role in the founding of the movement when he introduced Day to a whole body of European Catholic social thought which widened her vision of the church as a vehicle for social reform. Nevertheless, as historian Mel Piehl maintains, Maurin's importance was "more personal and symbolic than programmatic or intellectual."[20] In a pinch, it was Day who coped with concrete problems and made pressing decisions. As John Cogley, a Chicago Catholic Worker who had ample opportunity to watch the interaction between Maurin and Day, observed: "[Maurin] was obviously uncomfortable in the feigned role of leadership. Unless the questions were abstractly philosophical or sweepingly historical he would turn helplessly to Dorothy Day for an answer."[21] Moreover, Piehl reminds us, Maurin was also "strategically useful," a "symbolic helpmate" in a church which implicitly rejected the notion of female leadership.[22]

Ironically, Dorothy Day herself paid lip service to the same sexual stereotypes she refuted in her day-to-day life. She once wrote that "Men are the single-minded, the pure of heart in these movements. . . .Women by their very nature are materialistic, thinking of the home, the children, and all things needful to them."[23] It is significant to our discussion to note that this was written by Day, a single parent, who devoted almost half a century to one movement. Elsewhere, however, Day argued in favor of women's unique qualifications for the job the Catholic Workers were doing. "Perhaps it is easier for a woman to understand than a man," she affirmed, "because no matter what has occurred or hangs overhead, she has to go on with the business of living. She does the physical things and so keeps a balance."[24] From her own experience as a woman and as a mother, Dorothy could see that women's ineradicable link to "the physical things" was not a spiritual liability but a responsibility and a gift.

In a church with clearly delineated lines of authority, Day openly urged others to pursue alternative channels, to bypass established authorities in the interests of justice and peace. "When I started *The Catholic Worker*," she affirmed, "I asked no permissions, expected no recognitions."[25] In 1963 she urged Catholic activists in Los Angeles:

We must follow where the spirit leads. So go ahead, . . . don't look for support or approval. And don't always be looking for blame either, or see opposition where perhaps there is none. . . . I beg you to save your energies to fight the giant injustices of our time, and not the Church in the shape of its Cardinal Archbishop.[26]

During the New York City gravediggers' strike in 1949 Day had chosen the same approach and supported the strikers while Cardinal Spellman had openly opposed them. Nevertheless, Day could still maintain that "if the Chancery ordered me to stop publishing the *The Catholic Worker* tomorrow, I would."[27]

For all of her ideological independence Dorothy Day was a traditional Catholic who staunchly upheld the authority of the church amidst the turbulence of the 1960s. Daniel Berrigan recalls how she supported the church's position on sexual ethics to the letter and ". . . broke friendships, tossed free-loving hippies out on their ears, forbade Catholic deviants access to her paper." Only later did she mellow and renew her old friendships with married priests like Berrigan's brother Philip.[28] Dorothy Day also remained aloof from the drive for democracy and lay rights in the church in the 1960s and the Catholic women's movement which gained momentum in the following decade. Doris Grumbach, an observer at a conference on women in the church held in Westchester, New York in November 1970, noted that seventy-two-year-old Dorothy Day appeared out of place among "the smartly suited nuns and laywomen and men . . . and nattily dressed priests." Nonetheless, Grumbach maintained that Day was "in action and practice the most liberated [woman]" in a room which included such figures as Sidney Callahan and Betty Friedan. All Day had to do was to reiterate what she had said all along:

Yes, we have lived with the poor, with the workers . . . the unemployed, the sick. . . . We have all known the long loneliness and we have learned that the only solution is love and that love comes with community.[29]

Here we reach the heart of Dorothy Day's approach to the leadership of her movement, her emphasis upon community. Looking back upon her experiences in the late 1920s when she was a freelance writer taking care of an infant daughter, she recalled the profound loneliness she had experienced and she reflected:

> I was to find out then, as I found out so many times, over and over again, that women especially are social beings, who are not content with just husband and family, but must have a community, a group, an exchange with others. A child is not enough. A husband and children, no matter how busy one may be kept by them, are not enough. Young and old, even in the busiest years of our lives, we women especially are victims of the long loneliness.[30]

When Day referred to the long loneliness, she meant not only her own situation, but the human condition in general. And yet, for Day, there was a special female dimension to the long loneliness as the above quotation indicates. Day originally encountered the phrase in the writings of the English nun, Mary Ward. Ward had written: "We women especially are victims of the long loneliness."[31]

The underlying goal, to fight against the long loneliness, explains much about why Dorothy Day's movement is an anomaly in the institutional church and why Day's style of leadership contrasts with that exercised by bishops and cardinals. Granted, Day could occasionally take control and wield power *as if* she were at the helm of a hierarchy. When John Cogley and some Chicago Catholic Workers disagreed with Day's absolute pacifism during the Second World War, Dorothy Day issued an ultimatum to the dissenters: either distribute *The Catholic Worker* (which propagated Day's position) or split with the movement.[32] John Cort, a convert who joined the Catholic Workers in the 1930s after his graduation from Harvard, has called the movement "an extraordinary combination of anarchy and dictatorship."[33] On the issue of pacifism Day appears to have inclined in the direction of dictatorship. This is part of what Daniel Berrigan had called her "absolutely stunning consistency."[34] Day categorically rejected all forms of violence, war and bloodshed. And yet, this very position which she felt so intensely and furthered so heavy-handedly is, upon closer examination, deeply rooted in her larger vision of the Catholic Worker movement as a community intended to stave off the long loneliness.

As Abigail McCarthy, a close follower of the movement since her college days in the 1930s, has observed, a salient trait of the Catholic Worker houses and farms has been their separate, autonomous, family-like structure. The Houses of Hospitality were homes in which Dorothy Day played the role of mother and sister.[35] Because her goal was community and peace and justice Day eschewed all formal structures and institutionalized means of control. As Mel Piehl puts it:

> For Dorothy Day, a social revolution would be worthwhile only if it was also homelike. By making the themes of community and domesticity that had always been important to her parts of the fabric of Catholic Worker life, she made its radical Christian idealism seem homey as well.[36]

If life with the Catholic Workers was homey, it was also rigorous and physically uncomfortable. Writing in 1952 Day reported that many Houses of Hospitality still lacked central heating and indoor toilets. The Philadelphia House still used oil lamps and shared its water faucet, located in the alley, with several other residences.[37]

Notwithstanding, Catholic Worker houses attracted a variety of volunteers during the forty-seven years in which Day stood at the center of the movement. Julia Porcelli, who joined the Catholic Workers in New York in the 1930s, did so because she "didn't see many people living by faith, and . . . was very hungry for things of the spirit." Porcelli confessed: the Catholic Workers were "the people I wanted to be with. There was brotherhood, there was unity, there was family, . . . I felt strongly that they were my own family."[38] The movement also attracted a growing minority of Catholic college students, male and female, who were full of idealism but without an outlet for their energies during the Depression.[39] The Catholic Workers represented a way to be involved in the struggle for social justice and still avoid the more radical movements condemned by the church. Ex-seminarians rethinking their vocational plans found homes in the Houses of Hospitality as did working-class Catholics like Margaret, a young Lithuanian woman from a mining town in Pennsylvania who came with her infant daughter Barbara and tended the stove when she was not hawking *The Catholic Worker* on the New York City streets during the early years of the movement.[40]

Then, especially in the years following the Second World War, there were college educated upper-middle-class Catholics like Michael Harrington who came to the Catholic Worker fresh from Holy Cross and sought to recover in the movement a Catholic social justice tradition which was slipping out of the sight in an American Catholic Church increasingly enamored with militarism and bourgeois culture. Ultimately Harrington chose to follow Day's example in reverse; he moved from the Catholic Church to socialism. But he never forgot Dorothy Day and he readily acknowledges his debt to Day and to the movement.[41]

Dorothy Day had an uncanny ability to persuade people to confront themselves and thus to find their own vision and their own power. Wilfrid Sheed relates that during the Vietnam War Day persuaded several young men to go to jail rather than face induction into the army. While they were in jail, the men lost their faith. Sheed underlines the irony: "the fact that those young men had lost their faith was heartbreaking to [Day]. And she had urged them into it!"[42] Day's pacifism and her pivotal role in the Catholic Worker movement were both rooted in her boundless maternal instinct. When, during the Korean War, a reader of *The Catholic Worker* castigated her for her lack of compassion for "the poor kids in Korea," she re-

sponded trenchantly: "If it refers to our soldiers, the phrase is maudlin, and I don't think it means the children being killed by our bombs."[43]

The volunteers came to the Catholic Worker not merely to give but also to receive. With Julia Porcelli they came for the family. Wilfrid Sheed recalls that "every possible blueprint for a Catholic left was hammered out in the back room while Dorothy doled out soup in the front. . . . Yet the talk *was* the movement as much as the soup."[44] Day certainly did not confine herself to the task of ladling soup, but there was a touch of domesticity to every aspect of life in the Houses of Hospitality. When the seamen went on strike in New York City in 1936–37 Day housed as many strikers as she could and set up a store-front commissary near the waterfront especially for the strikers. She raised four thousand dollars to feed them for several months. When strikebreakers threw a paving stone through the commissary window Day informed readers of *The Catholic Worker*: "half the stone is used to bolster up the stove and the other half is used to keep the bread-knife sharp, as we are slicing up 150 loaves of bread a day."[45]

Typically, Dorothy Day sought to bring her readers into the kitchen with her, to share her work and her community and to help them to stave off the long loneliness. Strictly speaking, Day did not administer or lead the Catholic Worker Movement; she mothered it in the best, most profound sense of the term. In collaboration with Peter Maurin she conceived it and brought it to term. From 1933 until her death in 1980 she remained the center of the movement, its constant source of life and strength. Volunteers came, attracted by Day, her vision and her community. Even if they disagreed with Day they left enriched, with a new sense of their own identity and their own power.

In an expanded footnote in *Bare Ruined Choirs* Garry Wills describes Dorothy Day as a "Catholic earth mother" who "mothered her principal charge [Peter Maurin] and then mothered a whole succession of others through the years."[46] Wills calls the Catholic Worker houses "way stations" for "troubled young men" in transition. As Julia Porcelli reminds us, the houses were more than remedial units; they were homes. Nevertheless, Wills correctly calls attention to the transient character of the Catholic Worker population. Dorothy Day was the only constant; the other members were in transit.

Wills's choice of the earth mother archetype also focuses our attention upon other important aspects of Day's function within the community. Day brings to mind the earth mother at the center of the ancient religions which preceded the rise of Yahwism, "a powerful female figure who was at once virgin and mother, wife and sister, and who rescued the dying God from the power of the underworld." Like Day and the Catholic Workers the ancient earth mother religions celebrated "the release of captives, justice for the poor, and security against invasion, as well as the new rain, the new grain, the new lamb and the new child."[47] Although the image may not be a perfect fit, it is an apt metaphor for Day's pervasive maternal presence at the center of the Catholic Worker movement for so many years. It also calls to mind other important moments earlier in Day's life: her childhood dreams of a raging God soothed only by the warm presence of her mother by her bed, her adolescent walks with her baby brother through Chicago's West Side empathizing with the poor and marveling at the beauty of their tiny gardens, and finally her ambivalent relationship with the cold, shivering, dependent Eugene O'Neill during the winter of 1917. Motherhood was a revelation to Dorothy Day. When she became a mother she realized her own special need for a community beyond her daughter and discovered her own special ability to help others through the long loneliness.

Dorothy Day was not a Catholic earth mother simply because of her selfless service to others; the earth mother archetype is far richer than that. Dorothy Day was not Mother Teresa, an unquestioning daughter of the church content to bathe the wounds inflicted by the present system without asking how we might shut off the source of the pain. Daniel Berrigan calls attention to Day's primal power and to the penetrating critique of the status quo which she came to symbolize simply by being utterly consistent in her refusal to accept war, injustice and poverty. He compares Day to Christ and Buddha and explains: "At length, all was said and done. So she stood there, or sat down, like Christ, like Buddha." Dorothy Day stayed put; her movement revolved around her. And yet, as Berrigan insists, staying put can be a revolutionary act. He thanks Day for paving the way for the destruction of the nuclear reactors at King of Prussia, Pennsylvania, in September 1980. "The best tribute that we could offer Dorothy is that we too would stand somewhere or sit down."[48]

What can Dorothy Day's life teach us about women's power in the Roman Catholic Church? It shows that it is at least possible for a woman to form and lead a decentralized movement for peace and justice and still remain a faithful, even a devout Roman Catholic. It indicates that the hierarchical model of authority does not exhaust the possibilities open to the church; the extended family model might, in fact, be more compatible with a strong stand on peace and social justice. Implicitly, Day's experience illustrates the wisdom and practicality of confronting the issues rather than the authorities whenever possible. Granted, Dorothy Day had no trouble making this clear-cut distinction because for her, the authority structure was not one of the issues.

The power Dorothy Day wielded as earth mother bears little resemblance to the type of power required to run a tight ship or a competitive corporation. From Day's maternal style of leadership we learn that movements are best served by leaders who, like the best mothers, train others to move beyond them to claim their own power and vision. When Dorothy Day died, many wondered whether the Catholic Workers could survive without her. Clearly they have,[49] and the current editors of *The Catholic Worker* have rather self-consciously set out to move beyond Day and Maurin in order to remain within the spirit of the original movement. From Dorothy Day the Catholic Workers have learned to seek the source of renewal and growth within their own communities rather than asking for direction from above or without. The power epitomized by Dorothy Day, the Catholic earth mother, is the kind that empowers others rather than entrenching itself. Ultimately it is the only kind of power that can be passed on with confidence to future generations of women (and men).

Notes

1. Pope John Paul II is another matter. He has chosen to publicly ignore at least one outspoken American churchwoman, Sister Theresa Kane, a strong advocate of women's ordination. As theologian Hans Küng has observed ("Will the Pope Win Over Women?" *The New York Times*, 16 November 1983, A31): "The Pope, who receives even atheists and Communists, has consistently refused [Kane] a private audience."

2. *Commonweal* has been especially attentive to Dorothy Day over the years. Some important articles on Day which have appeared elsewhere include: a symposium on Day and the Catholic Worker movement in *America* 127 (11 November 1972); Dwight MacDonald, "Profiles: The Foolish Things of the World," *The New Yorker*, 4 October 1952, pp. 37–56 and 11 October 1952, pp. 37–52; Colman McCarthy, "On Dorothy Day," *The New Republic* 168 (24 February 1973), pp. 30–33.

3. Biographical information on Day's life is drawn from William D. Miller, *Dorothy Day: A Biography* (San Francisco: Harper and Row, 1982); Mel Piehl, *Breaking Bread: The Catholic Worker and the Origin of Catholic Radicalism in America* (Philadelphia: Temple University Press, 1982); Dorothy Day, *The Long Loneliness: An Autobiography* (San Francisco: Harper and Row, 1952; rpt., 1981).

4. Day, *Long Loneliness*, p. 20.

5. Ibid., p. 21.

6. Ibid., p. 23.

7. Ibid., p. 37.

8. For a discussion of the context in which Dorothy Day found herself see Leslie Fishbein, "The Failure of Feminism in Greenwich Village before World War I," *Women's Studies* 9 (1982): 227–89.

9. New York: Viking Press, 1951, p. 69.

10. Miller, p. 110.

11. Ibid. Day revealed this to a companion in February 1974. Miller (p. 111) maintains that Day recognized some of herself in O'Neill's character, Josie Hogan, in *Moon for the Misbegotten*.

12. See Day's account of the prison experience in *The Long Loneliness*, pp. 72–83.

13. New York: Albert and Charles Boni, 1924.

14. Miller, pp. 112–13.

15. Day, *Long Loneliness*, p. 134.

16. Ibid., p. 136.

17. Ibid., p. 165.

18. Leo R. Ward, *Catholic Life U.S.A.* (St. Louis: B. Herder, 1959), p. 189.

19. Nancy L. Roberts, "Building a New Earth: Dorothy Day and 'The Catholic Worker'," *The Christian Century* 97 (10 December 1980): 1217; *The New York Times* (1 December 1980, D12) estimated 85,000 subscribers while *Newsweek* (15 December 1980, p. 75) supplied another figure: 90,000.

20. Piehl, p. 64.

21. Quoted in Abigail McCarthy, "Confronting Dorothy Day," *Commonweal* 104 (13 May 1977), p. 297.

22. Piehl, p. 65.

23. Ibid.

24. Quoted in McCarthy, p. 318.

25. Quoted in Piehl, p. 915.

26. Quoted in Piehl, p. 92.

27. Quoted by Dwight MacDonald in "Profiles," *The New Yorker*, 4 October 1952, p. 39.

28. Daniel Berrigan, "Introduction" to *Long Loneliness*, xiv.

29. Doris Grumbach, "Father Church and the Motherhood of God," *Commonweal* 93 (11 December 1970), pp. 268–69.

30. Quoted by Miller, pp. 211–12.

31. Quoted by Piehl, p. 83.

32. See Piehl, pp. 155–6.

33. "My Life at the Catholic Worker," *Commonweal* 107 (20 June 1980), p. 364.

34. Berrigan, "Introduction" to *Long Loneliness*, xix.

35. McCarthy, p. 318.

36. Piehl, p. 80.

37. Day, *Long Loneliness*, p. 187.

38. Quoted in Miller, p. 270.

39. Day, *Long Loneliness*, p. 186.

40. Ibid., p. 185.

41. See, for example, *The Boston Globe*, 6 October 1983, p. 2. On Harrington's experience with Day and the Catholic Workers see Harrington's *Fragments of the Century* (New York: Saturday Review Press/E.P. Dutton, 1972, 1973), pp. 17–23; Piehl, pp. 172–8.

42. Wilfrid Sheed, "Dorothy Day," *The Nation* 231 (20 December 1980), p. 661.

43. Quoted by Piehl, p. 81.

44. Sheed, p. 661.

45. Quoted by Cort, p. 365.

46. Garry Wills, *Bare Ruined Choirs: Doubt, Prophesy and Radical Religion* (New York: Dell/Delta, 1974; c 1971, 1972), p. 59.

47. Rosemary Radford Ruether, "Motherearth and the Megamachine: A Theology of Liberation in a Feminine, Somatic and Ecological Perspective," in *Womanspirit Rising: A Feminist Reader in Religion*, eds., Carol P. Christ and Judith Plaskow (San Francisco: Harper and Row, 1979), p. 47.

48. Berrigan, "Introduction" to *Long Loneliness*, xxii-xxiii.

49. In May 1982 *The Catholic Worker* published an impressive list of affiliated Houses of Hospitality and farming communes in the United States and Canada.

Further Readings

Coles, Robert. *Dorothy Day: A Radical Devotion.* Reading, Mass.: Addison-Wesley/Merloid Lawrence Book, 1987.

Ellsberg, Robert, ed. *By Little and By Little: The Selected Writings of Dorothy Day.* New York: Alfred A. Knopf, 1983.

Forest, Jim. *Love Is the Measure: A Biography of Dorothy Day.* New York: Paulist Press, 1986.

Klejment, Anne and Alice Klejment, eds. *Dorothy Day and the Catholic Worker: A Bibliography and Index.* New York: Garland Publishing Company, 1986.

Roberts, Nancy L. *Dorothy Day and the Catholic Worker.* Albany, N.Y.: State University of New York Press, 1984.

For the history of the discussion of women's power in the American Catholic community, see Mary Jo Weaver, *New Catholic Women: A Contemporary Challenge to Traditional Religious Authority* (San Francisco, Calif.: Harper and Row, 1985).

II

WOMEN EXPLODE

Ritualized Rebellion for Women

We who have been raised in some of the more formalized Western traditions are accustomed to thinking that people choose, of their own volition, to join a religious movement or pursue a religious career, as demonstrated by the example of Dorothy Day. However, the accounts of Julia and Jnanananda have shown that, when women follow an extraordinary calling, they often find that they are chosen as much as they make the choice. Experiences of possession by gods or ecstatic seizures like theirs are widespread in women's religious lives. Many people who study religion have observed how often women serve as shamans or mediums in a variety of cultures. Religious movements valuing possession experiences and ecstasy seem more open to women than are the formal, structured traditions often described in textbooks on religion. Religious laws and bureaucracies can dictate that only men shall be priests, but the gods choose whom they will. Consequently, these callings and movements often seem to function as an important means of self-expression for women denied such opportunity through other institutions. Their pent-up energy, intelligence, and frustration are released as they literally explode.

When such explosions occur, it is not uncommon that they become a source of family or public scandal. At the same time, however, they may function as a kind of religious safety valve. Everyone knows that some women—perhaps the whole society—would disintegrate without these vehicles for self-expression. Therefore, women's breakdowns are often interpreted in religious terms and are channeled through acceptable ritual and cultural expressions. As a result, both the women themselves and their families avoid disintegration.

In this section we study two instances of ritualized rebellion on the part of women in two cultures widely separated in time and space. Some modern Korean housewives who are ill-suited to their traditional roles suffer breakdowns. Korean folk psychiatry knows how to foster a recovery: the women are recognized as shamans—psychic advisors and healers—who are sought out by other Koreans who pay for the aid they receive from them. After accepting their shamanic callings, the women no longer face the situation that sparked their breakdown. Some seemingly scandalous aspects of the ancient Greek cult of the god Dionysus can probably be understood in a similar manner. This cult, in which the god possessed large numbers of women and made them into temporary antihousewives, has long mystified classicists, who wondered how this could have happened. Unlike the Korean possession sickness, however, initiation into Dionysus' mysteries probably brought Greek women only temporary relief.

4

Possession Sickness and Women Shamans in Korea

YOUNGSOOK KIM HARVEY

K orea has a long-standing tradition, probably reaching into prehistoric times, of women serving in the religious role of *mudang*, or shaman. Two different types of *mudang* are found in Korea. The first is a kind of family priestess whose role is usually inherited. The second may be called a "professional" shaman, whose services may be engaged by anyone willing to pay a fee. Unlike the family priestesses, these professional shamans acquire their role through individual experiences of spirit possession and subsequent rites of initiation conducted by qualified professional shamans. The professional shamans can enter into trance states and are believed to possess supernatural

---

YOUNGSOOK KIM HARVEY was born in Korea and came to the United States at the age of seventeen. She studied, worked, and lived on the East Coast and Hawaii. When this study was written, she was serving as Associate Professor of Anthropology at Chaminade University and as Assistant Clinical Professor of Psychiatry at the University of Hawaii School of Medicine. She wrote a monograph on *Koreans in Hawaii*, and also *Six Korean Shamans: the Socialization of Shamans*, from which the material in this chapter was selected (see Further Readings at the end of the chapter). We deeply regret to inform our readers of Dr. Harvey's untimely death in 1983.

Author's Note An earlier version of this article was presented to the 76th annual meeting of the American Anthropological Association, Houston, Texas, 1977, as part of the session on Religion, chaired by Ruth Wangerin. I am indebted to Dr. W. P. Lebra for reading the manuscript and suggesting certain changes. Responsibility for the article, however, rests with myself alone.

powers, which they use to perform a variety of services for the clients who have hired them. Although some professional shamans are men, the overwhelming majority are women.[1]

To understand the position of present-day shamans, some historical background is necessary, for the institution of professional shamans resulted largely from actions taken under the Yi Dynasty (1392–1910). The Yi Dynasty government was founded by neo-Confucian scholars and government officials, who were fanatically determined to bring about a total and radical reform of Korean society. To its founding fathers, the Yi government represented the political triumph of neo-Confucianism, which was seen as the design for rational society. Its exponents immediately launched a comprehensive national program of social reform in which shamans and shamanistic cults were quickly identified as foremost targets of attack. The new regime saw shamanism as appealing to nonrational aspects of humanity; thus, for a rational society to be achieved, it had to be eradicated.

Initially the government attempted to isolate shamans from the populace by banning them from cities and towns and penalizing government officials who failed to keep them out. Such government efforts to stamp out shamanism and replace it with neo-Confucianism resulted in merely driving it underground. In no small part, the program of eradication failed because neo-Confucianism could not minister to the emotional and religious needs of the people. Eventually the government recognized the futility of its program and shifted its policy from total eradication of shamanism to severe restrictions aimed at containing it. Although the government allowed shamans to exist, it licensed them for purposes of taxation and then officially ascribed the social status of outcastes to shamans and their families. This outcaste status had the effect of severely restricting shamans' ability to use their influence and economic power for personal or family social mobility.

Since the fall of the Yi Dynasty in 1910, subsequent governments, including the present one, have continued the traditional policy of persecuting shamans to some degree. Thus, shamans and their families continue to suffer the ostracism directed against outcastes in Korea. Notwithstanding, professional shamans have been, and continue to be, in persistent popular demand to serve as religious functionaries and ethnopsychiatrists. Clients call upon them to find out whether their ancestral spirits are comfortable, to arrange reunions between the dead ancestors and the living descendants, to pick auspicious days for weddings or burials, to reveal causes of marital and family strife and to advise on their resolution, to perform rituals that guarantee continued prosperity, to open up the "gates of good fortune" for those in difficult circumstances, and to heal those who are broken in body or soul.

In the life of a professional shaman, *sinbyŏng* ("possession sickness") is a crucial experience. It often causes great hardship both to the victim and to her family, but it is also a crucial prerequisite to becoming a shaman. Given the disadvantages of the shaman role in Korean society, it seems that *sinbyŏng* may actually be a face-saving mechanism that permits Korean women to acquire the shaman role and their families to accept it. At the same time *sinbyŏng* reflects tensions within the family. Its diagnosis and subsequent cure, which occurs when the shaman role is assumed, relieve some of those tensions.

Sinbyŏng, represented by two Chinese ideographs—*sin* (spirit) and *pyŏng* (sickness)—is the term that Korean researchers of shamanism use to refer to a range of bodily, mental, and behavioral symptoms that, in the Korean folk view, are a supernatural summons to the afflicted that she should assume the shaman role. Koreans view *sinbyŏng* as the most critical prerequisite experience to becoming a professional shaman. The decisive symptom for the diagnosis of *sinbyŏng* is a possession state in which the afflicted person experiences hallucinations and manifests inappropriate behavior. Koreans say that such behavior is the result of possession by spirits. The Korean folk terms for *sinbyŏng*—*sin-chip'yŏtta* and *sin-naeryŏtta*—in fact focus on the possession state as the critical element in *sinbyŏng* experience and can be translated literally as "caught by spirits" and "spirits have descended," respectively.

Symptoms of *sinbyŏng* are at first vague and, therefore, difficult to diagnose. Initially the symptoms are physical. At first, victims have feelings of listlessness and later complain of many or all of the following conditions: anorexia, circulatory distresses such as extreme coldness and/or numbness of hands and feet, diarrhea, faintness or dizziness, headaches, aches in the joints, insomnia, nausea, palpitations of the heart, respiratory congestion experienced as "heaviness of the heart" or "tightness of the chest," acutely painful ringing in the ear, sudden fevers, and weight loss. These physical symptoms do not respond to treatment by the usual home remedies, Chinese herbal medicine, or modern Western medicine and are eventually compounded by mental and behavioral symptoms.

Mental symptoms generally include auditory and/or visual hallucinations and strange dreams, which later prove to have been prophetic of the shaman role destined for the victim. Behavioral symptoms include a variety of actions that would be judged inappropriate or shocking, such as bathing in midwinter with cold water in an open courtyard in direct violation of female modesty and sensible health-care practices, traveling in the cheapest public conveyances in warm weather dressed in extravagantly luxurious winter clothes, or stopping strangers on the streets and telling them their fortunes. Worst of all, as far as the community is concerned, victims may speak too frankly and accurately about things going on in the community that would normally not be openly discussed. They may, for example, say that the chronic illness of a young housewife is due to bottled-up resentment toward her abusive mother-in-law or toward her husband, who will not curtail his gambling or extramarital affairs. Or they may refer to the well-known, but never publicly discussed, history of a man who repeatedly fails in his business ventures and puts the blame for his failures on the disturbance created in his household by his nagging wife. They sometimes reveal adulterous affairs among neighbors that, in all likelihood, everyone has known about but no one has openly acknowledged.

Behavioral symptoms are usually the last to emerge; they ultimately invite the diagnosis of *sinbyŏng* because of their socially disruptive nature. Typically, people are either angered or frightened by these behavioral symptoms. They will think that the women who display them are morally reprehensible or "crazy," with the latter perhaps the more common response. In fact, according to the Korean folk view, it is extremely difficult to differentiate the shaman recruit in possession state, or *sinbyŏng*, from a "crazy" person. Very frequently the diagnosis of *sinbyŏng* is first seriously considered when the victim starts to act as though she were insane.

As the two Chinese ideographs representing the term imply, Koreans believe that *sinbyŏng* is of supernatural origin. Its outcome, on the other hand, is thought to depend on human responses to it. The victims who suffer *sinbyŏng* cannot be blamed for it personally, nor are they free to deny it. Any attempt to resist or deny the call, it is believed, will inevitably invite life-threatening supernatural retaliation on the victims, their families, or both and is therefore ultimately meaningless. Resistance only intensifies *sinbyŏng* and makes it last longer. Furthermore, if the victim dies without assuming the shaman role, the role will be transferred to another member in the lineage, either at once or in the future. If, on the other hand, the victim accepts her calling, she can obtain immediate relief and protect her kinfolk from potential supernatural harm. Thus, refusing to become a shaman can be viewed as an act of futile selfishness on the part of the victim, while assuming it can be interpreted as an act of altruism that will protect others at the same time it alleviates the victim's own suffering.

However, because a shaman in the family brings that family outcaste status, the decision making becomes complicated. Here another folk belief may furnish further motivations for the family to urge that the victim accept her shamanic calling. Koreans believe that, when spirits are searching for humans to possess and use as their mediums, they are particularly attracted to individuals whose *maŭm* (heart/soul) has been "fractured" by experiences of exploitation and tragedy caused by others. Implied in this belief is the suspicion that families of *sinbyŏng* victims may have predisposed them to possession by mistreating them. Such suspicion places the families of victims in a socially embarrassing and psychologically defensive position within the community. It makes them more vulnerable to the implied moral obligation to rescue the victims from *sinbyŏng* as well as to their obligation to urge the victims to assume the shaman role. At the same time, their willingness to assume outcaste status in order to relieve the *sinbyŏng* victim of her affliction makes the family seem altruistic, thus countering the possible suspicions about its earlier treatment of the victim.

In analyzing the life histories of six women shamans, I have traced the spiraling development of their *sinbyŏng* through at least the following phases: (1) The victim experiences severe conflict between her sense of self and her housewife's role, as well as significant conflict with important members of the family, such as her husband, mother-in-law and/or sister-in-law. (2) The victim attempts to cope with these conflicts but feels overwhelmed and helplessly trapped by them. (3) The victim falls ill with vague symptoms and is given "time out." (4) The illness persists, and the family reduces or completely eliminates its normal demands on the victim while mobilizing its resources to

rescue her from her sickness. (5) Under these circumstances, the victim recovers and resumes her usual functions. (6) Now reassured by her recovery, her family reassumes old patterns of interacting. (7) The cumulative strain of living with the conflicts again becomes unbearable, and the victim again becomes sick. This oscillatory process may be repeated several times, as it did with all of my informants, until an impasse develops between the victim's repeated illness and her family's rescue efforts. At this point of impasse, the attending shaman diagnoses the victim's afflictions as *sinbyŏng*.

In one case history, this process took twenty-eight years and two marriages. When she was seventeen, Namsanmansin was forced into an arranged marriage. She tried several times to sabotage the marriage by running away but was caught each time; the last time she was kept a prisoner in her room until the wedding. She felt so violated by the marriage that she refused to consummate it for four months, and when the consummation occurred, she felt raped by her husband. She had not consented; he had simply overpowered her physically one night. When it became apparent that she was pregnant, she tried valiantly to accept her marital role and even to excel in some of her tasks. To her dismay, she found that she simply could not put her "heart into it," and she fell ill with vague symptoms in a recurrent pattern. She had hoped that her child's birth might change things, but she felt no emotional attachment to him when he was born. He was conceived, she says, as a result of rape.

In quick succession, she had two more babies, both girls. The first was stillborn, and the second died when two years old. Namsanmansin felt numb after her daughter's funeral, for she had become fond of the girl, whereas she still felt estranged from her son. Shortly after her daughter's funeral, she began to feel ill again with the same symptoms she had had before, but this time they were much more severe. Her parents-in-law finally called in a shaman to attend her, after the treatments of the Chinese herbalist and the modern doctor from town proved totally ineffective. The shaman declared that Namsanmansin was suffering from *sinbyŏng*, thereby confirming rumors that had been whispered for some time among the elderly women of the village. Namsanmansin's parents-in-law urged her to accept the call and put an end to her own afflictions and the drain on the family's resources. However, the prospect of becoming a shaman was so horrifying to Namsanmansin that she fled from the house that very night and became a peddler in a distant town.

Within a year, she was living in common-law marriage with a North Korean refugee who had a young son. She was very much in love with him and wanted to have their union legalized in marriage, especially after the birth of a daughter. However, her "husband" already had a wife, who had remained in North Korea to look after his aging parents when he fled with their son to South Korea during the Korean War. Although Namsanmansin understood the circumstances of her "husband's" resistance, she herself could not accept being a common-law wife and the mother of a "bastard." She was determined to legalize their relationship.

Knowing that her common-law husband dreamt constantly of big business ventures but lacked the capital for implementing any of them, she underwrote his first big business scheme by adroit investment of her own savings in several mutual aid societies. Shortly afterward they were legally married. However, when his business became stabilized and generated enough income for her to quit her business and become the conventionally ideal Korean wife and mother, her husband became involved in a series of extravagant extramarital affairs that eventually brought financial ruin to them. In the meantime Namsanmansin fell ill with symptoms similar to those that had once been diagnosed as *sinbyŏng*. She consulted a shaman and was told that she was destined to become a shaman. However, she recovered from her illness when her husband's financial ruin was complete and the family was on the brink of starvation. She was a capable businesswoman and soon was able to subsidize her husband's business venture again.

This pattern repeated itself many times during their marriage, until her husband's erratic and extravagant behavior with women finally placed them in such dire financial straits that Namsanmansin had to abandon their fourth child, a month-old girl, at the gate of a prosperous-looking house that she had picked out some weeks before when she feared she might have to give up her baby. She felt she could not care for an infant as well as provide for the older children. She broke down again shortly thereafter. This time, however, she did not recover from her illness and was not able to go to her husband's and children's rescue, as had been the pattern before. Instead, she sat staring into space and hallucinating intermittently for six months, completely oblivious to the needs of her family. Her husband tried all of his previously effective ploys and strategies to motivate her to return to business; but this time he failed completely. Desperate, he called in a shaman who, like others before her, diagnosed Namsanmansin as suffering from *sinbyŏng*.

When they owned nothing more that could be sold, Namsanmansin herself suggested that she must become a shaman, that she was so predestined, and that all the afflictions that she and her family suffered had been for the purpose of breaking her will and making her accept her calling. Her husband acquiesced, especially since the spirits possessing his wife were identified as those of his own ancestors. In 1973, when I last visited her, Namsanmansin had, in two short years after her decision to accept the shaman role, built up a moderately thriving practice in Seoul and was supporting her children and her chronically unemployed husband. Her husband, for his part, totally accepted his dependence on his wife as a predestined "curse" that befalls husbands of shamans. He still talked about going into business for himself and hoped that his wife would underwrite him just once more. She no longer gave him substantial amounts of money, keeping him on a daily allowance doled out just before he left home to join his cronies for yet another idle day.

The developments that typically occur after *sinbyŏng* diagnosis are as significant as those that precede the diagnosis. In general, post-*sinbyŏng* developments involve drastic changes in the previously conflict-ridden relationships between the victim and her family. These new developments manifest themselves in several ways.

First, the mutual antagonisms between the daughter-in-law and her family are eased. Her family drops or suppresses any suspicions it might have harbored about the victim's faking illness to avoid work. In her eyes, the family must also be absolved of any responsibility for the illness, because it has accepted the implied accusation and consented to the proper remedy, despite the liabilities that will be suffered by its members.

Second, since both the victim and her family are now viewed as fellow victims of supernatural phenomena that are beyond their control, a new bond of mutuality emerges between the victim and her family. This bond offers them new possibilities for collaboration as they respond to the diagnosis of *sinbyŏng* and the shaman role it implies for the victim. This happened with five of the six informants I worked with. The sixth returned to her mother's family for support. These reconciliations can be quite dramatic. In one case, a shaman had initially been evicted from her mother-in-law's house when she became a shaman. But the verbal taunts and physical abuses that her children, as children of a shaman, had to endure from the other children in the neighborhood finally brought reconciliation between her mother-in-law and herself. One day the mother-in-law happened upon one of her grandchildren who was crying piteously because her playmates hurled insults at her about her shaman mother. The grandmother became so angry that she picked up a piece of firewood and chased after all the children, shouting insults about their parents and daring the whole neighborhood to come out and face her. She finally took her crying grandchild by the hand to her daughter-in-law's house and made peace with her "for the sake of the children."

Third, the diagnosis transforms the afflictions of *sinbyŏng*, albeit retrospectively, into "sensible" and "meaningful" experiences for the victim and her family. They can now "see" that their suffering had a purpose. For another shaman in my sample, the official diagnosis enabled the entire family to live more comfortably with the fact that they had survived the previous winter by begging on the streets.

The spirits possessing the victim are extremely important in changing the relationship between the shaman and her family. They must be consulted about any actions taken concerning the *sinbyŏng*, its termination, and the victim's assumption of the shaman role. With their entrance into the family situation, the possessing spirits transform the previously dyadic power relationship between the new shaman and her family into a triad, with themselves in the controlling position. However, since the new shaman alone, among the family members, has direct access to the spirits, judgments will be at least somewhat susceptible to the needs and interests of the shaman. Since the possessing spirits are often ancestral ghosts from the lineage of the victim's husband, the coalition between the shaman and her possessing spirits is very powerful. Other family members are quite helpless in this situation, for in Korea descendants do not generally deny the advice and counsel of their ancestral ghosts or ignore their demands.

Thus, it is clear that, once the diagnosis of *sinbyŏng* is acknowledged, the old patterns of interaction within the family cannot be resumed. Metaphorically, one could say that *sinbyǒng* is analogous to the spirits' "kidnapping" the victim from her ordinary but conflict-ridden role within the household. The spirits, from their position of superiority, then bargain for the ransom they demand, which is that the shaman recruit must serve as their medium and that, additionally, her family must support her in this role.

The experience of another shaman I interviewed illustrates well the changes in family relationships that occur after the *sinbyǒng* diagnosis is accepted and the shaman role is assumed. When she publicly accepted the call to become a shaman by receiving clients, this woman initially saw thirty to forty visitors a day. She would begin shortly after dawn and work almost nonstop until nine or so every evening. Her husband had to take over most of her housekeeping and child-caring chores. He and his daughters prepared the family's food; he would call her in at mealtimes to feed the baby. Her mother-in-law, distressed beyond description by the sight of her son doing women's work, began to come over and relieve him of many of these tasks. Today the mother-in-law not only supervises the general housekeeping chores of her older granddaughters but also takes full charge of all the hired women who prepare ritual food for her daughter-in-law's shamanistic activities. Thus the roles have been completely reversed, not only between the shaman and her husband but also between the shaman and her mother-in-law.

Such a reversal of power positions is common among the families of shamans, and the former victim often eventually achieves de facto household headship. As a shaman, she bargains with her family from a position of strength based on her earning power, spiritual superiority, and recovered health and self-confidence. This change in the family's power structure is much more pronounced, if, as is usually the case and was with five of my informants, the family's economic resources have been exhausted in the course of her *sinbyǒng*. Circumscribed by their outcaste status, the members of her family tend in such instances to become almost totally dependent on her for economic support.

I suggest, therefore, that *sinbyǒng* is a symptomatic representation of an impasse in both the victim's conflicted self-image and in her friction-ridden relationship with her family. When *sinbyǒng* results in her assuming the shaman role, she and her adversaries in the family are extricated from the impasse. Thus they can remain together as a family unit by redefining their roles. This solution, however, begets other problems. Members of the shaman's family are permanently held hostage by their fear of supernatural retaliation and by the social stigma of their outcaste status. The shaman, on the other hand, must deal with the social and personal sacrifices that her family must make. Furthermore, she suffers the frustration of not being able to use her power to restore them to their proper standing in society.

Note

1. Male shamans are considered by Koreans as marginal men and were customarily expected, until about three decades ago, to practice transvestism. They are not necessarily homosexuals.

Further Readings

Harvey, Youngsook Kim. *Six Korean Women: The Socialization of Shamans.* St. Paul, Minn.: West Publishing Company, 1979.

Janelli, Roger L. *Ancestor Worship and Korean Society.* Stanford, Calif.: Stanford University Press, 1982.

Joe, Wanne J. *Traditional Korea: A Cultural History.* Seoul: Chung'ang University Press, 1972.

Kendall, Laurel. "Korean Shamanism: Women's Rites and a Chinese Comparison." *Religion and the Family in East Asia*, ed. by George A. DeVos and Takao Sofue. Berkeley, Calif.: University of California Press, 1984.

_____. *Shamans, Housewives, and Other*

Restless Spirits: Women in Korean Ritual Life. Honolulu: University of Hawaii Press, 1985.

Lee, Jung Young. *Korean Shamanistic Rituals*. The Hague: Mouton, 1981.

Yu, Chai-shin and Richard Guisso. *Shamanism: The Spirit World of Korea*. Berkeley, Calif.: Asian Humanities Press, 1988.

5

Ecstasy and Possession: Women of Ancient Greece and the Cult of Dionysus

ROSS S. KRAEMER

A mong the cults of classical antiquity, the worship of the Greek god Dionysus is one of the most intriguing. Modern scholarship has devoted considerable energy to the study of Dionysiac religion. But very little attention has been paid to one of the most striking aspects of the cult—namely, the very conspicuous role that women have played within it. This chapter considers the participation of women in the worship of Dionysus and suggests a possible explanation for women's attraction to Dionysiac rites and myths.

The worship of Dionysus, god of the vine and of life-giving liquids, appears to go back at least to the seventh century B.C. in Greece; in early times it was associated with rural agricultural festivals of spring. The

---

ROSS S. KRAEMER   holds a Ph.D. from Princeton University in History of Religions and writes and lectures on women's religion in Greco-Roman antiquity. Her more recent work focuses on Jewish women in the Diaspora. She presently holds a faculty appointment at the Medical College of Pennsylvania and a research appointment in the Department of Religious Studies at the University of Pennsylvania.

Author's Note   A fuller discussion of certain issues raised in this chapter appears in the *Harvard Theological Review* 72 (1979).

representations of Dionysus in myth and art depict, alternatively, a young child, a smooth-faced, androgynous young man with beautiful curls and fair skin, and a bearded mature figure. In addition to the well-known symbols of the grape cluster and the ivy vine, Dionysus is often associated with phallic representations. Dionysiac festivals exhibit the temporary license of drunkenness and sexual expression that characterizes agricultural festivals in other cultures as well (such as the activities at the harvest festival described in the biblical book of Ruth). Virtually from his appearance as a divinity, Dionysus was associated with various fertility motifs and was one of a number of Greek deities called upon to ensure the fruitfulness of fields, flocks, and human beings. As far as we can tell, these rural festivals in honor of Dionysus were in no way restricted to one sex or the other.

However, relatively early, the worship of Dionysus was also associated with other rites, apparently of a more restricted nature, for which the best description comes from a play by Euripides, written at the turn of the fourth century B.C. The *Bacchae*, whose title means "female worshipers of the god Bacchus" (another name for Dionysus), dramatizes the legend of the introduction of Dionysus' worship to Thebes, a city in northern Greece.

According to the play, which appears to combine elements of fixed myths with Euripides' own observations of contemporary practices, Dionysus was the product of a liaison between Zeus, the head of the Greek pantheon, and a mortal woman, Semele, daughter of Cadmus, the king of Thebes. While Semele was pregnant with Dionysus, she was killed by one of Zeus' lightning bolts, the apparent victim of a jealous plot devised by Hera, the wife of Zeus. The unborn Dionysus was snatched from his mother's womb and finished his gestation period in Zeus' thigh. Upon his maturity, he spread the cult of his worship through Asia Minor and the Orient. Although a Theban by blood and birth, in Euripides' *Bacchae* Dionysus comes to Thebes from the east to introduce his rites to all of Greece. In the opening lines of the play, the god explains that he has chosen Thebes as the first Greek city in which to inaugurate his rites so that he may redeem his mother's honor and punish her family for refusing to believe the paternity of her child. Semele's sisters, we are told, doubted that Zeus had fathered their sister's child and spread the rumor that Semele, having been impregnated by a mere mortal, was prompted by her father to ascribe the loss of her virginity to Zeus. This lie, they asserted, resulted in her death by Zeus' thunderbolt.

Dionysus' revenge on his mother's sisters was exacted in very specific form—a divinely induced madness that caused the women to engage in various unusual activities which are described in the play.

> Suddenly
> I saw three companies of dancing women
> one led by Autonoë, the second captained
>   by your
> mother Agave, while Ino led the third.
> There they lay in the deep sleep of
>   exhaustion,
> some resting on boughs of fir, others
>   sleeping
> where they fell, here and there among the
>   oak leaves—
> but all modestly and soberly, not, as you
>   think,
> drunk with wine, nor wandering, led
>   astray
> by the music of the flute, to hunt their
>   Aphrodite
> through the woods.
>
>   But your mother heard the lowing
> of our horned herds, and springing to her
>   feet,
> gave a great cry to waken them from
>   sleep.
> And they too, rubbing the bloom of soft
>   sleep
> from their eyes, rose up lightly and
>   straight—

a lovely sight to see: all as one,
the old women and the young and the
  unmarried girls.
First they let their hair fall loose, down
over their shoulders, and those whose
  straps had slipped
fastened their skins of fawn with writhing
  snakes
that licked their cheeks. Breasts swollen
  with milk,
new mothers who had left their babies
  behind at home
nestled gazelles and young wolves in their
  arms,
suckling them. Then they crowned their
  hair with leaves,
ivy and oak and flowering bryony. One
  woman
struck her thyrsus against a rock and a
  fountain
of cool water came bubbling up. Another
  drove
her fennel in the ground, and where it
  struck the earth,
at the touch of god, a spring of wine
  poured out.
Those who wanted milk scratched at the
  soil
with bare fingers and the white milk came
  welling up.
Pure honey spurted, streaming, from their
  wands.[1]

                    Then at a signal
all the Bacchae whirled their wands for the
  revels
to begin. With one voice they cried aloud:
"*O Iacchus! Son of Zeus!*" "*O Bromius!*"
  they cried
until the beasts and all the mountain
  seemed
wild with divinity. And when they ran,
everything ran with them.

                    It happened, however,
that Agave ran near the ambush where I
  lay

concealed. Leaping up, I tried to seize
  her,
but she gave a cry: "Hounds who run with
  me,
men are hunting us down! Follow, follow
  me!
Use your wands for weapons."

                    At this we fled
and barely missed being torn to pieces by
  the women.
Unarmed, they swooped down upon the
  herds of cattle
grazing there on the green of the meadow.
  And then
you could have seen a single woman with
  bare hands
tear a fat calf, still bellowing with fright,
in two, while others clawed the heifers to
  pieces.
There were ribs and cloven hooves
  scattered everywhere,
and scraps smeared with blood hung from
  the fir trees.
And bulls, their raging fury gathered in
  their horns,
lowered their heads to charge, then fell,
  stumbling
to the earth, pulled down by hordes of
  women
and stripped of flesh and skin more
  quickly, sire,
than you could blink your royal eyes.
  Then,
carried up by their own speed, they flew
  like birds
across the spreading fields along Asopus'
  stream
where most of all the ground is good for
  harvesting.
Like invaders they swooped on Hysiae
and on Erythrae in the foothills of
  Cithaeron.
Everything in sight they pillaged and
  destroyed.
They snatched the children from their
  homes. And when

they piled their plunder on their backs, it
    stayed in place,
untied. Nothing, neither bronze nor iron,
fell to the dark earth. Flames flickered
in their curls and did not burn them.
    Then the villagers,
furious at what the women did, took to
    arms.
And *there*, sire, was something terrible to
    see.
For the men's spears were pointed and
    sharp, and yet
drew no blood, whereas the wands the
    women threw
inflicted wounds. And then the men *ran*,
routed by women! Some god, I say, was
    with them.
The Bacchae then returned where they
    had started,
by the springs the god had made, and
    washed their hands
while the snakes licked away the drops of
    blood
that dabbled their cheeks.[2]

The collective madness of Agave, Ino, and Autonoe culminates in the murder and dismemberment of Agave's son Pentheus, whom she and the other women mistakenly perceive to be a wild animal. At the end of the play, Agave goes into exile, the house of Cadmus is destroyed, and the worship of Dionysus is firmly established in its cult center of Thebes.

Compelling though Euripides' description is, it is difficult to determine the extent to which these activities of the possessed women reflect actual ritual practices in the orgiastic cult of Dionysus. But the *Bacchae* itself does provide some relatively straightforward information about the rites. From Euripides' play, we may infer that Euripides knew of Dionysiac rites that were restricted to the initiated, that were celebrated by night, that involved dancing, and that carried with them the suspicion of sexual misconduct. References in the play suggest that the initiates were primarily women, though a line to the effect that the god wishes honor from all suggests that men were not altogether banned from the cult—a point to which I will return. From the detailed descriptions in Euripides' play, one might argue that the *Bacchae* describes actual rituals practiced by Greek women before or during Euripides' own lifetime. Such rites might have included wandering on the mountain at night; nursing wild baby animals; dancing frenziedly; consuming wine, honey, and milk; and possibly performing a two-part sacrificial ritual— the *sparagmos* (ripping apart) and *omophagia* (raw consumption) of a wild beast identified simultaneously with the god and with one's own son (Agave dismembering Pentheus). While engaged in the Bacchic rites, the participants might have worn appropriate ritual clothing, including perhaps a fawn skin, and carried the wand called a *thyrsus*.

Most classical scholars, however, contend that there is virtually no evidence for such ritual practices in Athens of the fifth or fourth century B.C. Some believe that Euripides utilized a myth of the origins of Dionysiac worship at Thebes whose form was fairly well fixed and whose specifics thus need not reflect actual Greek practice, while others suggest that such interpretations are open to question. Another potential witness for classical *orgia* comes from the wealth of Attic red-figure vases depicting Dionysiac scenes. One scholar who studied these vase paintings extensively concluded that they indicate a high degree of interest in rituals of collective ecstasy focusing on Dionysus early in the fifth century, prior to the writing of Euripides' play.[3]

While we cannot be sure of the precise nature of any fifth- or fourth-century orgiastic worship by women in a cult that may clearly be identified as Dionysiac, we have a better picture of the cult and its organization during the later Hellenistic period.[4] Apollodorus' *Library* contains various forms of most of the myths describing the importation of Dionysiac rites into various regions of Greece. Diodorus

of Sicily devoted extensive sections to Dionysiac lore in Greece and included a detailed description of Dionysiac practices, although it is
not clear whether Diodorus was referring to
the practices of his own time (first century B.C./
A.D.) or quoting from a source describing earlier customs.

> In many Greek cities the women assemble
> to celebrate Bacchic festivals every other
> year, and . . . it is customary for the maid-
> ens to carry thyrsi and join in the frenzied
> revels with shouts of Evo, while the matrons
> sacrifice to the god and celebrate the
> Bacchic festivals in groups, and in general
> extol with hymns the presence of Dionysus,
> in this manner acting the part of the Mae-
> nads who, as history records, were of old
> the companions of the god.[5]

The first-century philosopher Plutarch also
refers to the Dionysiac rites many times. He
tells of one occasion when a search party was
sent out to rescue women who, while engaged
in the midwinter celebrations, became caught
in a severe winter storm. Elsewhere he records
how the women of a town called Amphissa
protected sleeping maenads from the unwanted
attentions of soldiers and provided them with
a safe escort home.[6]

The Hellenistic period also yields inscriptions relating to the Dionysiac cults; one, from
Magnesia on the Meander, a city in Asia Minor, dates from the second century B.C. and
deals with the origins of the worship of Dionysus in the city. Apparently, an image of the
god was found in a plane tree—a portent that
was interpreted to mean that Dionysus wished
the people to institute his worship. Accordingly, they sent for women initiated into the
cult to establish the orgiastic rites and Bacchic
associations.[7] Another inscription from Miletus, also in Asia Minor, regulates the practices
of ritual sacrifice, discusses financial questions,
and describes the priestess' role in Dionysiac
initiations.[8]

These texts and inscriptions, taken together, confirm the existence of well-regulated

Dionysiac cults, with relatively tame rituals
consisting of dancing, snake handling, and
nocturnal mountain wanderings. These cults
appear to have had both private and public
dimensions. Such practices are well attested in
the first century by various Greek writers and
as early as the third century by the epigraphical
evidence. In this period the cult of Dionysus
was apparently widespread and flourishing.

Thus, all in all, our evidence about the orgiastic worship of Dionysus—that is, about the
private, ecstatic, nonagricultural cult of Dionysus rather than the public agricultural
rites—yields an intriguing but incomplete picture. However, despite our imprecise evidence,
enough traces remain of the myths, rituals, and
symbols to let us attempt some analysis and
interpretation. In particular, we may discern
two major motifs: that of insanity and possession on the one hand and that of sociobiological
roles and status on the other. In the many
myths of the introduction of the worship of
Dionysus, including those retold in Euripides'
play, the reversal of sanity and insanity predominates. Those who yield to the divine madness of Dionysiac possession are the truly sane,
while those who resist the holy insanity are the
truly insane. Those who accept the call of the
god and surrender to the temporary possession
suffer no harm, while those who struggle
against the god invoke a second level of possession far more dangerous than the first. It is
insane to be sane, sane to be insane.

This motif of the reversal of normal states
and judgments occurs in the sphere of sociobiological roles as well. Women possessed by
Dionysus are compelled to abandon, at least
temporarily, their domestic obligations of
housework and child rearing in favor of the
worship of the god. While in the service of
Dionysus, their activities express a marked ambivalence toward the neglected roles. On the
one hand, the Bacchae mimic their normal
roles, in a transmuted form, as they nurse baby
wild animals with the milk intended for their
own young. But the death and dismemberment

of Pentheus reflect the inversion of their maternal loyalties; the slaughter of Pentheus is the vicarious slaughter of each woman's own offspring.

A temporary escape from marital sexual obligations is also reflected in the activities attributed to the worshipers of Dionysus. Although the maenads are repeatedly accused of sexual immorality while in the possession of Dionysus, often elsewhere in the same myths, and in the *Bacchae* itself, they are defended from such accusations. If a historical truth is to be extracted here, it may be reflected in Dionysus' speech to Pentheus, when he proclaims that the Dionysiac rites do not compel a woman to be unchaste, at the same time conceding by implication that the rites afford the opportunity for such activities. But we should also keep in mind that accusations of unchastity are themselves a form of social control; therefore, we should be extremely cautious in seeing such accusations and their refutation as rooted in actual historical practices of either chastity or unchastity.

Further indications of sex-role reversal in the Dionysiac rites appear in the maenads' hunting activities, climaxing in Agave's slaughter of Pentheus and her victorious boasts to her own father, Cadmus, on her return to Thebes. In a speech we might expect more from a Greek son than from a Greek daughter, and one most tragic in its irony, Agave addresses her father:

> Now, Father, yours can be the proudest
> boast of living men.
> For you are now the father of the bravest
> daughters in the world.
> All your daughters are brave, but I above
> the rest.
> I have left my shuttle at the loom; I raised
> my sight to higher things—
> to hunting animals with my bare hands.[9]

In this brief passage, Agave makes clear the values of Greek society and the roles normally appropriate for each sex. Agave has become,

in her own mind, a hunter, rejecting the pursuits of women for the higher achievements of men.

Elements of male sex-role reversal also occur in the *Bacchae*. Cadmus (the grandfather of Pentheus) and Teiresias (the blind seer) don the ritual clothing of women to worship Dionysus, as does Pentheus under the spell of the god. Further, the god himself embodies the form of both sexes simultaneously. An essentially androgynous figure, Dionysus aptly represents sex-role reversal for both sexes.

These symbolic and ritual reversals so abundant in the orgiastic worship of Dionysus provided significant releases to the adherents of the cult. It is important to stress, however, that, although the cult of Dionysus reverses the standards for social judgment and appropriate behavior, such reversal is necessarily temporary. As anthropologists have observed, one of the primary functions of ritual reversal is to affirm the ultimate appropriateness of that which is reversed.

Although the symbolic and ritual reversals in the cult of Dionysus seem primarily restricted to women, there is some evidence that men also participated to some degree in the orgiastic cult. The evidence for male participation in the classical period is scant. Outside of the *Bacchae* there are only a few references that may be interpreted to indicate that men did participate in the rites. In the *Bacchae* itself, though, three male characters other than Dionysus participate, or attempt to participate, in the Dionysiac rites. In an early scene of the play, Teiresias and Cadmus meet to prepare themselves for the Dionysiac dance. Teiresias comes knocking on Cadmus' gate dressed in a fawn-skin cloak, wearing an ivy garland, and carrying a thyrsus—three elements typical of the Bacchic cult. Cadmus is similarly prepared, and together they plan to set off to dance to Dionysus. The same scene contains a reference suggesting that of all the males in Thebes only they worship the god. Cadmus asks Teiresias,

"Shall we be the only ones in Thebes who dance to Bacchus?" and the seer replies, "We alone are right-minded; the rest are perverse." Surely this text cannot mean that of all the people in Thebes only Cadmus and Teiresias dance for Dionysus, since earlier passages have already described how Dionysus has possessed all the women of Thebes and driven them out of their homes and up onto the mountains to celebrate his rites. Rather, the passage must mean that of all the males in Thebes only Teiresias and Cadmus worship the god.

Of what specifically, then, does the service of these two men consist? In the scene just discussed, they speak of two and possibly three elements of the cultic activities outlined elsewhere: they wear the prescribed clothing and carry the ritual wand, they propose to dance, and they intend perhaps to do so on the mountains. Neither of them mentions any possession experience, spontaneous or induced, and, in this scene and the following one with Pentheus, the two men seem singularly in their everyday minds. Nor do we find any reference to the sacrifices that are characteristically associated with the orgiastic worship of the god. I am tempted to suggest that some Greeks, whether men or women, participated in the cult only to the extent of wearing ritual clothing and performing certain dances. Such differentiation may be evidence of levels of cultic initiation, and it may be possible that men were allowed to participate only in the lesser activities, while full initiation with its practices of possession and sacrifice was denied to them.

The other male character in the play who participates in the rites in honor of Dionysus is Pentheus; but his involvement cannot be taken as evidence for usual male cultic activity, although it raises some interesting questions about the identity of the sacrifice. For Pentheus is variously the slaughtered animal, the dismembered child, and perhaps the torn and rent god. Far from being a celebrant, he is the hapless victim of the celebration, who is punished for his refusal to accept and permit the rites of the god in what is perhaps an unusual mode for a god whose usual revenge is insanity.

The Hellenistic period has produced more certain evidence of male participation. Diodorus described the company of Dionysus as both male and female and stated that the god instructed all pious men and initiated them into his mysteries—a statement juxtaposed with one concerning the god's special identification with women.[10] The cult inscription from Miletus is even more interesting, since it discusses men's and women's participation somewhat differently. One verb, meaning "to sacrifice," "to offer," or "to celebrate," is used in connection with activities performed by both men and women. A different verb, which connotes initiation, is used only in reference to women's activities. This may further support the implications in the *Bacchae* that, although men participated in the cult, they were limited to certain practices, while only women could become full initiates. Thus, it appears that, at least until the late Hellenistic period, the primary participants in the Bacchic orgiastic rites were women; where there is evidence for male participation, it is almost always of a limited nature.

It seems clear that the rites of Dionysus either appealed primarily to women or were restricted in some ways to them. Thus the major question is to explain the special appeal of these rites to women.

I wish to propose an explanation that draws on the work of the anthropologists Kenelm Burridge and I. M. Lewis. Burridge has pointed out that all societies have measures of worth by which individuals are judged and on the basis of which the rewards of privilege and prestige are meted out. The society remains stable as long as most people in it can perceive their own activities as prestigious and valuable according to these measures and can, at least to some extent, have access to the rewards.

However, when enough of a society's members are deprived of its rewards and praise, movements often emerge that provide alternative norms.[11]

In most societies few, if any, activities are judged as appropriate for both women and men, and the standards of worth are different for the two sexes. Even today in many cultures—especially the traditional ones—men are usually judged in terms of learned achievements (hunting prowess, education, artistic accomplishments, or accrued wealth), while women are normally evaluated primarily on the basis of their reproductive success and on the basis of whose wife, mother, daughter, or sister they happen to be. The sign of a successful man is frequently his wealth or his skills; that of a successful woman, her husband and her sons. Given such sex-role differentiation, the social deprivation of men will frequently revolve around different issues than the social deprivation of women. Whereas men will experience social deprivation and seek some kind of redress over issues ranging from physical and military prowess to money and political power, women will experience deprivation primarily in regard to their biological status. A man will perceive himself as inadequate if he is poor, or unlettered, or unsuccessful as a hunter, depending on the criteria of his particular culture, but a woman will perceive herself as inadequate unless she enters into an acceptable marriage and bears many healthy children, preferably sons. Women who fail to meet this standard—unmarried women over a certain age, childless women, and often widows—are by definition marginal. While both "deprived" men and "deprived" women may seek redress in religious settings, women who fail to meet the standards that their society sets for them are likely to be attracted to religious activities that provide them with an alternative sense of worth.

The implications of all of this for women in ancient Greece and for their participation in the cult of Dionysus are twofold. First, we

might expect that Greek women who could not meet Greek standards for successful womanhood might be attracted to activities, particularly religious ones, that dealt with women's concerns. More important, the overall status of women in ancient Greece comes into play. As many historians have noted, the status of women in classical Greece ranks among the worst of women in Western society at any time. It is likely that many women could not meet their society's measure of a "good" woman. Even if they did, a tremendous disparity remained between the rewards a "successful" woman could expect and those awarded to the successful man. This disparity may have threatened the entire social fabric of ancient Greece and increased the vulnerability of Greek women to the cult of Dionysus.

In the light of this analysis, the work of the anthropologist I. M. Lewis provides another useful model for interpreting Dionysiac ecstasy. Lewis was most interested in the sociological function of ecstatic cults, which he studied extensively in Africa and the Caribbean. According to Lewis, these cults are fundamentally mechanisms through which the powerless express aggression and hostility against the powerful. Through the cult activity, members find some redress while permitting the basic social fabric to remain unaltered. Lewis himself notes that the orgiastic cult of Dionysus falls into this category, although he does not pursue the observation.

Another major aspect of these cults, according to Lewis, is their peripheral character. The possessing spirits are believed to originate outside the society whose women they typically plague, and those whom they afflict—women and socially powerless men—occupy a "peripheral" position within the social structure. Furthermore, the possessing spirit is typically considered to be amoral, a conception that Lewis sees as crucial. Therefore the possessed individual cannot be held morally responsible for his or her possession. Being morally blameless, the possessed are able to take advantage of the special privileged position in which possession places them.

> In his state of possession [the] patient is a highly privileged person: he is allowed many liberties with those whom in other circumstances he is required to treat with respect. . . . Clearly in this context possession works to help the interests of the weak and downtrodden who have otherwise few effective means to press their claims for attention and respect.[12]

Since the possession illness is never fully cured and is likely to recur, its victim is provided with additional social leverage. In the cultural systems that Lewis analyzed, as in ancient Greece, women are the primary participants in these possession cults.

Thus, it seems that the system of possession can serve to redress some of the grievances of oppressed women in male-dominated societies. Lewis also suggests that the system is able to function precisely because the men recognize, at least up to a point, the legitimacy of the women's grievances and thus permit the syndrome to go on.

> Hence, within bounds which are not infinitely elastic, both men and women are more or less satisfied; neither sex loses face and the official ideology of male supremacy is preserved. From this perspective, the tolerance by men of periodic, but always temporary, assaults on their authority by women appears as the price they have to pay to maintain their enviable position.[13]

Possession thus appears to neutralize the potentially destructive emotions felt by oppressed individuals of a society by permitting these emotions to be vented through highly institutionalized and regulated forms.

Lewis' findings are illuminating for the study of the Dionysiac cults, although the correspondence between the Dionysiac cults and the cults he studied is far from one to one. The primary affliction in Dionysiac cults is not illness, with physical symptoms, but rather madness, or a kind of trance possession,

marked by the urge to dance and to abandon home and hearth to follow the god. Nevertheless, it is clear that possession occurs and that it can be cured only through participation in the ritual dancing and perhaps also through the rites of killing and eating. In any case, the language of possession and cure is unmistakably present in Dionysiac rituals.

Unlike the cults studied by Lewis, it might be argued that Dionysiac possession was not wholly "amoral." The possession of Agave, her sisters, and Pentheus in the *Bacchae* is clearly not amoral; it is a direct response to their failure to acknowledge the liaison between Semele and Zeus and the divinity of Dionysus, their child. However, the nature and consequences of the affliction of Semele's sisters are qualitatively different from that of other women who follow Dionysus.

Lewis' model also clarifies another aspect of the Dionysiac myth that scholars have vigorously debated—namely, the alleged foreign origin of Dionysus. Although the historical evidence on this point is unclear, Dionysus was known in the tradition as a foreign god. If Lewis' understanding of the function of amoral possession is correct, then Dionysus almost *has* to be foreign. His "foreignness," both mythical and psychic, means that the possession cannot be seen as evidence of the victim's moral deficiency. If the possession were not something foreign that overwhelmed the maenad, not only would it fail to alleviate the stress due to the woman's social position, but it would result in even greater social disapproval. Thus, far from being an arbitrary element of the myth, Dionysus' alleged foreign origin emerges as part of a coherent, forceful pattern.

The possession and cure of Greek women did in fact produce temporary, socially sanctioned respite from the pressures of Greek life and familial obligations. Unfortunately for the maenad, however, such respite does not seem to have carried over into everyday life in the same way that initiation into the possession cults studied by Lewis permanently ensured

the African and Caribbean woman some redress. On the other hand, one scholar argues
that there probably were small household cults
that arose from participation in the Dionysiac
rituals. We may speculate that these household
cults in some way perpetuated the possession's
social benefits.

Lewis' work, especially when combined
with Burridge's theory, gives us another valuable insight into the function of Dionysiac possession and cult. According to Lewis, the
initiation of women into peripheral possession
cults was almost always precipitated by a recent or impending change in their sociobiological status. In particular, Lewis noted that
women whose husbands were about to take a
new wife (in polygamous societies), new-
lyweds, or women who had recently had children seemed especially vulnerable to possession. Many of the women afflicted with the
Dionysiac madness, especially in the myths,
also seem to have been women whose sociobiological status was in some way being threatened or radically altered. The daughters of
Minyas, discussed by Apollodorus, refuse to
worship Dionysus because they are concerned
about getting husbands. Thus they are roughly
at the age of puberty, anticipating the major
transition from girlhood to womanhood.[14] For
their refusal, they are afflicted with the second
stage of Dionysiac madness. Driven from their
homes by ivy and honey dripping from the
walls, they rend apart a child. In the *Bacchae*,
Agave and her sisters, who have grown sons,
are all approaching old age and the problems
of widowhood.

Thus it is possible to suggest that women
whose sociobiological status is in flux are more
vulnerable to possession and need its therapeutic advantages more than women whose social
roles are relatively stable. Since possession
brings its victims some social prestige and ma-
nipulatory powers, those most attracted to the
possession cult would be women temporarily
in limbo and in need of some way to deal with
their uncomfortable situation. This is not to
suggest that all the women who participated in
the Dionysiac rituals were experiencing
changes in their sociobiological roles but that
such situations might have provided the cata-
lyst for many, if not most, women's possession
by Dionysus.

Two other interesting parallels between the
cults Lewis studied and the Dionysiac mysteries ought to be mentioned. First, in the cults
that Lewis studied, the possession cult usually
meets at a fixed date about the time of the
main festivals of the official religion. This observation strengthens Lewis's thesis that the
cult is an alternative to the normative male-
dominated worship. Interestingly, the biyearly
Dionysiac festival was also celebrated in close
proximity to the main Greek cult festival, perhaps for the same reason. Second, Lewis
pointed out that in some cases the possession
trance is experienced as sexual union with the
possessing spirit. This sheds interesting light
on the allusions to sexual activity between
Dionysus and the women-initiates as well as
on the allegations of unchastity leveled against
them.

In conclusion, participation in the Dionysiac rituals afforded Greek women a means of
expressing their hostility toward and frustration with a male-dominated society by temporarily abandoning their homes and household
responsibilities and engaging in activities outside the limits of their usual ones. This occurred within a framework that prohibited any
serious sanctions against them, since the possession was in most instances understood to be
amoral and irresistible. Both the women and
the men were able to participate in the game;
the women could temporarily disrupt the domestic routine, and the men could acquiesce
to a limited expression of hostility and frustration, in part because they too accepted the
authority of the god and believed that he punished resistance to the possession. Thus a cult
whose origins lie in other concerns, especially
the perpetuation of the life force in the cosmos
and the complex human feelings associated

with it, becomes a mechanism for coping with and providing some relief for the Greek devaluation of women.

Notes

1. Euripides *Bacchae*, lines 680–711 (trans. W. Arrowsmith), in *Greek Tragedies*, ed. David Grene and Richmond Lattimore (Chicago: University of Chicago Press, 1958), vol. 4.
2. *Bacchae*, lines 723–768.
3. Lillian Lawler, "The Maenads: A Contribution to the Study of the Dance in Ancient Greece," in *Memoirs of the American Academy in Rome* 6 (1927); see also Lawler, *The Dance in Ancient Greece* (Middletown, Conn.: Wesleyan University Press, 1964).
4. Although the term *Hellenistic* is often used to denote the period from Alexander the Great to the reign of Augustus, I prefer to use it to designate the period from Alexander to the fall of Rome, since the influence of Greek culture can hardly be said to cease with the advent of the Roman Empire.
5. Diodorus Siculus *Library* 4. 3. 3.
6. Plutarch *De Primo Frigido* 953D; *De Mulierum Virtutibus* 249E.
7. M. P. Nilsson, *The Dionysiac Mysteries of the Hellenistic and Roman Age* (Lund: C. W. K. Gleerup, 1957), p. 6.
8. Nilsson, p. 6 n. 7.
9. *Bacchae* 1232–38.
10. Diodorus Siculus 4.2.5; 3.64.7.
11. Kenelm Burridge, *New Heaven, New Earth* (New York: Schocken Books, 1969), p. 43.
12. I. M. Lewis, *Ecstatic Religion: An Anthropological Study of Spirit Possession and Shamanism* (Harmondsworth, Middlesex: Penguin Books, 1971), p. 32.
13. Lewis, p. 86.
14. The French classicist Henri Jeanmaire has also noted an apparent connection between puberty and the point at which young women entered the cult; in *Dionysos, Histoire du Culte de Bacchus* (Paris: Editions Payot, 1951), p. 208.

Further Readings

Cole, Susan G. "New Evidence for the Mysteries of Dionysos." *Greek, Roman and Byzantine Studies* 21 (1980) 3:223–28.

Henrichs, Albert. "Greek Maenadism from Olympias to Messalina." *Harvard Studies in Classical Philology* 82 (1978) 121–60.

Keuls, Eva. *The Reign of the Phallus: Sexual Politics in Ancient Athens* (San Francisco: Harper and Row, 1986).

Kraemer, Ross S. "Women in the Religions of the Greco-Roman World." *Religious Studies Review* 9 (1983) 2:127–39.

Kraemer, Ross S. *Maenads, Martyrs, Matrons and Monastics: A Sourcebook on Women's Religion in the Greco-Roman World* (Philadelphia: Fortress Press, 1988).

Pomeroy, Sarah B. (with Ross S. Kraemer and Natalie Kampen). "Selected Bibliography on Women in Classical Antiquity." In John Peradotto and J. P. Sullivan, eds., *Women in the Ancient World: The Arethusa Papers* (Albany, N.Y.: State University of New York Press, 1984), pp. 317–72.

Segal, Charles. "The Menace of Dionysus: Sex Roles and Reversal in Euripides' *Bacchae*." In John Peradotto and J. P. Sullivan, eds., *Women in the Ancient World: The Arethusa Papers* (Albany, N.Y.: State University of New York Press, 1984), pp. 195–212.

III

IN THE WINGS

Rituals for Wives and Mothers

U nlike the women of extraordinary callings who enliven many pages of this
volume, the women in this section are primarily involved in everyday concerns.
In five of these studies, there is little tension between their religious and their
mundane lives. Rather, their religious concerns often validate these women's
ordinary concerns and help to give them meaning. In the sixth case, religion helps
women bear the frustrations of their everyday lives. At least in terms of sheer
numbers, these are probably the more common patterns of women's religious
lives.

One of the least known aspects of women's everyday religious lives relates to
the many rites and ceremonies that women celebrate on their own. Yet these
rituals are as much a part of the religious milieu as are the much-better publicized
rites and gatherings of men. Often women will organize them, prepare for them,
and celebrate them, with little or no male participation or intrusion. It is important
for us to review these practices, because, more than any other aspects of women's
religious lives, they reflect women's most common concerns and experiences.
Virtually any woman in most traditional cultures could find something in the
descriptions included here that would parallel some significant aspect of her own
religious world.

We have offered six samples from four cultures. Although the heritage of Hindu
women's rites and festal occasions has scarcely been studied in the past, it offers
an exceptionally rich sampling of women's practices. The first three chapters in
this section describe three very different types of rituals practiced by Hindu
women in different regions of India. These three chapters show how rich women's
ordinary religious world can be even in a culture like India's, in which men control

almost exclusively so many public and formal religious practices and institutions. Childbirth provides a significant religious occasion for women of central India as it does for women in other regions of the world. Chapter 6 allows us to share in this experience. Chapters 7 and 8 describe how wives and mothers of a north Indian village engage in numerous rituals to protect their families and household interests and how middle-aged women of a village near the eastern Indian coast protect their husbands through a month-long discipline in which they joyfully worship the deity Krishna.

In many cultures death seems as much a special women's province as birth. Chapter 9 carries us halfway around the globe to Central America to witness another group of older women who organize and celebrate traditional rituals of mourning.

The two final chapters of this section describe practices connected with cults of saints in Iran and Morocco. In a practice popular in pre-revolutionary Iran, women of all ages made requests to the Muslim saints. These requests were related to their various domestic concerns; as part of this practice, women also vowed to provide a ritual meal for their friends if the request was met. Though sometimes criticized, these vows and feasts were important occasions for women, both socially and religiously. In Morocco, the saints are also important in women's religious lives, even though the saints and their sanctuaries are not part of official Islam. In this case, the tombs of saints serve as a place of refuge and solace for women overtaxed by the demands and stresses of their family roles.

6

Golden Handprints and Red-Painted Feet: Hindu Childbirth Rituals in Central India

DORANNE JACOBSON

The cry of a newborn child sounds faintly from within the thick mud-plastered stone walls of a house in an Indian village. Barely audible in the night air, this tiny cry gives evidence of a major event in the lives of those who dwell within the walls of that house.

While this birth is but one of about 58,000 that occur each day in India (21 million every year), it is the focus of much concern, some of which is manifested in a set of rituals performed by women before and after the arrival of the baby. Centering on the infant and its mother, these rituals involve kinswomen of the baby, other women of the village, and, tangentially, some men. The rituals serve a number of purposes: they announce the baby's arrival to the world, magically strengthen and protect

DORANNE JACOBSON received her Ph.D. in Anthropology from Columbia University and is currently Director of International Images, Springfield, Illinois. She has focused her anthropological research on changes in women's roles in Central India, where she has conducted research for a total of five years. She has published a book and more than twenty articles on women, the family, development, and religion in India. She is also a widely published photographer.

Author's Note   The data on which this chapter is based were collected during three years of field research in India (1965–1967, 1973–1975). I am grateful to the American Institute of Indian Studies and the National Institute of Mental Health for supporting the research. A grant from the National Endowment for the Humanities supported the writing of the article. For their essential assistance, I wish to thank the residents of Nimkhera village and Ms. Sunalini Nayudu, Dr. Leela Dube, Dr. Suzanne Hanchett, and Dr. Jerome Jacobson.

mother and child from evil influences, mark the passage of mother and infant from one stage of life to another, provide the new mother with approval and support, contribute to women's sense of solidarity with other women, and publicly recognize women's vital roles·in perpetuating and enhancing the prosperity of the family and the larger community. In a culture in which women typically enjoy fewer privileges than men, the rituals serve to remind women—and men—of the fact that women, after all, produce children, the one thing without which no kin group or society could long exist.

This chapter discusses the Hindu practices and rituals surrounding pregnancy and childbirth that are observed in Nimkhera, a village in Madhya Pradesh State, Central India. These rituals, summarized in Table 1, are primarily life-crisis rites, or rites of passage, centering on a major transition in the lives of the newborn infant, its mother, father, and other kin. Typically, in all cultures rites of passage—ceremonies marking birth, coming of age, marriage, and death—note momentous changes in the lives of individuals. Rites of passage are remarkably similar the world over. Those undergoing a major transition are formally separated from their old status and routines, and they assume their new roles, often in isolation. Finally, a ceremonial reintegration into the larger society recognizes their changed status and resulting changes in social relationships.

In Indian childbirth ceremonies, although the infant is important, most of the ritual focuses on the parents, especially the mother. Childbirth rituals are unique in the degree to which they are the domain of women in a culture where men often seem to dominate. The contrast is seen, for example, in a Hindu wedding; when the bride is given to the groom and his family, a male Brahman priest chants Sanskrit verses and directs the rites, while veiled women sing on the sidelines. In childbirth rituals, however, men play only minimal supporting roles. Giving birth is a skill in which

no man can claim expertise. This is the heart of the domestic sphere, the women's domain par excellence. In dramatizing one of women's most vital roles, the rituals contribute to harmonious cooperation among women brought together to live in the patrilineal joint family, the key social unit in rural India.

NIMKHERA VILLAGE AND THE CULTURAL SETTING

Nimkhera village is in Raisen District, about 50 miles east of Bhopal, the capital of Madya Pradesh, India's largest state. The village is similar to hundreds of others in the region. The population of the village was 621 in 1974, approximately 80 percent Hindu and 20 percent Muslim. The villagers belong to 21 different ranked Hindu castes and 5 Muslim caste-like groups. A few of the village men work outside Nimkhera, but most villagers derive their support from the abundant wheat crop grown on the village fields.

Raisen District is almost completely rural, and most of its villages are small. The district has a relatively low population density and is underdeveloped agriculturally and educationally. Fewer than 8 percent of district women can read. As in many other parts of India, there are fewer women than men (900 to 1,000), reflecting the special physical hazards to which women are subject in a region where good medical care is difficult to obtain. The rate of infant mortality is declining but remains high.

Hindu parents arrange the marriages of most girls before puberty and most boys before age twenty-two. The young couple—usually strangers to each other—do not normally begin living together until after the consummation ceremony, about three years after the wedding. Dressed in fine clothes, ornamented with glistening jewelry, and modestly cloaked with a white shawl, the weeping bride is led from her parental home and borne in a bullock cart or taxi to her marital home, usually in a village one to forty miles distant from her parents' home. There she meets alone with her husband for the first time. She begins to spend much of her time in her husband's home as the lowest-ranking member of his joint family. However, most women enjoy long, refreshing visits in their natal homes until late in life.

In most joint families the young wife is expected to observe purdah: she stays inside the house most of the time and veils her face from elders. She is usually responsible for cooking

Table 1 *Summary of Childbirth Rituals and Practices in Nimkhera Village*

Occasion or Timing	Ritual and Practice	Sociological Interpretation
Pregnancy	Minimal restrictions on food and activity	Gradual separation of pregnant woman from group
Delivery and 3-day pollution period (*Sor*)	Strong restrictions on food and activity	Definite separation of mother and child from group; recognition of their lineage membership
Day of birth	Placement of the *charua* pot; special foods for the new mother	Psychological support for the new mother
Evening after birth	*Charua* songfest	Announcement to village of the birth; tacit public recognition to new mother; symbolic sharing of her fertility
3 days after birth	Lifting of 3-day pollution period (*Sor*); ritual cleansing	First step in reintegration of mother and child into group
7–10 days after birth	*Chauk* ceremony: blessing of mother and child; worship of sun and water pots; ethno-birth control	Recognition and support of the new mother; introduction of mother and child to outside world; symbolic extension of her fertility
	Chauk songfest	Announcement to village of infant's successful completion of most dangerous period of life
	Grass Celebration (*Duba Badhai*): celebration of first son; gift distribution	Display of generosity; averting of envy
About 40 days after birth	Well Worship	End of postpartum pollution period; final reintegration of mother into group; symbolic extension of her fertility to village water supply
2½ or 5 months after birth	First feeding of solid foods	A milestone in the child's growing individuality
No set itme	*Pach* gifts from mother's natal kin	Recognition of importance of kinship ties with maternal relatives
No set time	Head shaving	Final separation of child from physical attachment to mother; acknowledgment of importance of mother's care for child's survival; introduction of child to life outside the home

and other time-consuming chores. Some women—usually not the youngest brides—go to the village well twice daily to bring back heavy pots of water atop their heads. Women's duties also include plastering and painting the house and courtyard. Many women work in the fields and perform myriad other tasks.

But in the eyes of all, a woman's prime role is to be a mother, particularly a mother of sons. Every girl receives early training in child care, and girls love to carry young children about. A young woman is brought as a bride into her husband's family to produce children for the family. Through bearing children she finds social approval, economic security, and emotional satisfaction. Every young bride knows of old women who lack children; with houses empty of sons and grandchildren, they have no young hands to depend upon for support and aid. Even having daughters is not enough, for daughters marry and go to live with their husbands' kin. Adoption is possible only under very limited circumstances. Fortunate women are those who are fed from their sons' earnings and cared for by daughters-in-law. The message is clear: to be barren brings grief; to bear children brings joy. Thus every bride looks forward to becoming pregnant. Even women with several children are usually happy about new pregnancies. Contraception and abortion are very rarely practiced. Given the high infant-mortality rate in the region and the advantages of having children, the lack of enthusiasm for birth control is not surprising.

Childbirth rituals are almost the same for a baby boy as for a baby girl, but the greater enthusiasm surrounding rituals for boys shows a strong bias in favor of sons. Women say they love boys and girls the same; after all, they suffer equally painful birth pangs for both. "But we feel great pleasure if a son is born," one woman said. "A son remains part of our family. A daughter will belong to others."

Throughout the birth rituals certain materials appear again and again as symbols, expressing cherished values and desires. Cow dung is commonly used for cleaning and purifying. Produced by the sacred cow, dung is used daily in the form of dried cakes for cooking fuel; as a paste that dries to form a resilient film, it is used to plaster earthern walls and floors. Only women make cow-dung cakes and apply cow-dung paste. Golden turmeric, used in many Hindu rituals, is especialy noticeable in ceremonies involving women. Wet turmeric is used to help effect transition from one state to another, and in childbirth rituals it also symbolizes female generative powers. Items of red and russet hue are often part of women's rituals along with the turmeric; these, too, symbolize female fertility. Wheat and objects used by women to produce wheat foods appear frequently—hardly surprising in this area where wheat is literally the staff of life. Chilis, pulse, and salt, classic accompaniments to a meal of wheat breads, are also evident. Brown-sugar and the more expensive puffed white-sugar candies are highly desired treats used in many rituals and also distributed at births and weddings to express the joy of the family. Water is a key symbol signifying both purification and fertlity. In this region the water supply is limited throughout much of the year, and the vital link between water and survival is keenly felt by the villagers. Since one of women's particular duties is to bring water into the house, women and water are often connected in ceremony and symbol.

PREGNANCY

Since women's overriding concern is to produce offspring, no effort is spared to encourage pregnancy. Brides who remain childless too long are given every opportunity to be with their husbands by night and to worship Matabai, the village Mother Goddess, by day. The childless wife also offers special oblations to Lord Shiva or fasts every week in honor of the Goddess Santoshi Mata. Concerned relatives may take her to visit the shrines of other deities of the region, particularly the temple of the Goddess Narbada Mai. Silently begging the Goddess for a son, the woman wets her hands with cow-dung paste and makes inverted handprints on the base of the Goddess's temple. If her prayers are answered, she gratefully returns to make upright handprints in golden turmeric on the temple and to make other offerings to the Goddess. The childless woman may also visit a shaman, or medium, who will divine the cause of her problem and seek to cure it. The shrines of such mediums are thronged by worshipers, many of whom return to express their thanks for newly born offspring. A few villagers also consult women gynecologists.

Generally, failing to conceive is regarded as a feminine defect. A childless daughter-in-law is criticized, and may be replaced. Barrenness may be seen as punishment for sins committed in a past life or as the result of educating a girl too highly. Husbands are virtually never blamed for childlessness, despite the fact that most villagers believe that a baby grows out of the man's seed alone, developing like a plant's seed in the fertile field of the womb. On the other hand, a woman is not blamed if she gives birth to babies that die; people say that it was not her husband's fate to have living children.

Once she suspects that she is pregnant, the happy young woman shyly refrains from mentioning the joyous news to anyone. She delicately leaves it to others to notice that she has not observed the usual monthly pollution period, is sometimes nauseous, or is widening at the waist. Her husband and other relatives gradually recognize the situation, and she begins to receive special treatment.

The pregnant woman is advised not to eat certain foods that are regarded as possibly harmful to the baby, and she may be given special delicacies. A major concern is shielding the expectant woman and her unborn child from malevolent magic and spirits. The pregnant woman is encouraged to remain home as much as possible. She is not allowed to wander about after dark, for fear of evil spirits. The woman may wear a tiny jacknife on her belt: a sharp iron object wards off ghosts and spirits. She also does not wear the usual auspicious substances with which women paint themselves, for fear that they may attract an evil spirit. A pregnant woman stays shut up inside her house during an eclipse of the sun since her appearance would be an "offense to God," and the child would be born with a defect. Conservative villagers feel that sexual relations should be avoided for the latter months of pregnancy. These protective practices serve to gradually set the pregnant woman apart and to inform others of her special and valued condition.

Particularly for the first birth, the woman must be at her husband's rather than her parents' home for delivery. If a woman bears her first child in her parental home, it is strongly believed that misfortune or tragedy will befall her relatives. For example, one young woman bore her first child in her natal home, and villagers shook their heads knowingly when her teen-aged brother suddenly died the next day. Furthermore, a woman giving birth is almost never attended by her mother but by her female in-laws.

DELIVERY

When labor begins, the prospective mother is suddenly and radically separated from others. In Hindi, the language of the region, a woman who is in labor or has just given birth is called *jachcha*. A *jachcha* is in a highly polluted and polluting state, similar to that of the lowest untouchable castes. Anyone who touches her or her newborn infant becomes ritually polluted and must take a bath before contacting others. Therefore, when labor begins, the *jachcha* retires to a little-used room or curtained-off area, separated from all other members of the household. A man of the family is sent to call the midwife.

The midwife who delivers most babies in Nimkhera lives in a nearby village. Like traditional midwives in much of India, she belongs to a very low-ranked caste, because of the ritually defiling nature of her work. Four generations of women in her family have been midwives. She has received some training in modern methods and sterile technique at the district hospital, but she completely ignores this training in her practice. A nontraditional nurse, trained in midwifery and employed at a government health station in a nearby village, is also available. This post is usually filled by a Christian woman from the southern state of Kerala, to whom ritual-pollution concepts are relatively unimportant or even irrelevant. The traditional midwife's fees are lower than the government nurse's, and her methods are more familiar, so most villagers call the nurse only in a very difficult case.

During labor some women undo their buttons, braids, knots, and trunk locks to "open the way" for the baby. The *jachcha* may be fed water in which the idols in the village temple have been bathed. This sacred water is said to alleviate labor pains and bring about a speedy delivery.

Inside the dimly lit birth room, the *jachcha* squats on the cowdung-plastered earth floor and clings to a rope or house post. If delivery is difficult, the midwife or nurse may encourage her to lie on her back. One woman from her marital family and the midwife are with the *jachcha*. The assisting relative hands things to the midwife and watches to make sure that the midwife does not perform magic on the *jachcha*. No matter how great the pain, the *jachcha* is expected to endure the pangs of labor stoically. Silence is ideal, low moans are tolerated, but shouting or crying are strongly disapproved of and ridiculed.[1] One woman who had been in labor for nearly twenty-four hours was seen crying and clutching her husband in a desperate embrace. The village women gossiped for weeks about this shameless indiscretion. Furthermore, the woman giving birth is expected to retain her modesty as much as possible by draping her sari adroitly, and she should take care not to soil any garments or bedclothes, since the Washerwoman[2] objects to laundering cloth defiled with uterine blood. In childbirth, as in other facets of life, restraint is the keynote.

Finally, the baby emerges. No exclamations or cries of delight are heard; only a quiet statement is made: "It's a boy" or "It's a girl." Emotions are kept in check; to compliment or admire the baby would surely draw the evil eye.[3] A man with a watch is asked the time, so that an accurate horoscope can be prepared later. Otherwise, no announcement is made.

The midwife lays the slippery babe on a rag on the floor and waits for the placenta. Then, without care for aseptic technique, she ties a string or bit of rag around the umbilical cord and cuts it with a sickle (or, in recent times, sometimes an old razor blade). The act of cutting the umbilical cord is considered to be extremely polluting and is done only by the midwife. Even if the midwife's arrival is delayed for hours after the birth, the cord is left uncut until she arrives.

After the mother and child are cleansed, the newborn baby is placed for a moment in a winnowing fan along with a sharp metal object and a handful of uncooked wheat, lentils, salt, and red chilis "to make the child's mind sharp." The midwife then digs a shallow hole in the earthern floor near the mother's cot and buries the placenta and severed unbilical cord there to keep them safe from the clutches of malevolent magicians. (A bit of placenta, manipulated magically by a childless woman, could help the woman produce a healthy child but would cause harm to the original baby.) The midwife scapes up the other remnants of the birth from the floor and later discards them. Then she plasters over the area with a new layer of purifying cow-dung paste. A broken earthern pot is put beside the mother's bed for a urinal, as she will not leave the birth room for several days. The birth sari is given to the Washerwoman to be laundered (and thus purified). The midwife may give the new mother an oil massage. Still in a very polluted state, not to be touched by anyone other than the midwife and assisting relative, the sequestered mother and child rest. Outsiders are not invited to see the baby, and even when the midwife makes follow-up calls on the mother, the baby is covered with a cloth to avoid the evil eye (and, unknown to the villagers, extra germs). The fear of illness or death striking the baby is so strong that no visitors, and not even the parents, ever openly admire the child. Instead they exaggerate complaints about the baby's health.

CEREMONIES FOLLOWING DELIVERY

On the day of the birth, a small ceremony is held for the new mother. At an auspicious time, selected by the family Brahman priest, an herbal tea is ritually brewed for the mother. Only women of the extended family are invited to this event. The sister of the baby's father purifies an area of the floor with cow dung, and, using wheat flour, draws an auspicious design (*chauk*) on it. Then a special new pot, called a *charua*, is decorated with red paint, cow dung, turmeric, and grass. It is then filled with water, special herbs, and fruits and set on the design. After that, five or seven women from the family carry the pot into the kitchen, where the sister of the child's father places it on the stove. The reddish herbal tea that results is the *jachcha*'s main drink for many days. The new mother must also be fed other special foods that are very expensive but that miserly in-laws can hardly balk at providing.

That evening a women's songfest is held at the home of the new infant. These songfests bring women together as women to celebrate a uniquely female achievement and to honor the new mother. Women and girls from the neighborhood—or the whole village—are invited by the Barber woman on behalf of the host family. As darkness settles over the village, the women gather in the *jachcha*'s courtyard to talk, spread news, reminisce about other pregnancies and other births, and sing special childbirth songs. The *jachcha* and the infant remain hidden and unheard in their polluted isolation, but they can hear the sounds of the gathering. Most of the birth songs refer to the *jachcha* and the pain she has suffered, as well as to tensions between the new mother and the in-laws with whom she lives. A typical song is the lament of a woman in labor, with her husband away, and her mother-in-law and husband's sister providing her with no help or sympathy. None of the songs center on the child, presumably to avoid the evil eye, but in a few songs the child is referred to as "jewel-like." In one song Lord Krishna's adoring mother is singing a lullaby to her beautiful divine infant. Thus, indirectly, women can express the joy they feel in holding their own precious babies—their one great consolation for having to live among unfamiliar and often unloving in-laws. Listening to the conversation and to the songs, young girls at the songfest receive early training in what to expect when they reach childbearing age. As refreshment the singers receive sugar candies and also swollen boiled wheat, suggestive of the *jachcha*'s formerly swollen body and hence symbolically extending her fertility to the other women.

For three days after the birth the new mother and child are in an especially great state of pollution, "because nine months' menstrual blood comes out at a baby's birth." During these three days, called *Sor*, no one but the midwife touches the mother and infant. All members of the father's family are also polluted, though less so than the mother and child. Even if the child is born away from its paternal home, members of the patrilineage are still polluted. This pollution observance emphasizes to kinsmen the significance of the arrival of a new member of the kin group. At this time, the father of the baby may glimpse it but not hold it. Any contact whatsoever between husband and wife is forbidden during these three days. They may not have any intimate contact for forty days.

During *Sor* mother and child are given sponge baths and oil massages each day by the midwife. Then, on the third day after the birth, a ritual ends this state of greatest impurity. The midwife breaks the mother's old glass bangles, polluted by the birth, off her wrists. She rubs the mother with an ointment of turmeric, wheat flour, oil, and water to cleanse her skin. The baby is rubbed with a ball of turmeric and dough and given an oil massage. Then the midwife gives both mother and child complete purifying baths (the mother's first real bath since the birth), and they don clean clothes. Other family members also bathe. The bedding and dirty clothes are either washed by the Washerwoman or thrown away. The midwife purifies the birth room by applying cow-dung slip to the floor and up onto the base of the walls.

After *Sor*, since the new mother has moved a step closer to her normal state, the untouchable midwife no longer takes care of her. Instead, the middle-ranking village Barber woman now takes over. The Barber woman cuts the new mother's nails and applies another layer of cow dung to the floor of the room. If the new mother wants to become pregnant again soon, she asks the Barber woman to apply the cow-dung slip so that it covers only a narrow band at the base of the walls. But if she wants to postpone her next pregnancy, she asks the Barber woman to smear the slip higher on the wall. Women members of the family apply cow dung to the other floors of the house, and all earthen water pots (which are absorbent and hence polluted by the birth) are replaced with new pots. The sickle used to cut the umbilical cord is purified with fire by the blacksmith.

After this purification, the members of the kin group, as well as the infant, emerge in a clean and renewed state. The new mother can now enter the main room of the house and be touched by others, but she is still not pure enough to engage in normal household tasks. In particular, she avoids cooking and any jobs involving contact with dampness; in fact, she should not even wash her own baby, for fear of her catching cold. Also, she still avoids eating certain foods. Not until forty days after the birth will she achieve a completely normal state.

THE CHAUK CEREMONY

The major ritual following childbirth is the *Chauk* ceremony, held about a week to ten days after the birth. The exact time is selected by the Brahman priest according to astrological calculations. The *Chauk* takes its name from the four-sided design drawn in wheat flour to mark the central location of the ritual.

The infant's paternal aunt, who should be present for the occasion, plays an important role in the *Chauk*. Through that role she reaffirms her involvement in the home of her birth and the importance of her continuing bonds with her parents' family. If she is not available, another female relative—usually a young girl—can substitute. If the child is a boy, the aunt makes two designs out of wet cow dung, one on each side of the house's main door. Otherwise, the *Chauk* ceremonies are the same for boys and girls. In the late afternoon, after the designs have been made, the Barber woman arrives to prepare the mother for the *Chauk*. She bathes her, cuts her nails, does her hair in fresh braids, and fits new mirror-studded lacquer bangles on her wrists. The baby too is bathed.

The *Chauk* ceremony itself takes place at dusk, around 6 or 7 P.M. It is a private ceremony, normally attended only by women and girls of the household and by the Barber woman, who physically guides the new mother through the ceremony. Boys and men are usually excluded.

The aunt uses cow dung to cleanse a spot on the floor in the center of the main room of the house, just in front of the door, and then draws the *Chauk* design in wheat flour on the spot and arranges other ritual paraphernalia. The new mother appears, her face covered by a veil, and sits down on a wooden platform, which has been placed over the design, facing the door of the house. She is wearing all her fine jewelry and best clothing, over which she wears a white cover-all shawl. Held in the crook of her right arm and completely covered with her sari and shawl is her baby, dressed in new clothes that were blessed by having a maiden step on them.

The Barber woman rubs the mother's feet with wet turmeric and, using red paint, draws an auspicious design on them. Garbed in finery, modestly cloaked in white, with only her ornamented hands and gold-and-red painted feet protruding, the new mother looks as she did when she first arrived at the door of the house as a bride on the occasion of her consummation ceremony. Then she stood outside the door, facing the house, with her white veil tied to her new husband's shawl, while he stood on the wooden platform. Now, holding her baby, she sits on the platform inside the door, facing out. In her new role as mother she is fulfilling the promise that was inherent in her role as bride.

Guided by the Barber woman, the sister of the baby's father holds a platter filled with ritual paraphernalia and stands before the veiled mother and child. With her finger she carefully paints a turmeric swastika (an ancient Hindu auspicious design) on the white cloth over the woman's head and on the cloth over the baby. The swastika on the mother's head is said to help ensure that she will enjoy a long married life. The swastika over the baby is intended to "keep her lap full of babies." The aunt then slowly swings the brass platter back and forth over the woman's head, in an arc from one shoulder to the other, five or seven times. As she moves the platter, she puts her hand over the glittering oil lamp and then onto the mother's shoulders and the baby, blessing them. This gesture, called *arti*, is a key feature of the worhsip of deities by their devotees and in addition to being an act of adoration may also provide protection from the evil eye.

Carrying her baby, the mother rises from her seat over the auspicious design on the floor and goes out the door. She quickly turns and hands the baby back in through the door to a relative who puts the baby in a wheat-filled winnowing fan and covers it with a cloth. Out in the dark courtyard, the Barber woman guides the new mother through several additional rituals, one of which is believed to determine how long it will be before the new mother conceives again. She herself makes the determination when she throws lumps of food eastward "as an offering to the sun." The farther she throws them, the longer it will be before her next pregnancy. In another part of the rite, the new mother worships and blesses the family water supply by placing her own golden handprints—symbols of her fertility—on the family water pots. She then reenters the house.

The entire *Chauk* is performed without any particular verbal expressions or prayers. Formalized ritual utterances are the province of the male priests; women's rites involve doing, not talking except for their songs.

In the *Chauk* the woman clearly emerges in her new role as mother of a child and as a woman who has fulfilled her duty to her marital lineage. Leaving the door of the house with her baby, both mother and child make a formal entry into the outside world. The *Chauk* stresses the beneficent and creative powers of the female. In her new role as a child-producing member of the household and lineage, the mother is reminded that she upholds the strength of the family group through chaste behavior and devoted motherhood. Much depends on her.

Although the *Chauk* has brought them a step closer to normal life, the mother and child are still in a state of vulnerable transition. They are shrouded by layers of cloth and darkness throughout the ceremony, and the child must not even glimpse the lamplight. They remain sequestered for the rest of the forty-day post-partum period. The infant is not yet individualized to the point of being given a name. Although it has survived the most dangerous days after birth, its grip on life is still not deemed to be a sure one.

That night, after the *Chauk* ritual itself is over, many women are invited to a *Chauk* song-fest. If the family is prosperous and high ranking, a drummer is hired to announce the start of the event, and a crowd of perhaps forty women and girls gather in the courtyard to sing childbirth songs. The mother and child are still not seen or heard from. Here too, as in almost all other situations involving childbirth, the new father is not at home and is nowhere to be seen. The women sing the usual songs, many of which stress a woman's alienation from her conjugal kinfolk. One song, about Bemata, a goddess who gives babies to women, declares:

As a scorned basket is useful in carrying cow dung,
A scorned daughter-in-law is useful in producing sons.

The birth of a first-born son in a prominent and prosperous family may be marked with a special celebration, to which all the villagers are invited. This celebration, held on the night of the *Chauk* festival, is called *Duba Badhai* (Grass Celebration) in reference to the sacred *duba* grass that the village Barber sticks in the turbans of the male guests as a kind of blessing. The men sit and chat while the women, sitting separately, sing. Guests may give money or clothing to the Barber to be presented to the baby.

To the sound of beating drums, the celebrating family distributes gifts—clothes and money to the family Brahman priest and his wife, the family guru (religious teacher) and his wife, the village temple priest and his wife,

the Barber and Barber woman, the Sweeper woman, the Potter woman, and even the Tanner woman. Sisters and daughters of the family often receive clothing. All the male guests are given brown-sugar lumps or sugar candies, and the women receive sweets and boiled wheat. In the privacy of the courtyard, away from the eyes of the men, women guests may dance in celebration. In addition, women of the higher castes may be feasted as special guests on the *Chauk* day. The family head may also present cows to the village tailor, the Barber, the Sweeper, and, as an act of religious merit, to a poor maiden. All of this largesse reaffirms the family head's position as a prominent and generous person and suggests that the newborn infant may follow in his footsteps. The generosity also helps to fend off envy, as the good fortune of the family in having a new male member is shared with others.

After the *Chauk*, the mother can again eat most normal foods; in addition, she may continue to eat the special foods that are prescribed for new mothers. She can now do many routine household tasks, such as cleaning grain and sweeping. But she should still refrain from fetching water or touching wet cow dung, for fear she might catch a chill. For the same reason, she does not take a full bath again until the forty days are over. Because she is still somewhat polluted, she does not enter the kitchen or cook, except sometimes for herself on a small stove outside the kitchen. Grinding flour, too, is usually avoided. She does not participate in any worship services for Gods or Goddesses or touch the household's holy images. Except for going out to eliminate at the edge of the forest or fields, she stays home. Very poor women, however, may not be able to afford so many days of idleness and may return to their jobs in the fields much earlier.

Finally, the postpartum pollution period ends about forty days after the birth. The exact date is set by a Brahman. The mother bathes, her room is cleansed with cow dung, and her clothes and bedclothes are washed again. She is now ready to resume normal life. The return to normalcy is marked in some castes with a ritual called Well Worship. In some of the middle castes, women perform the Well Worship ceremony after the birth of a first child, and Brahman women perform it after the birth of every child. Women of other castes may perform a tiny ceremony at the well side before drawing water for the first time, or they may not bother with any ceremony at all.

For her Well Worship, the bejeweled and white-shrouded Brahman mother goes at night to the village well, preceded by a drummer and accompanied by the Barber woman, a few women members of her household, and a few relatives and neighbors. After a fairly complex ritual in which the new mother makes auspicious diagrams at various points around the well's rim, she pushes all the ritual offerings into the well, draws some water in the household water pots, and carries it home. Women who have gathered there sing and receive sugar treats. The new mother has thus symbolically extended her fecundity to the village water supply. The woman's transition to her new status as the mother of her child and her reintegration into the normal life of her family and community are now complete.

THE CONTINUING CYCLE OF CEREMONIES FOR THE CHILD

The ceremonies following the Well Worship center on the child, its gradual achievement of individuality, and its relationships with others. In the *Pach* ceremony, held at any convenient time within the first few months after the birth of a first child, members of the mother's natal family arrive at her marital home with gifts of clothing, jewelry, toys, and perhaps even a fancy cot for the baby. The visitors also ceremonially present clothing to the child's parents and other men and women of the child's paternal household. Thus, the bond between a

child and its mother's parents, its mother's brother, and other maternal relatives is acknowledged and strengthened. At the same time the importance of the link between a woman's natal family and her conjugal kin is recognized. When they leave, the visitors take the new mother and the baby home with them for a lengthy stay. Most children and their mothers visit their maternal kin often, and some children live in their maternal uncle's home for years at a time.

A small ceremony is held when the child is fed solid food for the first time—generally, at two and one-half months for a girl and five months for a boy. Tiny portions of wheat breads, fritters, sweet milk-and-rice pudding, or other foods (ideally, thirty-six varieties of food) are fed to the child from a silver rupee coin by the child's paternal aunt or a stand-in. The aunt then receives a present from the baby's father. The child usually continues to suckle until it is about two years old, gradually increasing the amount of solid food it consumes.

At some time in the first year or two of life, a child's head must be ritually shaved to remove the polluted "birth hair." Among many high-caste families in Nimkhera, the Head-Shaving ceremony is held near the Matabai (Mother Goddess) shrine. The mother and child are dressed in good clothes; accompanied by female relatives, neighbor women, and the Barber couple, they parade to the shrine in late morning. An auspicious design is made on the ground in front of the shrine. The mother sits on a wooden platform over the design, with her baby cradled in her lap. A worship service (*puja*) is performed; then the Barber shaves the baby's head with a wicked-looking straight-edged razor, and the baby's head is anointed with turmeric, usually by the mother. The hair cuttings are collected to be thrown into a sacred river as an offering.

The hair cutting is the first public ceremony involving the child and serves to introduce the child to the village Mother Goddess and to the village. While the earlier rites are performed in dark protective privacy, the hair-cutting ceremony takes place in open sunlight. Here, for the first time, a male (the Barber) representative of the world outside the home acts as the child's attendant. The simple *puja*, with offerings put into a small fire, is typical of scores of other rituals involving male participants. This ceremony mediates between the dangerous period of infancy and the less dangerous period of childhood. With the removal of the birth hair, the child is finally separated physically from the mother and achieves individuality. Offering the hair to the divine may act to consecrate the child and help protect him or her from harm. The mother's anointing the child's head with turmeric is a blessing, a visible symbol of a belief often stated by village women: "A child needs his mother's hand over his head; then he grows fast, sustained by her love." Not until the child's wedding, when he himself steps on the path to parenthood, will he again be rubbed with turmeric. Then the child—bride or groom—will be anointed with the golden ointment by young women of the family, while the mother protectively holds her hand on the child's head.

CONCLUSION

During the total of thirty-seven months I spent in Nimkhera, at least seventy-six Hindu babies were born, sixty-seven of whom survived the first two weeks of infancy. Thus, Hindu childbirth rituals were performed at the rate of about twenty-two complete sets per year, involving the women of the village again and again in the rites and practices surrounding initiation into motherhood. Childbirth rituals are certainly the most frequently performed life-cycle ceremonies; among all Hindu ritual observances in Nimkhera only the short daily worship services held in the temple and at some homes and shrines outnumber them. In a situation in which modesty and fear of unseen evil forces militate against public discussion of childbirth, these ceremonies provide public recognition to women as they contribute their procreative capacity to the family and to society. Indeed, except for her wedding, there is virtually no other situation in which a woman can legitimately achieve recognition at all. Ideally quiet and—in her marital home—veiled and secluded, the woman is the center of attention only in new motherhood. The never-ending sequences of childbirth ceremonies continually tell her that, above all, women should be mothers and that only in motherhood will she find satisfaction.

Within the family-oriented village society, there is little room for following individual preferences; all must work together for the family's strength. Women must dutifully carry out their assigned tasks in the home and in the fields and, most important, make their unique contribution of new members for the group. As anthropologists Yolanda and Robert Murphy have written, "The woman remains the custodian and perpetuator of life itself. Those who would question the worth of this trust must first ask if there is anything else in human experience that has an ultimate meaning."[4]

Notes

1. No painkillers are used. Indian women could benefit greatly from knowledge of Lamaze childbirth techniques, in which a series of breathing exercises direct the pregnant woman's mind away from feelings of pain or discomfort.
2. The terms "Washerwoman" and, later, "Barber woman," have been capitalized in this chapter because they designate the women's caste rank as well as the service that they perform. The term "midwife," however, designates only a service; the woman who performs it may come from a number of different caste groups.
3. Excellent sociological and ecological analyses of the evil-eye beliefs found in many parts of the world are presented in Clarence Maloney, ed., *The Evil Eye* (New York: Columbia University Press, 1976).

4. Yolanda Murphy and Robert F. Murphy, *Women of the Forest* (New York: Columbia University Press, 1974), p. 232.

Further Readings

Jacobson, Doranne. "The Women of North and Central India: Goddesses and Wives." *Many Sisters: Women in Cross-Cultural Perspective*, ed. by Carolyn J. Matthiasson, 99–175. New York: The Free Press, 1974.

——————. "Songs of Social Distance: Women's Music in Central India. *Journal of South Asian Literature* 11, nos. 1 and 2 (1975): 45–59.

——————. "You Have Given Us a Goddess: Flexibility in Central Indian Kinship." *Aspects of Changing India*, ed. by S. Devadas Pillai, 315–26. Bombay: Popular Prakashan, 1976.

——————. "Purdah in India: Life Behind the Veil." *National Geographic Magazine* 152, no. 2 (August 1977): 270–86.

——————. "The Chaste Wife: Cultural Norm and Individual Experience." *American Studies in the Anthropology of India*, ed. by Sylvia Vatuk, 95–138. New Delhi: American Institute of Indian Studies and Manohar Publications, 1978.

——————. "Purdah and the Hindu Family in Central India." *Separate Worlds: Studies of Purdah in India*, ed. by Hanna Papanek and Gail Minault, 81–109. Columbia, Mo.: South Asia Books and Delhi: Chanakya Publications, 1982.

——————. "Studying the Changing Roles of Women in Rural India." *Signs: Journal of Women in Culture and Society* 8, no. 1 (1982): 132–37.

Jacobson, Doranne and Susan S. Wadley. *Women in India: Two Perspectives*. Columbia, Mo.: South Asia Books and New Delhi: Manohar Book Service, 1977 (reprinted 1986).

Hanchett, Suzanne. *Coloured Rice: Symbolic Structure in Hindu Family Festivals*. Delhi: Hindustan Publishing Corporation, 1987.

7

Hindu Women's Family and Household Rites in a North Indian Village

SUSAN S. WADLEY

S lap! Slap! The sound of the winnowing fan being beaten reverberates through the house and courtyard as Jiya, the mother, rids the family living quarters of evil spirits and chases away poverty. It is late on a dark night, the no-moon night of the month of Kartik (October-November), and everyone else is asleep. Earlier in the evening the entire family has celebrated Divali,

the Hindu festival honoring Lakshmi, the goddess of prosperity. Divali is also known as the Festival of Lights because Lakshmi is called to homes throughout India by lighting rooftops and windows with clay lamps. It is a joyous festival, also celebrated with fireworks and special foods. But even though the main celebration is over and the family is sleeping, Jiya performs this one last task. As is the case for

SUSAN S. WADLEY, Professor of Anthropology at Syracuse University, received her Ph.D. in Anthropology from the University of Chicago in 1973. Her research interests range from women's ritual and folklore to regional epic traditions to socio-economic change, especially as it affects women in rural north India. She has published several books and numerous articles on women, folklore, and rural north India.

Author's Note I conducted the research on which this paper is based during 1967–1969 and 1974–1975 and was supported by grants from the National Science Foundation; the South Asia Committee, the University of Chicago; and the American Institute of Indian Studies. I also wish to thank my colleagues Barbara D. Miller, William Houska, and Bruce W. Derr, whose insights and suggestions aided me in writing this paper. Last, the women of Karimpur deserve the most thanks. I can never repay them for their hospitality and kindness; I only hope that I do them justice.

many other women's calendrical rituals in north India, she, as the eldest female in the family, has to protect her family's health and welfare.

Whereas men's rituals are aimed primarily at general prosperity or good crops and at the world outside the house itself, women's rituals focus more specifically on family welfare and prosperity within the walls of their homes. In this chapter I will examine how women deal with these concerns by discussing the calendrical cycle of rituals practiced by the high-caste Hindu women of Karimpur,[1] a village of North India.

Karimpur is located approximately 150 miles southeast of Delhi. In 1968 it had a population of 1,380 divided among 22 hierarchically ranked castes. Jiya belongs to the highest-ranking group, the Brahman caste. In Karimpur members of this caste, though nominally priests, are actually farmers. They dominate the village ritually and economically. Most people in Karimpur live by farming. The men work the fields with their bullock-drawn plows, while the women process the food through winnowing, husking, grinding, and cooking. Women work in the fields only rarely, and it is a sign of a family's low status if the women work outside of the home.

Most Karimpur families are joint families—families in which sons, sons' wives, and grandchildren all live with the parents. Married daughters live with their husbands' families in other villages and only periodically visit the home of their birth. Most of the women in Karimpur, especially wealthier and young married women, follow *purdah* restrictions. In north India *purdah* requires that females should be secluded in their family courtyards and houses. When outside these quarters, they must cover their heads and faces with their saris or shawls. Even inside they must cover their faces before their husbands and husbands' older male relatives—fathers, uncles, and older brothers.

Essentially, men and women in Karimpur occupy separate worlds. For the most part, women live and work in their homes and have little mobility outside of them. The physical structure of Karimpur houses is important in understanding women's activities. Most homes are built of mud bricks and have an outer room with a verandah adjoining the village lanes. Behind this room is an open courtyard with one or more rooms attached to it. This courtyard and the rooms around it form the women's world. Men must cough or otherwise announce their presence before entering it. Within the confines of their homes, women cook, clean, care for children, visit with neighbors (who come by crossing over rooftops rather than by using the "public" lanes), weave baskets, knit, and celebrate their rituals. Men use the courtyard primarily for eating and bathing. They entertain their guests on the front verandah or in the outer room. Much of the time the men sleep there as well.

In many aspects of life, even in the content of songs and the way they are sung, men and women express their separate worlds. It is not surprising, then, that women's desires, as expressed in their rituals, are those of their world—the household—while men's concerns are focused primarily on the outer world. Since the world affects women differently than it does men, women's symbols of hope and prosperity are also different from men's symbols. On a more theoretical level, we could say that the calendrical rituals of Karimpur express women's most vital moods and motivations. Whether by beating the winnowing fan on Divali night or by worshiping a banyan tree during Marriage Worship or by offering milk to snakes, women in Karimpur symbolically, yet very powerfully, state the longings and ideas that are vital to their women's world. They express these longings and concerns in the twenty rites they perform every year.

Of these twenty rituals performed by women, three involve the direct worship of male relatives. In these rituals the male relative is actually the deity worshiped, and offerings are made directly to him. Four rituals involve the worshiping of a deity for the protection of a particular family member. Another four annual rituals are concerned with obtaining protection for one's family in general. Nine more rituals seek household prosperity. (See Table 2 for a complete list of these rituals.)

Before going on to examine these rituals in detail, three points should be clarified. First, living human beings can be, and often are, deities in Karimpur, as are plows, snakes, bullocks, and wheat seedlings, in addition to the normally recognized pantheon of mythological gods and goddesses. The basic rule is that any being that a person considers more powerful than himself or herself in any particular realm of life can become an object of worship. Thus for any given individual the religious pantheon of Karimpur is potentially enormous, since it could consist of all other beings. Moreover any action that is undertaken because of another being's power (*shakti*) is religious action. The implications of this point for women's religion will become clearer later.

Second, all the rituals listed in Table 2 are performed by women and/or girls. None of these rites requires the services of a priest or other religious specialists (who are almost exclusively male). All the rules for proper worship and all the stories and songs that accompany worship are orally transmitted from women to women for women's use.

Third, women in Karimpur practice three major forms of religious activity: *vrat* (fasts), *puja* (worship), and *bhajan* (devotional singing). Fasting implies greater devotion than that associated with mere worship. Worshiping means honoring the deity as one would a guest: food is presented, the image may be bathed and perfumed, and new clothes are given. To further symbolize her humble subordination to the deity, the worshiper then eats the god's leftover food (*prasad*). The third ritual form, devotional singing, is both entertainment and serious religious activity. Women's religion in north India is primarily devotional. The deities are worshiped with love and respond with boons for the devotees. Devotional singing accompanies the worship.

I will examine in detail five of the twenty rites practiced by women. I will also look in depth at those aspects of the women's world that give meaning to their ritual actions. The five rituals to be discussed are Brother's Second, Marriage Worship, Lampblack Mother, Snake's Fifth, and the Festival of Lights. Male kin—brothers, husbands, and sons—are the focus of the first three; general family health is sought in the fourth; and family prosperity, in the fifth.

BROTHER'S SECOND

Brother's Second occurs in the fall, two days after the Festival of Lights. On this day women worship their brothers, if the brothers are present in the village, or images of their brothers, if they are not present. To understand the ritual significance of brothers, we need to learn why brothers are important to Karimpur women. To do this, we shall focus on the roles and activities of women, for it is what women are and do that makes their brothers so important.

Two crucial factors in the lives of Karimpur women affect their relationships with their brothers. First, all girls must marry out of the village of their birth (village exogamy); second, they must marry into families considered to have higher ranks than their own (hypergamy). As a result of becoming a part of her husband's family and hence "taking on" his higher status, a married woman has higher status than her own brothers, father, and other natal kin. Because of his lower status, her father does not visit her new relatives or receive any hospitality from them. Yet, since women of north India may not travel alone, some male relative must fetch her from her husband's home when she makes her annual visit to her natal home. Normally, brothers are entrusted with this task. Hence a woman's brothers symbolize her

Table 2   *Women's Rituals in Karimpur*

Deity Worshiped	Name of Festival	Purpose	Date*
Worship of Kin			
Brother	Tying on Protection (*raksha bandan*)	Obtaining his protection	Savan 2:15 (July-Aug.)
Husband	Pitcher Fourth (*Karva chauth*)	Obtaining his protection	Kartik 1:4 (Oct.-Nov.)
Brother	Brother's Second (*Bhaiya duj*)	Obtaining his protection and his long life	Kartik 2:2 (Oct.-Nov.)
Worship on Behalf of Kin			
Savitri Banyan tree	Marriage Worship (*barok ki puja*)	Long life of husband	Jeth 1:15 (May-June)
Gauri	The Third (*tij*)	Brother's welfare	Savan 2:3 (July-Aug.)
Devi	Nine Nights (*neothar*)	Happy marriage for girls	Kuar 2:1–9 (Sep.-Oct.)
Siyao or Sihayo Mata	Lampblack Mother (*siyao* or *sihayo mata*)	Having sons; children's welfare	Kartik 2:1 (Oct.-Nov.)
Worship on Behalf of Family			
Devi	Goddess Worship (*Devin ki puja*)	Protection for family	Chait 2:9 (Mar.-Apr.)
Snakes	Snake's Fifth (*nag panchmi*)	Deliverance from snakes	Savan 2:5 (July-Aug.)
Krishna	Cow Dung Wealth (*gobardhan*)	Protection for family	Kartik 2:1 (Oct.-Nov.)
Devi	Goddess Worship (*Devin ki puja*)	Protection for family	Chait 1:8 (Mar.-Apr.)
Worship for Prosperity			
Grain, Vishnu	Grain Third (*akhtij*)	New crops, shelter	Baisakh 2:3 (Apr.-May)
Devi guru	Asarhi (*asarhi*)	Protection from rains	Asarh 2:15 (June-July)
Hanuman	Eternal Fourteenth (*anant chaudas*)	Protection	Bhadon 2:14 (Aug.-Sep.)
Lakshmi	Elephant Worship (*hathi ki puja*)	Wealth, fruits	Kuar 1:8 (Sep.-Oct.)
Lakshmi	Festival of Lights (*divali*)	Wealth	Kartik 1:15 (Oct.-Nov.)
Vishnu	Awakening Gods (*deothan*)	Prosperity	Kartik 2:11 (Oct.-Nov.)
Vishnu	Full Moon of Kartik (*Kartik purnamashi*)	Wealth	Kartik 2:15 (Oct.-Nov.)
Shiva	Shiva's Thirteenth (*Shiva teras*)	Protection	Phagun 1:13 (Feb.-Mar.)
Holi Mata Krishna	Holi	Crops, removal of evil	Phagun 2:15 (Feb.-Mar.)

*The religious calendar in India is reckoned by lunar months, with each month divided into a dark half (full to new moon) and a light half (new to full moon); this column specifies the date by month, then half (1 = dark half; 2 = light half), then day within the half (1–15).

links to her natal village. They bring her back for her first visit after her marriage, and they come at times of distress or bring gifts when a child is born or married. This cultural rule makes a great deal of sense. Given the Indian life span of approximately forty-four years for males, it is the brother and not the father who will more likely live to carry out these tasks; only rarely would a woman's father be alive into her middle age.

Conditions of life in a husband's household, as well as stereotypes about it, add to the brother's significance. In rural north India all marriages are arranged by the male kin of bride and groom. Neither the girl nor the boy will have ever seen the other before the wedding day itself, and even then *purdah* restrictions require that the bride be cloaked in heavy shawls. The wedding takes place in the bride's home. Afterward the groom and his male relatives (no female relatives can take part in the journey from one village to the other) remove the bride from the family that she has known since birth and take her as a complete stranger to her new family. Here she is a *bahu* (wife), and is subordinate to all until either she has a child or a yet younger "wife" is added to the family. As a servant to her elders, locked into strict *purdah*, and under the tyranny of a mother-in-law, the woman sees her husband's home as a trying and often lonely and unhappy place.

In contrast, the time spent in her father's home, ideally at least one month a year, gives a woman joy, happiness, and a feeling of being loved and cherished. While she is again a daughter, not a wife, *purdah* restrictions are lifted, childhood friendships are reestablished, and freedom is gained from imprisonment in servile relationships with everyone above her. Thus the emotional tone of a woman's life undergoes a complete turnabout when she moves from one house to the other. Many women's songs recognize this fact, particularly those of Savan, the rainy-season month when daughters should return home. Swings are hung in trees, and daughters of all ages gather

to sing of swinging in the cool air of the monsoon, gazing at the green of the fields, and listening to the peacock. Many of the Savan songs lament the fate of women whose brothers did not bring them home.

A brother's importance is further enhanced by his gift-giving role. Beginning with engagement gifts and ending only when she dies, a woman's natal family is expected to give gifts to her husband's family. Gifts should be given yearly and also on special occasions, such as the birth of a child and children's marriages. For example, the mother's brother provides his sister's children with their wedding clothes. Gifts are especially important during the first years of marriage, when gifts from the bride's family, given via the brother, are almost like bribes to ensure that the bride will be well treated in her new home.

Brothers are necessary for women's long happiness. A girl without a brother is considered only slightly better off than a widow. A girl with many brothers is most fortunate. Brothers shelter their sisters from afar. Thus, in the rituals called Brother's Second, The Third, and Tying on Protection, women work to ensure the health and welfare of their protectors.

In the fall, after the Festival of Lights, sisters worship their brothers by putting an honorific *tika* (auspicious mark) on their foreheads and by offering them food, especially sweets, and water. The brother responds by giving his sister gifts of money or clothing, symbolizing his protection for the coming year. When the brother is not present, his sister draws a figure of him in flour paste on the courtyard floor and offers food and water to the image. Some women also make a figure out of cow dung that represents their brothers' enemy. They crown this figure with thorns, take it to the door of the house, and smash it with a rice pestle. Having thus demolished their brothers' enemies for the year, the women conclude their ritual.

Although ritual actions during Brother's Second suggest that the sister seeks the brother's protection, stories told in connection with the rite emphasize that in fact the sister protects the brother. She destroys his enemies for him and thus ensures him a long life. There are two common stories.

Once upon a time, a brother came to his sister's house to take her to his marriage. She made food for him in the middle of the night; but by accident she ground a snake into it. When later she discovered that the cakes she had prepared were bad, she promptly replaced them. Having saved him from the poisonous food, she learned of a thorn (*sahe*) that would rid him of all misfortunes. So, when he got married, she put *sahe* thorns on all the offerings and used them at all the ceremonies, thus giving everybody the impression that she was mad. She even insisted on sleeping in the same room as the bride and groom. When a snake sneaked into the room and tried to bite her brother, she killed it and saved him and his bride. Thus, she shielded her brother from many troubles. When she told her story, she was highly praised. So all sisters worship their brothers and ask for their brothers' long life.

Yamuna and Yamraj were sister and brother. Every day Yamuna went to her brother's house and gave him food. One day Yamraj came to Yamuna's house instead. This day was the second day of the light half of Kartik (the day of Brother's Second). Seeing her brother, Yamuna greeted him with reverence and great happiness. After worshiping him, she gave him food. Yamraj was very pleased by her signs of respect and gave her gifts of ornaments and clothes. When he left, Yamraj said "Sister, I am very pleased with you. Ask any boon; I will fulfill all your wishes." Yamuna said, "Brother, if you are truly pleased with me, come every year on this day and I will feed you. And may a long life be given to those people who go to their sisters and take food on this day." Saying, "It shall be this way," Yamraj left, and Yamuna's every wish was fulfilled.

These stories highlight the main elements of a brother's importance to a Karimpur woman. In the first story, the brother has come to fetch his sister, and she in turn seeks his long life. In the second, the brother not only visits his sister but also gives her gifts. We have seen how important both these elements are to Karimpur women.

MARRIAGE WORSHIP

However important a brother may be, the husband is even more important to a woman's general happiness. A variety of factors, both religious and social, contribute to a husband's importance.

According to Hindu teachings, a good woman is devoted to her husband. The ideal wife is Sita, heroine of the Ramayana, an epic widely read and known throughout India. In the Ramayana, Sita follows her husband Rama into twelve years of exile in the forest. She is kidnapped by a demon, whom Rama eventually destroys. When Sita's virtue is questioned, she mounts a lighted pyre to prove her continued chastity. The gods recognize her purity, and the flames do not burn her. The Ramayana's message is explicit, as illustrated by this quotation from the version commonly read and recited in Karimpur.

[A sage's wife speaks to Sita] Though a husband be old, diseased, stupid, or poor, blind, deaf, bad-tempered or in great distress, yet if his wife treats him with disrespect, she will suffer all the tortures of hell. This is her one religious duty, her one vow and observance—devotion in thought and word and deed to her husband's feet. . . . The wife who honestly fulfills her wifely duty wins salvation with the greatest ease; but she who is disloyal to her husband, wherever she be born, becomes a widow in her early youth.[2]

Thus a woman's hopes for salvation also depend on her marriage.

Traditional Hindu teachings also deal with women who are widowed. Ideally, the widow should commit *sati* by throwing herself on her husband's funeral pyre; this actually occurred quite rarely even in the past. However, by committing *sati*, the widow eliminated two problems: her own inauspicious presence and potential charges of unfaithfulness. Upper-caste widows traditionally were not allowed to remarry, and the sad status of widowhood was displayed for all to see. Widows could no longer wear jewelry, they had to wear plain cotton saris, and their heads were shaved. They could not attend marriages, childbirth celebrations, or other auspicious occasions. In fact, even today, widows are often considered to be witches or carriers of the evil eye.

The conditions of the extended family also make a husband vital to a woman's happiness. Although a husband should not intercede with his mother on his wife's behalf, having a husband around to note mistreatment is considered crucial for a woman's protection. A popular myth associated with the goddess Santoshi Mata iterates this theme. According to this myth, the husband has gone to a foreign land to make his fortune. Meanwhile his wife is abused by her mother- and sisters-in-law. The goddess herself intervenes on behalf of the wife, but fair treatment is meted out only when her husband returns.

Since Hindu women believe that husbands are necessary for their own religious salvation and for a better day-to-day life, it is not surprising that women direct much of their yearly religious activity toward them. Three rituals directly concern husbands. *Barok ki puja* (Marriage Worship) seeks the husband's long life. Young girls perform *neothar* (Nine Nights) in order to secure a future good husband. Performing *karva chauth* (Pitcher Fourth) makes the husband protect his wife, while incidentally asking for his long life. These rites differ from rites honoring brothers in that the two performed by married women (Marriage Worship and Pitcher Fourth) are deemed absolutely necessary. They are part of a wife's duty (*dharma*). In order to be a *pativrat* (worshipful wife)—a state requiring chastity, virtue, and the worship of one's husband—these two rites must be performed.

In Marriage Worship, which occurs during the hot season, women seek long lives for their husbands. The Hindi name for this ritual is revealing—*barok ki puja. Barok* literally means "the gifts given to the groom's family by the bride's relatives at the time of marriage." In this ritual the gift given to the groom's family is his long life. And only a faithful, worshipful wife can give this gift. On this day, women fast and worship the goddess Savitri and a banyan tree in order to ensure a long married life, health for their husbands, and many sons.

The well known story of Savitri captures the essence of this important celebration. I give a summary here.

A daughter, Savitri, named after the goddess, was born to a wise king. When the time came for her marriage, her father told her to choose her own husband. She selected Satyan, son of King Dumtsen, who had lost his kingdom and his eyesight. Satyan cared for his parents by collecting firewood in the jungle. Later, a great sage told Savitri about Satyan's fate. He said that Satyan was a very great man but that he would live only one year. Nevertheless, Savitri married him and served him and his parents well. Three days before he was due to die, she started fasting, and on the third day she insisted on accompanying him to the forest. There, under a banyan tree, he died and Yama (God of Death) came to take him. Savitri followed. Eventually Yama noticed her and tried to send her back, but she refused to go. Noting her devotion, Yama allowed her one wish—anything but her husband's life. She asked for King Dumtsen's kingdom and eyesight. Her wish was granted. Again she followed, and again she received a boon—a hundred brothers—because she was a true and faithful wife. Yet another boon was given—one hundred sons. Still Savitri followed. Yama again stopped her, and she said, "Having a hundred sons without a husband is not right. How can I, a true and faithful wife, have a hundred sons if I have no husband?" Outwitted, Yama conceded defeat and returned Satyan to life. His father's kingdom was restored, and eventually Savitri gave birth to one hundred sons.

By worshiping Savitri, the women honor their marriages and claim recognition as loyal and faithful wives. As they well know, those who worship their husbands and worship on behalf of their husbands will be rewarded. The truly devoted wife can even save her husband from the arms of the god of death. Wifely duties and worldly happiness are intertwined in this ritual.

LAMPBLACK MOTHER

In their worship of Lampblack Mother (Siyao Mata), women seek the welfare of a third set of important kin—their sons. Having sons is considered vital by women for several reasons: sons are needed to perform the ancestral rites, they provide "insurance" in one's old age (especially crucial if a woman should be so unfortunate as to become a widow), and they also make up the family labor force. Equally important is the emotional support that sons provide. Daughters marry and leave home, but sons remain. And whereas in rural India husbands and wives are not supposed to have close emotional attachments, mothers and sons have the strongest emotional affinity of any kinship pair. It has been noted that Indian women's devotion to their sons surpasses that to their husbands.

For a young [Indian] wife, her son in a quite literal sense is her social redeemer. Upon him she ordinarily lavishes a devotion of an intensity proportionate to his importance for her emotional ease and social security. . . . Even when a woman has several sons, she cherishes and protects and indulges them all to a degree not usually known in the Western world.[3]

This joy in sons is reflected in the songs women sing to honor their sons' births:

Jasuda gave birth to a son, bliss spread in Gokul.
Came outside the call for the midwife;
The midwife cut the cord, bliss spread in the palace.
Now the queen gave birth to a son, bliss spread in Gokul.

Women's desire for sons is expressed in the ritual known as Lampblack Mother, in which women express their desire for sons and also seek their sons' continued welfare. At dawn on the morning following the Festival of Lights, women rise early to perform their rites before beginning the day's work. Mornings are chilly in October. While everyone else sleeps, the married women gather, shivering, at designated spots felt to be auspicious to their family—most often the site or doorway of the ancestral home. They make a rough figure of a cow with a heap of fresh cow dung. Then a lamp is lit, and a silver coin is immersed in the lamp's oil. Finally a spoon is held over the lamp to collect the soot (lampblack), which is applied around the eyes of children to ward off evil spirits. Symbolically Lampblack Mother is the cow mother, who in this case is clearly related to women's fertility. After these preparations the women in turn take a bunch of sacred grass and, while "sweeping" it behind them with one hand, say, "Give me wealth. That which is bad, run away." They then each take a *puri* (fried bread) and, while holding it under their saris at the womb, say, "Siyao, don't give daughters, give sons. Keep all well in the next year." Or, if they already have sons, they say, "Keep my sons alive and give them many children." After each woman in turn has sought the goddess's favor, the rite ends with a short session of devotional songs.

Stories told during this ritual are about women who have no sons. In the stories someone tells the unfortunate woman about Lampblack Mother and how to worship her. She does so and has many healthy children. To the Karimpur women having many healthy sons is extremely important. Equally important is their belief that the goddess will give them sons and will help them keep their sons healthy.

SNAKE'S FIFTH

On *nag panchmi* (Snake's Fifth) women ask the snakes to keep away from their families. This ritual takes place in July during the moonsoon season. Because of flooding, snakes often seek refuge on higher land—in many cases inside someone's house. As a result, snake bites increase.

Early in the day, women draw a picture of snakes on the wall of the house. These symbolic snakes are offered milk (believed to be a favorite food of snakes) and flowers. The oldest woman in the family usually makes these offerings. The snakes are asked not to harm family members. The rite itself is brief, and generally no songs and stories are associated with it. Similarly, the request itself is less weighty than those made to other deities.

FESTIVAL OF LIGHTS

I have already described how Jiya concludes the Festival of Lights; it is enlightening to put her activities in a larger context. The Festival of Lights is widely celebrated throughout India. Preparations are made for several days. Houses are repaired and freshly whitewashed, new clothes and ornaments are bought, and sweets and special foods are cooked. Most of the day itself is spent in further preparations. The potter has brought numerous tiny clay lamps that must be filled with oil. The cotton brought by the cotton carder is made into wicks. The courtyard is cleansed once more with a fresh layer of cow dung.

Finally darkness descends. While the women and children arrange the unlit lamps on an auspicious square marked on the courtyard floor, the head of the household, with his wife at his side, worships Lakshmi, the goddess of prosperity. This ritual takes place in the small walled space forming the family "kitchen." This area is the heart of the home physical structure, and family heads often conduct their rituals in it. Here, in sacred space, Lakshmi is entreated to visit the household during the coming year. To encourage Lakshmi's arrival, clay lamps are then lit and placed around rooftops, in windows, and on or near items that could benefit from Lakshmi's gift of prosperity, such as the cattle yard, a student's books, or the granary. Where a lamp burns, Lakshmi's way is lit. To spell out the invitation to her, fireworks, rockets, sparklers, and pinwheels are set off. Men dominate these activities. But men cannot deal with the spirits of the house—the women's world. Hence, when all other activity ceases, Jiya bangs her winnowing fan and shouts, "Get out, poverty" as she roams the courtyard and rooms where her family sleeps. This act, dealing with the immediate family and house, is women's work. Her husband and sons have sought Lakshmi's protection, but she must ensure that evil spirits are chased from the nooks and crannies of *her* house.

CONCLUSION

Hinduism is nominally a male-dominated religion. According to the Sanskrit scriptures, women cannot study the most sacred texts or engage in rituals without their husbands. Furthermore, the most important rituals should be performed by a male religious specialist—the Brahman priest. Yet, as the evidence from Karimpur shows, women are very actively religious. Devotional religion does not require priests. The rites of Karimpur's women are all devotional in character; therefore, they can be conducted by women.

By studying these rituals, we can see which ones are most important to Hindu women. Only in the case of three rituals performed for specific relatives does each woman perform her own ritual herself. The female head of the family conducts two more general rites for all the other women. Two of these five rituals involve fasting—Brother's Second and Marriage Worship. The fast for Marriage Worship is longer and more rigid. Ritual preparations, including the making of special foods, are more demanding for Brother's Second, Marriage Worship, and the Festival of Lights. Thus, it is clear that Marriage Worship is given the greatest weight, followed in order by Brother's Second, Lampblack Mother, and Snake's Fifth. The Festival of Lights is an anomalous case, because it is actually a family ritual in which men also play an important role.

In all these rituals, women, who should ideally be submissive and passive, become instead active. Such rituals may give psychological support to the women themselves, because they allow women to have active control of events rather than depend completely on their male kin. Ritually, only a wife or a sister can really save a husband or brother from death; only Jiya can in fact finally chase poverty out of her house. The rituals performed by Karimpur's women clearly reflect the women's social world—the world of the family and household. Their attempts to have active control over these most important facets of their lives may in fact be most critical for our understanding of Karimpur women's rituals.

Notes

1. Karimpur is a pseudonym. The village has been described in William Wiser and Charlotte Wiser, *Behind Mud Walls* (Berkeley: University of California Press, 1972) and in Susan S. Wadley, *Shakti:* *Power in the Conceptual Structure of Karimpur Religion* (Chicago: University of Chicago Department of Anthropology, 1975).

2. W. Douglas P. Hill, *The Holy Lake of the Acts of Rama* (London: Oxford University Press, 1952), pp. 297–298.

3. David Mandelbaum, "The Family in India," in *The Family: Its Function and Destiny* (New York: Harper and Brothers, 1949), p. 104.

Further Readings

Archer, William G. *Songs for the Bride: Wedding Rites of Rural India.* New York: Columbia University Press, 1985.

Babb, Lawrence Alan. *The Divine Hierarchy: Popular Hinduism in Central India.* New York: Columbia University Press, 1975.

Egnor, Margaret T. "Internal Iconicity in Paraiyar 'Crying Songs.'" *Another Harmony: New Essays on the Folklore of India*, ed. by Stuart H. Blackburn and A. K. Ramanujan. Berkeley, Calif.: University of California Press, 1986.

Gold, Ann. *Village Families in Story and Song: an Approach through Women's Oral Traditions in Rajasthan.* Teaching Unit Available from the Outreach Office, South Asia Center, University of Chicago.

Jacobson, Doranne and Susan S. Wadley. *Women in India: Two Perspectives.* New Delhi: Manohar Books, 1977.

Wadley, Susan S. "The Katha of *Sakat.* Two Tellings." *Another Harmony: New Essays in the Folklore of India*, ed. by Stuart H. Blackburn and S. Ramanujan. Berkeley, Calif.: University of California Press, 1986.

———, ed. *The Powers of Tamil Women.* Syracuse, N.Y.: South Asia Series, Foreign and Comparative Studies Program, Syracuse University, 1980.

———. "Vrats: Transformers of Destiny." *Karma: An Anthropological Inquiry*, ed. by Charles F. Keyes and E. Valentine Daniel. Berkeley, Calif.: University of California Press, 1983.

———. "Women as Mothers, Wives, and Daughters in North Indian Folklore." *Asian Thought and Society* 6: 4–24.

8

The Ladies of Lord Krishna: Rituals of Middle-Aged Women in Eastern India

JAMES M. FREEMAN

During my most recent anthropological study of a village in Orissa, India, I became fascinated by the *habisha* rituals associated with the Jagannatha temple in the pilgrim town of Puri. These rituals, performed mainly by women, are remarkable for the intense religious fervor they inspire, for their grace and beauty, and for their complex symbolism. Despite the importance of these rituals for women, no existing description of the Jagannatha cult gives the *habisha* more than passing mention.

The *habisha*, like many Hindu rites, is a *brata* (or *vrata*) rite—a vowed observance. Historically, vows have been an important part of Hindu ritual life for centuries. People make vows mainly to secure something in this world, such as progeny, wealth, good fortune, health,

JAMES M. FREEMAN (Ph.D. Harvard), Professor of Anthropology at San Jose State University, is author of many articles and two books on India, including the award-winning *Untouchable: An Indian Life History*. His most recent publication on women's religion is "Turnings in the Life of a Vietnamese Buddhist Nun," which in expanded form is included in his latest book, *Hearts of Sorrow: Vietnamese American Biographies*.

Author's Note I am grateful to the following institutions for their generous support of my research, of which this article is one result: The American Institute of Indian Studies, Senior Faculty Fellowship, 1970–1972; The Joint Committee on South Asian Studies of the Social Science Research Council and the American Council of Learned Societies, Grant, 1976–1977; The Center for Advanced Study in the Behavioral Sciences (with funds from the Andrew W. Mellon Foundation), Fellowship, 1976–1977; San Jose State University, Sabbatical leave, 1976–1977.

fame, or long life; sometimes people make vows to secure something in the next world; and occasionally, as in the *habisha* rites, people make vows to gain something both in this world and in the next. Some vows last only a day; others, a lifetime. But whether they be long or short, failure to fulfill a vow is said to lead to dire consequences. Hindu scriptures known as *puranas* contain detailed descriptions of rules for vow makers. Among others, these rules include fasting, worshiping of gods, frequent purificatory baths, sexual abstinence, refraining from drinking water and from chewing betel nuts, and not sleeping during daylight hours. Proper fulfillment of vows not only brings the vow maker the rewards that he or she seeks but also invests that person with great spiritual power. For example, a virtuous wife who fulfills certain vows is said to gain the power to prevent the death of her husband—a power that plays an important role in *habisha* rites.

In the village that I studied, which is located three miles from Bhubaneswar, the capital of Orissa, the rite that people call *habisha* seems to be a combination of many vows and ceremonies. The village rites that I witnessed differed significantly from descriptions found in both Western and Indian literature on the topic. In particular, although written sources state that the *habisha* is especially a widows' rite, the village women informed me that widows were not supposed to perform *habisha* rituals, and, in fact, I found that they rarely did so. Most *habisha* participants were menopausal women whose husbands were still alive. Although several women informed me that their main purpose for performing *habisha* rites was to protect their husbands, they also revealed other important religious motivations. In general, the village women's *habisha* rituals were far more elaborate than already available descriptions might suggest.

My principal research in the village consisted of taking a census of each household and collecting life histories from a number of villagers. Two of the women who narrated their life histories to me in their native language of Oriya described the complex details of their *habisha* rituals. Tila Sahu, the younger of the two women, was fifty-five years old, married, and a member of the Confectioner caste. She was lively and talkative, and, when she discovered my interest in her *habisha* rituals, she offered to show me how she performed them and urged me to photograph them. In October–November, 1971, I witnessed Tila's performance of these rites.

The older woman, Padma Bewa, was the seventy-year-old widow of a temple priest. She introduced herself to me one morning by pulling me into her tea shop and offering me some sweets. When, at my suggestion, she later narrated her life history to me, I learned that she had followed the *habisha* fasts, as well as many others, for thirty years, stopping only a year earlier, when her husband had died. Because she was a widow, she believed that she should no longer perform the rituals. Nevertheless, she did tell me in great detail her recollections of the ceremonies that she had performed in the past.

Both women, who were deeply religious followers of the Jagannatha cult, spoke of their *habisha* experiences, especially their pilgrimages to Puri, as high points of their lives. Every year Padma Bewa and Tila Sahu, as well as many other elderly middle- and high-caste Orissan women, would observe *habisha*. For a period of thirty-five days in October–November, women vow to the deity Jagannatha (a form of Vishnu or Krishna) that they will perform purificatory rituals and fasts to protect their families or to improve themselves spiritually. During the *habisha* rites, women worship Jagannatha as the young Krishna, the cow herdsman surrounded by his female devotees, or *gopis* (milkmaids). Frequently they create ephemeral, stylized, but intricate and individualized rice-powder paintings of the god and his followers. Replicating the activities of the *gopis*, the devotees churn milk, offer Krishna coconuts and cowrie shells, and dance ecstatically to demonstrate their devotional love of Krishna.

Whenever possible, the rite concludes with a forty-mile pilgrimage to the temple of Lord Jagannatha in the holy city of Puri. One of the holiest and most famous shrines in India, this temple is best known for its annual chariot festival in July, which draws over 100,000 pilgrims. However, the religious cult of Jagannatha is also the focus of many other ceremonies, like the *habisha*, throughout the year.

HABISHA RITUALS OF TILA SAHU AND OTHER VILLAGE WOMEN

Because *habisha* rituals are expensive and often inconvenient for other family members, Tila Sahu, like all prospective vow makers, asked and received permission from her family before beginning her *habisha* vows. Six days before the month of Kartik (October–November), I watched a barber trim Tila's fingernails and toenails as a preliminary act of purification. After bathing, Tila summoned a Brahman family priest who customarily performed ceremonies for her family.

To purify Tila further, the Brahman—a tall, thin man—sprinkled cow-dung water on her head. The Brahman then turned to me and said that people ought to purify themselves for *habisha* vows by drinking *panchagavia*, "the five holy substances of the cow"—milk, curds, clarified butter, urine, and dung—but that nowadays few people did it. After putting on a new sacred cloth, Tila offered her Brahman priest gifts indicating that she would be his disciple and follow his instructions on the performance of the rituals and that she would listen to his daily recitation from a sacred book during the month of Kartik. She also promised to fulfill her vows of fasting, purification, and sexual abstinence.

On the following day Tila Sahu began the predawn bathing and purificatory rites of the *habisha* devotee. With nine other elderly and middle-aged Hindu women, only one of whom was a widow, she walked slowly into the chilly waters of the village pond. Facing north, waist deep in the water, they called out to three deities—Brahma, Vishnu, and Maheswar (Shiva)—asking them to witness their *habisha* vows. Turning east, the most sacred and auspicious direction, each woman scooped up a handful of water and called to all the holy rivers of India, venerated as Goddesses, to attend the women's sacred activities. Each woman threw this sanctified water over her head and body and then bathed. Facing south, the direction of death, sin, and pollution, each woman called to her ancestors to take a holy bath and witness the sacred events. Turning west, the direction symbolizing the completion of auspicious rituals, the women offered water to the deities of the ten directions (the cardinal directions, the ordinal directions, the zenith, and the nadir). Finally each woman dipped beneath the water three times, each time calling to the god Vishnu. The water of the pond was especially purifying because it was the water of a sacred place where the village deity had been bathed.

Dawn had nearly arrived as the women scooped up handfuls of mud and climbed out of the village pond. They shivered in their thin, wet, clinging saris as the biting October wind whipped past them. On the stone steps above the pond, the women, following Tila's lead, patted the mud into little images of Damodar, a form of the deity Vishnu as a child, and then uttered prayers and sprinkled offerings of flowers and water over them. Standing and facing east, they offered prayers to the rising sun. Next they prayed to the *tulasi*, the holy basil plant sacred to Vishnu, that grew in a stone pot on the steps. Finally they entered the village temple next to the pond, where they waved burning wicks in tiny clay oil lamps before each of twenty-six deities and chanted songs describing their desire to merge their souls with the souls of the deities.

I asked Tila why none of the women were young. She replied, "A *habisha* woman should be fifty years or over, so that menstruation has stopped. A woman who menstruates becomes 'untouchable' for four days and must stop her vow activities during that time. While she is impure, another person who is pure performs the rituals for her. A woman gets more *dharma* [merit] if she starts her vow rituals while her husband is alive, but she receives *papa* [demerit] if she performs the *habisha* while menstruating."

The other women smiled and nodded in agreement. They were in a joyous mood, as befit the occasion. It was the beginning of their holy period of one-meal-a-day fasting, praying, and purifying themselves—a period when, as they pointed out to me, they put aside animosities and jealousies and ceased gossiping, turning instead to cooperation, expressions of good will, and religious devotion.

The women went to their homes and cooked their meals. During the *habisha* they would eat only once a day, before sundown, or not at all if they so desired. Tila had previously collected the white unparboiled rice, required for ritual practice, which would be her main food during her *habisha* days. (Rice used for everyday purposes is often partially cooked before final boiling.) Besides rice, she could eat only certain other foods considered to be pure: a variety of lentil, green plantain, taro, cucumber, ginger, and custard apple. The devotees were supposed to prepare their own meals, which had to be boiled. No spices were allowed, but each meal had to contain clarified butter, a substance considered holy because made from cow milk.

After cooking her meal, Tila bathed again in the village pond and waved burning wicks at the deities of the temple. When she returned home, she washed her legs, hands, and face. Next she sprinkled water containing holy basil

leaves—the sacred food of Vishnu—around the food pots and into the food, transforming it into Vishnu's *prasad*, (sacred food).

Then she ate, talking to no one but silently uttering the name of Vishnu at each bite. The *habisha* food is considered even more sacred than ordinary sacred food, so much so that the Brahman family priest, who ordinarily must not eat food cooked by persons of castes lower than his, regularly eats the food cooked by his *habisha* disciples. After offering some food to the Brahman, Tila gave the rest to her husband and son, as well as her daughter and granddaughter, who had come for a visit.

Tila observed purificatory rules not only when she ate or bathed but when she performed other activities as well. She avoided touching and talking to untouchables and low-caste people. If she stepped on human urine or feces or on the feces of animals such as dogs, chickens, or goats, she bathed and sprinkled cow-dung water on her head. She was supposed to avoid gossiping and arguing, as well as begging and borrowing. At all times she carried with her two nuts representing Krishna and his brother. Throughout the day she prayed to these symbols of God and sang prayers to Vishnu that she had learned over the years by listening to others. "The month of Kartik is a religious month," she said. "Affection for God comes in that month. During Kartik I never feel away from God but devote my days to God."

On the first day of the month of Kartik, the full *habisha* ceremonies began. After bathing in the pond and praying in the village temple, Tila and the other women brought ritual articles to a holy basil plant in the front yard of the house where Usha, the Brahman woman, lived. Donated by the women's husbands, these articles were offerings for the ceremonies honoring Krishna. While Usha directed the collection of the articles, Tila, using colored powders made from rice, charcoal, turmeric, and vermilion, created a picture around the holy basil plant. She drew Krishna in the form of Jagannatha, his brother Balabhadra and his sister Subhadra. Then she added a large *garuda* bird (the symbolic vehicle of Vishnu), footprints of Lakshmi, the goddess of wealth and wife of Vishnu (Jagannatha), and two bodyguards. She completed her picture with a ladder leading to the sea of eternity, a lotus plant (associated with Lakshmi), and a conch shell and a discus, symbols of Vishnu.

Usha, the leader, began praying. She made the ululating *hulahuli* sounds that women utter at auspicious or holy occasions. The others then followed with other *hulahuli*. While ringing a bell, Usha threw offerings of flowers on the holy basil plant and water from the conch shell onto the sacred food. Then she raised her eyes to the sun and prayed. The other women presented their offerings by placing them in a brass plate that all of them held together, and they made the *hulahuli* sounds as they held onto the plate.

Then the women reenacted the familiar legend of Krishna and the milkmaids. One woman in the role of a milkmaid churned milk in a small clay bowl. Tila, playing the role of Radha, the chief milkmaid and divine lover of Krishna, placed the pot of churned milk on her head. The women, holding hands, formed a circle, danced, sang loudly, and clapped their hands, imitating the devotional worship of the milkmaids for Krishna. One of the women, in the role of Krishna, reenacted the practical jokes he played on the milkmaids—hiding their clothes while they were bathing in the river, moving the boat that would ferry them across the river, and delaying its return. Pretending not to know who he was, the milkmaids loudly criticized the boatman until he revealed himself as Krishna, beloved to all of them. One of the women, in the role of Krishna's mother, played with her son and tried to prevent his mischievous pranks, while the other milkmaids danced, sang, and laughed noisily.

To end the ceremony, the women placed flowers and sacred water on the sides of one another's faces and on the tops of their heads. Then they prostrated themselves, touched their foreheads to the mound around the holy basil plant, and dispersed.

Each day Tila and the other women performed their Krishna dances and games, increasing the tempo of the singing and dancing, twirling and leaping around the holy basil plant. Except for myself, adult males were not permitted to watch.

On the final day Tila presented her Brahman family priest with a gift of cloth and food. The next day she invited her immediate family and relatives to a feast of goat-meat curry, reversing her month-long diet of bland vegetarian food. While all her relatives were sitting together and eating, Tila announced, "I have fulfilled my vow. God should bless me. I should receive that for which I performed my vow."

Padma Bewa, the old widow, did not participate in the *habisha* rituals on this occasion. "For thirty years I followed the rites of many vows, including *habisha*," she said to me, "but after the death of my husband, I forgot all about them. Women observe their vows until their husband dies; then they stop, as I did. This is what women should do. My *habisha* was for my husband [to protect him]. When I first started *habisha*, I did it only occasionally, fasting for twenty of the thirty days, eating only one meal of white rice at night. My husband was a temple priest. He often observed the *habisha* rites because the pilgrims he served would appoint him to perform *habisha* for them for five, seven, or even twenty-one days—sometimes even for the entire month. So I vowed to perform the full *habisha* ritual with him, even though it was improper because I was too young. But our village deity had appeared to me in a dream and ordered me to do it, so I knew it was all right." Padma Bewa did continue to observe some vows for her son. "These days I carry out several fasting vows to protect my son. I will do this until my life ends."

THE RELIGIOUS EXPERIENCES OF TILA SAHU

Tila Sahu, the Confectioner's wife, said to me with regret that she had visited Puri only twice in the month of Kartik but that both visits had been memorable experiences. "Thirty years ago I visited Puri during *habisha* for the first time," she said. "I longed to participate, but I just watched others. I was not in *habisha* because I was too young—a new wife without children.

"Ten years ago during the month of Kartik I went to Puri to see a dance in the temple of Lord Jagannatha. I hardly saw it because of the thousands of people there. Although I had traveled to Puri with relatives, I stayed alone that night in the temple. I watched how different *habisha* people worshiped. They became ecstatic, and in their devotional fervor they forgot all about the world. They tried to merge their souls into that of the deity.

"When morning came, I returned to my uncle's house in Puri. Then I bathed in the temple's tank. Afterward I went with my relatives to the Gate of Heaven on the beach where the dead are cremated. We saw several women doing their *puja* [ritual]. I joined in and sang for them a *habisha* song that the milkmaids sang when Jagannatha and his brother went to help the king of Puri fight a war against the king of the south. All the *habisha* people were surprised at how much I knew. They happily pulled me into the center of their group, dressed me as Radha, and dressed another woman like Krishna, while the others became milkmaids for the drama. We danced and sang on the beach, and the others praised me. Many groups of women were singing and dancing; one after another they invited me to dance and sing with them. I continued for twelve hours.

"I returned home by bus. In the village we dance and sing but not like in Puri. Men and women in the village criticize *habisha* people because, they say, it is improper to sing and dance publicly. Those villagers are wicked. They have no power of devotion."

I asked Tila why she longed to go to Puri and why she performed her village *habisha* rituals so faithfully. Tila said that she had been trying to reach God since her childhood. When she was eleven years old, she met a *babaji*, an ascetic holy man of marvelous powers, who lived in a forest dwelling near her village. She brought him an offering of milk, sent by her mother. The *babaji* blessed her. "From that day," she said, "my religious devotion increased, and I wanted to serve that *baba*." She returned each day with offerings of milk. Her mother, a devout woman, excused Tila from her ordinary household tasks so that she could serve the *babaji*. "I was happy because I preferred to be with the *babaji* than to do household chores," said Tila. "So every day I went, and after a while I didn't need friends to go with me and play. I became very familiar with the *babaji*, like a disciple. The *babaji* never let the shadow of a mature or married woman fall across him. He ate sour meditation medicine to bind his body [prevent sexual discharge]."

Tila said that the holy man used his religious powers to help villagers appease the Goddess Bimala so that she would not burn down their villages in the dry season. According to Tila, his powers astonished people. "What can I say about that *baba*?" said Tila. "I was too young at that time. I did not follow any religious faith. I did not learn anything from him. I did not receive any remarkable abilities or magical powers. So when I think about him, I feel very unhappy. Tears come to my eyes. What a powerful deity I lost! You can't imagine his qualities and abilities!"

Tila served the holy man for three years. Then, when she was fourteen years old, a marriage proposal came to her house from a family in a nearby village. She was married soon after. After staying for a few days in her husband's house, she returned to the home of her parents. She said, "That evening I remembered about the *baba* and decided to visit him the following morning. In the middle of the night, however, the *babaji* came and sat near my head. He said, 'Tila, look at me well; this is the last time you will see me. No matter how much you want to, you can never visit me again. You are married, so you must stay away. If you come near me, I'll beat you and drive you away!' I cried and suddenly woke up. I never saw my *babaji* again. I heard that four months later he left the forest and that two months after that he left his mortal body. Since that time I have been searching through my *habisha* vows for someone like the *babaji*."

THE RELIGIOUS EXPERIENCES OF PADMA BEWA

Padma Bewa, the old widow who had performed her *habisha* rituals in Puri for thirty years, usually walked to that holy city. Each year Padma and about fifty or sixty women from her village, carrying their small grandchildren, their own food, and some cooking utensils, trudged the forty miles from their homes to the city of Puri, stopping and praying at holy shrines along the way. A couple of elderly men usually went with them. At Puri the women first visited several shrines and performed the prescribed purificatory rites. Then they walked to the beach and joined other groups of women who were singing, swaying, and dancing. When Padma joined them, she was swept up in wild exultation and lost all sense of self, time, and place. "While bathing or dancing," she said, "I never felt tired. I was so happy from being in Puri that I felt no weariness." Some villagers returned home after one or two days; Padma usually stayed on the beach for many days and sometimes during the entire month fasting, praying and dancing.

I asked her how she had become a religious person. Padma said that from childhood she had believed strongly in various gods and god-desses. As a young childless wife, she visited temples all over Orissa, praying that the deities of those temples would bless her with a child. Although her prayers went unanswered, her faith remained strong. As she grew older, she visited various shrines whenever she could afford to. She planted fruits and plants sacred to different deities, and in her yard she worshiped Lord Vishnu's holy basil daily. Each day she prayed to two gods and to twelve goddesses, all forms of the Mother Goddess.

She said, "I prayed to them to pull me to their feet. I desired to visit their shrines. I thought about nothing but gods and goddesses. I enjoyed listening to the stories from the *puranas* [old books]. Each night, when I had no other obligations, I gathered with other women at the house of a Brahman woman who could read. She read us stories from the old religious books.

"From her I learned about the powers of the gods and goddesses. I learned that by prayer and devotion people can receive whatever boons they wish. I had always had religious feelings, but now they grew in my heart more and more. I attended the nightly readings regularly because I liked it so much. I liked all of the gods and goddesses.

"Then one night I had a dream in which Sri Lokanatha, one of Puri's deities, said, 'Why do you delay visiting Lord Jagannatha at Puri? You have never seen him. You should go and visit him.' I told my husband about my dream, and I persuaded him to come with me. That was my first trip to Puri. Soon after, I began going each year for *habisha*.

"One year during *habisha*, while we were bathing on the Puri beach at the Gate of Heaven, the undercurrent took one of our women, swallowing her body into the womb of the sea. Although she was very old, we still cried at her death. We sent a woman back to our village to inform the drowned woman's son.

"When he arrived, he ran into the sea to drown himself, but the fishermen pulled him back. We tried to cheer him up, saying that, because his mother had been pious, she had received the gift of dying in the holy abode of Vishnu and Lakshmi. We tried to convince him that his mother's death was a significant and noble one and that her fortune had guided her to die in this most sacred place, next to the Gate of Heaven, where the soul could reach heaven without any death ceremony.

"The next morning all of us *habisha* women looked for the body along the seashore. Late in the morning a wave washed her onto the beach. Her son held her body and cried, and so did we. Then we collected bamboo and branches, carried her to the Gate of Heaven, and cremated her.

"During those two days, instead of eating one meal a day, we ate nothing. How could we eat, thinking of the death of one of our companions and the sorrow of her son? We all prayed to Lord Jagannatha that he would bless us so that we might meet a death like that of our companion. But we are unfortunate. How can we get that sort of death?

"Several people from that group have since died, but all of them died in the village. Several times I have dreamed that I died in Puri and that I saw my own funeral procession and ceremony. I liked that death. So every year I want to go to Puri to die, but only God knows whether I will be able to die in Puri."

THE SIGNIFICANCE OF HABISHA AS A HINDU RITUAL

Habisha rituals, like practically all Hindu rituals, are concerned with the opposing themes of purity and pollution. This was evident in Tila Sahu's performance of her month-long vow as she sought to increase purity and avoid pollution and polluting substances even more than usual. Closely linked with the concern about purity and pollution is a concern to increase the auspicious and to drive away the inauspicious—a concern that runs through most Hindu rituals. In rituals that enhance the auspicious, such as the *habisha*, marriages, and many calendrical celebrations of deities, worshipers acquire a high degree of ritual purity (eliminating more pollution than usual) in part by using purifying substances. Then, as Tila Sahu did, they share their high state of purity with their families by giving them sacred food. Thus auspiciousness radiates from the woman performing *habisha*. As part of the same theme, the *habisha* rites end with an abrupt reversal that returns the *habisha* worshipers to their ordinary state; they cook and share with their relatives a meal of goat-meat curry that, like all meat, is much less pure than the diet permitted during *habisha*.

Habisha rituals, like all Hindu rituals, also involve sacred space and sacred time. Villagers like Tila Sahu and Padma Bewa believe that the region in which they live is itself a sacred space, and they replicate this space in their rituals. When the *habisha* followers make rice-powder paintings of deities, they, in effect, create a sacred altar. The women believe that, by purifying themselves and praying, they draw together the divine powers within themselves. They then transfer these powers to the inanimate pictures, bringing them to life as the deity, who is invited to the ritual as a friend. All Hindu worshipers engage in rituals to bring deities to life, whether in temples, houses, or, as the *habisha* women did, out in the yard next to the holy basil plant. The *habisha* worshipers are involved not only with sacred space but also with sacred time. The month of Kartik is a special holy time that heightens religious consciousness and releases worshipers from ordinary daily activities. The women deliberately drop what they consider to be bad behavior, such as gossiping and quarreling, and try to be cooperative. More importantly, during this month women engage in behavior that is normally forbidden—emotional public displays of dancing, singing, and worship.

Habisha rituals fit neatly into the complex

of theistic, devotional Hinduism. The beliefs and activities of the women closely parallel practices in devotional Hinduism that have usually been studied and discussed by Western scholars as performed by men. The *habisha* women worship Vishnu, a popular deity of contemporary Hinduism, who has many forms and hundreds of different names. They identify most closely with the north-Indian deity Krishna, one of the most widely known forms of Vishnu. In Orissa, however, Krishna and his legends have been merged with Jagannatha, "Lord of the World," a local deity probably of tribal origins who has his own distinctive traditions, stories, and art forms. The women's worship of Krishna through art and ritual is typical in Hinduism. The women who make the powder paintings create individualistic representations that are part of a distinct regional style of women's ephemeral art (the paintings are rubbed away and recreated each day of the ritual). However, the paintings also contain symbols that are widely recognized throughout India—the conch shell, the *garuda* bird, the footprints of Lakshmi, and the discus. The women also retell and reenact, through dance and drama, all the beloved stories of Krishna and Jagannatha.

THE SIGNIFICANCE OF HABISHA IN THE LIFE CYCLES OF WOMEN

Habisha is performed most often by menopausal, married, upper-caste women. All three adjectives are crucial to understanding the significance of *habisha* in women's life cycles.

Only upper-caste women are allowed to, or have reason to, perform *habisha*. To understand why, we must remember that one of the main stated reasons for performing *habisha* is to keep husbands alive. This is important to high-caste women both because of the difficulties an upper-caste widow faces and because of

her economic dependency on her husband. A high-caste woman from the village of Tila Sahu and Padma Bewa most often remains at home, without outside employment, supported by her husband's family. Once widowed, she becomes inauspicious, an object of scorn and a source of potential sexual scandal. She is expected to remain at home doing household chores, faithful to her deceased husband. But often she is assumed to be secretly involved with other men. Ordinarily, she must not attend auspicious rituals like marriages, and she may participate only in penance and purification rites. No wonder these women want to keep their husbands alive!

By contrast, women from low and untouchable castes are not expected to perform the *habisha* rituals. Many of these women live in poor households, become wage earners outside of the house, and consequently have greater economic independence from their husbands than do high-caste women. Furthermore, lower- and untouchable-caste widows are not expected to remain faithful to their deceased husbands; instead, they are allowed to remarry and frequently do so.

Almost all of those who perform the full thirty-five-day ritual are older wives, not yet widowed, who no longer menstruate. This suggests that the *habisha* marks an important transitional stage in the life pattern of a high-caste Hindu woman of Orissa—the stage between menopause and widowhood—and meets her distinctive needs. The most important question is why the *habisha* has become a ritual for older wives rather than younger ones. If *habisha* is performed in part to protect husbands, why do young high-caste wives of childbearing age rarely perform the full *habisha* rituals, waiting instead until they become fifty years old? Surely young high-caste wives have as much at stake in keeping their husbands alive as do older wives. Whether young or old, a high-caste widow becomes inauspicious, is not allowed to remarry, and usually suffers greatly.

There are at least five possible reasons why

younger women usually do not perform *habisha*. The first, which Padma Bewa and Tila Sahu stressed, is that young wives will be menstruating during some of the days of the full *habisha*. Women in such a condition are considered polluting and should not perform the ceremony themselves, although it would be permitted to have the rites performed by a proxy during the days of actual menstruation. Second, young wives may be prohibited from performing the full *habisha* also because public singing and dancing are considered particularly inappropriate, if not scandalous, behaviors for young women. By contrast, women beyond the age of childbearing are allowed much greater freedom in speech and action. Third, the *habisha* is an expensive, time-consuming ceremony. Young women, who have a greater workload than older women in a joint household, are less likely to be released from their daily chores for thirty-five days than are older women, whose daily tasks are not as time consuming. Fourth, historically the rites were performed by widows and have only recently become rites for older married women. Enough of their previous association with inauspicious widows may linger on to make the rites seem inappropriate for young, childbearing women. Fifth, with improvements in nutrition and health care, particularly for higher-caste and wealthy people, fewer husbands die young. The wives of young men may not consider their husbands to be as vulnerable to harm as do older women who are married to older men. The older wife, on the other hand, has strong reasons for performing the *habisha* ritual. Recognizing their aging husbands' increasing vulnerability to disease and death, elderly women make and fulfill *habisha* vows to forestall the dreaded onset of widowhood with all its negative implications, including the expectation that they will no longer perform *habisha*.

These menopausal wives are in a unique phase of their life cycle—a phase that allows and encourages them to engage in such rituals for the first time in their lives. It is also a phase that almost demands that they perform *habisha*, because through *habisha* they hope not to lose the status of older wives by becoming widows. Also, they are at a moment in their lives when they have passed through the stage of childbearing, which is associated with the polluting conditions of childbirth and menstruation. Menopause gives a woman greater ritual purity (absence of pollution) and frees her from the numerous ritual proscriptions placed on women of childbearing age. Thus it is easier for older women to perform a ritual that will intensify their purity. Furthermore, menopausal women are released from many social obligations required of younger women. They enjoy the highest degree of domestic, social, and ritual freedom that any adult Hindu woman ever knows. Thus they have the time and the energy to perform *habisha* rites. The opportunities afforded to *habisha* women, who have completed all their worldly obligations, are similar to those offered to men who have completed their worldly occupations and can withdraw into a stage of the life cycle that is more concerned with spiritual growth. This parallel is quite important in the study of women's life cycles.

There is, however, a negative side. Menopausal women are increasingly vulnerable. The performance of marriage duties and childbearing—historically the primary functions of Hindu women—are mostly things of the past. More important, their husbands are aging, a fact that increases the threat of widowhood, with its concomitants of pollution and inauspiciousness. Thus these women have a great stake in prolonging this relatively free and fortunate phase of their life cycle. Consequently, they are increasingly concerned about husband and family protection, as well as with their own spiritual purification.

The *habisha* has, therefore, come to symbolize an unusual period of freedom from men and their demands, as well as from the social obligations and ritual prohibitions that men ordinarily impose on women. But such freedom comes at the cost of increased vulnerability to widowhood. Although the women perform the rituals in part to protect their husbands, they perform the rituals mainly for themselves. The *habisha*, by reversing ordinary behavior, gives these women the opportunity to look after their own spiritual development before the ritual prohibitions of widowhood again limit their religious expressions.

Further Readings

Babb, Lawrence. *The Divine Hierarchy: Popular Hinduism in Central India.* New York: Columbia University Press, 1975.

Das, S. R. "A Study of the Vrata Rituals of Bengal." *Man in India* 32 (October–December 1952): 207–45.

Eschmann, Anncharlott, *et al.*, eds. *The Cult of Jagannath and the Regional Tradition of Orissa.* New Delhi: Manohar Books, 1978.

Freeman, James M. "Trial by Fire." *Natural History Magazine* 83 (January 1974): 54–63.

———. *Scarcity and Opportunity in an Indian Village.* Prospect Heights, Ill.: Waveland Press, 1985 (1977).

Kane, Pandurang Vaman. *History of Dharmasastra.* Vol. 2, part 1. Poona: Bhandarkar Oriental Research Institute, 1941.

———. *History of Dharmasastra.* Vol. 5, part 1. 2d ed. Poona: Bhandarkar Oriental Research Institute, 1974.

O'Malley, L. S. S. *Puri District Gazeteer.* Patna: Government Printing Press, 1929.

9

Garifuna Women and the Work of Mourning (Central America)

VIRGINIA KERNS

In 1840 an Englishman named Thomas Young traveled through several of the Garifuna (Black Carib) settlements that lie along the coast of Central America. In his *Narrative of a Residence on the Mosquito Shore,* published several years later, he mentioned that the Garifuna, practicing Roman Catholics, took great pains to see that their children were baptized. But even then they also held ceremonies for their dead that were not sanctioned by the Church. These death rites were (and still are) misunderstood by outsiders, who suspected that the Garifuna engaged in "devil worship" and even cannibalism on these occasions. They did not, as is clear from Young's account of the "feast" that he attended in one community. Apparently he was unaware of the religious significance of this mourning ceremony, known as *dügü*.

Today women are very prominent in *dügü* and the other death rites. Their participation seems to be a long-standing feature of Garifuna religious life. In his brief account Young pointedly remarked that the women "in great numbers" danced and sang at the "feast" and that

VIRGINIA KERNS holds a Ph.D. in Anthropology from the University of Illinois and currently teaches at the College of William and Mary. She is the author of *Women and the Ancestors: Black Carib Kinship and Ritual* (Urbana, Ill.: University of Illinois Press, 1983), and co-editor, with Judith K. Brown, of *In Her Prime: A New View of Middle-Aged Women* (South Hadley, Mass.: Bergin and Garvey, 1985).

Author's Note I wish to acknowledge the generous support of the Fulbright-Hays Commission and the Wenner-Gren Foundation for Anthropological Research, which made my fieldwork possible.

the men were concerned with sharing "strong spirit," or rum—a necessary ingredient of any death rite even today. Older women organize most of these ceremonies; they contribute their labor to the time-consuming preparations, and their expertise to the actual performance. Aside from singing and dancing, they also assume major ritual roles. In theory, any adult may take part in any of the major death rites; in fact, it is largely older women who choose to do so.

During 1974–1975, and again in 1976, I observed and participated in dozens of death rites in several communities in Belize (the former British Honduras). Like Thomas Young, who had witnessed one of these ceremonies well over a century before, I was struck by the prominence of women, and especially older women, as ritual performers. The following account of the participation of women in death rites and its importance is based on my experiences in Belize.

COMMUNITIES IN BELIZE

The Garifuna have an unusual history, too complex to relate in detail here, which explains the fact that they speak Carib, an Amerindian language, although they are also obviously of African descent. The first of those to settle in Belize entered the territory early in the nineteenth century. Today there are six Garifuna settlements in Belize, ranging from villages of several hundred to towns with several thousand inhabitants. These are the northernmost of the more than fifty settlements scattered along the low and sandy coastline of the Caribbean Sea. Eighty thousand or so Garifuna live in these communities in Belize, Guatemala, Honduras, and Nicaragua.

In Belize, the villages are rural and quite isolated, but the people who live in them are not peasants. Today farming provides relatively little food or income. Some men work

at nearby plantations and return home to their families on a frequent and regular basis. Many other men and young women work as unskilled laborers all over the country, coming home only occasionally. Most of the older people who live in these villages are men and women who cannot find work, either because of physical disability or, in the case of women, because of age discrimination in the labor market. The government of Belize sets no compulsory retirement age, and, because of a chronic shortage of male labor, most men can find jobs as long as they are physically able to work. Some are employed into their sixties and even early seventies. Fewer jobs exist for women, especially for those who are older. After the age of forty or fifty a woman finds it very difficult to obtain any regular employment aside from the lowest-paying kinds of domestic work. Most older women must depend on others for support—either their grown children or, if they are married, their husbands.

While marital relationships are relatively unstable, the Garifuna consider the parent/child bond to be perpetual, one that even death cannot sever. Deceased men and women may request private or public offerings from their children and other descendants. Older women—the daughters and granddaughters of the dead—usually see to these offerings, as well as to the other mourning ceremonies.

DEATH AND RITUAL

Beliefs about the supernatural are highly syncretic and quite intricate. Villagers believe that a plethora of spirits, both human and nonhuman, frequent the local landscape. Most of the nonhuman spirits are entirely hostile to the living, while the spirits of lineal kin can either protect or harm their living descendants. Interaction between the living and the dead is highly reciprocal. If the living neglect their dead kin, they can expect to suffer for it: their ancestors may cause them to sicken and even to die. The only protection against such misfortune, and the only cure for it, is careful attention to the needs and demands of the dead.

The needs of the dead are met through ritual. Two rites, deemed to be absolutely necessary, are held after the death of any adult. These are the wake (and burial) and the ninth-night wake, which is a major ritual and social occasion.[1] Three additional minor mourning ceremonies may be held. These are *tagurun ludu*, which ends the period of formal mourning by close kinswomen of the deceased; a ritual bathing, *amuidahani*; and a requiem mass with a small "feast" afterwards. The dead typically request these last two ceremonies through dreams, often within a year or two of burial. Finally, spirits also occasionally ask for two other major rituals, *chugu* and *dügü*, voicing their requests by speaking through a shaman. As shown in Table 3, they may request these as soon as a few years or as long as half a century after death.

The three intermediate rituals listed in Table 3 are minor ones. They last for only a few hours and attract no more than one or two dozen participants, most of them older women who live in the community. Minor ceremonies also entail far less expense than the major rites, which draw larger and more heterogeneous crowds, including visitors from other communities. Several hundred women and men may attend ninth-night wakes and *dügü*. Despite the differences in scale, all mourning rituals share the same serious purpose—satisfaction of the dead and protection of the living. But the usual ambience is not solemn; they are festive occasions enjoyed by the living as well as, it is believed, by the dead. Rituals are also work. The preparations require the efforts of at least several women and sometimes of several dozen women.

THE WORK OF MOURNING

The sound of women wailing is the first public signal of a death in a Garifuna village. Kinswomen of the deceased begin their customary display of grief as soon as they hear of the death, and they continue to wail at intervals until burial the next day. Preparations for the wake are under way almost immediately. Women of the community, who volunteer their help to the bereaved family, start to prepare the food that they will serve at the wake.

Table 3. *Sequence of Death Rites*

Rite	Timing
Beluria (wake) and *abunahani* (burial)	Obligatory, within 48 hours of death
Arisaruni (novenas) and *beluria* (ninth-night wake)	Obligatory, usually within 2 or 3 weeks of death
Tagurun ludu (end of mourning ceremony)	Obligatory, 6 months or 1 year after death of parent or spouse
Amuidahani (bathing the spirit)	Obligatory if requested, usually within several years of death
Helemeserun hilaña (requiem mass) and *efeduhani laugi lemesi* (feasting after mass)	Obligatory if requested, usually within several years of death
Chugu (feeding the dead)	Obligatory if requested, usually more than 10 and less than 50 years after death
Dügü (feasting the dead)	Obligatory if requested, usually more than 10 and less than 50 years after death

While a few elderly women work in private preparing the corpse for burial, several men hastily construct a coffin. When the wake begins after dark, the coffin is finished and has been placed in the main room of the house. Men, women, and children go there to view the body, and many of the adults linger to express their "appreciation" of the deceased. The men speak eloquently but briefly, the women speak more tearfully and at greater length. When they wail, they eulogize the deceased and lament the death.

People are subdued as the wake begins. Some men sit together and gamble; others converse. Women talk quietly among themselves or help to distribute food and rum. The size and conviviality of the crowd grow in proportion to the amount of rum that the women pass around. Later in the night a few men begin to drum on wooden crates, providing the musical background for the traditional dances that are staple ingredients of nearly any public occasion in Garifuna communities. Men and women of all ages join in these dances. If the wake is a "good" one, with a generous supply of food and rum, many of them will remain throughout the night. Even if refreshment is in short supply and most of the people depart early in the night, older women will keep their vigil by the body until dawn.

The next day people gather briefly in the church to pray. Then a procession of women, children, and a few men follows the male pallbearers and coffin to the burial ground. As the men lower the coffin into the grave, kinswomen of the deceased begin to wail again. One or two of the women may be so overcome with grief that other women and men must physically support them and help them away from the site.

In most cases novenas for the deceased begin on the first or second Friday after burial. Following Roman Catholic tradition, this nine-day period of prayers assures repose for the soul and separates the dead person from the living. Shortly before dusk each day, ten or fifteen older women gather to say prayers at the house where the ninth-night wake will be held. The leader of the prayers, who may be either male or female, must be fluent and literate in Spanish, the preferred medium for novenas.

People explain that the ninth-night wake is a kind of farewell party for the dead man or woman, who "resurrects" on the third day after burial and then wanders about aimlessly, "bothering" the living, unless given a proper send-off to the next world. Many of the older women who have attended the novenas also help with food preparation on the Saturday of the ninth-night wake. They finish their work before dusk and then attend the final prayers, held inside the house at 8 P.M., at midnight, and at dawn on the following morning. Outside the house a crowd of men and women enjoy themselves during the night, singing and joining in the traditional dances performed on festive occasions. After the midnight prayers women serve the food they have prepared; the people who attended the midnight prayers are fed first, then those outside the house. The women also distribute rum throughout the night. After the prayers at dawn, they abruptly tear down the novena altar while kinswomen of the deceased wail briefly one final time. This marks the end of the ninth-night wake.

Close kinswomen of the deceased do not take part in dancing on this occasion, nor do they join in any festivities for some time after it. As part of the formal mourning observances prescribed only for women, they abstain from all such merrymaking and put aside their normally colorful clothing for more somber dress. This period of formal mourning continues for six months or a year after the death, depending on the woman's relationship to the deceased.

Tagurun ludu, which literally means "throwing off the mourning cloth," is a ceremony that marks the end of these observances. On the day before this end-of-mourning ceremony, women prepare food for the occasion. Shortly before dawn on the appointed day, the mourning women enter the church for brief prayers. Accompanying them is a throng of older women, and perhaps a few men. After the prayers end, the crowd leaves the church and gathers on the beach to watch the mourning women ritually bathe. Each woman has a female partner whom she has selected to walk with her into the sea. Linking their arms together, and fully dressed, the pairs wade out beyond the breakers. There the companions of the mourning women submerge them completely, then help them up, repeating this twice again. After the third submersion they leave the water and walk home. As each of the mourning women stands in the doorway, about to enter the house, other women grasp the back of her wet dress. With a sudden pull, they tear the garment open and away from her body. The woman removes her underclothing, screened from public view by the women clustered around her, and then walks to another room to dress. There she and her kinswomen, who have shed their mourning dresses in the same manner, all put on brightly colored new garments and jewelry, adorning themselves for the first time since their relative's death. In the same room, by a burning candle, the women place a small plate of food and some rum as an offering for the spirit of the deceased. In the main room of the house a few begin to serve food, and later rum, to the twenty or thirty older women who have assembled there. After they eat, the women begin to sing *abaimahani* songs—songs of remembrance that the women themselves compose to sing on such occasions. Outside the house there is the inevitable crowd of spectators—young women, men, and children—that gathers during any ritual event.

Occasionally, perhaps even before the end-of-mourning ceremony, the deceased appears in a dream to a relative, requesting a bath. The journey to the next world is long and arduous, and spirits of the dead often desire the refreshment of a bath. *Amuidahani* is held in response to this request. The day before the ceremony a few kinswomen of the deceased prepare the necessary food. The next morning, in the predawn darkness, a small group of people gathers by the house where the deceased man or woman lived. Some of them are close relatives of the deceased, and the remainder are older women who are interested in the event. Standing by a shallow pit, which represents a grave, each of the men and women in turn throws a bucket of water into it. Addressing the spirit by the appropriate kin term, they say simply, "Here is water for your bath." Then they fill the pit with sand, and some of the women begin to distribute the food and rum to the others. The *abaimahani* songs of remembrance, and later some festive singing and dancing, follow. Inside the house the women have set some food and rum next to a burning candle as an offering to the spirit.

Like the preceding ceremony, a requiem mass is held if a spirit requests it in a dream. After the mass older women, and perhaps a few old men, gather at the house of the woman who arranged the mass. Then, as a small "feast," food and rum are served. The women usually sing the remembrance songs for some time and then perhaps add other traditional songs and dances. In a back room of the house a small offering of food and rum for the spirit stands beside a burning candle.

Chugu and *dügü* differ from the preceding ceremonies in many details of performance; but, as in the other ceremonies, older women are very prominent, and an individual spirit is the focus of ceremonial attention. In most cases a series of misfortunes precipitates the elaborate offerings of *chugu* and *dügü*. One person, or a number of relatives, may fall seriously ill or develop some chronic sickness. The afflicted person is usually an adult and is more often female than male. Only a shaman can identify the particular ancestor who is responsible for the misfortune; having done so, the shaman tries to determine what sort of offering the spirit wants. Although shamans may be either male or female, those in Belize are mature women, over the age of forty.

Chugu is a one-day event, an elaborate offering of food and prayer. Throughout the day a shaman leads prayers, alternately addressing them to God, the Virgin Mary, Christ, and the afflicting ancestor. Women prepare the food, which is usually offered in the afflicted person's house. The offerings of fish and meat, bread, fruits, and vegetables are set on tables in the morning and left there during the day for the spirit to eat. Other older women in the community represent their children and grandchildren by bringing smaller offerings, usually a single plate of food, for their own ancestors. *Chugu* is a quiet event, without drums or dancing. The music is limited to remembrance songs, which the older women sing.

All the mourning ceremonies entail some "feasting"—sharing food and drink among the living and, usually, offering food and drink to the dead. In the minor ceremonies, and some of the major ones as well, the food is quite simple: bread, coffee, and rum. But *dügü* far eclipses the other ceremonies, both in the lavishness and in the length of the feast. Moreover, unlike the other rites, *dügü* takes place in a temple, not in an ordinary house, and the ancestral spirit may request that a new temple be built for the occasion. Preparations sometimes require as much as a year's work. The organizer, nearly always an older woman, must collect the necessary funds and foodstuffs for *dügü*: a hog, great quantities of cassava bread, dozens of chickens, gallons of rum, and various other staple items. A rather small portion of this food is offered to the spirit and then buried or discarded at sea. The sponsors of the ceremony distribute most of the food among the living. Some is given as a gift to the drummers and to those who helped to procure and to prepare food for the occasion. Women cook the rest and serve it to the dancers at *dügü*.

A *dügü* typically lasts for three days and nights. Each day several older women prepare the food; the nights are devoted to dancing, drinking, and dining. These festive qualities do not obscure the serious purpose of *dügü*. Like *chugu*, its stated purpose is to appease an ancestor who is afflicting the living. This ancestor is the guest of honor, so to speak, at the ceremony; the dancing and offering of food are intended to placate the spirit and thus to cure the afflicted person. Other spirits of the dead also attend *dügü*, at the invitation of the ancestor for whom it is held. These spirit guests require offerings, albeit very small ones, from their own descendants. To neglect them is to court future misfortune at their hands. The older women who provide the small offerings serve as intermediaries between their living kin and their ancestors.

Women typically outnumber men ten to one as singers and dancers in the temple; there they perform eight or more dances of placation to the ancestor each night of *dügü*. Led by the shaman, to the accompaniment of drums, they sing to the spirit, whom they address as *nagütu*, "my grandmother," regardless of the spirit's gender. Between the dances of placation, they sing songs and perform other dances specific to *dügü*. At midnight they stop to share a meal and then continue to sing and dance until dawn.

Possession by ancestral spirits, usually occurring in the early hours of the morning, is a distinctive feature of *dügü*. As the drummers and most of the dancers pause briefly to rest, one or two dance on, having been possessed by a spirit guest. Those possessed are usually women. Very few men, aside from the drummers and some of the sponsors of the ceremony, participate in the dancing and possession. Some men say that they depend on their kinswomen to represent them to the ancestors. More men choose to stand outside the temple as transitory spectators than to enter it and dance. The few men who do enter the temple rarely linger for more than an hour or two, in contrast to the many women who remain through the night.

OLDER WOMEN IN RITUAL

Older women figure in the whole gamut of death rites in a number of important ways. They organize and provide most of the necessary labor and expertise for the events, and they represent their kin in certain ones. In many rituals they predominate as singers and dancers. Religious specialists are typically women, whether they are shamans or simply women who are consistently sought out as advisers because of their knowledge about the various rites.

Why older women predominate in ritual life is something that the Garifuna, including the women themselves, can explain only in personal terms. Although they insist that anyone may take part in the death rites, they say that women, and especially older women, simply happen to take greater "interest" in them. They do not explain this interest as an inevitable outcome of declining activity at home. No one suggests that older women "have more time" for ceremonies, and, in fact, many of the most active women have very heavy domestic responsibilities.[2] Nor do people see older women as being "cleaner" than younger women or spiritually better suited for these activities. It is true that menstruating women are supposed to avoid public gatherings in general and rituals in particular. But many young women scoff at the idea that they attract malevolent spirits when they menstruate, and some claim to disregard any monthly restriction. More to the point, few of them choose to participate in mourning ceremonies, aside from wakes and ninth-night wakes, even when they are not menstruating. As a rule, women

begin to take active part in ceremonial life after their mothers cease to do so (either because of death or extreme infirmity). This may be before or after they reach menopause, in their mid-to-late forties.

There is no specific age at which women begin to participate in mourning ceremonies, but their interest seems to develop slowly with age. Many young women are openly skeptical about the need for some of the ceremonies. They confess to little interest in them, and they lack the ritual knowledge and skills that their mothers or grandmothers possess. Standing outside a temple during *dügü*, watching the older women dance inside, young women and men routinely admit that they do not even understand the meaning of the songs being sung. Most older women, in contrast, are true believers who are well versed in the large body of belief and protocol associated with the death rites. By their own accounts, their expertise and personal belief grew slowly over the course of many years, primarily through observing and occasionally taking part in the ceremonies. Many concede that they were once skeptics themselves. But over the years, they explain, they saw cures effected by shamans and by ritual means; they witnessed countless cases of possession, or, more startling and convincing, they experienced it themselves. This cumulative evidence finally persuaded them that what they had once questioned, as some of their own daughters and sons now do, was in fact true.

To take a broader view of these personal experiences, women, as they age, may well be more easily persuaded of the importance of ritual. The whole pattern of Garifuna life, and especially the interdependence of generations, seems to "predispose" older women to take interest in the death rites. As a women's personal circumstances change with age—as her children grow up and her parents die—the ceremonies assume greater meaning for her. She can no longer depend on her mother to represent her in ritual; now she must represent herself, and her children and grandchildren as well.

Moreover, like her mother before her, the older woman increasingly depends on her daughters and sons for support. And while there is no law that compels their support, morality demands it, and women do their best to encourage it. For the Garifuna, a moral person is a generous and responsible one who honors the obligation to "help" kin, in whatever manner necessary. An immoral person is a stingy and negligent one. As young mothers, women instill the traditional values of generosity and sharing in their children; from a very tender age a child's refusal to share brings swift punishment. Later in life, when their sons and daughters are grown, women organize the rituals that express these values. In many of the death rites the living make offerings to the ancestors: they tangibly demonstrate concern for the well-being of their (deceased) elders. Two of the ceremonies, *chugu* and *dügü*, show how elder kin, even after death, can punish neglect.

Whether older women consciously recognize that their position of dependence parallels the ancestors' is debatable. But they obviously find the entire moral thrust of ritual life more meaningful than men or young women do. For older women the traditional values represent survival, and it is scarcely surprising that they take such interest in ceremonies that express them.

Older women do consciously recognize a very practical reason for taking part in death rites. They consider ritual activity to be one of a number of caretaking services that they can provide for their grown children in return for economic support. By organizing and cooperating in these ceremonies, they claim to protect their sons and daughters and grandchildren from possible harm at the hands of neglected ancestors. Of course, this amounts to self-protection as well, since a woman's own economic welfare is so closely bound to her children's

productive abilities and, ultimately, to their general health and well-being.

Paradoxically, the economic dependence of older women helps to explain not only their interest in these rituals but also their ability to organize them. Only these women have the economic and social means to stage the elaborate and expensive ceremonies with any degree of ease. Despite the fact that they are excluded from the labor market, older women potentially have greater economic resources at their disposal than other adults because they are entitled to contributions from their grown children. All the major rituals are quite expensive, and a man or a single household usually finds it impossible to meet the expense. When an older woman assumes responsibility, as is usually the case, the expense is divided among a number of sponsors—her grown daughters and sons. Older women also have the "human capital" that is often required. Female cooperative labor, which is indispensable to any major ritual undertaking, is founded on reciprocity. Any older woman who has helped others when they organized events can expect their help in the future when she needs to organize a mourning ceremony. Women work to create an elaborate and enduring network of mutual obligations with other women, and they draw on this network as necessary.

It bears repeating, in closing, that both men *and* women, by cultural concensus, are equally eligible to take part in nearly all of the rituals. Yet for the most part only women, and more specifically older women, choose to participate in them. A whole array of very concrete circumstances—women's lifelong caretaking roles based on a principle of female responsibility for lineal kin, the loss of a family representative in ritual when their own mothers die, increased economic dependence in later life—all induce them to join in these activities. Social circumstance everywhere shapes the personal experiences and colors the perceptions of individuals, and in many societies it affects male and female, or young and old, in different ways. Among the Garifuna the differing life experiences and perceptions of women and men, of old and young, are manifest in the pattern of ritual activity.

Notes

1. The Garifuna hold only a very simple wake and burial for an infant or child who dies. There are no further mourning ceremonies for them.

2. Many older women foster some of their grandchildren, whose parents work in other districts or even abroad. Rather few live in households without any dependent children.

Further Readings

Brown, Judith K. and Virginia Kerns, eds. *In Her Prime: A New View of Middle-Aged Women.* South Hadley, Mass.: Bergin and Garvey, 1985.

Cohen Stuart, Bertie A. *Women in the Caribbean: A Bibliography.* Leiden, Netherlands: Department of Caribbean Studies, Royal Institute of Linguistics and Anthropology, 1979.

González, Nancie L. *Black Carib Household Structure: A Study of Migration and Modernization.* Seattle, Wash.: University of Washington Press, 1969.

———. *Sojourners of the Caribbean: Ethnogenesis and Ethnohistory of the Garifuna.* Urbana, Ill.: University of Illinois Press, 1988.

Justus, Joyce Bennet. "Women's Role in West Indian Society." *The Black Woman Cross-Culturally,* ed. by Filomena C. Steady. Cambridge, Mass.: Schenkman, 1981.

Kerns, Virginia. "Structural Continuity in the Division of Men's and Women's Roles among the Black Carib (Garifuna)." *Sex Roles and Social Change in Native Lower Central American Societies,* ed. by Christine A. Loveland and Franklin O. Loveland. Urbana, Ill.: University of Illinois Press, 1982.

———. *Women and the Ancestors: Black Carib Kinship and Ritual.* Urbana, Ill.: University of Illinois Press, 1983.

10

The Controversial Vows of Urban Muslim Women in Iran

ANNE H. BETTERIDGE

Relatively little has been written in the West about Islamic ritual. Scholarly attention has been devoted largely to Islamic history and textual traditions, while the religious life of the Moslem has gone unstudied. Still less has the religious life of Moslem women been the object of study. This results not only from lack of interest in women's activities; for the most part these activities are inaccessible to the Western male researcher. Even what a Moslem man knows of women's religious activities is usually re-stricted to his experience with women of his own family, particularly during his childhood.

As a woman anthropologist studying Islamic ritual in Iran, I have been able to observe and participate in a wide range of ceremonies in which women take part. Women's religious activities are not a pale imitation of those engaged in by men. In addition to the formally enjoined participation in prayer and pilgrimage, women are signficantly involved in marriage-contract ceremonies, funeral observances, pilgrimages to local shrines,[1] and in the making and ful-

ANNE H. BETTERIDGE   (Ph.D. Anthropology, University of Chicago) is currently working as a Research Associate at the Southwest Institute for Research on Women at the University of Arizona, where she is also Adjunct Assistant Professor at the Center for Middle Eastern Studies. Dr. Betteridge's research interests include women in Middle Eastern society, especially Iran, and women and Islamic ritual. She is planning a research project on women in the Iranian immigrant community in the United States.

Author's Note   This chapter is based primarily on research conducted in Shiraz, Iran, between December 1974 and November 1976. The second *rowzeh* and ritual meal described in the article was attended in June 1977.

filling of vows, including the preparation of special foods having religious significance.

Men usually belong to formal religious organizations. These may be connected with a mosque or local shrine, or they may be occupationally based. Women, often lacking the extradomestic existence of men, are less likely to belong to organized groups that meet outside the home on a regular basis. This is not to suggest that women's activities are unstructured. Rather, women tend to use informal means in organizing and communicating with others about any ritual event. Women's ritual events are usually held in the home; news of them is spread through informal networks of family and friends. Women regard word of mouth as an effective means of publicizing a gathering. It is thought that news about gatherings for women should not be placed in public view. The large numbers of women attending the gatherings, and the still larger numbers aware of them, attest to the correctness of the women's assumption; formal publicity is unnecessary.

Even women's religious education has traditionally been informal. Although girls may now attend religious schools in the theological center of Qom in Iran (as of 1976), this was not true in the past. Thus, for example, the one woman in Iran currently to reach the highest Shi'a Muslim clerical rank of *mujtahid* was educated at home by private tutors.[2] Some girls' schools do exist; like parochial schools in the United States, they place great importance on teaching religion in addition to the usually required subjects. Also, many knowledgeable older women, often those whose children have grown or who are childless, conduct classes in Qoran reading and principles of religion in their homes.

Such women may also function as leaders in the various religious ceremonies sponsored by women. As is the case with the ceremonies themselves, these women do not announce themselves publicly. They dress no differently from the laity, while male clergy can readily

be identified by their robes and turbans. Women do not have to signal their status by outward means; they know who among them is knowledgeable in religious matters and who occupies a position of clerical eminence.

The majority of Iranians adhere to the Shi'a sect of Islam. It is distinguished from the more common Sunni sect by dispute over rightful succession to the leadership of the Islamic community. Shi'a Muslims, unlike Sunni Muslims, believe that the Prophet's successor should not have been elected and that the Prophet Mohammad intended to appoint Ali, his trusted companion, cousin, and son-in-law, as the next leader of Islam. Ali was the first in a sequence of twelve leaders, or Imams. The Imams are regarded as having had the ability to interpret divine law for Shi'a society. The twelfth and last Imam disappeared when he was a child but is regarded as still alive. Shi'a society now awaits the return, when God wills, of the twelfth Imam. Until his return, religious leaders are responsible for interpreting and administering divine law.

The esteem and affection in which the Imams are held give a distinct character to Shi'a Islam. Popular ritual practices, addressed to the Imams and their relatives, recount the sufferings that these holy individuals endured during their lifetimes. Such rites are performed in addition to the formally prescribed ritual duties of daily prayers, fasting, and pilgrimage to Mecca. These popular practices are not obligatory, but are considered religiously commendable.

Among important Shi'a popular rituals is the *rowzeh,* a ceremony of great significance to many women. The *rowzeh* is a very common ritual attended by people of all social classes. Men and women, either at one gathering or in single-sex assemblies, convene to hear a sermon and to mourn for the cruelly slain members of the Prophet's family. The sermon may concern any topic of the speaker's choice, but it always ends by recounting the tragedies that befell the Imams. *Rowzeh* ceremonies emphasize especially the third Imam's martyr-dom at the Battle of Kerbela. This last part of the *rowzeh* provokes great sadness and mourn-ing activity among members of the audience. Both men and women weep, beat themselves, and call out to the Imams and their relatives. In general, the women are far more demon-strative than the men, sobbing and beating their thighs, heads, and chests. At *rowzehs* at-tended exclusively by women, the reciter of *rowzeh* is often a woman. Women who recite at these ceremonies are known for their ability to read Arabic well and often for their religious learning. In many cases they are the same women who conduct religious classes for women and children in their homes.

In theory, the *rowzeh* provides an opportu-nity for communicating religious ideas and his-tory to the audience. In practice, however, the *rowzeh* has come to serve other functions, which have made it the center of often heated controversy. This has been especially true of the women's *rowzehs*, which are criticized not only by men but by many of the more devout and better-educated women. Objections focus on both the mercantile attitude reflected in making *rowzeh*-connected vows and the ten-dency to emphasize social aspects of the cere-mony rather than sincerely expressing devotion to God.

Both objections require more explanation. The first objection involves the fact that often, in recent times, the *rowzehs* have been used as vehicles for registering personal requests with God. In return for attending the ceremony and mourning for the Imams, people hope that such requests will be answered. This is partic-ularly true of women's *rowzehs*, which are often performed in connection with a vow. Vow making has a prominent place in women's re-ligious activities; a woman may vow that, if a particular request is granted or a difficulty remedied, she will sponsor a specific kind of religious ceremony. One women has illustrated this for me by saying that, if one's child were

in a car accident, one might make a vow to sponsor a ceremony on condition that the child recover. Another woman cited her own vow: "I asked that my youngest son, about thirty-two years old, should get married. I declared it in my own heart, and that this should happen within the month, by the first of Ramazan. If my request is answered, then I will fulfill my vow." Should her petition go unanswered she is under no obligation and can make another vow.

Because of what is felt to be their basically emotional nature and because of their involve-ment in the home, women are charged with the care of domestic and personal problems. Nevertheless such ritual transactions are read-ily viewed by some as perverting the true na-ture of Islam. One Shirazi woman, well edu-cated in religious matters and very much opposed to most *rowzehs* and vows, says that practices like these make the relation between humans and God "commercial." Rather than requesting strength of character and other kinds of spiritual help from God, people have come to expect material rewards—children, spouses, employment, houses, health—and are prepared to pay for these goods by fulfilling vows. The objection is made that ceremonies are not sponsored out of religious feeling but as payment for services rendered. The rela-tionship is contractual, not devotional.

To understand more fully the second com-mon criticism—that women performing *rowzeh* also engage in socializing (or "recreation," as one priest has called it)—it is perhaps easiest to examine one type of *rowzeh* in performance. One of the most heated controversies about women's *rowzeh* concerns a vow called *sofreh-ye Hazrat-e 'Abbas*. If the woman's request is granted, the woman who made this vow is obliged to give a ritual dinner along with a *rowzeh* in the name of a very popular saint of Shi'a Islam, 'Abbas, the son of the first Imam and younger half-brother of the second and third Imams. Because of his youth and the tenderheartedness shown in his compassionate deeds in warfare, this saint is regarded as more easily approachable than his brother, the third Imam. He has, as a young shrine helper told me, "less endurance": he cannot bear to refuse and is hence more likely to answer the pleas of distraught believers. Still another informant referred to 'Abbas by his title—"the gate to needs," or "the path by which one can achieve one's desires." Hence a wide variety of petitions can be addressed to him; virtually any kind of request can be made in connection with a promise to sponsor a rite in the name of 'Abbas.

The *rowzeh* and *sofreh*, or ritual dinner given in the name of 'Abbas, have a set form and menu, although they can be done in a more or less elaborate fashion. The ritual dinner is given in the home. Its date and time are important; either major religious holidays or Mondays are preferred, and it is usually held in the late afternoon and early evening. The ceremony may begin with a reading of a long prayer in Arabic. I was told that this prayer assures a favorable divine response to any needs or requests that those attending the ritual dinner might have. Following this, the *rowzeh* leader will deliver a sermon, ending with a *rowzeh* about the martyrdom of 'Abbas. During this time the women will have been sitting around a white cloth. When the *rowzeh* is finished, special foods are placed on this cloth, and everyone begins eating.

The ritual meal provides an opportunity not only for the hostess to celebrate the successful conclusion of her vow but for her guests to make their own vows as well. Generally, this is done by lighting a candle. A hostess may provide a metal tray filled with sand to hold the candle. Alternatively, individual candles in candlesticks may be placed on the white cloth for guests to light if they wish.

Thus described, this religious observance seems straightforward enough. The major source of criticism centers on the way it is put

into practice. The ritual meal may also be an occasion for showing off finery, gossiping, bawdy storytelling, singing, and dancing. Needless to say, the fine spread of food is also greatly enjoyed. Furthermore, the occasion is undoubtedly used for social competition. For example, a woman who conducts classes in religion for girls and women told me that she had once received invitations to two such celebrations to be given on the same day at the same time. They were to be held on opposite sides of the street by wives of two brothers; clearly, it was a contest.

I attended my first ritual dinner and *rowzeh* given in the name of 'Abbas on the eve of the Prophet's birthday in the company of my friend Homa and her mother. The hostess was a local doctor's wife. I was somewhat surprised when I was told to put on my best clothes and jewelry; I knew that the entire ceremony would include *rowzeh* and had assumed that black clothes would be appropriate. We left at about 5:45. I took my see-through *chador* (veil) for the first time, feeling somewhat uneasy about it.

We parked the car, put on our *chadors*, then entered the house. As we walked through the door, Homa took a deep breath and happily announced, "I smell food." The hall was filled with shoes, much jazzier than those I was used to seeing gathered in a hall when a *rowzeh* was in progress. Near the door to the living room was a metal tray filled with sand, with lighted colored candles standing in it. I was told that any woman who wished to make a vow could light a candle and place it in the tray.

As Homa's mother disappeared into another section of the living room, we took our seats on the floor along the back wall by the door. The entire floor was spread with white cloths decorated with vases of flowers. Some of the food was already set out. Homa started eating the pickles immediately; she had them polished off by the time the *rowzeh* was over. No one else was eating, however, and I later learned that Homa's action had brought a scolding from her mother.

Reading in Arabic was in progress when we entered. The *rowzeh* leader sat at the juncture of the two sections of the L-shaped room. A low wooden table, spread with a lovely cloth, had been placed in front of her. I recognized her as Khanom-e Rohani, a *rowzeh* leader whom I had seen previously at a different ceremony in town. Her veil was down around her shoulders throughout the reading and *rowzeh*. She was dressed in black, and her hair was parted in the middle. She looked very severe in comparison to the other women. They were made up, wearing colorful suits and dresses; most of them had on printed or light-colored veils. It was hot in the room; one very pregnant woman fanned herself vigorously throughout the ceremony.

Two women at the head of the room took turns reading in Arabic. Khanom-e Rohani corrected their reading and would sometimes take over for a while. I was surprised to see a young, very pretty, and well-dressed woman with frosted hair take her turn reading from the text. Her reading was loud, nasal, and forceful; I noticed that her hand shook as she read. When not reading, she followed along in her text, unlike the other women. Most of the guests did not have prayer books and spent their time sitting, watching the children they had brought along, and talking among themselves. Homa asked me if this was my first time at such a ceremony. When I told her it was, she assured me that I would get whatever I wanted.

From time to time the children interrupted. Some tried to snatch packets of *ajil*—a special vowed food consisting of nuts and candies—from the tray where it was stored. Homa frightened off one little girl by shouting in a gruff voice, "Don't touch it!" As the girl ran shaking to her mother, Homa tossed two packets of *ajil* over to her. While the women around me laughed, the *rowzeh* leader joined in by asking everyone to send a blessing for

the child.

The *rowzeh* leader then gave a brief sermon. She reminded all the women that on the Day of Judgment each must answer for herself and be responsible for her own actions. One cannot get any outside help and must bear the weight of one's own deeds. Her speech included recitations of two brief prayers in Arabic, each repeated five times; all those present joined in repeating the prayers. Following the prayers, the *rowzeh* leader asked all the women to say the response, "*amin*" (amen), in unison. Several women by the back door continued talking throughout the sermon; they were not in the least fazed by the *rowzeh* leader's fierce glances. A series of blessings was recited for those who had read in Arabic and for the mothers and fathers of those who were present. Every now and then the *rowzeh* leader would encourage the women to be vociferous in their blessings. Homa responded very loudly. At one point she was busy teasing the children and just managed to come in at the end for the last phrase. When the *rowzeh* leader began to speak about the happy occasion of Mohammad's birth, some women began to cry, pulling their veils down over their eyes.

The *rowzeh* leader then told the lady of the house, "You can turn the lights out now," something that I had never seen before in an Iranian ritual. Once the lights were off, she launched into a *rowzeh* about 'Abbas, recounting the details of his bravery and martyrdom. The women sat in the dark sniffling and weeping. Very shortly the *rowzeh* wound to a close, the lights were turned on, and our hostess removed the table in front of the *rowzeh* leader.

In the break that followed, Homa told me that the year before the *rowzeh* leader had been very entertaining. She had told all those present that any woman who did not make love with her husband when he wanted to would be hung by her breasts in hell. Homa's apt comment to the women seated around her had been, "If a man doesn't make love with his wife when she wants to, what do they hang him by?" Homa said that last year's *rowzeh* leader had been invited by mistake; the hostess had heard her complimented undeservedly and had invited her on the basis of what proved to be false praise. A woman across the way laughed when she heard the story and told that she had come this year in hopes of hearing the same woman speak. An older woman next to me, the mother of one of Homa's friends, told me not to believe what the woman had said about wives being punished in hell, because it probably wasn't true. She was afraid that I might take it seriously and didn't want to see Islam so misrepresented.

At that point the food began to arrive—platters of chicken, rice, and flatbread. Homa managed to wangle from the hostess some of the tasty crust at the bottom of the rice. The sweets came soon after. Homa advised me to take out my plastic bag; it turned out that a good-sized plastic bag had been neatly folded and placed under everyone's plate. We were served several kinds of cookies and candy, then fruit; all the participants popped the sweets into their bags. After the fruit had been passed the first time, Homa told me to hide my bag behind me so that they wouldn't realize we had been served. I did as she recommended and, sure enough, we were served again, ending up with twice as much as our fair share.

I noticed that Homa's mother had come back for yet another round of food. She wasn't talking with anyone, just quietly stuffing her bag. She poured the excess oil off a plate of *halva*, scooped all of it onto a piece of bread, rolled it up, and tucked it into the bag. She later told me that she had wanted to take the chicken from a plate in front of her but had restrained herself; a few minutes later it had disappeared into the bag of the *rowzeh* leader.

The ritual meal was over. As we prepared to leave, Homa captured a final plate of *halva* and a pair of daffodils that she later gave to me. As she offered an extravagant thank-you and good-bye to the *rowzeh* leader, her mother was talking the hostess out of the last of the exceptionally good soup. Driving home, Homa congratulated her mother on their haul; they

had gathered more than enough to feed Homa's brothers that evening. Like many other guests, we had removed our veils on leaving; most of the guests were doctors' wives or doctors themselves and wore their veils only for special religious occasions.

The basic framework of the ritual meal with its *rowzeh* provides a great deal of opportunity for elaboration; thus each celebration tends to have its own distinctive style. This can be seen in a second ritual meal I attended. This time the ceremony was held on the eve of the thirteenth of Rajab, birthday of the first Imam. The meal's sponsor was a woman from a family well known as members of a Sufi order. I attended with Simin, a friend visiting from Tehran, and her mother; a friend of Simin's mother had arranged the invitation.

This time the ritual meal was for men and women; men were seated in the house and women in the courtyard. This had been covered with a canvas tent, while green lights, crepe paper, and metallic garlands were draped between and through the branches of the courtyard's trees. The ground was covered with carpets spread with white cloths set for dinner. My friend Simin commented that this was a very well laid out and classy affair. She drew my attention to the fact that no plastic had been spread over the white cloths, a tacky measure practiced by some who give such dinners. Other aspects of the setting were also very richly embellished, but with more of an attempt to evoke the religious theme of the occasion than was the case with the first ritual meal I attended. A finely woven carpet with a picture of 'Abbas on horseback hung on the courtyard wall; a picture of Ali was above it. Black-and-white postcards portraying 'Abbas on horseback had been placed on top of each china plate on the white cloth. Ali was represented on a gold-colored coin placed to the right of each setting. When dinner was served, we would also find the names of members of the Prophet's family inscribed in icing on cakes. The white cloths were strewn with one-rial coins and silver candy balls that women gathered up during the course of the evening to take home for their children. Green candles stood on the white cloth for the use of any woman who might wish to make a vow.

As befitted a mixed occasion, the principal invited speakers were men. They spoke from a porch at the far end of the courtyard, facing the house, and their sermons were broadcast through a loudspeaker. The first man delivered a general sermon, assuring us that we would all get whatever we wanted; he concluded with a traditional chanted remembrance of 'Abbas' suffering on the field of Kerbela. The second, an esteemed priest known for his mystic inclinations, chose to tell us about Islam's famous women. He referred to the womb of Ameneh bearing the Prophet as a shell containing a pearl and recounted the stories of other famous women in the early history of Islam: the Prophet's first wife, Khadijeh, his daughter Fatimah, wife of the first Imam Ali and mother to the second and third, and, finally, Husain's sister Zainab, who had been present at the Battle of Kerbela. The priest next turned to the subject of Ali's search for a suitable wife after the death of Fatimah: she had to be lovely, intelligent, and able to bear him fine sons. Ali's search ended when he married Omm ol Banin, who subsequently gave birth to 'Abbas and six other sons. This time the speaker did not follow with the usual account of 'Abbas' death; for the lament had already been performed by his predecessor. The last man to recite chanted beautiful verses about Ali; Simin knew all the words and chanted along softly, crying as she chanted.

One striking feature of the evening was a brief speech by the hostess, in which she told her own reasons for sponsoring the ritual dinner. She said that she had been very sick during the month of Muharram. On the day of 'Ashura (the tenth of Muharram, anniversary of Imam Husain's martyrdom), she had made a vow to Ali and 'Abbas that she would sponsor a ritual meal and *rowzeh* in the name of 'Abbas on Ali's birthday if she recovered. She explained that she had made this vow rather than

any other because it would provide a chance for all her friends to get together. In so saying, she acknowledged the dual social and religious function of the ritual meal. Simin, who had given the same ceremony some years before, confirmed our hostess's estimation of the ceremony's social virtues. Women begin working together at least a week ahead and enjoy themselves in preparing for the meal. In fact, many of the women present had helped our hostess to get ready for the celebration. Some also served during the dinner, while others brought flowers or cakes and boxes of sweets to be served after dinner.

The formal part of the ceremony ended as a friend of the hostess read her own poem in honor of Ali. The dinner was served and cleared, with plastic bags stuffed as before. Then the evening's socializing began in earnest. A tray was handed to a very plump and jolly friend of our hostess. She began to beat on the tray, dance around, and sing gay, bawdy songs, much to the delight of the clapping audience of women, who joined in the refrains. Gradually some of the women, including our hostess and her poet friend, began dancing, each in turn. During the singing and dancing, many of the women got up from their places and moved around to visit friends. They caught up on the news, found out who had married, who had had children and how many, who had been sick, and on and on. This continued until people started to leave.

The preceding descriptions should give some idea of why a Shirazi plaster worker I know told me that the ritual meal is not "real Islam." He said that he had a relative too poor to keep a decent carpet underfoot but that the same person had spent some 10,000 *toman* (about $1,500) to sponsor a *rowzeh* and ritual meal in the name of 'Abbas. He himself charged that the ritual was being pushed by low-level priests in search of a free meal; he could also not see why such money should be spent in serving persons whose bellies were already full. A devout woman of my acquaintance has called such events "silly ladies' parties." She objects to the way women pounce on their food and stuff their plastic bags. She herself no longer attends them, describing the behavior of those who attend as "disgusting."

In general, however, one finds a striking difference between men's and women's responses to the ritual meal and similar women's ceremonies. Men may condemn women for their display, overeating, and gossip and yet are often willing to tolerate such practices. The reason is unflattering: women's excesses and failings are attributed to their more "emotional" nature, while men's own ritual practices are seen as being more "rational." In effect the men are saying that women's ceremonies are abused but that this can't really be helped. Women, on the other hand, are much more likely than men to press for "reform" of these ceremonies.

The women's ceremonies can also find intelligent defenders. My friend Simin is an example. She agrees that this occasion can be misused, but she does not find this a reason to condemn the practice as a whole. Simin sponsored the entire ceremony, both *rowzeh* and ritual meal, when her aunt returned from the United States, where she had successfully undergone a serious operation. Her aunt and her friends, many of them members of her Qoran reading group, attended the ritual. In this way Simin was able to celebrate her aunt's recovered health in the company of good friends, most of whom shared her religious views. In answer to the charge that the ritual meal is irreligious because it gives food to people who are not in need, Simin told me that, as part of her vow, much of the food prepared for the ritual meal was given away to the poor. She had cooked special large pots of rice with this in mind and had them distributed at a local shrine. Simin feels that her actions were properly devout, but she also thinks it important that she could share with friends the happy resolution of a worrisome event in her life.

A popular Shirazi *rowzeh* leader annually sponsors three weeks of *rowzehs* in his home during the month of Sefar. One morning I was surprised to hear him condemn the practice of women's vows and ritual meals in the course of his sermon. His remarks provoked a furor among the women who were listening that day. During sermons in his home on succeeding mornings, quite a few women interrupted to question the *rowzeh* leader himself and other speakers about their views on women's vows. The women were very fond of the practice and reluctant to give it up; they argued with each of the male preachers in turn during the next few assemblies, always defending the ritual meals. I had never seen a stronger audience reaction to any sermon topic in Iran.

Since so much can be said against the way the vow is currently practiced, we must consider why some women remain so firm in its defense. The women's ritual meals are a major part of the social lives of many Iranian women. As Robert and Elizabeth Fernea say about an Iraqi ceremony that is very similar to the Iranian ceremonies I studied, religious gatherings offer women "one of the few community-sanctioned opportunities for meeting socially in each other's homes, in groups that cut across the ordinary kin grouping and which include representatives from all segments of the community."[3] In Iran it is true that women of educated families and upper-class groups are no longer very restricted in their visiting patterns and movements about town. But, especially for lower-class women and for those who come from more traditional families, religion offers a much-needed opportunity to assemble. It is also one of the few occasions in which a sizeable amount of money can be properly spent on a women's gathering. Once a vow has been made and answered, a woman is bound to fulfill it; her family will support her financially in completing the obligation.

Chapter 12 of this volume describes the situation of women in one Iranian village. I am struck by the absence of group ritual occasions for women there. Women seem to be isolated in their homes, have little religious education, and seldom gather, lest they be accused of frivolity and laziness. Their lives are the more desolate for lacking communal gatherings.[4]

It is perhaps unfortunate that women are obliged to justify their socializing by placing it in a religious framework. However, this is a common feature of women's religious lives in much of the Middle East. Only modern, educated, or upper-class women can move about easily in a secular context. Such women are divided in their opinions about women's vows and ritual meals. Those with deep religious orthodoxy tend to oppose these ceremonies. However, because it is easier for them to get together in nonreligious settings, it is also easier for them to condemn the practice of women's *rowzeh* and ritual meals. Such practice does not play as important a part in their social lives as it does for most women, who favor it. Other upper-class women, less orthodox in temperament and background, see no contradiction in holding a festive social event in connection with a religious ceremony. What, in their view, is wrong with combining religion and enjoyment?

What is actually at stake in these controversies over women's ceremonies is the definition of the proper boundaries of religion. Overall in Iran, women's religious activities fall into several categories, ranging from the more contemplative and intellectual quests to group-oriented social affairs such as those I have described. Members of either group may be equally sincere in their religious motivations, but they are defining religion differently. While some women define religion in a strict and formal sense as a way of life and thought centering around certain beliefs and commandments, others may agree with this view but include a more social dimension as well. For many women religion pervades all aspects of social life, as witnessed by the variety of occasions on which vows may be made. To separate religion from social life would be to make a distinction not recognized in practice by many Islamic women.

The opportunity to gather on religious occasions and combine fellowship with worship is not to be condemned out of hand. It is in the nature of much religious practice to draw people together and to promote understanding and sympathy among them. That such occasions provide a chance to visit with friends is part and parcel of the nature of women's religious lives in traditional Islamic society. Women share many common problems: the effort to find a good husband and bear a child, the threat of barrenness and children's sickness, and hopes for the success of their children and husbands. Women often seek resolution to these problems through religious means and celebrate such resolutions through group activities. Many of those who participate in a given ritual share certain beliefs and, by sharing them, support one another's faith. As an outside observer, one may distinguish social activities and see their place in religious behavior. However, in the daily course of women's religious lives, the two are so interwoven that their conjunction seems correct, desirable, and even necessary to many women who join in ritual activity.

Notes

1. Fatima Mernissi has described women's visits to local shrines in Morocco in her article "Women, Saints and Sanctuaries," which follows in this volume.
2. A *mujtahid* is one learned in religious sciences whose learning and abilities have been formally recognized and certified by the Shi'ite religious leaders (*'ulama*) of the time. A *mujtahid* is unique in having the right to make independent decisions in the interpretation of religious law. This distinguished woman, now in her eighties, is Khanom-e Amin; she received her degree of *ejtehad* on the basis of her writings, which were read by the *'ulama* then centered in Najaf, Iraq.
3. Robert and Elizabeth Fernea, "Variations in Religious Observance among Islamic Women," in *Scholars, Saints, and Sufis: Muslim Religious Institutions Since 1500*, ed. Nikki R. Keddie (Berkeley: University of California Press, 1972), pp. 394–395.
4. See Erika Friedl, "Islam and Tribal Women in a Village in Iran," in this volume.

Further Readings

Betteridge, Anne H. "*'Aqd*" (marriage contract). In Ehsan Yarshater, ed., *Encyclopaedia Iranica,* vol. 2 (London: Routledge & Kegan Paul, 1982), pp. 189–91.

———. "*'Arūsī*" (wedding celebration). In Ehsan Yarshater, ed., *Encyclopaedia Iranica,* vol. 2 (London: Routledge & Kegan Paul, 1982), pp. 666–70.

———. "Domestic Observances: Muslim." In Mircea Eliade, ed., *The Encyclopedia of Religion* (New York: Macmillan, 1986).

———. "Gift-Exchange in Iran: The Locus of Self-Identity in Social Interaction." *Anthropological Quarterly* 58(4), October 1985: 190–202.

———. "To Veil or Not To Veil: A Matter of Protest or Policy." In Guity Nashat, ed., *Women and Revolution in Iran* (Boulder, Colo.: Westview Press, 1983), pp. 109–28.

Early, Evelyn A. "Catharsis and Creation: The Everyday Narratives of Baladi Women of Cairo." *Anthropological Quarterly* 58(4), October 1985: 172–81.

Jamzadeh, Laal and Margaret Mills. "Iranian Sofreh: From Collective to Female Ritual." In Caroline Walker Bynum, Stevan Harrell and Paula Richman, eds., *Gender and Religion: On the Complexity of Symbols* (Boston: Beacon Press, 1986), pp. 23–65.

Mills, Margaret. "Sex Role Reversals, Sex Changes, and Transvestite Disguise in the Oral Tradition of a Conservative Muslim Community in Afghanistan." In Rosan A. Jordan and Susan J. Kalcik, eds., *Women's Folklore, Women's Culture* (Philadelphia: University of Pennsylvania Press, 1985), pp. 187–213.

Tabari, Azar and Nahid Yeganeh, eds. *In the Shadow of Islam: The Women's Movement in Iran.* London: Zed Press, 1982.

11

Women, Saints, and Sanctuaries in Morocco

FATIMA MERNISSI

. . . The next morning I went to see my mother. I had a snack with her and the children and then I went to spend the day at the Marabout [a sanctuary]. I lay down there and slept for a very long time.

Q *Do you go to the Marabout often?*

A Yes, quite often. For example, I prefer to go there on the days of *Aïd* [religious festivals]. When one has a family as desperate as mine, the shrine is a haven of peace and quiet. I like to go there.

Q *What do you like about the shrine? Can you be more precise?*

A Yes. The silence, the rugs, and the clean mats which are nicely arranged . . . the sound of the fountain in the silence. An

FATIMA MERNISSI was formerly Professor of Sociology at Muhammad V University in Rabat, Morocco, and currently holds a research appointment at Morocco's Institut Universitaire de Recherche Scientifique. Her numerous writings on Muslim women include *Beyond the Veil: Male-Female Dynamics in Modern Muslim Society* and *Le Maroc raconte par ses femmes*. Dr. Mernissi has studied and lectured extensively in the United States.

Author's Note Gathering of historical data on saints, mainly female saints, was done with the collaboration and critical supervision of the Moroccan historian Halima Ferhat, a Maître de Conférence at the University Mohammed V.

enormous silence where the sound of water is as fragile as thread. I stay there hours, sometimes whole days.

Q *The day of* Aïd *it must be full of people.*

A Yes, there are people, but they are lost in their own problems. So they leave you alone. Mostly it's women who cry without speaking, each in her own world.

Q *Aren't there any men at the shrine?*

A Yes, but men have their side, women theirs. Men come to visit the shrine and leave very quickly; the women, especially those with problems, stay much longer.

Q *What do they do and what do they say?*

A That depends. Some are happy just to cry. Others take hold of the saint's garments and say, "Give me this, oh saint, give me that. . . ." "I want my daughter to pass her exam . . ." [she laughs]. You know the saints are men, human beings. But sometimes, imagine, the woman gets what she asks for! Then she brings a sacrifice . . . she kills an animal and prepares a meal of the meat and then offers it to the visitors. Do you know Sid El Gomri?

Q *No.*

A [laughs] Salé is full of shrines . . . full, full. You know, there is a proverb, "If you want to make a pilgrimage, just go around Salé barefooted . . ." [laughs]. They do say that. . . . All of Salé is a shrine. There are so many that some don't have names [laughs]. My father is a native of Salé. He knows the shrines and talks a lot about them. When you are separated from someone or when you have a very bad fight, the saint helps you overcome your problem. When I go I listen to the women. You see them tell everything to the tomb and mimicking all that took place. Then they ask Sid El Gomri to help them get

out of the mess. They cry, they scream. Then they get hold of themselves and come back, join us, and sit in silence. I like the shrine.

Q *Are you ever afraid?*

A Afraid of what? In a shrine, what a question? I love shrines.

Q *And when do you go?*

A They are shut in the evenings except for those that have rooms, like Sidi Ben Achir, for example. You can rent a room there and you can stay a long time.

Q *Rent a room for how much?*

A Oh, fifteen dirhams.[1]

Q *Fifteen dirhams a night?!*

A No, for ten dirhams you can stay as long as you like, even a month. You know, they call Sidi Ben Achir a doctor. Sick people come with their family; they rent a room and stay until they are well. You know, it's not Sidi Ben Achir that cures them, it's God, but they think it's Sidi Ben Achir.

Q *Can anybody rent a room?*

A Not any more. Now you have to have the authorization of the *Mokkadem* [local officials]. They want to know where you live and be sure that you are really sick. Once a woman rented a room and told them she had a sick person, but it was her lover. Since then they've made renting rooms more difficult.

Q *Are there young people your own age at the shrine?*

A Yes, but they don't come for the shrine, only for the view. A lot of young men from the neighborhood come to the shrine for picnics during the spring and summer. You should see the shrine then: the Hondas, the motors roaring, the boys all dressed up, the girls with short skirts, all made up and suntanned. It's beautiful. It's relaxing . . . the silence inside of the shrine, and life outside . . . it's crawling with young people. You know they have even made a slide in the wall that goes down to the beach. I will show it to you when we go. It's faster. You jump off the rampart, go down the slide and you're on the beach. You know some people come to the shrine during the summer for their vacations instead of going to a hotel where you pay ten or fifteen dirhams a day. In the shrine a whole family pays fifteen or twenty dirhams a week or month. It's especially the people who live outside of the city and come from far away, the north, the south, all corners of Morocco. For them the shrine is ideal for vacations. The old people can pray and the young can go to the beach. In the summer I meet people from all over Morocco. It's as if I were in Mecca, but I'm in Salé! You must come and see it. We can go in the summer if you want, it's more pleasant. You don't have to come to pray, you can just come and look. I told you, when I go to the shrine its's not to pray. I never ask for anything. When I want something I'll ask God directly, but not the saint . . . he's a human being like I am.

This excerpt from an interview with a twenty-year old maid, who works in a luxurious, modern part of Salé and lives in its *bidonville* section, suggests the great variety of experiences which take place in the sanctuary according to individual needs. Although they vary throughout the *Maghreb* (North Africa) from a humble pyramid of stones to a pretentious palace-like building,[2] all sanctuaries have one element in common: the saint's presence is supposed to be hosted there, because it is his tomb, a place he inhabited, or the site of an event in his life. The sanctuary testifies to the saint's welcomed presence in the community, but as an institution in a dynamic developing society it also reflects the society's economic and ideological contradictions.

SANCTUARIES AS THERAPY

For women, the sanctuary offers a dramatic contrast to their subordinate position in a bureaucratic, patriarchal society where decision-making positions are held by men. In the courts and hospitals, women hold a classically powerless position, condemned to be subjects, receptacles of impersonal decisions, executors of orders given by males. In a public hospital, the doctor is the expert, the representative of the bureaucratic order, empowered by the written law to tell her what to do; the illiterate woman can only execute his orders. In the diagnosis process, she expresses her discomfort in awkward colloquial Arabic and realizes, because of the doctor's impatience and irritation, that she cannot provide him with the precise, technical information he needs. Moreover, the hospital is a strange, alien setting, a modern building full of enigmatic written signs on doors and corridors, white-robed, clean, and arrogant civil servants who speak French for all important communications and only use Arabic to issue elementary orders (come here, go there, take off your dress, etc.).

In comparison to the guardians who stand at the hospital's gates and in its offices, the saint's tomb is directly accessible to troubled persons. Holding the saint's symbolical drape or another object like a stone or a tree, the woman describes what ails her, and it is she who makes the diagnosis, suggests the solution or solutions which might suit her, and explains to the saint the one she prefers. Saints know no French and often no literate Arabic; the language of this supernatural world is colloquial dialects, Berber or Arabic, the only ones women master. The task of the saint is to help her reach her goal. She will give him a gift or a sacrifice only if he realizes her wishes, not before. With a doctor, she has to buy the prescription first and has no way of retaliating if the medicine does not have the proper effect. It is no wonder, then, that in spite of modern health services, women still go to the sanctuaries in swarms, before they go to the hospital, or simultaneously, or after. Saints give women vital help that modern public health services cannot give. They embody the refusal to accept arrogant expertise, to submit blindly to authority, to be treated as subordinate. This insistence on going to saints' tombs exemplifies the North African woman's traditional claim that she is active, can decide her needs for herself and do something about them, a claim that the Muslim patriarchal system denies her. Visits to and involvement with saints and sanctuaries are two of the rare options left to women to *be*, to shape their world and their lives. And this attempt at self-determination takes the form of an exclusively female collective endeavor.

In the sanctuaries, there are always more women than men. They speak and shout with loud voices as if they are the secure owners of the premises. Men, although allowed in, often have to shorten their *Ziara* (visit) because they are overwhelmed by the inquisitive and curious looks of ubiquitous female visitors. Women gather around each other at the saint's supposed tomb and feel directly in contact with a sacred source of power that reflects their own energies. Distressed and suffering, these women have a very important bond: the will to find a solution, to find a happier balance between themselves and their surroundings, their fate, the system that thwarts them. They know they are *wronged* (*Madluma*) by the system. Their desire to find an answer to their urgent needs is a desire to regain their rights. That other women are in exactly the same situation creates a therapeutic network of communication among them.

When a woman enters the sanctuary, she goes directly to the tomb, walking over the stretched feet of sitting women, the stretched bodies of sleeping women. If women have already cried and screamed, they often lie in a fetal position with their heads on the floor. The newly arrived woman will put her hand on the tomb, or on the drape over it, and will explain her problem either in a loud voice or silently. She might go into great detail about her son who failed his examination or was driven away from her by his bride. When describing an intimate fight with her husband, the woman will mimic what happened, name the actors, explain their gestures and attitudes. After she has expressed her needs, she will come to sit among the other women. Eventually, they will gather around her, ask her more details, and offer her the only expertise these women have: experience in suffering. Outraged by her situation and encouraged by this female community, the woman may fall on the floor and scream, twisting her body violently. Some women will rush to her, hold her, hug her, soothe her by talking to her about their own cases and problems. They will massage her forehead, cool her off with a drink of water, and replace on her head her displaced headgear or scarf. She recovers quickly, regains her composure, and leaves the scene to the next newcomer. Undeniably therapeutic, the sanctuary stimulates the energies of women against their discontent and allows them to bathe in an intrinsically female community of soothers, supporters, and advisors.

SANCTUARIES AS ANTIESTABLISHMENT ARENAS

It is primarily as an informal women's association that the sanctuary must be viewed. It is not a religious space, a mistake which is often made. Most saint's sanctuaries are not mosques. With very few exceptions, they are not places where official orthodox Muslim prayer takes place. As Derminghem remarks,

In principal, the *cubba* is not a mosque (*Mesjid*) where one does *soujoùd*, the prostration of ritual prayer (*çala*), even less so, the *Jam'*, the cathedral mosque where Friday service is held. One can do the *dou'a*, prayer of supplication and optional invocation, but not the *sala*, sacramental prayer before a grave.[3]

The institution of saints that is enacted in the sanctuary has an evident antiorthodox, antiestablishment component which has been the object of a prolific literature. But studies of the woman-saint relation have placed excessive emphasis on its magical aspect. Western scholars who investigated the institution were fascinated by the "paralogical" component of the "Moroccan personality structure" and the importance of magical thinking patterns in the still heavily agrarian Moroccan economy and paid little attention to what I would call the phenomenological aspect, namely, what the practitioners themselves derive from their involvement with the saint and the sanctuary.

Such practices have also been interpreted as evidence of the mystical thinking of primitives as opposed to the secularity of the modern mind. As Mary Douglas points out,

Secularization is often treated as a modern trend attributable to the growth of cities or to the prestige of science, or just to the breakdown of social forms. But we shall see that it is an age-old cosmological type, a product of a definable social experience, which need have nothing to do with urban life or modern science. Here it would seem that anthropology has failed to hold up the right reflecting mirror to contemporary man. The contrast of secular with religious has nothing whatever to do with the contrast of modern with traditional or primitive. The idea that primitive man is by nature deeply religious is nonsense. . . . The illusion that all primitives are pious, credulous and subject to the teaching of priests or magicians has probably done even more to impede our understanding of our civilization.[4]

Women, in particular, who are always the ones to be kept illiterate (and 97 percent of rural Moroccan women still are),[5] are described as simple-minded, superstitious creatures, incapable of sophisticated thinking, who indulge in esoteric mysticism. This view of women has gained even greater support with the advent of the development and nascent industrialization in Third World economies. If women in industrialized societies are granted some capacity for rational thinking, women in Third World societies are still described as enthralled in magical thinking, despite the fact that their societies are leaping into a modernity enraptured with rationality, technology, and environmental mastery.

SAINTHOOD AS AN ALTERNATIVE TO MALE-DEFINED FEMININITY

Far from magical, a visit to a saint's tomb, an ongoing relation with a supernatural creature, can be a genuine attempt to mediate one's place in the material world. Interaction with the saint can represent an effort to experience reality fully:

The sacred is the real *par excellence,* at one and the same time power, efficiency, source of life and fertility. The religious desire to live within the sacred is in fact equivalent to the desire to be in objective reality, not to be paralyzed by endless and purely subjective experience, but to live in a world which is real and efficient, and not illusory.[6]

At bottom, women in an unflinchingly patriarchal society seek through the saint's mediation a bigger share of power, of control. One area in which they seek almost total control is reproduction and sexuality, the central notions of any patriarchal system's definition of women, classical orthodox Islam included.[7] Women who are desperate to find husbands, women whose husbands have sexual problems, women who have lost their husband's love or their own reproductive capacities go to the saint to get help and find solutions. One of the important functions of sanctuaries is precisely their involvement with sexuality and fertility. Indeed, if power can be defined as "the chance of a person or a number of persons to realize their own will in a communal action, even against the resistance of others, who are participating in the action,"[8] then women's collaboration with saints is definitely a power operation. Excluded from ritualistic orthodox religion, women walking in processions around saints' tombs express their quest for power in the vast horizons of the sacred space, untouched, unspoiled by human authority and its hierarchies:

> Pale young girls throw red flowers into the spring, others sugar or honeycombs, so that their voice may become sweet, spiritual, persuasive. The women who throw musk dream of being loved. . . . None goes to the spring without henna, without benjamin. While burning her green or red candle, the virgin says, 'Master of the spring, light my candle' which means 'marry me,' or else 'give me splendid health.' The power to which they speak is capable of granting them all the goods of the world: life, strength, fortune, love, children.[9]

Now this quest for power that underlies the woman-saint relation is further confirmed by the fact that there are women saints who occupy a preeminent place and who specialize in solving problems of sexuality and reproduction.[10] They assume what Freud would certainly have called a phallic role and function. Some female saints go beyond the stage of penis envy and reverse traditional patriarchal relations: they are the ones who give penises to men suffering from sexual disturbances; such is the case of the Algerian female saint, Lalla Nfissa.[11] But this is not their only function. Unlike the emphasized passivity of women in the material, real world, supernatural women lead intensively active lives, perform all kinds of acts, from benign motherly

protection to straightforward aggression, such as rape of men.[12] These women in the supernatural realm do not respect the traditional Muslim sexual division of labor which excludes women from power in religion and politics. In the supernatural realm, women may refuse to assume domestic roles and play active roles in both religion and politics.

In one of the most respected saint's biographies, the thirteenth-century *At-Tasawwuf Ila Rijal At-Tasawwuf*,[13] the biographer, Abu Yaqub At Tadili, makes no specific reference to the fact that some saints were women: they enjoy exactly the same rights and privileges and assume the same characteristics as male saints. At one point, a woman saint, Munia Bent Maymoun Ad-Dukali, says, "This year, hundreds of women saints visited this sanctuary." At another, a male insists that, "In Al Masamida [a region], there were twenty-seven saints who have the power to fly in the air, among whom fourteen are women."[14]

Female saints seem to fall into two categories, those who are saints because they were the sisters, wives, or daughters of a saint[15] and those who were saints in their own right.[16] Many of these saints have strikingly "unfeminine" personalities and interests. Imma Tiffelent, for example, literally fled her domestic condition:

> Not wanting to marry, Imma Tiffelent took the shape of a dove, escaped, and became a prostitute. . . . Twenty-seven young men disappeared after having loved her. Then she became an ascetic, in a hut, at the top of the mountain. . . . Ragged, unkempt, she preached religion in the valley, returned to her hut, shed even her rags, lived nude, and prophesied. It is forbidden to touch the trees around her grave, to kill the birds, to take the partridge eggs from the nest.[17]

The same identical flight from patriarchal "womanhood" can be seen in Sida Zohra El Kouch, "who was as wise as she was beautiful, resisted Moulay Zidane, died a virgin, and was visited only by women."[18] No less important, a prolific body of literature shows a number of female saints played important roles in the political arena.[19] One of the most famous is certainly the Berber saint Lalla Tagurrami, who played a strategic role in her region's history as a referee in conflicts between tribes and between tribes and the central authority.[20] Politically, she was so influential and successful that the king imprisoned her:

> As she was among the most beautiful girls of the village, she was sought after for marriage, but refused all suitors. . . . Her reputation as a saint grew and extended far. The sultan wanted to meet Lalla Aziza and asked her to come to Marrakesh. Once there, she continued to distinguish herself by her piety and the good she did. She was very honored, but her influence became so great that the sultan took offense and had Lalla thrown into prison. She was poisoned and died.[21]

It is of course possible that her fate was devised by myth tellers to discourage other women from taking such paths.

MALE SAINTS AS ANTIHEROES

Male saints, on the other hand, were profoundly concerned with what we would call a housework issue: how to eat without exploiting somebody else's work. Most analyses of the saints' lives fail to emphasize their constant preoccupation with food and its preparation; that they walk on water, fly in the skies, are given more weight than their efforts not to exploit the traditional domestic labor force available—women. Around this question clustered all other issues, such as the repudiation of possessions, privileges, political power, and the condemnation of wars and violence, the very characteristics of a phallocratic system. Most saints fled urban centers and their sophisticated exploitative lives, tried hunting, fishing, gathering, and cooking for themselves.[22] Some fasted as often as they could[23]

and trained themselves to eat very little; one went as far as to feed himself on one mouthful.[24] Still others had supernatural help which ground their own wheat or simply which gave them food.[25] They all tried to do without housework and to avoid food cooked by others,[26] and they also tried, to the community's dismay, to perform daily domestic chores themselves, such as taking the bread to the neighborhood oven.[27] One of the most famous of saints, Bou Yazza, went so far as to assume the appearance of a female domestic and to serve a woman for months.[28]

Some saints have families and children, some abstain and live in celibacy. But those who marry are unsuccessful fathers and husbands and live like embarrassed heads of families who can't provide properly for their dependents.[29] Others, especially elderly saints, did not hesitate to renounce their marital rights when these appeared to be totally opposed to the woman's happiness.[30] They definitely did not play the patriarchal role well. Among those who did not marry, one saint explained he was afraid to be unjust to his wife;[31] for him, apparently, marriage was an unjust institution to women. Another said he saw a beautiful woman walking down the street and thought he was in paradise; she was exactly like a *houri*, females provided to good Muslim believers in paradise.[32] Although he secluded himself because he was afraid females would turn him away from God,[33] he did not identify them with the devil, as classical Muslim ideology does, but with paradise, the most positive aspect of Muslim cosmogony.[34] Another saint fainted when he found himself alone with a woman in a room,[35] an unmasculine gesture to say the very least. Indeed, all these fears are not those of a self-confident, patriarchal male.

Like the women who come to visit their sanctuaries, a large number of saints were of humble origin and were involved in manual or physical activities as shepherds, butchers, or doughnut makers.[36] Others had no jobs and lived off nature, eating wild fruits, roots, or fish. Some saints were learned men, even judges, who refused to use their knowledge to obtain influential positions and accumulate wealth, or even to teach,[37] and encouraged illiterates to be proud of their illiteracy. Like the women in the sanctuaries, however, many of them were illiterates. They reminded their communities, which respected them, of their illiteracy,[38] perhaps in order to demystify knowledge as a prerequisite for decision-making positions. Moulay Bou Azza made a point of not speaking literate or even colloquial Arabic.[39] Moulay Ábdallah Ou Said, for example, tried to practice a teaching method for the masses "without the intervention of written texts."[40] Although it shocked the learned mandarins, the illiterate female saint Lalla Mimouna constantly insisted she did not use the customary complicated Koranic verses in her prayers because she did not know them. "Mimouna knows God and God knows Mimouna"[41] was the prayer she invented. This resistance to hierarchical knowledge is a persistent characteristic of saints' lives and their battles, which finds sympathy with the oppressed of the new developing economies: the illiterates, who are predominantly women. It is, therefore, no wonder that in the disintegrating agrarian economies of the Maghreb, sanctuaries, among all institutions, are almost the only ones women go to spontaneously and feel at home in. The sanctuary offers a world where illiteracy does not prevent a human being from being a wholesome, thinking, and reasonable person.

The psychic and emotional value of women's experience in sanctuaries is uncontested and evident. Sanctuaries, which are the locus of antiestablishment, antipatriarchal mythical figures, provide women with a space where complaint and verbal vituperations against the system's injustices are allowed and encouraged. They give women the opportunity to develop critical views of their condition, to identify problems, and to try to find their solution. At the same time, women invest all of their efforts and energies in trying to get a supernatural force to influence the oppressive structure on their behalf. This does not affect the formal power structure, the outside world. It has a collective therapeutic effect on the individual women visitors, but it does not enable them to carry their solidarity outside, to affect the system and shape it to suit their own needs. For these needs spring from their structural economic reliance on males and on the services they must give them in exchange: sex and reproduction. The saint in the sanctuary plays the role of the psychiatrist in the capitalist society, channeling discontent into the therapeutic processes and thus depriving it of its potential to combat the formal power structure. Saints, then, help women adjust to the oppression of the system. The waves of resentment die at the sanctuary's threshold. Nothing leaves with the woman except her belief that her contact with the saint triggered mechanisms which are going to affect the world, change it, and make it suit her conditions better. In this sense, sanctuaries are "happenings" where women's collective energies and combative forces are invested in alienating institutions which strive to absorb them, lower their explosive effect, neutralize them. Paradoxically, the arena where popular demonstrations against oppression, injustice, and inequality are most alive become, in developing economies, the best ally of unresponsive national bureaucracies. Encouragement of traditional saints' rituals by administrative authorities who oppose any trade unionist or political movement is a well-known tactic in Third World politics.

Notes

1. A dirham is roughly equivalent to $0.20 (U.S. dollars).

2. Emile Derminghem, "Les Edifices," in *Le Culte des saints l'Islam maghrébin* (Paris: Gallimard, 1954), p. 113.

3. "En principe, la cubba n'est pas une mosquée, Mesjid, où l'on fait le soujoùd, la prosternation de la prière rituelle, çala, encore moins, la Jam', la

mosquée cathédrale où se fait l'office du vendredi. On peut faire la dou'a, prière de demande et d'invocation facultative, mais non la sala, prière sacramentale devant un tombeau." Ibid.

4. Mary Douglas, *Natural Symbols: Exploration in Cosmology* (New York: Random House, Vintage Books, 1973), p. 36.

5. *Recensement général de la population et de l'habitat, 1971* (Rabat: Direction de la statistique, Ministère de Planification, 1971), 3:5. The illiteracy rate is evaluated to be 75 percent for rural women between the ages of ten and twenty-four and between 93 percent and 97 percent for older women.

6. "Le sacré c'est le réel par excellence, à la fois puissance, efficience, source de vie et de fécondité. Le désir de l'homme religieux de vivre dans le sacré équivaut en fait à son désir de se situer dans la réalité objective, de ne pas se laisser paralyser par la réalité sans fin des expériences purement subjectives, de vivre dans un monde réel et efficient et non pas dans une illusion." Mircea Eliade, *Le Sacré et le profane* (Paris: Gallimard, 1965), p. 27.

7. Fatima Mernissi, *Beyond the Veil* (Cambridge, Mass.: Schenkman Publishing Co., 1975), esp. the chapter entitled, "The Traditional Muslim View of Women and Their Place in the Social Order."

8. Max Weber, *From Max Weber, Essays in Sociology*, trans. and ed. with an introduction by H. Gerth and C. Wright Mills (New York: Oxford University Press, 1958), p. 180.

9. "Des jeunes filles pâles jettent dans la source des fleurs rouges, d'autres du sucre, des rayons de miel, pourque leur parole devienne douce, spirituelle, persuasive. Les femmes qui y lancent du musc rêvent de se faire aimer . . . nul ne s'y rend sans henné, sans benjoin." En brûlant son cierge vert ou rose, la vierge dit, "Maître de la source, allumes-moi mon cierge" ce qui veut dire "mariez-moi," ou encore "donnez-moi une santé brillante." La puissance à laquelle on s'adresses est capable de donner tous les biens de ce monde: vie, force, fortune, amour, enfants." Desparmet, "Le Mal magique," in Derminghem, p. 44.

10. Léon L'Africain, *Description de l'Afrique*, trans. from Italian by A. Epaulard Adrien (Paris: Maison Neuve, 1956), p. 216; and E. Doutté, *Magie et religion dans l'Afrique du Nord* (Alger: Typographica Adolphe Jourdan, 1908), chap. 1, p. 31.

11. Derminghem, p. 43.

12. Vincent Crapanzano, "The Transformation of the Eumenides: A Moroccan Example" (unpublished manuscript, Princeton University, 1974), and "Saints, Jinns and Dreams: An Essay on Moroccan Ethnopsychology" (unpublished manuscript, Princeton University, Department of Anthropology).

13. Abu Yaqub Yusuf Ibn Yahya At-Tadili, *At-Tasawwuf Ila Rijal At-Tasawwuf; vie de saints du sud Morocain des V, VI, VIIIème siècles de l'Hégire. Contribution à l'ètude de l'histoire religieuse du Maroc*, ed. A. Faure (Rabat: Editions Techniques Nord Africaines, 1958). I will refer to this work as *Tasawaf* and cite the number of each saint's biography.

14. *Tasawaf*, no. 160, p. 312; no. 209, p. 397.

15. See *Tasawaf*, no. 240, p. 431; no. 7, p. 70; no. 25, p. 111; and Derminghem, Lalla Mimouna, p. 68; Lalla Aicha, p. 125, Mana Aicha, p. 107.

16. See *Tasawaf*, no. 160, p. 312, no. 209, p. 397; no. 207, p. 394; no. 210, p. 398; no. 167, p. 331.

17. "Ne voulant pas se marier, Imma Tiffelent s'échappa sous forme de colombe et se fit prostituée dans la montagne. . . . Vingt-sept jeunes gens disparurent après l'avoir aimée. Puis elle devint ascète, dans une hutte, au sommet de la montagne . . . déguenillée, hiruste, elle prêche la religion dans la vallée, revint à sa hutte, quitte même ses haillons, vit nue, prophétise. Il est interdit de toucher aux arbres autour de sa tombe, de tuer les oiseaux, de dénicher les oeufs de perdrix." Trumelet, "Blida," and "Saints de l'Islam," as quoted in Derminghem, p. 53.

18. "qui fut aussi savante que belle, resista à Moulay Zidane, mourut vierge, et n'est visitée que par les femmes." Derminghem, p. 49.

19. Jacques Berque, *Structures sociales du Haut Atlas* (Paris: Presses Universitaires de France, 1955), p. 296.

20. Ibid., pp. 281, 286.

21. "Comme elle était parmi les plus belles jeunes filles du village, elle fut recherchée pour le mariage, mais refusa tous les prétendants. La réputation de sainte de la jeune fille en grandit et s'étendit au loin. Le sultan voulut connaître Lalla Aziza et la fit demander à Marrakech. Elle s'y rendit et continua dans la ville à se faire remarquer par sa piété et par le bien qu'elle faisait autour d'elle. Elle fut très

honorée, mais son influence devint tellement grande que le sultan en prit ombrage et Lalla Aziza fut jetée en prison. Elle mourut empoisonnée." Ibid., p. 290.

22. *Tasawaf*, no. 73, p. 186; no. 67, p. 170; no. 13, p. 88; no. 87, p. 217; no. 12, p. 86; no. 59, p. 162.

23. *Tasawaf*, no. 68, p. 76; no. 96, p. 228; no. 33, p. 124.

24. *Tasawaf*, no. 25, p. 111.

25. *Tasawaf*, no. 93, p. 223; no. 63, p. 171; no. 54, p. 156.

26. *Tasawaf*, no. 62, p. 166; no. 132, p. 184.

27. *Tasawaf*, no. 93, p. 224; no. 77, p. 197; no. 162, p. 321.

28. *Tasawaf*, no. 77, p. 200.

29. *Tasawaf*, no. 92, p. 222; no. 51, p. 152; no. 48, p. 144; no. 34, pp. 125–26.

30. *Tasawaf*, no. 99, p. 233; no. 56, p. 158.

31. *Tasawaf*, no. 45, p. 141.

32. *Koran*, Sourate 44, verses 53–54.

33. *Tasawaf*, no. 84, p. 214.

34. Abu Hasan Muslim, *Al-Jami' As-Sahih* (Beirut: Al Maktaba at Tijaria, n.d.), 8:130.

35. *Tasawaf*, no. 94, p. 224.

36. *Tasawaf*, no. 10, p. 79; no. 26, p. 115; no. 96, p. 228.

37. *Tasawaf*, no. 17, p. 95; no. 69, p. 178; no. 6, p. 69.

38. *Tasawaf*, no. 93, p. 223; no. 77, p. 197.

39. V. Loulignac, *Un Saint Berbère—Moulay Bou Azza; Histoire et légende* (Rabat: Hesperis, 1946), 31:29.

40. Jean Chaumel, *Histoire d'une tribu maraboutique de l'Anti-Atlas, le Aît Abdallah ou Said*, vol. 39, ler et 2ème trimestre (Rabat: Hesperes, 1952), p. 206.

41. Derminghem, p. 69.

Further Readings★

Davis, Susan Schaefer. *Patience and Power: Women's Lives in a Moroccan Village.* Cambridge, Mass.: Schenkman Press, 1983.

Fernea, Elizabeth, ed. *Women and the Family in the Middle East: New Voices of Change.* Austin: University of Texas Press, 1985.

Mernissi, Fatima. *Beyond the Veil: Male-Female Dynamics in Modern Muslim Society.* Rev. ed. Bloomington and Indianapolis: Indiana University Press, 1987.

———. *Le Maroc raconté par ses femmes.* Rabat: Société Morocaine Editeurs Réunis, 1984 (translation forthcoming by The Women's Press, London).

———. "Virginity and Patriarchy." *Women and Islam*, ed. by Azizah al-Hibri. Elmsford, N.Y.: Pergamon Press, 1982.

———. "Zhor's World: A Moroccan Domestic Worker Speaks Out. *Feminist Issues* 2, no. 1 (1982): 3–31.

———. "Women and the Impact of Capitalist Development in Morocco." *Feminist Issues* 2, no. 2 (1982): 69–104.

Rassam, Amal. "Women and Domestic Power in Morocco." *International Journal of Middle East Studies* 7, no. 2 (1980): 171–79.

Smith, Jane I. *Women in Contemporary Muslim Societies.* Lewisburg, Pa.: Bucknell University Press, 1980.

★ Selections primarily from a list compiled by Mary Jo Lakeland for the 1987 edition of Dr. Mernissi's book *Beyond the Veil* (Bloomington, Ind.: Indiana University Press).

IV

OUT OF THE SHADOWS

Women in Male-Dominated Systems

Several of the studies included in the preceding sections refer to the special obstacles that women confront when they act within religious or cultural systems that normally justify patterns of male domination. This section gathers together a number of studies that focus especially on these obstacles.

Chapter 12 continues the exploration of ordinary women's religious lives begun in the preceding section but shows how religion can alienate women instead of providing them with an avenue of self-expression and validation. Muslim tribal women of a village in Iran live with traditional and male-defined religious ideals and norms that they cannot possibly hope to meet. They also find little opportunity to participate in public religious life. Their situation invites comparison with that of the urban Iranian women discussed in Chapter 10, who, like them, confront some degree of misogyny and exclusion. But the outcome is different, for the urban women have created an alternative religious life of their own, while the tribal women seem more prone to conclude that religion is "made for men" only. It should be noted that both these situations involve the same Shi'a sect of Islam in Iran. Thus we see that it is quite difficult to make blanket judgments about how a given religion affects the lives and attitudes of women, since much depends on subtle local variations.

The next three chapters are quite different, for they follow the ventures of extraordinary women. Furthermore, from one point of view they may be considered success stories, for the women they study challenge conventional expectations to create a new kind of place in the world for themselves. However, in each case the traditional system eventually reasserts its claims and in one way or another undercuts their achievements.

In the middle of this century, a middle-aged Japanese countrywoman named Sayo Kitamura declared herself the instrument of God, chosen to usher in a new divine age. The "new" religion that she founded still thrives in Japan as well as in a number of other countries. Sayo herself achieved an extraordinary personal liberation through her experiences and career as founder. Nonetheless, the inevitable dilemmas caused by her own teachings as well as by traditional Japanese patterns of religious and managerial leadership seem already to ensure that men will eventually dominate and shape her movement's direction.

Perhaps we should call Empress Wu of classical China a political rather than religious figure, although she appears to have drawn much of her own self-understanding from models provided by Chinese Buddhism. Furthermore, she successfully manipulated the symbolism of two religious systems to validate her brilliant reign as the only woman emperor of China. Despite her success at filling that role, later Chinese historians drew on more conventional norms to condemn her reign as scandalous.

The fourth study assesses the history of the order of Buddhist nuns in India. For more than a thousand years the order provided refuge for Indian women who found the everyday concerns of housewifery and motherhood not their calling. However, by the time of Buddhism's brilliant final centuries in India, it faded to a pale shadow beside the much more prestigious and better-supported order of Buddhist monks.

The final two chapters of this section, returning again to a discussion of ordinary women's ventures, record success stories whose long-range prospects seem more hopeful. These women have reappropriated the traditions for themselves, using the most central values and beliefs of the system to do so. We are most familiar with this process as seen in contemporary Judaism and Christianity, but it is also occurring in other traditions, such as Buddhism and Islam. Our chapter on women in the Sunday school movement shows that such appropriation by women is not confined to the current feminist movement. In nineteenth-century mainstream Protestantism, young women educated themselves for a career of Christian service, thereby finding meaning and autonomy for themselves. By the 1970s, the women's movement was strong in both Judaism and Christianity. Marian Neudel traces the development of an unusually egalitarian Jewish congregation, the Upstairs Minyan of the University of Chicago Hillel Foundation, from 1965 to the present. Women used traditional Jewish values and skills to earn for themselves a place of respect and equality within the congregation.

12

Islam and Tribal Women in a Village in Iran

ERIKA FRIEDL

Religion is said to be less restrictive to Muslim tribal women than it is to Muslim urban women.[1] For example, the harem system was never successfully instituted in nomadic tribal societies, and the necessity for mobility and outdoor work made it unfeasible to seclude women, as is often done in towns. In small rural-tribal communities, especially nomadic camps, which are organized along lines of kinship, the distinctions between stranger and kinsman, outdoors and indoors, and public and private are somewhat artificial and do not influence the organization of the social environment. In these communities, colorfully dressed women go about their work rather freely, often not even veiled. They seem to have considerable influence in all affairs and to hold their places next to the men,[2] despite their lack of prominent political or economic positions. Tribal women are considered immoral in religiously conservative circles, which condemn the social setup that allows women such freedom.

ERIKA FRIEDL holds a Ph.D. from the University of Mainz in West Germany and currently is a Professor of Anthropology at Western Michigan University. For a total of nearly six years out of the past twenty-five, she has lived with a tribe in Iran, studying, among other topics, the status and self-images of women, family-related issues, and popular philosophy. She has published several articles and a book on various aspects of this people's culture.

Author's Note Various stages of the research underlying this chapter were supported by grants from the Wenner Gren Foundation for Anthropological Research, the Social Science Research Council, and Western Michigan University.

These impressions of tribal women's relative freedom have been formed by foreigners and city people, who tend to base their judgments mainly on outward signs of appearance and behavior. However, they are only impressionistically formed stereotypes. To the best of my knowledge, there is no systematic study of women's religious lives in a tribal or rural Shi'ite Muslim community in the Middle East.

Between 1965 and 1976 I conducted a total of four years of anthropological fieldwork in a tribal area in Southwest Iran in the southern range of the Zagros mountains.[3] During my visits I became especially interested in the ways religious knowledge is learned and transmitted, the roles women play in religious rituals, the criteria for judging morally good behavior in men and women, and the relationship between women's self-images and their worldviews. I was able to gather a wealth of information on these topics by participating in numerous and often very intimate informal discussions with women and men, by collecting and analyzing over two hundred proverbs and close to seventy tales and legends,[4] and by observing women's participation in many kinds of religious activity. Drawing on these data, I will describe the religious system in which women of this area operate.

Given that at present we know very little about the various aspects of women in Islam, we have to be careful about drawing generalizations from one particular case. We know that, since many cultural and economic factors are reflected in religious beliefs and practices, we can expect to find a variety of religious systems in different Shi'ite communities. We also know that town women live with different religious frameworks than do villagers, to say nothing of middle-class city women.[5] However, from the first-hand experience I have of other Iranian villages, I would expect that the religious system in which they operate is very similar to the one described here. Only further research can reveal the exact similarities and differences.

The tribal area I studied is inhabited by several Luri-speaking tribes who are Shi'a Muslims. Traditionally they lived on a mixed economy of sheep and goat herding and agriculture. The area is relatively isolated and only recently has been opened to the economic, sociopolitical, and cultural developments of the outside world.[6] The fieldwork for this study was done in the largest village in the area, which has more than 2,700 residents. During the last ten years the village has lost its economic self-sufficiency and is now rapidly being tied into the general Iranian cash-crop and wage-labor economy. Therefore an increasing number of men are away from their families for much of a year, if not for several years. The result of men's intimate and prolonged contact with the outside is a "cultural cleavage" between men and women in the village. Inevitably, men come in contact with many different religious trends in the towns, ranging from the fundamentalist views of pious bazaar merchants to the atheistic Western philosophies of the sophisticated intelligentsia at the universities. In contrast, even educated women in the village cling to more or less uniform patterns of belief and ritual, more from lack of alternatives than by choice. The returning men will eventually have an influence on the religious climate in the village and on their wives' religious views, but this influence cannot yet be discerned.

Islam is a book religion, and reading the Qoran and religious literature is considered indispensable to religious education and knowledge. In the village older and middle-aged women are nearly 100 percent illiterate, while about 20 percent of the younger women have learned to read (schooling for girls has only recently become popular). In all age groups illiteracy is considerably more common for women than for men. Thus, most women are barred from the major source of religious knowledge; even those who can read do not have easy access to religious literature—or to any other, for that matter. Even now, although roads are being built, transportation into the area is cumbersome, and books are not among the things people feel a need to import. Today one sometimes sees a few women listening to their children read religious stories from schoolbooks, but this trend is so recent that its impact on women's religious education cannot yet be ascertained. The written word, so important in a book religion, does not reach women directly.

The *mullah*, or preacher, and participation in mosque-centered religious rituals are women's other possible sources of religious teaching. The village has both a *mullah* and a mosque of its own. The *mullah*, however, gives few sermons and provides no formal religious education for women. In the summer a guest *mullah* may reside in the village for several weeks and offer regular Qoran lessons, but only for boys. The *mullah* has little professional contact with the village women. He views them as uneducated and superstitious and therefore unable to grasp religious knowledge. He regards himself as a theologian rather than as a teacher and missionary, and women benefit the least from his knowledge.

Occasionally, itinerant preachers or snake handlers give a performance in the village, during which they dramatize legends about saints. Gaudy pictures illustrate the high points of their narratives. Most of the spectators are women and children; men usually "don't have time" to watch these displays and would consider it undignified to attend the spectacle. The information women get from these shows is at best not of particular educational value.

The ceremonial side of Islam is also largely closed to village women. Ceremonies in the mosque are attended by only a few women. If asked why this is so, the *mullah* and the more traditional religious men quickly explain that women in general do not pay much attention to religion and that they are not "good Muslims." The women, however, will say that they cannot go to the mosque when they are ritually unclean (for example, during menstruation),

when they have urgent business at home, and when the children are around, because they cannot leave them alone at home and they cannot take them with them to the mosque. If they did, the children would make a lot of noise there and disturb everybody, which would be a sin. Thus, the women explain their neglect of this religious duty with a moral conflict. In fact, however, women are never an integrated part of any mosque ritual. Those who do attend sit in a room adjacent to the main assembly hall, where they cannot see the preacher and often cannot even hear him well. They are never included in the distribution of tea or food in the mosque. Separated from the men, they are tolerated only if they stay within their boundaries, but even there they have no function. They are unseen and never directly addressed. Women draw very little social or religous meaning or satisfaction from participating in mosque services. Thus it is not surprising that they will use any pretext to avoid going there.

In rituals that take place outside, like some ceremonies mourning the death of the Shi'a martyr Husain, women watch, hidden on rooftops behind their veils. Many more women attend these rituals than the prayers at the mosque. Although participating in such rituals in any form, even if only as a compassionate spectator, is considered meritorious, some people question the women's motives for attending. Pious elders accuse the women spectators of man-watching and of enticing youths into sinful displays of virility during the ritual flagellation and chest beating.

During a funeral—another open-air religious ceremony—women function as mourners, crying and singing around the body in the cemetery, while the men dig the grave. As soon as the body is buried and the prayers begin—in other words, as soon as the ceremony takes on a distinctly religious character—the women must leave.

Unlike women in towns, the village women have no religious rituals that are exclusively or specifically for them and no religious gatherings in which they receive instructions or can actively engage in a communal religious activity. Therefore, they have no means to complement the men's ritual activities from which they are almost completely excluded. It is not surprising that, when women discuss their access to religious knowledge and to rituals, they often emphatically declare that religion was "made for men" and not for women.

There are however a few religious activities in which women can and do act independently. These activities relate to the use of powers thought to be inherent in plants and minerals, as well as special prayers and rituals to overcome problems such as the sickness of a child or economic hardship. Since most of these rituals are private, occur locally, and entail minimal expense, women are relatively free to act according to their own knowledge and judgment. Because women are more exposed to the nitty-gritty of everyday life than are men, they are more involved than men in the use of religion (or magic) to alleviate these hardships. It is mostly women who resort to such devices as fumigating against the evil eye, having a powerful prayer written in an amulet to cure a headache, or preparing a string of amulets for a newborn baby against the influences of bad spirits. But this involvement is greater only in quantity, not in quality.

For the same purpose, women also make vows and go on pilgrimages. Vows are usually made to specific saints. They consist of a promise to make a pilgrimage to a saint's shrine and/ or to give a certain amount of money or goods to a saint asking for the saint's help in exchange. Saints, both male and female, are said to be favored by God. Out of pity, kindness, and compassion, they can use their privileged position to influence God to help human beings in distress. Although they serve as intermediaries between God and humans anywhere and at any time, it is especially effective to invoke their help at their shrines. The small shrines scattered throughout the tribal area are popular among local people. But the big, famous shrines of the most powerful saints—the ones that attract pilgrims from all over the country—are in the cities. A visit to one of them requires special efforts and major expenses for a villager.

I have heard women state that they can make vows to saints without consulting their husbands and that a husband must honor the vow of his wife by giving her the means to fulfill it. Actually, however, most women are very careful not to overstep their husbands' means when they make vows and not to pledge something they know their husbands will not agree to. In the case of a vow that would involve major expenses, such as a pilgrimage to a major shrine, a village woman will request or suggest to her husband that he make it in her behalf. This approach is meant to avoid any potential conflict with him. However, the strategy doesn't always work. For example, one woman in the village wanted her husband to offer a goat as a sacrifice to a saint to strengthen her plea that her fractured leg should heal better. The husband was reluctant to give up a goat, because it had been a bad winter and spring for his herd. When her leg got worse, the woman complained bitterly about her husband's reluctance, but she could not change his mind and did not dare to dispose of a goat herself.

When making vows and pilgrimages to the saints' shrines, a woman feels equal to a man. Her ability to communicate with the saints, to evoke their pity, and to elicit their help is the same as a man's. Among all the saints, certain female saints are considered to be especially open to women's problems, because they have insights into women's difficulties that no man, however sympathetic, could have. Many women have a deep emotional attachment to these saints. They invoke their names in times of distress, make vows to them, promise pilgrimages to their shrines in return for help, and tell many legends about them.

Most religious education for villagers—men and women—is informal, unspecific, and, unlike informal education in other areas such as housekeeping or plowing, largely nondirected. Children learn about religion just as they learn proverbs or songs. Even before they know the text of a prayer, they will imitate the adults' prayer gestures and ablutions. These are the only formal religious rituals a girl will ever perform. Children learn some basic religious concepts, like the names and functions of saints, from the adults' frequent exclamations and admonitions. They learn that God will punish them if they are lazy, disrespectful, or disobedient; they learn that certain things are sinful and therefore "bad," while others have religious merit and thus will help one be admitted to paradise after the Day of Judgment. The information the children get this way is sketchy, diffuse, and often contradictory. Furthermore, it is not backed up effectively by the actual behavior of their elders, which often conflicts with their pious statements.

Very little theology is taught to the children, either formally or informally, since the emphasis is on morality and not on theology. The format is the same for boys and girls, but the religious messages conveyed in the moral code are quite different for the two sexes. For men, good conduct is defined quite generally, and the commands are few and dramatic: above all, a man has to care for his dependents; he must avoid murder, theft, and lies; he may not commit adultery, he is required to be charitable and hospitable; and he must fast and perform the required rituals. Some commandments are more important than others, and offenses against a less important commandment can be justified if they are deemed necessary in order to fulfull a more important one. Thus, it may be argued that a lie said to safeguard one's family's interests will be pardoned as a kind of "necessary" lie. An urgent agricultural task is sufficient reason for not saying the prayers. The evil of stinginess is offset if a man is actually saving for his son's education. For major crimes, like robbery or murder, the claim of coercion is used to justify oneself. Thus, a man may argue that he was ordered to commit a major crime, that he had no choice but to

comply, and that therefore he has to be excused. Adultery, which is very rare, is not pardonable by any of the above arguments. However, it is blamed on the permissive or provocative behavior of the woman involved and therefore considered much more of a sin for her than for the man.

For a woman the boundaries of good behavior are narrower, and the moral code is more specific than for a man. Obedience to her husband and submission to the authority of men are absolutely essential. Taking care of her children and husband competently and industriously, behaving modestly, being peaceful and kind, minding her own business, not gossiping, and not giving others any reason for gossiping about her are the next most important commandments for a woman. Saying her prayers and performing the ritual ablutions and fasts are last on the list. Theft and murder are not considered typical crimes of women and are of little relevance in the women's moral code. Unlike men, women are not usually allowed excuses for failure. There is, for example, no valid excuse for disobeying a husband, for fighting with a neighbor, or for any of the other "typical" female sins.

For a woman, relating properly to her husband, family, and neighbors is of prime importance. Here the ideal standard is very high. The following legend I heard in the village describes quite dramatically a wife's correct attitude toward her husband.

One day the Prophet Mohammad sent his daughter Fatme to visit a woman who, he said, was the best wife in town. Fatme went there but was not admitted by the woman, because her husband was not at home. The woman asked Fatme to come back the next day so that she could first ask her husband for permission to receive Fatme as a visitor. Next day Fatme went there again, this time taking her little son with her; the woman refused to admit her because she had been given permission to receive Fatme but not her son. This happened again the next day, because Fatme took both her sons with her rather than only the one whom the woman now had permission to admit. Finally, on the fourth day, Fatme was let in. She found the woman sitting in the courtyard near the door with her skirts gathered strangely, a stick next to her, a cup of water standing in the sun, and some hard, dry bread in her lap. Asked for an explanation, the woman said that she drank only tepid water and ate only hard bread because her husband, a shepherd, had nothing better to eat either; she had a stick ready in case her husband found something wrong and wanted to beat her when he came home; and she gathered her skirts to be ready in case her husband was overcome by desire when he saw her.

Obedience, compassion, and total subordination, the legend suggests, are the most noble virtues in a wife. Measured against these standards, women in the village find themselves sadly lacking the correct attitudes, especially total subordination. Although women actually do attend to their husbands like servants in their homes, they nevertheless often act on their own judgment, speak their minds freely, and disagree with their husbands to the point of open quarrel. They are, in short, "bad wives" when judged strictly by these ideal standards.

Men and women expect the same worldly results from good or bad behavior. A blameless life does not necessarily lead to health and prosperity, just as evildoing does not necessarily lead to immediate hardships. Men's and women's expectations about the afterlife, however, are substantially different. For men, promises of reward are specific and detailed. From the fragrance of heavenly flowers to the shining faces of the *huris* (sort of angelic fairies), from the refreshing gurgling of clean springs to the taste of delicious fruits and the sweet sounds of music, men can describe their eternal pleasures very concretely. For women, the same paradise is rather vague and general. They will "see the angels" and "never be hungry" or simply "have no more worries." Although theoretically the fruits and fragrances should be the same for men and women, neither men nor women describe paradise as the same for both. For example, women will have no counterpart for the beautiful *huris* men will enjoy. A woman will not even be together with her husband. "What would a man want his wife for," one woman declared, "when he has all the *huris* to play with?" Men and women are not at all sure what women can expect from paradise beyond leisure and a general bliss.

On the other hand, punishment in the afterlife for wrongdoing on earth is described in general terms for men ("He will go to hell," "He will burn in the fire," "He will have great pains") but is very specific for women. A woman who nursed another woman's baby without her husband's consent will be hung up on a hook by her breasts; a woman who gossiped will have her tongue pierced with a hot iron rod; her ears will be cut to tiny pieces for eavesdropping, and so on.[7]

As we have already seen, legends, as well as religious stories and folktales, are important sources of religious and moral knowledge for both women and men. Although their purpose might be simple entertainment, such tales always convey information about the prevailing moral code and what is expected of people. Most of them present a negative image of women: women are bad wives, evil forces, antagonists of the hero, or just ridiculous figures.[8] Through these tales women learn that they are unimportant, foolish, or threatening to men. This little story about Adam and Eve, told by an elderly man to a largely female audience, is a good example.

One day Eve was sulking (as women always do, the narrator remarked). God had pity on the lonely and neglected Adam and opened the door to paradise just a little bit, enough for Adam to take a good look at the beautiful *huris* inside. Eve—nosy like all women—risked a glance too. What she saw made her run back to Adam immediately, falling all over herself to be at his service. With this little trick God had shown Adam how to make a stubborn wife pliable.

Women, as well as men, hear these stories and accept the implications that women are "weak" in a physical, intellectual, and moral sense and that they are more prone than men to commit sins. When asked, for example, how many women there are in paradise in relation to men, one woman went so far as to say that she thought there were no women in heaven or perhaps just a few female saints. She added that this was God's will, otherwise He would have arranged things so that women wouldn't be ritually impure so often and wouldn't have bad, sinful characters. "When we are young," another woman said, "we cannot help being unclean all the time from menstruation, childbirth, and the babies who soil us. When we are old, it is easier to keep [ritually] clean; but the older a woman gets, the worse her character becomes. So what can we do?"

For the people of the village being a "true believer" is largely a matter of satisfactory conduct. Believing in Islamic dogma and performing rituals but not exhibiting proper moral or ethical behavior would mean, in the critical eyes of the villagers, that one is a heathen or an infidel—not a Muslim. The local people use such charges generously in their judgments of fellow villagers. Given the strictures of the women's moral code and the demands of everyday interaction with family and neighbors, women are especially open to these charges. A man irrigating his fields alone all day long will hardly meet with opportunities to sin; his wife at home will be challenged to gossip, hit a misbehaving child, quarrel with a neighbor, neglect a crying baby, forget to feed the chickens, or do something against her husband's will. These are all sinful actions. Because women are believed to easily succumb to the lures of evil anyway, the fact that they have many opportunities to commit sin in the course of a day makes their "sinning" unavoidable. Therefore, the women in the village regard themselves, and are regarded by others, as bad Muslims and even as "heathen."

The moral code states that it is not "good" to quarrel or gossip. Yet it is believed that it is women's nature to gossip and quarrel. Therefore women feel that there is not much point in trying to refrain from gossiping or quarreling, because it is in the very nature of things that they be quarrelsome. The fact that women often are actually bad tempered is taken as proof of their innate inclination toward shrewishness—a vicious circle of expectation and fulfillment.

Just as quarreling is a sin typical of women, so is suicide. And just as the label "sin" is not a deterrent to bitchiness, so it is not a deterrent to suicide attempts either. Presently there are about four suicide attempts per year in the village, all by women. These attempts take place within the framework of the village's moral and religious code. Women who do attempt suicide are not irreligious, nor would they deny that committing suicide is a sin. But villagers assume that it is part of women's inferior nature to be ignorant and weak and thus prone to do foolish things, like committing suicide. Nevertheless, such behavior is regarded as sinful, and a woman who attempts suicide is scolded by everybody, including the doctor. She gets no sympathy from anyone, although most women will understand her situation very well, and some will even concede that, given her circumstances, she really had "no choice."

One informant told me that a woman's weak character is as unalterable as man's inability to fly or as man's need to worry about clothing although none of God's other creatures need to do so. Like other problematic conditions in this world, a woman's disposition cannot be changed much and has to be accepted. For women, then, free will and choice are almost nonexistent, and even religion cannot provide an effective incentive for choosing certain morally good behaviors, since religion also teaches that these behaviors contradict women's nature.

Despite their predicament, however, women are not pardoned by God or man for any improper behavior caused by their weak and inferior character. A gossipy woman, for example, is considered "bad" in a moral sense by both women and men, and she is expected to be punished for her shortcoming either in this world or in the next. No form of a woman's bad behavior is ever excused because of the generally inferior stuff women are made of. It is only explained by it. How is it that women are made of such inferior material? The legend of Noah's daughter explains it.

When Noah got the order to build an ark, he could not find anybody to help him in this unusual task. So he promised his only daughter to three different craftsmen in exchange for their help. After the ark was built, each of the three men wanted the promised bride, and Noah was in serious trouble, since he had only one daughter. In his despair, he implored God to help him—after all it had been His command that got him into trouble—and God told Noah to lock the girl in a room overnight together with a dog and a donkey. This was a strange request indeed, because both these animals are looked down upon, and a dog is considered ritually impure. Ordinarily neither animal would be let into a house. Nevertheless Noah obeyed, and in the morning the donkey and the dog had turned into exact replicas of his daughter. Thus he could satisfy his three craftsmen. But the girl who had been a dog was very bitchy and the one who had been a donkey was a stupid ass; only Noah's own daughter was a good woman. The moral of the story is that all women are descendants of these three and retain the basic characters of their respective ancestresses. This explains why most women are either loose and bitchy like dogs or stupid and stubborn like donkeys and why only a few are decent.

Here, then, lies an obvious and very great conflict for every woman of the village; she is part of a religious universe that centers around men. She is largely excluded from their religious rituals, although participation in them is highly meritorious. She is considered inferior by nature and prone to sin; yet she is also held fullly responsible for the moral offenses that she will inevitably commit.

Every woman I talked with found it hard to come to terms with these conflicts, even when she could not articulate the problem in abstract terms. In their attempts to deal with such dilemmas, these women construct an astounding variety of individual philosophies and worldviews. Through these personal views they try to clarify for themselves, with more or less satisfactory results, their own position within their religion. These views range from simple resignation to their alleged spiritual and physical inadequacy, usually coupled with hopes for the mercy of God, to forthright denial of the validity of the present order.

This denial was expressed, for example, by an illiterate and rather poor woman with an amazingly assertive personality. Although deeply religious and unusually knowledgeable in religious matters, she declared very firmly to me that she thought that religion, as preached and practiced, was not made by God but by men in order to suppress women! God himself had meant men and women to be equal, she said, but, if taken seriously, this would mean the end of the men's superiority. Therefore men do not follow His command. Equally extreme, but more frequent, is a zealous, exaggerated version of the view held by the most orthodox men—namely, that women are the evil of the world and will congregate in hell, where they belong, leaving paradise to men. Other women look at the world from a quasiexistentialist point of view. They see their basic situation as senseless and often cruel but unavoidable. Every person must carry his or her own burden as best as he or she can, with no assurance that these efforts will ever be adequately compensated for in this or any other life. The most common attitude is a helpless and, at the same time, skeptical and grudging resignation to the status quo. Women who have this attitude feel that maybe not everything they hear has to be taken at face value. However, they feel that uneducated as they are, they are in no position to decide what is true and what is false. For this reason and because they have no authority, women must go along with the rules they are given.

There are no atheistic women in the village. Therefore God, although generally perceived as far away and aloof, is recognized by all as the ultimate and final judge of one's conduct. He alone is fully able to evaluate and understand a person's situation, and only He has the power to condemn and to pardon. Between the remote God and humans, however, stand the saints, who are more accessible and ready to intercede on one's behalf when matters in this life become unbearable. They can be invoked at any time, by anyone, and the women, whose resources in this life are especially limited, recognize them as their only recourse when they are in need of help. Although a plea to a saint guarantees nothing, at least it enables women to find temporary relief and consolation in times of distress.

Notes

1. See, for example, Raphael Patai, *Golden River to Golden Road: Society, Culture and Change in the Middle East* (Philadelphia: University of Pennsylvania Press, 1962), p. 120.
2. As described, for example, in Lois Grant Beck's paper "Theoretical Perspectives on the Position of Women in Iran," presented at the 7th annual meeting of the Middle East Association, 1974.
3. In 1965, 1969–71, and 1976.
4. Erika Friedl, "Tales from a Persian Tribe"; unpublished manuscript.
5. See Anne H. Betteridge, "The Controversial Vows of Urban Women in Iran," in this volume.
6. Reinhold Loeffler, "Recent Economic Changes in Boir Ahmad: Regional Growth without Development," *Iranian Studies*, 9, no. 4 (1976).
7. See also Jane Smith and Yvonne Y. Haddad, "Women in the Afterlife: The Islamic View as Seen from Qur'ān and Tradition," *Journal of the American Academy of Religion*, 43, no. 1 (1975).
8. Erika Friedl, "Women in Contemporary Persian Folktales," in *Women in the Muslim World*, Lois Beck and Nikki Keddie, eds. (Cambridge, Mass.: Harvard University Press, 1978).

Further Readings

Aït Sabbah, Fatna A. *Woman in the Muslim Unconscious*. New York: Pergamon Press, 1984.

Betteridge, Ann. *Ziärat: Pilgrimage to the Shrines of Shiraz*. Ph.D. dissertation, University of Chicago, 1985.

Friedl, Erika. "Division of Labor in an Iranian Village." *MERIP Reports*, no. 95 (March–April 1981): 12–18, 31.

———. "State Ideology and Village Women." *Women and Revolution in Iran*, ed. by Guity Nashat, 217–30. Boulder, Colo.: Westview Press, 1983.

———. "Parents and Children in a Village in Iran." *Women and the Family in Iran*, ed. by Asghar Fathi, 195–211. Leiden, Netherlands: E. J. Brill, 1985.

———. "Women in Contemporary Persian Folk Tales." *Women in the Muslim World*, ed. by Lois Beck and Nikki Keddie, 629–50. Cambridge, Mass.: Harvard University Press, 1978.

Hegland, Mary Elaine. "Political Roles of Iranian Village Women." *MERIP, Middle East Report*, no. 138, vol. 16, no. 1 (January–February 1968): 14–19, 46.

Higgins, Patricia J. "Women in the Islamic Republic of Iran: Legal, Social, and Ideological Changes." *Signs* 10, no. 3 (Spring 1985): 477–94.

Sara-Isfani, Kaveh. "Female-Centered World Views in Iranian Culture: Symbolic Representations of Sexuality in Dramatic Games." *Signs* 6, no. 1 (Autumn 1980) 33–53.

Tabari, Azar and Nahid Yeganeh, eds. *In the Shadow of Islam: The Women's Movement in Iran*. London: Zed Press, 1983.

13

No Women's Liberation: The Heritage of a Woman Prophet in Modern Japan

KYOKO MOTOMOCHI NAKAMURA

One striking feature of nineteenth- and twentieth-century Japan has been the emergence of many so-called new religions.[1] Crystallizing around the revelatory experiences of a central prophetic figure, they usually reinterpret and recombine older elements of the Japanese religious heritage. Much research has been done on various aspects of these movements, but little attention has thus far been paid to one of the movements' most remarkable features—namely, the very prominent role of women within them. Women have founded many of the new religions, and, according to Japanese tradition, it is generally expected that the founder's offspring, daughters as well as sons, will inherit the sect's leadership. This pattern might seem to suggest some sort of female dominance in the Japanese new religions.[2] However, the situation is much more complex, and, while it is indeed true that the new movements are often founded by women, the pattern of strong female leadership does not continue once the movements have been established. Nor do the new religions advocate dramatic changes in sex roles or power relationships between women and men.

In this chapter I will discuss the life and teachings of Sayo Kitamura, founder of the movement known as Tensho-kotai-jingu-kyo,

DR. KYOKO MOTOMOCHI NAKAMURA is Professor of History of Religions at Kawamura Gakuen Women's College in Japan. She holds M.A. degrees from both the University of Chicago (1962) and Tokyo University (1964) and has been a teaching assistant at Harvard and a Radcliffe Institute Fellow (1968–1970). She has published many articles and translations in Japanese and one book in English: *Miraculous Stories from the Japanese Buddhist Tradition* (Harvard University Press in 1973).

as well as important problems that her successor faces.[3] I hope to show some of the circumstances that have shaped women founders like Sayo and also some of the reasons why movements like hers revert so swiftly to patterns of male dominance.

SAYO KITAMURA, PROPHET OF TABUSE

Sayo was born on New Year's Day of the year 1900, exactly at the turn of the twentieth century, in the Ekimoto family of the village of Hizumi, in the Yamaguchi prefecture of western Japan. She had six years of education at a local primary school and took three years of lessons in sewing and handicrafts, as was the custom with most country girls of her day.

In 1920 Sayo married Seinoshin Kitamura (1884–1969), who lived with his mother in the village of Tabuse, not far from Sayo's home village. Seinoshin, with ten years' experience as an expatriate laborer in Hawaii, was an obedient son to his mother. The mother was notorious as a harsh taskmaster; she had already turned out five of her son's brides on the grounds that they were not good enough to be her daughter-in-law. In those days a bride had few legal rights; she was at the mercy of her husband and mother-in-law, and, once married, she had to obey them in any situation. Sayo, who was treated like a laborer, farmed many acres of land. She was given neither adequate food nor enough sleep. However, she survived the trial and served her mother-in-law until her death twenty years later. In the meantime Sayo gave birth to her only son, named Yoshito, and became a devoted mother. When her mother-in-law died in 1940, it was not her husband but Sayo who assumed financial responsibility for the family and began to manage the household.

The turning point in Sayo's life came when she experienced a catastrophe. The Kitamuras' barn was destroyed by fire on the night of July 22, 1942. This fire weighed heavily on Sayo's conscience; she viewed it not merely as a loss of personal property but as her personal failure in managing the household. She felt sorry for both the family ancestors and her son, who had been serving in Manchuria as an army veterinarian. At that time she became acquainted with an ascetic diviner in a nearby village, who received an oracle that attributed the fire to an arsonist. He urged Sayo to pay a monthly visit to the local Hachiman shrine for a year, but, instead of following his suggestion, Sayo vowed that she would make an ox-hour (2 A.M.) prayer for twenty-one days in succession. Each night she underwent the austerity of cold-water ablutions,[4] rode a bicycle to the shrine to pray, and stopped at the diviner's shrine on her way back. Because she began to feel an indescribable joy in these midnight devotions, she extended her disciplinary practices for thirty more days after the original vow had been fulfilled. Then she extended them again, disciplining herself in this way until the first anniversary of the fire. She had still, however, failed to discover the fire's real cause. After the diviner told her that her prayers had not fully reached God, she observed a continuous vigil for two weeks at the shrine.

From this time on, Sayo had a series of religious experiences that culminated on May 4, 1944, with her first experience of direct revelation. Now a strange One possessed her body and began to speak with her. Because she initially thought that it was an evil spirit, she sought the diviner's help to free herself. But she never succeeded. The possessing spirit first identified itself as "Tobyo" (a snake spirit in Japanese folk belief), then as "Controller of the Mouth," then as "Guardian Deity," and finally as "Tensho-kotai-jingu,"[5] whom she finally identified as the universal God. According to Sayo, Tensho-kotai-jingu had revealed himself through her as the God of the whole universe who demands complete surrender to his will; before her birth he had chosen Sayo as his temporary abode.

Under this influence, Sayo was transformed from a polite, modest, humble woman into a severe, critical, daring person. She began to offend old friends and relatives, as well as strangers, by reproaching them for injustice, dishonesty, and lack of faith. Sayo delivered her first sermon on July 22, 1944, exactly two years after the fire at her home. She declared herself to be the savior and redeemer of humanity and announced that the Kingdom of God was being established here and now. According to her, World War II was God's punishment inflicted on the corrupt Japanese; she condemned her countrymen for their lack of faith and for the corrupt morality that was especially conspicuous during the last stages of the war. Her words indicated that she saw herself as the chief actress in a divine drama whose curtain had already risen.

Tensho-kotai-jingu had descended into her body on November 27, 1944; on the night of August 11, 1945, at the end of the war, she experienced her adoption as heir to the Divine Couple of Tensho-kotai-jingu and Amaterasu-omikami, the female divinity of the sun who is one of the most important figures in traditional Japanese religion.

Seinoshin Kitamura had been a respectful son to his mother and a rather fastidious husband to his wife. Seventeen years older than his wife, he worked diligently, neither drinking nor smoking. But Sayo excelled him, even in farming or driving a cow. The Kitamuras had traditionally been Shin Buddhists. Every morning Seinoshin recited Shinto prayers in front of a family sanctuary, while Sayo recited the Shin Buddhist formula *Namu-Amida-butsu* ("I take refuge in Amida Buddha") to Amida Buddha and the Kitamura family ancestors. She reported all family affairs to the ancestors, including her own whereabouts. When the fire broke out in the Kitamura barn, she carried the ancestors' tablets outdoors to protect them in case the house, too, should catch fire.

On the morning of May 4, 1944, after Sayo heard the Inner One speak, her family life was dramatically altered. While praying, she was led to her husband's bedside. She kicked away his pillow, saying, "Listen, Seinoshin. Osayo's prayers have reached heaven as a result of her devotional sincerity. . . . How dare you sleep comfortably without praying? Get up and pray!"[6]

The good-hearted husband was greatly shocked at this sudden change in the wife who had served him so obediently all those years. From this time on, Sayo treated her husband as her follower. She addressed him by his first name, "Seinoshin" (which is not customary for a Japanese wife), instead of the more familiar "Daddy" that she had used for many years. However, although she no longer seemed to be a wife to her husband, she never abandoned her maternal love for their only son. She explained this apparent contradiction by saying that, when her son returned home from Manchuria, God had told her to say, "I have no parents nor any family ties," but he never asked her to say, "I have no son."[7]

Sayo herself had a great deal to say about appropriate family roles, both in her teaching and by the example of her life. Answering a question about the essence of her teaching, she once said, "Practical application of my teaching in your daily life is the way of advancing along the road to heaven. Home and society are the places where you should put my teaching into practice."[8] In other words, people come closer to God by fulfilling traditional human roles. The founder herself had tried her best to be a trustworthy wife and daughter-in-law, an affectionate mother, and later a mother-in-law and grandmother. At the same time, Sayo considered herself to be a prophet in the line of Sakyamuni Buddha and Jesus Christ. However, Sakyamuni and Jesus had left their families to fulfill their missions, while Sayo continued as head of the Kitamura family—a difference that was important to her whole message. Furthermore, since she refused to accept any remuneration for her teaching, she had to make a living by farming. She thus combined the roles of prophet and matriarch in her daily life. In the beginning this fact confused her family not a little, particularly her son, Yoshito, who had joined her followers and helped her manage the organization.

Sayo once prophesied that her teachings would be transmitted without much distortion as long as her son and grandchildren lived with cherished memories of her. Just as she believed that the home was the place where her teachings must be applied first, so, with this remark, she identified her own descendants as the best-qualified transmitters of her teachings.

As was the case with all of Sayo's words and actions, the choice of Sayo's successor was dictated by God. When her son's first child was about to be born, God told her that it would be a boyish girl or a girlish boy. They must name it Kiyokazu ("Pure and Peaceful"), which in Japan would ordinarily be a boy's name. Thus the baby was destined to become her successor before its birth. As the child's birth was being celebrated, Sayo publicly proclaimed that the little girl Kiyokazu would be her spiritual heir. She also asked for her congregation's help: "I shall raise this child myself, and it is God's will that she be my successor. I shall appreciate it very much if you, comrades, will help me bring her up properly. Please bear it in mind that she must not be spoiled, because she is to be my successor." Reportedly, the whole congregation was struck with a sense of joy and responsibility for the child. After the baby was forty-seven days old, Sayo began taking Kiyokazu with her to the prayer hall three times a day. When the child began to toddle, the founder would make her perform an "ego-free" dance in the hall following the afternoon prayer ("ego-free" dances will be discussed later in this chapter). Sayo took her granddaughter wherever she went, so that she could use every opportunity to prepare the child for her divine mission.

In a sermon on Kiyokazu's seventh birthday, Sayo said that she had trained her daughter-in-law and her granddaughter harder than anyone else, for the former was to be mother to the latter, who was to be God's instrument. Sayo contended that children of God are needed to establish the Kingdom of God and that worthy parents are needed to raise such children. Accordingly, she taught that the mother's responsibility is heavier than the father's, for the mother's influence on children is often stronger than the father's. The founder impressed not only her daughter-in-law and Kiyokazu but also her other grandchildren with her strict and yet loving discipline.

As the child matured, Sayo continued to supervise her training, even sending Kiyokazu for four years of study in England and the United States.[9] When Sayo felt that her last days were approaching, she also sent her son and daughter-in-law on a world tour to visit the foreign branches she had founded, in order to deepen mutual understanding. In this way the transition from the founder to her successor would not be a sudden change but an anticipated procedure in which Sayo's followers had participated. However, no matter how carefully Sayo had prepared for the change, the loss of her charisma was to be deeply felt. After becoming Sayo's successor, Kiyokazu has courageously led the movement herself, supported by her father, who manages the organization with its many spiritual, economic, political, administrative, and artistic functions. The two have so far tried to keep the founder's spirit alive in their community. Even younger members who have joined the movement after the founder's death are familiar with Sayo's taped sermons, played daily during prayer meetings at the headquarters and branches. Sayo's biography and teachings have also been edited and printed for circulation.

However, in spite of her successor's efforts and her faithful followers, the movement is confronted with the problem of trying to convert people without recourse to Sayo's striking psychic powers. Sayo herself placed little emphasis on healing or on the promise of worldly benefits; she stressed primarily the need for spiritual revolution to realize the Kingdom of God. But her followers' accounts of their conversion experiences reveal other sources of attraction, such as awe at her prophetic powers and experiences of healing as a result of her ardent prayers. Theoretically, her followers, too, can attain such powers through praying. But her powers seem to have had a different quality, for she was God's heir.

DOCTRINAL TEACHINGS OF SAYO'S MOVEMENT

Sayo insisted on the imminent need to establish the Kingdom of God on earth, a spiritual community of the faithful. By establishing such a Kingdom of God on earth, people would become free of all evil and would be able to achieve world peace through individual purification. Only those who were converted and lived a God-centered life might join the community as comrades. Those who did not were called "beggars" and "maggots," strong pejoratives that Sayo liked to use.

Several themes predominate in Sayo's sermons on the nature of the Kingdom of God and the means for establishing it on earth. One of the more important seems to be a new interpretation of traditional Japanese beliefs and rituals regarding the souls of the dead. In Japanese folk belief the souls of the dead are transformed into benevolent ancestral spirits through a series of rites—funeral and memorial services—mostly performed by Buddhist priests and bereaved families.[10] According to Sayo, today's world is afflicted with untransformed spirits who instigate quarrels among individuals, cause nations to war, inflict sickness on people, and arouse anxieties. By praying, she and her followers sought to redeem these destructive spirits. In effect, she taught

an internalization of traditional practice. She rejected all the old rites as degenerate and ineffective, because she felt that both Buddhist and Shinto priests were incapable of communicating with the psychic world. Instead, she insisted that faith in God, prayer to God, and a God-centered everyday life were the only means of gaining the power to communicate with the psychic world and thus to redeem the malevolent spirits of the dead.[11]

However, prayer to God and a God-centered life had, in Sayo's teachings, a far broader purpose than the transformation of the dead, for they were also seen as instruments of self-transformation. Like the Buddhist tradition from which she often drew, Sayo consistently emphasized the importance of overcoming egotism. The achievement of such a state was the reason for the ecstatic "ego-free" dancing revealed to Sayo through a vision, which had initially led mass media to label her movement "The Dancing Religion." As another avenue to the conquest of egotism, she enjoined her followers to "polish their souls." This central disciplinary practice combined resolute will, sincere prayer, constant self-reflection, and confession. Sayo stressed that her followers' loud and energetic prayers required faith, for without faith such prayers were just egotistic supplications. And, Sayo insisted, resolute prayer based on faith would bring the followers—as it had brought herself—to union with God.

At first glance, Sayo's movement appears to be new and unique among Japanese religions for its radical theocentrism and its rejection of all other beliefs and practices. On February 5, 1946, the first day of Sayo's new "Age of God," the founder burned Buddhist *sutras*, religious amulets, and the Kitamura family's ancestral records to symbolize her break with the past and its corruption. She ordered her followers to throw away their ancestors' tablets, to break off with the Buddhist temples whose cemeteries held their family tombs, and to refuse to join Shinto rites. It is not hard to imagine how much this iconoclastic action disturbed the local Buddhist monks and Shinto priests. As a consequence, Sayo's followers had a hard time living in local communities, where close human relationships governed all spheres of social and economic life.

Despite their emphasis on radical change, Sayo's teachings also preserve much traditional content. First of all, both her understanding of history and her own historical role are based on traditional Japanese ideas, especially the concept that time passes in repetitive cycles, returning again to the same point. A cycle of world history consists of four world ages; the present cycle (as well as the first age) began when the mythological first emperor of Japan, Jimmu, was enthroned. The age begun by Jimmu, which she called the "Age of Man," lasted for 2,605 years, until 1945, when World War II ended. We are now in the second age, the Age of God, or the Age of the Sun, which began on New Year's Day in 1946 and, Sayo has predicted, will last for 2,300 years. At the end of the Age of God there will be an Age of the Moon, which is to last for 1,999 years; then will come the Age of the Stars, which will last for another 1,526 years. The cycle ends in a phase that she called the "Waters." Each age is ushered in by the descent of God's heir— either male, as in the case of the Emperor Jimmu, or female, as in the case of Sayo—and ends in destruction and calamity. Just as Sayo was adopted by God to establish his Kingdom and save the nation, so, when the Age of God ends, she will be reborn as a fisherman's daughter to save the nation again.

As one can see from the preceding summary, much of Sayo's teaching was grounded in traditional and familiar Japanese Shinto mythology, and her view of history did not go beyond Japan and the Japanese nation. Also, she dwelt frequently on the well-known theme of the golden age of the Kami that starts at the beginning of Japanese mythical history. Apparently she identified the Age of God she was proclaiming with that first golden age.

Even the striking theocentrism and universalism of her teachings are more similar to traditional Japanese ideas than they at first seem to be. This can be seen quite clearly in the following literal translation of her most significant prayer.

> Tensho-kotai-jingu and eight million kami,
> May there be peace in the whole world.
> When all the nation complies with God's will,
> Give us a Heavenly Kingdom which is pleasant to live in.
> May the six functional elements in my soul be purified.
> The six functional elements in my soul are now purified;
> Since the six functional elements have been purified,
> It cannot be that this prayer will not be fulfilled.

This is my own translation, which differs from the English version authorized for use by the branches of her movement in the West. The authorized version begins with the line "Almighty God of the Universe and host of angels . . ." In this authorized translation we are impressed by Sayo's cosmopolitanism—an inclusive emphasis on which the founder herself insisted. However, in the Japanese original, both the opening phrase and Sayo's use of the term "nation" (*kokumin*) also communicate some nationalistic Shinto overtones. According to her successor's interpretation of Sayo's teachings, Japanese myths have nothing to do with modern nationalism; they are simply the ancestors' gift to the people.

But Sayo herself preserved a kind of balance between universalism and nationalism. She once asserted that the Japanese national polity (*kokutai*)[12] had never been changed after the end of the war. She interpreted this polity as a trinitarian unity of the Japanese land, the deity Tensho-kotai-jingu, and the emperor, who watches the country. The deity Tensho-kotai-jingu had revealed himself through her, Sayo, as the Universal God; she also calls him

"Heavenly Father," a title rather unfamiliar to the Japanese religious tradition. But concepts of this same deity are imbedded in traditional Japanese mythology. He was revealed to Sayo as consort to Amaterasu, the Sun Goddess and ancestress of the imperial family as well as the Japanese nation. Furthermore, in Sayo's teachings the universal God was not really viewed as fully transcendent; instead, Sayo perpetuated the traditional Japanese view of an immanent and personified God, thus retaining striking continuity with traditional Japanese mythology.

WOMANHOOD IN SAYO'S EXPERIENCE AND TEACHINGS

Different facets of Sayo's experiences and actions show different responses to her own femininity. When the goddess Amaterasu descended into Sayo's body to join her consort Tensho-kotai-jingu, the "Inner One," the two united as one God, making Sayo's body a temple for both male and female divinity. Thus, in a sense, she transcended her old female human nature and became androgynous. Sometimes she seemed to cultivate and emphasize deliberately a new, more "masculine" style, in contradiction to Japanese norms of "feminine" virtue. For example, Sayo sometimes sat cross-legged, a position few Japanese women dare to assume but that men often take when relaxed. After reversing her relationship with her husband in the pillow-kicking incident described earlier, Sayo began to wear masculine clothing, and a black pantsuit became her standard uniform several years later. Her speech and behavior became more aggressive. She started to call people "maggots" and "beggars," two strong epithets that not even men dared to utter; and she shocked her audiences with her fiery speeches, in a country where men and

women ordinarily speak quite differently and where women are expected to avoid impolite expressions.

At the same time, some of Sayo's statements and experiences show that her femininity remained part of her consciousness both during and after her transformative experiences. Between the descent of Tensho-kotai-jingu, her "Inner One," and the later descent of Amaterasu, Sayo underwent a rapid process of spiritual rebirth and maturation. This process was accompanied by physical symptoms. One was diarrhea, which, it was said, God inflicted on her to cleanse her dirty human stomach when she was about to become God's baby. Within about a month she developed into an "angel" with the mannerisms of a seventeen-year-old girl, and then into a young woman of twenty-five. God told her to sew a snow-white dress and to prepare a set of white bedding. When these were ready, she was told to wear the dress and to use the bedding to sleep before the altar on the night of August 11. On this night, by her own account, the Divine Couple adopted her as their only daughter and heir. In this respect, she continued to think of herself as a woman. It is interesting to note that, on her deathbed, she said that she was going to wed soon.

Sayo's advice to her women followers also reveals some ambiguity toward womanhood. It is clear that Sayo held high expectations for women. She taught that women who, like herself, have known many trials are very close to the Kingdom of God. In the coming Age of God, women would play a role more significant than the role they had played in the preceding era. This, she said, is a man-centered age in which power rules the world, while the coming age will be a wholesome one in which women will march in the vanguard on the road to the Kingdom of God. Her teachings to women, based as they were upon her own experiences, were realistic and substantial and contained detailed individual instructions; they also seem more strict than her teachings to men, for women must "polish their souls" more than men to meet the future's challenge.

Sayo taught all her followers, including the women, to speak frankly and directly like herself. When her followers put this teaching into practice, they ran into not a little trouble, as had Sayo herself. Her women followers especially had problems, since, traditionally, they had not been allowed to express themselves freely or to talk back to elders, husbands, or men in general. Their new boldness often seriously upset domestic harmony. However, Sayo tempered the impact of this new freedom by stressing the importance of traditional family responsibilities as *gyo*, disciplinary exercise. Thus she also taught her female followers to obey their husbands and elders, even if the women were right nine times out of ten. Emphasizing the different roles of the sexes, she used to say, "A husband has his own duty, a woman has her own, and parents have their own. After you perform your own duty, then you can demand your rights."[13]

The extent to which Sayo perpetuated conventional ideas about women's role can readily be seen throughout her references to women. In her teachings, women are never separated from the family; they remain dependent upon, and subordinate to, the family's traditional masters—father, husband, parents-in-law, and other male relatives; their role is to help men by carrying out miscellaneous tasks with divinely sanctioned motherly devotion. Sayo listed the human desire to love and be loved among the "six functional elements of the soul" that she challenged her followers to purify, and she taught that egocentric love should be abandoned. Maternal love, which traditionally has been valued in Japan, was highly valued also by Sayo because in her view it is the least egoistic love of all. Furthermore, maternal love was considered essential to the prosperity of the household and family line, which Sayo saw as important.

Thus, on the whole, Sayo's teachings about women follow the traditional, rather than the innovative, side of her message. It would be misleading to call Sayo a feminist. It is true that she taught women to speak out, and perhaps it is also true that she brought them a new sense of importance and mission. But she did not challenge the old patterns of authority that had been so oppressive for women like herself. Nor did she address herself at all to the new situation of women in a changing post-war society in which women's activities are no longer limited to the household.

CONCLUSIONS: FEMALE LEADERSHIP AND WOMEN'S LIBERATION

Like Sayo, several women have been important leaders in many new religious movements in Japan. They are regarded as human deities, or they act as mediums who deliver a divine message. Some work alone in the beginning, as Sayo did in her movement's earliest days. If the organization is small, and hence easy to manage, women may continue as sole leaders for a much longer time. More often they come to be assisted by some man, who is sometimes a husband, a son, or other relative, or just a spiritual friend, such as a teacher, a disciple, or other comrade. Many new movements have been jointly founded by a male and a female, with the woman serving as source of revelatory experiences.

Generally speaking, most women founders undergo their first transforming experiences in their later years. Thus they have experienced the whole life cycle of a woman, having lived as a girl, a wife, a mother, and sometimes a divorcee or widow. To put it another way, women begin to preach after they have raised their children or have parted with their husbands either physically or spiritually. By this time they are their own masters, free from family bondages. Because lay leadership has always been a prominent feature of the Japanese religious tradition, women rarely leave their families, who eventually come to assist them. Thus they also become the real heads of their families, even if their husbands are still alive. For female leaders the new position is a powerful personal liberation, won after the numerous hardships that result from living in a society in which women tend to be dependent on, and subordinate to, men and are traditionally discriminated against.

Many women founders have proved that women can be amazingly strong as charismatic religious leaders. They fight fiercely against the establishment, in which they have had no place from the beginning. They attack the government and willingly go to prison; having little to lose, they endure hardships without flinching. At the same time, they are able to guide their followers with down-to-earth individual advice from the accumulated wisdom, revelatory or otherwise, that they have acquired during a life full of hardships and trials. We must admit, however, that they tend to be poor in systematic thinking and self-expression.

Despite the founders' personal strength, the new traditions have thus far failed to realize their potential for women. Why? Four important problems, most of which are exemplified in Sayo's movement, seem to provide the answer.

The first two are byproducts of the standard mode of succession within the movements. In Japan callings and professions of all kinds, including religious ones, have traditionally been handed down through family lines. Thus it is natural for a woman founder like Sayo to name a family member as her successor—and also natural that the successor's family will continue to lead the organization. The successor may or may not be another woman. But even if a woman is chosen and trained very carefully, it is very unlikely that she can duplicate her predecessor's achievements, for the life experiences of the founder are very different from those of her successor. Nine times out of ten, the women founders have lived dramatic lives of material as well as spiritual oppression; their own sufferings allow them to attain a most penetrating insight into the sufferings of others. Can the disciplined education of a successor substitute for such hard realities and the psychic powers achieved through them? Doubtless the successor, like Kiyokazu, will faithfully follow her predecessor's path. But it may be extremely difficult for her to have genuine revelatory experiences without having experienced the human boundary situation. Thus the pattern of strong female leadership is sporadic and is generally limited to the founder's own lifetime.

In addition, the young woman successor faces the problem of marriage. She must marry and bear children to secure the line of succession and the transmission of leadership. But how can she serve God and be a wife at the same time? In Japan, where the tradition of lay leadership is prevalent—and the leader is, therefore, likely to be married—this conflict in roles is never a problem for male religious leaders, but it is often a problem for female leaders. Ideally, of course, a woman leader's husband should be her follower, content with a supporting role. Such a man is hard to find in the male-dominated Japanese society. The most common compromise is a husband with managerial talents or theological training, who then himself assumes a major role in running the organization. Thus the husband may come to overshadow the wife up to the point that she becomes a mere figurehead. In Kiyokazu's case, this problem has not yet been encountered. At the time of this writing, she is still single—a condition that causes her family not a little worry. It seems that she has not received a proposal from a suitable man.

The ease with which the husbands of religious leaders rise to power points to another important reason why women's initial prominence is often blunted or lost. As an organization expands, the founder or her heir can no longer manage it alone. She needs expert assistants—administrative, financial, theological, and secretarial. Because most Japanese women have less education and less training for public activity than men, more men than women move into key positions on the full-time staff as the movement grows. They build magnificent buildings, introduce high levels of efficiency, and give the founder's teachings much-needed systematization; but they often dilute the movement's initial radicalism and tend to make concessions to the prevailing social norms.

But perhaps the most serious obstacle to sustained female leadership is the new movements' own inherent conservatism. Most new movements are still based on traditional world views and are concerned with preserving the traditional family as an essential condition for maintaining society. Hence women's maternal function and family responsibilities are still considered of paramount importance, while their role in society as individual human beings is not. Historically, Japanese religions have offered only pacifiers to the frustrated women who have been boxed in by traditional family structures; this remains true, unfortunately, of the new religions as well. Furthermore, these religions' repeated sermons on the essential differences between the sexes and their respective roles have by now become too static for a society in transition. Looking back on her long, strenuous life, a woman leader like Sayo is likely to say that women who aspire to paradise should follow the model provided by the leader's own early life. But the society out of which such leaders have come is itself changing, and the traditional ideal of service to family is no longer adequate to meet women's changing roles and needs. This is why no constructive contribution to women's liberation has yet been made by the new movements in Japan,

despite the fact that women members usually outnumber the men, and women's missionary zeal has most often been responsible for the movements' success.

Notes

1. A comprehensive bibliography of Western-language materials on the new religions is found in H. Byron Earhart, *The New Religions of Japan* (Tokyo: Sophia University, 1970).
2. See Ichiro Hori, *Folk Religion in Japan* (Chicago and London: University of Chicago Press, 1968); Carmen Blacker, *The Catalpa Bow* (London: George Allen & Unwin, 1975).
3. For her life, see *The Prophet of Tabuse* (Tabuse: Tensho-kotai-jingu-kyo, 1954), an abridged English-language version of the still incomplete *Seisho* (vol. 1, 1951; vol. 2, 1967, vols. 3–6, forthcoming).
4. She got up about 1:30 A.M. and went out to the well in the yard to pour pails of cold water on herself there in the open before getting dressed for a visit to the shrine.
5. "Tensho" is another name for Amaterasu, the mythical ancestress of the Japanese imperial family, and "Kotai-jingu" is the inner sanctuary of the Ise Shrine where Amaterasu is enshrined. One tradition says that Amaterasu is a priestess in service of God and that Sayo made her consort to the universal deity (many deities are coupled in Japanese mythology).
6. *The Prophet of Tabuse*, pp. 30–31. "Osayo" is a politer form of "Sayo" with an honorific "o".
7. *The Prophet of Tabuse*, p. 71.
8. Sayo Kitamura, "Tensho Kotai Jingu-kyo" (The Dancing Religion), *Contemporary Religions in Japan*, 2, no. 3 (September 1961), p. 37.
9. Kiyokazu studied at Pitzer College, California from 1969 to 1971 and at Vassar College, New York in 1971–1972. Then she went to England for further education as well as to establish the London Branch.
10. See William H. Newell, ed., *Ancestors* (The Hague: Mouton, 1976); Robert J. Smith, *Ancestor Worship in Contemporary Japan* (Stanford, Calif.: Stanford University Press, 1974).
11. It is probably unwise to use Western analogies in trying to understand what Sayo meant by "praying to redeem the dead." She apparently did not

pray *to* them, or seek to assuage them, although sometimes she spoke of "converting" them. Nor did she intercede for them with the God who possessed her. Her prayers were viewed as a vehicle of spiritual power which worked directly to effect a transformation.

12. "National polity" was a favorite term of the nationalists before and during World War II and was explicated by State Shinto scholars. For its detailed discussion see D. C. Holtom, *Modern Japan and Shinto Nationalism* (Chicago: University of Chicago Press, 1943); David Magarey Earl, *Emperor and Nation in Japan: Political Thinkers of the Tokugawa Period* (Seattle: University of Washington Press, 1964), Appendix D: Kokutai.

13. *Ogamisama Says . . .* (Tabuse: Tensho-kotai-jingu-kyo, 1963), p. 29.

Further Readings

Davis, Winston. *Dojo: Magic and Exorcism in Modern Japan.* Stanford, Calif.: Stanford University Press, 1980. See especially chapter titled "Women and their Sexual Karma," pp. 161–200.

Hardacre, Helen. *Kurozumikyō and the New Religions of Japan.* Princeton, N.J.: Princeton University Press, 1986.

_____. *Lay Buddhism in Contemporary Japan: Reiyūkai Kyōdan.* Princeton, N.J.: Princeton University Press, 1984.

Lebra, Takie Sugiyama. *Japanese Women: Constraint and Fulfillment.* Honolulu: University of Hawaii Press, 1984.

_____. "Self-Reconstruction in Japanese Religious Psychotherapy." *Cultural Conceptions of Mental Health and Therapy,* ed. by Anthony J. Marsella and Geoffrey M. White, 269–83. The Hague: D. Reidel, 1982.

Nakamura, Kyoko. "Women and Religion in Japan: Introductory Remarks." *The Japanese Journal of Religion,* special number on Women and Religion, X, nos. 2–3, pp. 115–21.

_____. "Revelatory Experiences in the Female Life Cycle: A Bibliographical Study of Women Religionists in Japan." Japanese *Journal of Religious Studies* VIII, nos. 3–4 (September–December 1981): 187–206.

Nefsky, Marilyn Felcher. *Women and the Religious Character of Contemporary Japan.* Ph.D. dissertation, University of Toronto, 1984.

14

Empress Wu and the Historians: A Tyrant and Saint of Classical China

DIANA PAUL

In the long history of the Chinese empire, one remarkable woman stands out—Empress Wu Tse-t'ien (625–705) of T'ang China. She holds a unique position in Chinese history as the only woman to ever hold the title of emperor[1] rather than empress and the only woman ever to wield absolute power in the four-thousand-year history of China. She ruled during the zenith of China's international power and cultural activity, and it was during her reign that Buddhist art and scholarship achieved their highest expressions. Nonetheless, in China the name of Wu Tse-t'ien has become a denigrating epithet, suggesting someone who engages in Machiavellian strategies to implement her policies.

Several historians think that Empress Wu Tse-t'ien has been maligned. According to these historians[2] the *Chiu T'ang shu* and *Hsin T'ang shu*,[3] which are considered the "official" Confucian histories and which were written almost three hundred years after Wu Tse-t'ien's reign, are grossly prejudicial in assessing her political career. The reason for this prejudice is that the official Confucian historians were unlikely to look kindly on any powerful Buddhist figure—least of all a woman—in the most powerful political position in China.

To understand Wu's actual place in Chinese

DIANA Y. PAUL founded Interface Japan, Inc., in Palo Alto, California. The company specializes in U.S.–Japan business developments with support services in translation, interpretation, corporate seminars, and market research. Currently she writes for several newspapers on U.S.–Japan trade issues. Formerly she was Assistant Professor of East Asian Studies and Religion at Stanford University.

history, it is necessary to understand her relationship to Confucianism as well as Buddhism. According to the political and social norms of both, she was an anomaly. Yet she used each tradition, at least to some extent, to authenticate her position, although in the long run she drew on Buddhism more extensively. This may have been due in part to her own personal devotion to Buddhism.

Since her relationships to the two traditions were somewhat different, I will analyze them separately. First, I shall discuss two aspects of her role vis-à-vis the traditional Confucian establishment: (1) the difficulties that the Empress faced as a woman within the context of traditional Confucian ideals, and (2) her efforts to compensate for these difficulties by exploiting established women's roles and by manipulating traditional Confucian symbolism. Second, I shall discuss three aspects of her relationship to Buddhism: (1) the political factors contributing to her promotion of Buddhism as the state religion of the empire, (2) the dimensions of her personal relationship to Buddhism, and (3) some possible reasons why the Buddhist historians, too, finally rejected her. I hope that my analysis will provide a more balanced portrait of a brilliant and remarkably effective ruler.

WOMEN AND POWER IN TRADITIONAL CONFUCIANISM

To comprehend better the almost insurmountable difficulties that China's only woman emperor faced, it is necessary to summarize traditional Confucian ideas about the proper relationship between femininity and power. In China the norms of government organization and policy were for the most part dictated by Confucianism. Since Confucian teachings considered male authority to be axiomatic, any woman attempting to legitimize her own power had to make some concessions to the Confucian

value system. Confucianism considered femininity and public power as mutually exclusive terms. According to its most fundamental teachings, the female principle (*yin*) was to be ruled and to be submissive while the complementary male principle (*yang*) was to rule and to be dominant. Harmony would be disrupted and disequilibrium would ensue if flagrant deviations from that natural order were allowed to occur unchecked.

No Confucian classic, for example, ever sanctioned a woman in a powerful political position. Instead, the classics contain polemical warnings against the regency of empress dowagers who, even before the T'ang dynasty, had exerted considerable political influence.[4] The position of empress dowager had been reluctantly institutionalized as an expedient in situations of emergency. When the heir apparent was a child or when the emperor was unable to attend to affairs of state, the empress dowager could temporarily govern. Even with the position's official recognition, subtle distinctions were preserved between the man's and the woman's positions. If the emperor was ill, all decrees made by the empress dowager were issued "jointly" by both emperor and empress. If the heir apparent was a child, the decrees were also issued as "joint" proclamations.

The historical precedent of previous empress dowagers greatly helped later women rulers legitimize their positions. Empress Wu, however, had no precedent when she declared in 690 that she was the emperor of China, not the empress dowager. Historical records of the T'ang, written three hundred years after her reign, allege that she had usurped the throne by blasphemously ignoring the conventional laws of succession from father to son. Such records reflect more than bias against Empress Wu for defying the laws of the state and the tenets of Confucianism. According to the records, Empress Wu Tse-t'ien was an anomaly, for she attempted to be a "Son of Heaven" despite being a female. Since the title "Emperor, Son of Heaven" was a monopoly of the *yang* cosmic factor, no woman—who necessarily embodied predominately the *yin* cosmic factor—could rightfully claim a mandate to be emperor. A woman wielding imperial power defied the natural order; according to Confucian beliefs, such defiance would be the cause of catastrophic natural events and of social disruption.[5] It was even suggested that such a woman might be a sexually anomalous being, perhaps a male in female guise, with the male's natural expectations to rule and have power. Her official biography, in fact, suggests that Empress Wu might have had a sexually ambivalent character by describing her childhood predilection to dress in little boys' clothing.

POLITICAL AND RELIGIOUS CONFLICT: WU'S LIMITED USE OF CONFUCIANISM TO SUPPORT HER SOVEREIGNTY

To govern effectively as a woman emperor in Confucian China and to avoid continual threats to her reign, Wu Tse-t'ien had to accomplish two seemingly impossible tasks. First, she had to gain and consolidate the actual powers and titles of the imperial position. Second, she had to legitimize her role as the absolute head of state and reject the role of a mere political influence behind the scenes.

The first of these two tasks was ostensibly easier. The political structure allowed a woman to be the effective head of state within the designated roles of empress or dowager empress. Wu Tse-t'ien asserted her claim to exclusive imperial authority after a brilliant but largely conventional climb into traditionally established positions. First, she went through the ranks of concubinage to the emperor, a practice that other royal women before her had used to gain the opportunity to exert great influence at court. As a young girl, renowned for her beauty, Wu had received an invitation to become a moderately high-ranking concubine of Emperor T'ai Tsung. Favored because of her beauty, intelligence, and skills in music and literature, she was eventually promoted to a higher rank. The heir apparent, soon to become Emperor Kao Tsung, allegedly became sexually attracted to Wu while his father was dying. After T'ai Tsung's death, through intrigue and manipulation of sexual favors, she soon became Emperor Kao Tsung's favorite concubine.

Achieving the rank of first concubine to the new emperor required considerable political acumen on Wu's part. Since she had been a concubine of Kao Tsung's father, her role of concubine to the son could be viewed as incestuous; later historians, in fact, charged her with incest. In addition, according to conventional practices, all the emperor's concubines were relegated to secluded quarters after his death and required to spend the rest of their lives in quiet retirement. Wu Tse-t'ien, however, did not follow the traditional path laid out for concubines of deceased emperors. Her retreat was only temporary. From the secluded Buddhist convent of Kan-yeh, she made political allies among Kao Tsung's concubines, and she also cultivated his wife, Empress Wang. Furthermore, she was able to add to her list of allies powerful bureaucrats who hated Empress Wang.

Fortunately for Wu, Empress Wang was childless. Wu, therefore, based her strategy on the Emperor's need for an heir to the throne. By becoming the mother of a son, Wu could capitalize on a woman's only legitimate quest for power—namely, power for her son. Wu gave birth to several sons and was able to promote the idea that a natural son, rather than the adopted son of the existing empress, should be the heir to the throne. Using her role as mother and the influence of the political allies she had made, Wu maneuvered Wang's demotion and finally attained the title of empress in 655.

Five years later, Emperor Kao Tsung suffered a crippling stroke. Wu assumed overt administrative power, and during the next five years she gained increasing approval from Kao Tsung's cabinet. By 665 she was ruling from a position equal to Kao Tsung's, proclaiming state policies "jointly" with her consort. Although virtually functioning in the role of emperor, she still ruled within the limits of Confucian tradition, holding court from behind a screen, in agreement with the prescribed Confucian norms for empresses and dowager empresses. She also continued to nurture the support of the bureaucrats and the intellectual elite in spite of the fact that both were becoming increasingly uneasy about her political position.

During this period, Wu began to lay the groundwork that would eventually allow her to legitimate, in Confucian terms, her claim to absolute power of state when she later assumed the title of emperor. This task involved establishing some type of role model for a woman ruler that would, at least tentatively, legitimize her political power. This maneuver was crucial, because in the eyes of Confucians role models were of critical importance for effective government policy. If a ruler did not fit the role model of the virtuous sage-king, he could not possibly rule. Thus, without some kind of role model, Wu could never be considered a virtuous ruler by the population at large or by her political advisers. Therefore, she began to manipulate Confucian symbols to achieve some semblance of a role model for a woman emperor. She also began to support scholarship, particularly biographies of famous women, presumably to establish an elevated image of femininity. Unfortunately these biographies have not been preserved.

Wu also elevated the status of women, especially the status of mothers, by extending the length of the mourning period required for a deceased mother to equal that for a deceased father. In addition, she elevated the position of her mother's clan by constructing ancestral temples for its members, especially her mother,[6] and by appointing clan members to political posts. To further legitimize her in-

creasingly powerful position, she exploited the role of mother as well as her knowledge of traditional Confucian values. Adroitly utilizing Confucian principles in her treatise on the "Administration of Subjects" (*Ch'en kuei*), Wu effectively developed a model of government based on the metaphor of a mother's authoritative powers over her children.

> If one considers both the child and the subject, one's [ruler's] compassion and giving of incentives are without distinction. . . . Only the mother to her child has compassion and love which are especially deep. Although the child has already acquired loyalty and goodness, still she thinks of urging him [to be even better].[7]

By implication, she herself was the ideal mother ruler.

Empress Wu did not claim the full title of emperor until the year 690. In the meantime a number of other developments had occurred. Instead of following the Confucian tradition of quiet retirement, and in defiance of the traditional line of legitimate succession, Empress Wu deposed her older son from the rank of prince regent in favor of her younger son. She assumed the title "Holy Mother, Divine and August Empress," which was, for all practical purposes, the title of the emperor but with female gender. The importance of names and titles in Confucian society cannot be overemphasized. By assigning this title to herself, Wu was stating that she had the authority to rule with all the honor due an emperor. She was to settle for nothing less than the title "Emperor" itself in 690, when she explicitly demanded all the authority of a male sovereign.

However, in the final analysis, existing Confucian values could not legitimize such a daring political feat. Therefore, in addition to her manipulation of titles held sacrosanct to the maintenance of social, ethical, and political order, Empress Wu also began to manipulate traditional male and female cosmological symbols, especially as they were utilized in traditional divination practices. It was important to Wu that the results of divination be interpreted to declare that the Empress had received the mandate of heaven. Traditional *I Ching* divinations performed to predict the success of her reign resulted in a hexagram in which the feminine *yin* trigram was in the ascendant position. This particular configuration was interpreted as a prediction of protection, prosperity, and order—although *yin* in the powerful position of ascendancy would have normally predicted decay and chaos.

That the Confucian establishment accepted her regency certainly must have been due in part to her shrewd command of images and symbols. But, even more importantly, Wu was a brilliant administrator who achieved great military and political success during her regency. She selected her cabinet judiciously, was guilty of less nepotism than most of her predecessors, peacefully negotiated settlements with the Turks and Tibetans, and waged a victorious war against Korea. She was a masterful politician who, among other things, avoided peasant uprisings by relaxing the oppressive system of taxation. China was a far stronger and more united country as a result of Wu Tse-t'ien's regency, and, without her genius in governing the empire, the T'ang dynasty most probably would not have endured. In the face of such success, Confucian bureaucrats would accommodate themselves to the governmental policies decreed by a woman emperor, since it seemed that Wu did in fact justify her imperial name—"One Who Takes Heaven for Her Model"—with its strong Confucian connotations.

WU TSE-T'IEN'S ESTABLISHMENT OF BUDDHISM AS STATE IDEOLOGY

Nevertheless, despite her success with Confucian ideology, Wu herself turned more and more to Buddhism as she took the final steps in consolidating her unique position as secular and religious head of the Chinese empire. This culminated in 691, one year after she had proclaimed herself emperor, when she placed Buddhism over Taoism as the favored religion. Up until this time the T'ang dynasty had patronized Taoism as the religion of the emperor. After 691 Buddhism, in effect, enjoyed the status of state religion. Until the end of her life, Wu would zealously promote Buddhist institutions, scholarship, and art.

Traditional Chinese historians have, at various times, offered four explanations for her patronage of Buddhism: (1) Buddhism was a significant part of her personal history, since the Wu family clan had been devout Buddhists for generations. Her grandfather, a cabinet minister during the preceding Sui dynasty, had been a noted Buddhist patron. Her mother's connections to the tradition were even more dramatic, as she had personally intervened to avert an imminent persecution of Buddhists. This had happened during the early reign of Kao Tsung; the Emperor's armies were already mobilized to burn temples when Wu's mother marshaled popular support and forced him to recall them. As a child, Wu had learned Buddhist doctrine; she had also briefly secluded herself in a Buddhist convent during her days as imperial concubine. (2) Despite the fact that Taoist tradition was as rich as Buddhism in its feminine imagery and had potential as an ideology for a woman ruler, Wu may have wanted to disassociate herself from the preceding T'ang emperors who had favored Taoism. (3) It has been charged, without any supporting evidence, that Wu Tse-T'ien had a lover who was a Buddhist monk. His name was Huai-i, and he was a low-born monk who was said to have taken the vows in order to gain access to the imperial household. He became so notorious for his court intrigues, especially his baiting of Confucians, that the Empress herself finally ordered his execution. (4) It has also been charged that Wu supported Buddhist scholarship so that texts could be forged in her own support. It was said, for example, that Buddhist translators under her patronage interpolated a passage in the *Ta-yün*

Ching that was later used to justify her rule. Traditional historians have also claimed that Wu had her monk scholars compose this *sutra* describing a woman ruler.

The traditional explanations of Wu's patronage of Buddhism are not all valid. The influence of her family's commitment to Buddhism seems unquestionable. This was especially true of her mother, who, in many ways, was as formidable a figure as her daughter. The example of her mother's successful stand against an emperor must have provided Wu with a striking index of Buddhism's popular support. Even though the relations between the state and Buddhist institutions were deteriorating at this time, no regent dared ignore the political repercussions of refusing minimal patronage to Buddhist institutions, given Buddhism's popularity among the masses. Support of Buddhism therefore brought Wu a popular base that Taoism could not command, whatever its other advantages or disadvantages.

While the role of Huai-i, Wu's alleged monk lover, has been overemphasized, it nonetheless seems certain that the Empress was considerably influenced by her circle of Buddhist scholar advisers. This was especially true of the nine powerful monks who constructed her ideological platform. Modern scholars have cleared Wu Tse-t'ien of the charge of falsifying texts. Recent evidence has refuted that claim that the alleged interpolation in the *Ta-yün Ching* was a forgery.[8] However, her scholarly coterie was highly skilled at finding texts that could be reinterpreted to the Empress' advantage. This group of scholars wrote a number of commentaries shaping traditional Buddhist symbolism and models to the conditions of her reign. By far, their most significant contribution was to identify Wu with two familiar Buddhist figures: the *bodhisattva* and the *cakravartin*. This development deserves extensive explanation, for it seems that Wu believed that the Buddhist concepts of *bodhisattva* and *cakravartin* could better support her claims to the title of emperor than could Confucian ideology.

The *Commentary on the Ta-yün Ching*, which proclaimed that the Empress was a *bodhisattva*, was placed into circulation two months before Wu proclaimed herself emperor on October 19, 690. According to ancient forms of Buddhism then current in China, the *bodhisattva* was a being at an advanced level of spiritual development, progressing toward Buddahood, the highest Buddhist ideal. The career of a *bodhisattva* was a long and arduous one, requiring many lifetimes spent in the cultivation of virtue. The distinction between a *bodhisattva* and a Buddha rested in the fact that the former remained subject to rebirth and thus could practice the *bodhisattva*'s legendary qualities of generosity and compassion, helping lesser beings and striving to bring *dharma*, or truth and proper order, to the world. According to the traditional Buddhist teachings of Wu's time, *bodhisattvas* could assume a variety of forms as a means for converting people to Buddhist practice. Moreover, the literature and art of Chinese Buddhism had often used a maternal metaphor to describe the traits of certain *bodhisattvas*. The image of the maternal *bodhisattva* could, of course, be readily associated with the Confucian "Holy Mother" image that the Empress had tried to cultivate. At the same time, her apologists could counter Confucian objections to her unfeminine behavior and unnatural role by claiming that she was really a male *bodhisattva* in a female apparitional form. The sexual fluidity of this somewhat transhuman being was by this time a well-established concept.[9]

The other Buddhist concept that Wu used to support her claims was the *cakravartin*, or universal emperor (literally "wheel turner"— an image referring to an old Buddhist legend), which provided a solution to the bothersome problem of a role model for her regency. A *cakravartin*'s universal power was matched only by his virtue. Furthermore, in Buddhist legends, *bodhisattvas* frequently appear in *cakravartin* form. Thus Empress Wu was simultaneously identified as a savior *bodhisattva* and an ideal secular head.

This was a remarkable tour de force, which not only associated legitimate secular power with Buddhist religiosity but also evoked Confucian notions of motherhood and implied masculine power (*yang*) in feminine disguise. The Empress went so far as to include "*Cakravartin*" among her official titles in 693 and did not abolish the title until 700, under pressure from Confucian bureaucrats. This would be the first and last time in Chinese history that a sovereign officially adopted Buddhist titles and symbolism to signify the imperial reign.

WU TSE-T'IEN AS A BUDDHIST AND A BODHISATTVA

So far I have presented Empress Wu primarily as a shrewd manipulator of political ideology. This is the way the Confucian biographies describe her, and the materials they have preserved are, of course, materials that support their position. Buddhist historical records add very little information about Empress Wu's religious motivations; both scholars and the Chinese people have, for the most part, accepted the Confucian view of Wu. However, a few isolated and fragmentary comments on Wu Tse-t'ien, together with some writings attributed to the Empress herself, suggest a different side to Wu Tse-t'ien's character. These materials suggest that the Empress was also deeply committed to the Buddhist faith and that she probably did view her own reign as the reign of a *bodhisattva* and of an ideal *cakravartin*.

Let us consider the personal testimonies of two scholar-monks who were not a part of Wu's coterie. Fa-tsang and Hui-chih were known for their integrity and religious devotion; they had no need or political motivation to curry favor with the Empress. Yet each of them celebrated the Empress' spiritual qualities. For example, Fa-tsang, one of the most eminent and influential Buddhist scholar-monks of the T'ang period, assessed Empress Wu's spiritual character in his introduction to "Biographical Records of the Transmission of the Hua-yen Sutra" (*Hua-yen ching chuan-chi*) in terms reminiscent of the language of the Empress' own apologists:

> The holy, divine august Emperor of the Great Chou Dynasty [namely, Empress Wu Tse-t'ien] has planted the seeds of the [Buddhist] path for countless aeons of time and should be joyously esteemed by the common people. The Great Cloud [*Ta-Yün ching*] reveals that the Emperor turns the Golden Wheel [namely, she is the *cakravartin*] to govern them [the people]. . . . Holy and divine, she implements the six spiritual powers without reaching a limit. Boundlessly good and beautiful, she freely engages in the transformations of the ten good actions without any limitation.[10]

The other monk, Hui-chih, in "A Poem in Homage to the Bodhisattva Kuan-yin" (*Tsan Kuan-shih-yin p'u-sa sung*) presents a similar evaluation of Empress Wu.[11] In his description, too, the Empress (or Emperor) Wu has the spiritual powers and infinite goodness of a *bodhisattva* who turns the Golden Wheel of a *cakravartin*. She rules wisely by protecting Buddhism, and she gives of her merits to help all living beings through her *bodhisattva*hood.

Several literary works on Buddhist topics have been attributed to the Empress. Unfortunately, two collections that could probably throw some light on her religious views are no longer preserved. Their titles, however, are mentioned in the *Toiki dentō mokuroku* (TDM), an eleventh-century catalog of Chinese, Japanese, and Korean Buddhist texts, compiled by the monk Eicho. Chinese catalogs, too, attribute to Wu Tse-t'ien a number of introductions to *sutra* translations that she had sponsored. Even if these were not written *by* her, they were at least written *for* her; thus, they must have sufficiently reflected her own self-image for her to willingly attach her name to them.

Two of these introductions attributed to Wu Tse-t'ien are extant. Both reflect her desire to be known as a devout Buddhist, as well as her command of Buddhist doctrinal tenets or, at least, the knowledge that she wished to have attributed to her. Wu Tse-t'ien's introduction to the *Hua-yen ching* emphasizes her devotion to the principles of Buddhism. Again, she claims to be a *cakravartin* and a *bodhisattva*; she claims as well the power attributed to the sage emperor by orthodox Confucians and the omniscience attributed by Buddhists to the *bodhisattva*:

The Dharma-king, Sun of Wisdom, transcends the four great elements and is of lofty vision. The middle heaven is governed; the ruler steps beyond the ten stages [into Buddahood?], residing in honor, on the Cakravada mountain, extending over countless aeons of time. As for that one's essence, she neither arises nor ceases. As for the characteristics, she has no past or future. Correctly practicing the stations of mindfulness, the thirty-seven constituents [of enlightenment], is her practice. Sympathy, compassion, joy, and equanimity—the four unlimited virtues—move her heart. The power of expedient means is inconceivable, the unifying policy has many facets. Merging with the great Emptiness is the limit. How much less can the multifaceted [government] policy be exhausted? Entering the smallest infinitesimal point has no name which can be expressed. What is inexpressible—is this not the great enlightenment? I have planted, in past aeons of time, the causes for receiving the Buddha's prediction [of enlightenment].[12]

In this quotation the supreme powers of *bodhisattva*hood and the *bodhisattva*'s infinite variety of expedient means are deliberately associated with the Empress' absolute authority and the many facets of her unifying policy. Both reflect the inexpressible quality of the *bodhisattva*'s dawning enlightenment. The Empress' reference to a Buddha's prediction draws on an old belief that a *bodhisattva*, at a certain

stage of development, will have his or her final enlightenment predicted by a Buddha. Like other *bodhisattvas*, the Empress has planted in former lives the seeds of personal merit that led to such a prediction.

Finally, we must consider the testimony of her own religious deeds. Chinese Buddhism was to achieve its highest development under her generous imperial protection. Because she generously patronized Buddhist art projects, translations of *sutras*, and honoring of eminent Buddhist monks, scholastic Buddhism reached its apogee during her reign, and popular Buddhism continued to gain currency. Her financial support of temple constructions, cave sculptures, and translation activities may be seen as an attempt to carry out the religious practices of worship and generosity extolled in Mahayana Buddhist scriptures. Empress Wu's activities in support of Buddhist scholarship helped determine the trend of the doctrinal development of Chinese Buddhism. She personally sent emissaries to Central Asia to invite the most gifted Buddhist scholars to China and commissioned Fa-tsang to expound the works of Hua-yen Buddhism. During his lectures on Hua-yen philosophy at court, Empress Wu conferred special honors on Fa-tsang and paid him extreme deference by bowing before him at court. She welcomed other Chinese monks to court to give lectures and paid visits to Buddhist temples to attend lectures.

In the face of all this evidence, it seems that political considerations cannot entirely account for the intense and prolonged interest that Wu Tse-t'ien displayed in the Buddhist religion. Long after she had established a strong political base for her regency, her energetic support of Buddhist endeavors continued unabated. Wu Tse-t'ien's writings and continual support of Buddhist projects suggest that she fervently desired to meet the standards of *bodhisattva*-hood and to promulgate the teachings of Buddhism throughout the empire. Thus it seems most reasonable to conclude that Wu's use of Buddhist symbols and doctrine to develop her political image was not solely the invention of her political advisers but also reflected her own understanding of her sovereignty. It seems very likely that Wu did, in fact, identify with her own image; that is to say, she may well have sincerely believed that she *was* a *bodhisattva* and a *cakravartin*.

THE FINAL IRONY: EMPRESS WU AND BUDDHIST HISTORIANS

The negative portrayal of Wu in official Confucian histories is hardly surprising, having been motivated by outrage at Wu's defiance of prescribed feminine norms and by resentment on the part of Confucians at being replaced by Buddhist power brokers. On the other hand, one would expect a rather different portrait of the Empress by Buddhist historians. And yet, such is not the case. Although Wu had deftly taken advantage of Buddhist texts that provided a description of normative behavior for women rulers, Buddhist orthodoxy did not respond with wholehearted endorsement of women's legitimate use of power in the public sphere. Furthermore, Buddhist histories often present as negative a portrayal of Wu as do Confucian histories, even citing information exactly as it was found in Confucian chronicles. These negative portraits of Empress Wu Tse-t'ien in Buddhist chronicles are probably the by-product of the bitterness felt by Buddhist monks after Wu's death and the failure of their dream of an ideal Buddhist state. Buddhism's relations with the state rapidly declined after Wu's death in 705, and the Buddhists desperately attempted to remain in imperial favor. They did not succeed. As a result, later generations of Buddhist monks felt that they had to disassociate themselves from the policies and programs of Empress Wu for their own political survival. In that process the Confucian analysis and assessment of Empress Wu's reign were accepted without criticism and incorporated wholeheartedly in Buddhist records.

Nevertheless, to conclude, as did the Buddhist historians, that Empress Wu Tse-t'ien was an unscrupulous usurper is merely to accept the Confucian bureaucrats' claim that any woman in absolute power holds that power illegitimately. The tyrant Wu Tse-t'ien portrayed in the later Confucian histories and Buddhist chronicles is a reflection of the prejudice against a woman who challenged the value system of male sovereignty and of the bitter resentment of a religious elite that failed to realize its ambitions. At the very least, Empress Wu seems to have been a highly effective ruler and an enthusiastic devotee of the religion she promoted. At the most, she may well have identified personally with her *bodhisattva* and *cakravartin* models, attempting to make her own actions exemplify the virtues identified with these figures. Her actions themselves suggest this, as do the few words preserved of her own writing.

Notes

1. Instead of retaining the title *Huang-hou* ("August Empress"), Wu Tse-t'ien claimed the title *Huang-ti* ("August Emperor"), in 690. In this chapter I have retained the common practice among scholars of nevertheless referring to Wu Tse-t'ien as "Empress."
2. Antonino Forte, *Political Propaganda and Ideology in China at the End of the Seventh Century* (Ph.D. Diss., Institute Universitario Orientale, 1976), pp. 3–11 et passim; C. P. Fitzgerald, *The Empress Wu* (London: Cresset Press, 1968), pp. 92–93, p. 217 n. 6, et passim. I have used Fitzgerald's biography of Wu for information derived from the Confucian histories and drawn on Forte's criticism of Fitzgerald to some extent.
3. The *Chiu T'ang shu* is attributed to Liu Hsu (887–946) and was completed in 946. The *Hsin T'ang shu* was compiled by Ou-yang Hsiu (1007–1072) and others in the years 1043–1060.
4. Lien-sheng Yang, "Female Rulers in Imperial China," *Harvard Journal of Asiatic Studies* 23 (1960–1961), pp. 47–61.
5. In Confucian historiography Wu Tse-t'ien is held responsible for the strangest and most criminal

events of that time (Forte, p. 7). However, emperors who were believed to have lost the mandate of heaven were commonly held responsible for abnormal phenomena and catastrophes, sometimes manifested as droughts, earthquakes, eclipses, and birth anomalies (Kenneth Ch'en, *Buddhism in China: A Historical Survey* [Princeton: Princeton University Press, 1964], p. 23).

6. Wu Tse-t'ien had the first ancestral temple constructed for her deceased mother in 670 while she was still empress to Kao Tsung. She continued to pay homage at this Buddhist temple until her death in 705. This action probably reflects her admiration of her mother as much as her efforts to elevate motherhood in general.

7. *Ch'en kuei*, in *Ch'üan T'ang wen*, compiled by Tung Kao (1740–1818) among others c. 1814, 1000 *ch.* 20, vols. (Taipei: 1965), vol. 3, *chüan* 97, q.v. Kao Tsung Wu Huang-hou, p. 1256a, 3, 6–7.

8. The predominant scholarly consensus that Wu Tse-t'ien ordered the interpolation in the *Ta-yün Ching* has been forcefully challenged by Forte (pp. 19–50), who refutes this view in detail by comparing the *Ta-yün ching* with the Tun-huang manuscript that comments on it.

9. I have discussed at length the sexual transformations and apparitional forms of Bodhisattvas in *Women in Buddhism: Images of the Feminine in the Mahayana Tradition* (Berkeley, Calif.: Asian Humanities Press, 1979). One detailed text available in Chinese that discusses this theory is the *Chuan nü shen ching* ("Sutra on Changing the Female Body"), Taisho 564.14.

10. *Hua-yen ching chuan-chi* by Fa-Tsang (643–712), Taisho 2073.51. 164a12–16.

11. *Tsan Kuan-shih-yin p'u-sa sung* by Hui-chih, a monk who resided in the Fo shou-chi monastery during Wu Tse-t'ien's reign, Taisho 1052.20.68a8–12.

12. Introduction to Siksananda's translation of the *Hua-yen ching*, Taisho 279.10.1a5–13, a19–24.

Further Readings

Forte, Antonino. *Political Propaganda and Ideology in China at the End of the Seventh Century.* Naples, Italy: Institute Universitario Orientale, 1976.

Fitzgerald, C. P. *The Empress Wu.* London: Cresset Press, 1956.

Guisso, Richard W. *Wu Tse-t'ien and the Politics of Legitimation in T'ang China.* Bellingham, Wash.: Western Washington University Press, 1978.

Guisso, Richard W. and Stanley Johannesen, eds. *Women in China: Current Directions in Historical Research.* Youngstown, N.Y.: Philo Press, 1981.

Paul, Diana Y. *Women in Buddhism: Images of the Feminine in Mahāyāna Tradition.* Berkeley, Calif.: Asian Humanities Press, 1979.

Weinstein, Stanley. *Buddhism under the T'ang.* Cambridge Studies in Chinese History, Literature, and Institutions. New York: Cambridge University Press, 1987.

15

The Case of the Vanishing Nuns: The Fruits of Ambivalence in Ancient Indian Buddhism

NANCY AUER FALK

For a number of years I have been fascinated by a puzzling aspect of the history of ancient Indian Buddhism. The Indian order of Buddhist monks was still flourishing in 1198 A.D., when Turkish invaders began the series of raids that would destroy its greatest monasteries within the next forty years. Many centuries earlier, however, the parallel order of Buddhist nuns had virtually disappeared from the historian's view. Yet the order of *bhikshunis*, "female beggars," as these women were called—flourished in China and Japan until modern times. The very similar order of Jaina nuns that probably even antedated the *bhikshunis'* venture still prospers in Jaina regions of modern India. Furthermore, even as the nuns themselves became less prominent, other women remained important to the Buddhism of India. The generous gifts of great laywomen-donors are on record until the tradition's final days. And the same centuries that were so silent for the nuns

NANCY AUER FALK is Professor of Religion at Western Michigan University and was trained initially in History of Religions at the University of Chicago (M.A. 1963; Ph.D. 1972); her specialization was the religions of South Asia. Her principal research interest is the study of women's religious roles and lives, both in South Asia and cross-culturally; she has also written several scholarly articles on aspects of Buddhist popular practice in ancient South Asia.

Author's Note Portions of the research for this chapter were supported by the National Endowment for the Humanities (Summer Stipend, 1976) and Western Michigan University's sabbatical leave program (1977–78). An earlier version of this study was presented during the 1978 W. Y. Evans-Wentz Lecture Series at Stanford University.

produced the Vajrayana path with its women *siddhas*, who are described in Chapter 18 of this volume.

Materials on the nuns are very sketchy, and we will probably never know in detail what caused their decline. The most likely cause was a general decline in the Buddhist community's economic fortunes that had a long-term impact on the men's order as well. But bad luck hit the nuns first and disproportionately; thus we must look further to explain the reasons for the different fates of monks and nuns.

At the root, the major problem of the women's order probably rested in the Buddhist tradition's inability to affirm completely the idea of women pursuing the renunciant's role. This led to an institutional structure that offered women admirable opportunities for spiritual and intellectual growth, but not for the institutional and scholarly leadership that such growth should have fitted them to assume. The nuns' troubles were compounded by an ambivalent image created in a tradition of Buddhist stories that sometimes praised their achievements but just as often undercut and attacked them.

NOW YOU SEE THEM; NOW YOU DON'T

To appreciate the puzzle of the nuns' disappearance, one must have some minimal acquaintance with the sources and facts of the order's history in India. Overall, the history of the nuns, like that of the larger Buddhist community in India, can be divided into three phases.

The first, so-called primitive, period extends from the Buddha's first conversions (ca. later sixth century B.C.) and the early spread and consolidation of the tradition's teachings and institutions to the time when the great emperor Ashoka (ca. 272–236 B.C.) became a patron of Buddhism and facilitated its spread throughout and beyond the Indian subconti-

nent. Sources for this period are exclusively oral traditions; these were preserved by means of memorization and were recorded in writing only at later times. According to these traditions, the Master himself founded the women's order during the early years of his teaching career. The inspiration for its founding is said to have come from the Buddha's maternal aunt, Mahapajapati by name, who had raised him from birth after the death of his mother. The order was founded on the premise, affirmed in the Buddha's own teachings, that women were as capable as men of reaching *arhat*ship, the state of spiritual liberation characterized by total victory over desire. Memories of the early days testify to the order's thriving existence. It drew women from all walks and conditions of life, especially the mercantile and aristocratic classes that provided the entire tradition with its major bases of support. Many were matrons, turning to the order's rest after a full and exhausting life; others were young, moved by disgust for marriage or saddened by the death of children or other kin. Through the path of renunciation many of these women achieved the *nirvana* (coolness) that they sought. An extraordinary testimony to their accomplishment is a collection of stanzas preserved in Buddhism's southern, or Theravada, tradition, in which their most distinguished members celebrate their new spiritual freedom.[1]

The second period extends from the time of Ashoka through two later great empires, the one ruled by the Satavahanas in the south (ca. 55 B.C.–250 A.D.) and the other by Kushanas in the northwest (ca. 20 A.D.–240 A.D.) During this period, the Buddhist order became a significant religious force throughout India. Although the nuns' presence is still attested to in some works of literature that originated during this period, the most important historical testimonies to their existence are the numerous inscriptions left by donors to Buddhist building projects and monuments. These provide evidence of a thriving nuns' community in virtually all areas where the men's order is also well attested to. Especially in the south, the nuns seem to have been both numerous and wealthy. Their names are found in inscriptions in numbers almost equal to the monks' and they were able to offer generous gifts themselves as well as to receive donations.[2]

During the third period of Buddhist history in India, after the third century A.D., the nuns' fortunes deteriorated; the few traces of the women's order suggest that the order became much smaller. This was a time of general diminution for the Buddhist community as a whole, although it remained strong in some regions and kingdoms. It was also the best-recorded period in Buddhist history. One would expect, therefore, to find abundant materials on the nuns. Instead, they become almost invisible. I have found a few inscriptions: the last gift from a nun was recorded in 550 A.D. in the city of Mathura,[3] and a few donations reveal a small cluster of convents near the famous Buddhist "university" at Valabhi (last on record, 629 A.D.).[4] None of the famous philosophical treatises and commentaries that made the period so illustrious are attributed to nuns. Moreover, nuns rarely appear in the brief sketches of eminent figures' lives that are found so often in literary sources of the times. Once in a while we catch the nuns' shadow in the background: thus we learn that the Buddhist nun-mother of Kumarajiva, a famous scholar of northwest India who later made his home in China (ca. 344–413 A.D.), was an important influence in his life;[5] that another eminent monk, Vasubandhu, used part of the many gifts offered to him to build housing for nuns in the northern capital city of Patna, where he tutored members of a royal household (ca. 455–467 A.D.);[6] and that the widowed sister of the Buddhist emperor Harshavardhana *may* have taken the vows with her brother at the end of his rule (ca. 605–647 A.D.).[7]

Even the Chinese pilgrims who have otherwise provided such rich records of later Buddhist life in India have surprisingly little to say about the nuns. Fa Hsien, who traveled across northern India in 399–400 A.D., mentions the *bhikshunis* only once, in describing a rite at Mathura. Hsüan Tsang, who lived in India for more than twenty years (629–643 A.D.) and visited virtually all of its major centers, refers to nuns only in connection with the same rite described by Fa Hsien.[8] He must have seen nuns, however, for twenty-eight years later another voyager, I Ching, encountered them during his stay at Tamralipti in east India. I Ching noted how strictly they were supervised; they had to walk two by two outside the monastery grounds and traveled in fours if they visited a lay household. But he was most impressed by their poverty:

> Nuns in India are very different from those of China. They support themselves by begging food, and live a poor and simple life. . . . The benefit and supply to the female members of the Order are very small, and monasteries of many a place have no special supply of food for them.[9]

I Ching might have mentioned also that in India the nuns lived very differently from the monks. The monks he saw lived in richly endowed monasteries, and their lives could hardly be called poor or simple. Clearly the nuns had seen better days.

AN ECONOMIC MATTER

As brief as it is, I Ching's note on the nuns provides an important clue to the crisis in the women's order. Their singularly poorer state, as compared to the monks', indicates that they had problems in finding economic support. The record of Vasubandhu's contribution to the nuns in Patna probably means that the Patna community faced the same problem.

It is important at this point to examine the economic structure of the Buddhist monastic community.[10] The community had begun as a loosely knit group of mendicant wanderers. As early monks and nuns moved from town to town, they lived on handouts provided largely by lay members who had also taken refuge in the Buddha's doctrine. The beggar's life was essential to the community's discipline, for it helped the renunciants to sever their ties to all worldly things. Hence it was retained as an important part of the monastic rule even after the wanderers began to settle down in fixed and permanent monastic settlements. Thus monks and nuns remained dependent on donations. Lay persons built their monasteries, provided their robes and other modest possessions, and fed them, either as they went on daily begging rounds or by supplying food to monastery kitchens. Some of the wealthy made large endowments; a king, for example, might donate tax revenue from a village to ensure a favored monastery a continuing supply of basic requisites. Still, as in the Buddhism of Southeast Asia today, many of the renunciants' needs were cared for on a day-to-day or year-to-year basis. During times when Buddhism experienced a broad base of popular support, the whole monastic community flourished. This was especially true when the supporting community enjoyed an abundant surplus of wealth, as was the case, for example, in the southern empire of the Satavahana (or Andhra) dynasty, where the most successful nuns' community appears to have been located. When the economic bottom dropped out or popular support was eroded by competition from other religious teachings, the renunciants were in a less comfortable position. Both these negative forces were operating in the third century A.D., when the fortune of the nuns began to turn. The merchants and members of the Satavahana court, who had been the principal supporters of the Buddhist community, saw their profitable trade with ancient Rome decline and their empire fall to pieces. Furthermore, in many regions where Buddhism had been strong, devotional movements that honored Hindu gods were gaining new converts.

As Buddhism's popular base declined, a different source of support became preeminent. Kings and royal families had been conspicuous donors since the community's earliest days. Perhaps the most famous example of all was Ashoka, ruler of ancient India's largest empire. In those early days royal donors like Ashoka were motivated at least in part by personal commitment to Buddhism. Later, however, the records of royal grants show that many of the generous donors had taken Hindu names. Apparently, their donations had less to do with personal piety than with prestige. The Buddhist community was by now winning a high reputation for its scholarship. Learned stars like the brilliant Chinese visitor Hsüan Tsang were paraded by kings in public debates; famous philosophers like Vasubandhu were sought out to tutor royal families. Royal dynasties built up piece by piece the massive monastery-universities of these latter days, whose reputations shone throughout the Indian subcontinent. In this league, however, the nuns were at a decided disadvantage, for they were not stars, and their community had never enjoyed the lion's share of prestige. If the men's and women's communities had to compete for donations, there was no doubt that the men would capture the greater share of support.

ALMOST EQUAL

The reasons for the nuns' lower profile and lesser fame seem once again to lie partly in the institutional structure of the monastic orders. To find them, we must widen our circle of understanding. Our focus this time is on the Buddhist monastic Rule. According to the claims of the legendary histories that frame it, the Rule was the creation of the Buddha himself, who formulated its two-hundred-plus precepts in response to specific situations arising in his community. According to Western historians, the Rule probably developed slowly over a period of perhaps two centuries, becoming essentially complete around 350 B.C. The monastic Rule became one of the most stable features of the Buddhist tradition; although Buddhism developed many different sects and sometimes very different interpretations of the Buddha's teaching, the provisions of the Rule remained basically constant.[11]

The Rule provided a total framework for Buddhist monastic life. Many of its provisions expand and interpret the Buddhist renunciants' four major moral precepts: not to destroy life, not to take what was not given, not to have sexual relations, and not to speak wrongly. Other provisions spell out the prohibitions against luxury that were also an integral part of Buddhist practice. Still other portions of the Rule stipulate the fine organizational details that allowed the community to run smoothly and furthered its members' opportunity to pursue spiritual liberation.

In most respects the Rule approached monks and nuns with admirable equity. Before the monastic settlements were established, monks and nuns led the same wandering life, free of the domestic ties and labor that left neither men nor women in ancient India much chance for serious pursuit of spiritual discipline. Both monks and nuns went on the daily begging rounds; both held the important biweekly assembly in which the Rule's provisions were recited. Monks and nuns even looked alike; both shaved their heads bare, and both wore the same patchcloth robes dyed to earth color and draped identically over the left shoulder.

At times the Rule made special provisions to protect and help the nuns. Monks could not call upon the women's skills, for example, to sew or to dye and weave the small rugs on which they sat. Nor could the monks divert to themselves any food or robes that the nuns acquired as donations. For, it was said, "women come by things with difficulty"[12]— thus suggesting, incidentally, that economic problems were not new to the women of the order's later days.

It was important that nuns receive adequate instruction. To facilitate the observance of the rule on celibacy, monks and nuns usually led strictly separate lives; thus, for the most part nuns served as their own teachers. Those of early times sometimes gained brilliant reputations, such as the brahman Bhadda Kapilani, whom the Buddha himself praised for her knowledge of his teachings, or Patacara, whose insight into the meaning of suffering was deepened by a personal history of former rebellion and staggering loss. Nevertheless, the transmission of the teaching was for the most part in the hands of the men's community that had originally traveled with the Buddha; so the Rule allowed women to receive instruction from men as well as from other nuns. Ironically, this provision, so conspicuously designed to benefit the nuns, was probably one of the factors that worked ultimately to undo them, for the corresponding allowance was not given: monks could instruct nuns, but nuns could not instruct monks. Perhaps they did so anyway, informally; some early accounts seem to suggest that this happened at times. But no record of later times ever shows a man citing a woman as his *acharya,* or principal spiritual mentor. Thus the men owed nothing to the women, while that same provision justified their keeping the community's main educational apparatus in their own hands.

Other features of the Rule also play a part in the eventual decline of the nuns' order. In addition to the Rule they shared with the men, the nuns observed another, smaller Rule of their own.[13] Some of its precepts dealt with minor problems special to women—for example, how to cope with menstruation or how to handle the situation if a nun became pregnant. Many others elaborated the eight special rules that, according to legend, the Buddha had imposed on the women as a price for allowing them to found their order. These provided that the women would be permanently subordinated to the men:

1. Any nun, no matter how long she had been in the order, must treat any monk, even the rudest novice, as if he were her senior.

2. Nuns should not take up residence during the annual rainy-season retreat in any place where monks were not available to supervise them.

3. Monks would set the dates for the biweekly assemblies.

4. During the ceremony at the end of the rainy-season retreat, when monks and nuns invited criticisms from their own communities, the nuns must also invite criticism from the monks.

5. Monks must share in setting and supervising penances for the nuns.

6. Monks must share in the ordination of nuns.

7. Nuns must never revile or abuse monks.

8. Nuns must not reprimand monks directly (although they could and did report one monk's offensive behavior to another, who then might take the appropriate actions to correct it).[14]

We must avoid jumping to conclusions about the effects of these rules. Women of ancient India had always been subordinated to men. For the most part the nuns apparently did not find these rules oppressive, although one protest is on record against the rule of seniority. Nor, apparently, did they consider themselves inferior; what little record we have of their thoughts suggests that they either regarded themselves as equals or simply did not think to compare themselves with the men at all.

The extra rules did not hinder women in what was considered to be their most important pursuit—practicing the discipline that led to liberation. Nor did the special rules deny the nuns the opportunity, if they sought this out, to develop their minds and their insight into the tradition's teachings. In these respects,

especially when one considers the time and cultural context, the Rule's approach to women was extraordinarily open.

The damage inflicted by the special rules was of a subtler and worldlier nature. The discriminatory provisions meant that women would never be leaders in the life of the whole community or have any decisive voice in shaping its direction. They meant that the men would never be beholden to any of the nuns, in the way that students are beholden to the teachers whose efforts have helped them find meaning and direction. These negative effects became most pronounced in the days of the great universities and the royal patrons who built their own fame though these foundations. They communicated a damaging image to the greater world that picked up the monastic community's tab, because they affirmed that the monks were the more significant and worthier part of such a community. In other words, the discriminatory rules implied that the men deserved the richer offerings, the more elaborate buildings, and the greater opportunity to shine in court and in public confrontations.

ONE HAND GIVES; THE OTHER TAKES AWAY

Unfortunately this image of male superiority was reinforced from another direction as well, for the Buddhist literary tradition conveyed an ambivalence about the nuns that must have further eroded the order's standing. I am concerned here not so much with the sophisticated philosophical literature that was studied and taught primarily in monastic circles as with the many stories that once circulated, and still circulate, in the wider community. Ancient Buddhism, like all the traditions native to India, communicated its fundamental values and much of its understanding of human life and destiny through a rich storytelling tradition. We shall never know, of course, just exactly what form was given to these stories in the different times and regions of India where Buddhism was a living tradition, for the storytelling tradition was largely an oral one, with new versions constantly being shaped as the stories were told and retold. But some versions have been preserved, scattered in many places throughout Buddhist literature.

References to nuns appear in a number of Buddhist stories, especially those that tell about Buddhism's formative period. Such references come in two forms: (a) explicit evaluations of the nuns' spiritual capacities and of their role within the community, and (b) portrayals of their activities and spiritual accomplishments. The ambivalence that I have referred to pervades both types.

For example, one current in the Buddhist storytelling tradition unquestionably carries a strong positive image of the nun. The motif of the women's capacity for *arhat*ship is frequently iterated and is backed up by portrayals of *arhat*-nuns, such as biographical legends about many of the *theris*, famous *arhat*-nuns whose stanzas were mentioned earlier in this chapter. Some of the names and accomplishments of these nuns appear again in stories about the Buddha and his community that accompany accounts of the Buddha's sermons and dialogues with his followers. For example, in one old account the Buddha cites the most distinguished members of each of his community's four segments—the monks, the nuns, the laymen, and the laywomen.[15] Among the nuns we learn of Khema, most eminent in wisdom; of Nanda, first in meditation; of Sona, greatest in energetic effort; and of Sigala's mother, preeminent in faith. This list of distinguished members also includes the nun Dhammadinna, who is cited as the most skilled teacher of the Buddha's insights; Patacara, who knows best the rules of the discipline; and Kisha Gotami, who is first in the ascetic practice of wearing coarse robes. Uppalavanna is chief among those of supernormal powers; Sahula is first in clairvoyance; and Bhadda

Kapilani is best at remembering past lives. These are no second-rate achievements. Other narratives scattered throughout the literature recall further details of these women's careers. Mahapajapati, the nuns' founder, had a modest legendary cycle of her own, beginning, as most accounts of great Buddhists do, with stories of the deeds in former lives that brought her to her exalted role as the Buddha's aunt and the nuns' founder and ending with an account of her *parinirvana*, or final liberation.

Perhaps the strongest affirmation of the nuns' role is found in a little collection of stories that was apparently very widely known, since a number of versions have been found from quite different Buddhist times and regions. This collection contains the stories of ten nuns who, through wit, discipline, and purity of thought, managed to overcome the tempter Mara. All of them speak out strongly as Mara approaches and tries to awaken the lustful thoughts, painful memories, and past fears that would make a weaker person abandon the path of spiritual attainment. The message is clearest and strongest in the words that one of the sisters, Soma, speaks in answer to Mara's remark that she has just a woman's "two-finger intelligence" (enough to use a common and simple way of measuring rice). Soma's answer rings like a credo for all the nuns:

> What does the woman's nature do to us if
> the mind is well-composed
> If our knowledge progresses rightly, giving
> insight in the Teaching?
> Pleasure is completely destroyed for me;
> dark ignorance has been pierced.
> Thus know, Evil Death, you are
> destroyed!
> If a person still thinks to ask: "Am I a
> woman in these things? Or am I a
> man?"

This is the one to whom Mara can talk.[16] Offsetting the impact of such stories as those of Mahapajapati and Soma, however, is another series of accounts, which denigrate the nuns and their accomplishments. Many of these are clearly just tales of human foibles and failings and are not directed specifically at the nuns as such; similar stories are also told about the monks. A few have a gently humorous touch, such as the Vinaya tale of a country bumpkin nun who tosses the contents of her chamberpot over her convent's wall and hits a stuffy brahman on the head.[17] My own favorite is the story of Fat Tissa, who noisily celebrates the nuns' monk patron Ananda above the much more distinguished—but also woman-hating—Mahakassapa, thus bringing down the latter's wrath on poor Ananda.[18]

Other tales, however, strike quite a different and ominous note. Some accounts seem defaced, as though stories initially intended to celebrate the nuns' achievements had been altered to play down their accomplishments. Thus a very old story telling of the efforts of the founder, Mahapajapati, and her initial group of followers states that they very nearly attained insight on their first day of instruction. But, the story continues, unlike many of their male brethren, they didn't quite make it; thus they had to return for more teaching on the morrow.[19] The implication is that they were a little on the slow side. This didn't-quite-make-it theme appears several times. I know at least one instance in which both the celebratory and the denigrating versions of the same story have been preserved. This apparently popular story tells of a nun who wanted to be first in greeting the Buddha after he had spent a three-month rainy-season retreat in heaven. Not knowing quite how to accomplish this in the glorious company that was assembling for the occasion, she transformed herself into a universal emperor. One of my sources simply reports that she was, indeed, first—thus implying that hers was a great accomplishment. Another source, instead, states that, when she met the Buddha, he informed her that a male meditation master had in fact seen him first with his spiritual eye. And yet a third source reports that the Master censured her for abandoning her proper business of meditation.[20]

Certainly the most damaging of all must have been the story concerning the eight special rules that subordinated the nuns to the monks. It purports to tell how the nuns' order was founded over the Buddha's own objection to letting women renounce the world. To the Buddha's credit, the story may be a fraud, for it does not belong to the oldest stratum of Buddhist literature. But it was widely circulated as the authentic founding narrative; hence its charges must have cast a very long shadow on the nuns' endeavor. It is said that, when Mahapajapati and her retinue of five-hundred Sakya women first approached the Buddha to ask for ordination, he refused brusquely and sent them away in tears. They went home, shaved their heads, put on the renunciant's robes and then, with bare feet, followed the Master and his male disciples to a distant town to show their determination. The Buddha refused again; but this time Fat Tissa's hero Ananda intervened on the women's behalf. The Master finally relented, but he extracted the women's promise to observe the eight rules as a condition for their admission. Many versions of this story include a particularly vicious coda: because the women had been admitted as renunciants, the Master announced afterward, his teaching would last only five hundred years instead of the thousand that he had originally anticipated.[21]

Once upon a time I attributed these kinds of stories to simple misogyny among the celibate monks' community. Today, after many years of study, I believe that the explanation is probably not so simple. Another group of women—the Buddhist laywomen—comes off very well in Buddhist stories, in spite of the fact that the Buddhist lay community in general was considered spiritually inferior to the monastic community. Buddhist laywomen tend to be presented in much more positive terms than the nuns, and their deeds and virtue are almost invariably praised. The stories that relate to laywomen are far more numerous and more lavishly and enthusiastically developed than those that relate to nuns. The grand heroine of Buddhist storytelling is not the nuns' founder Mahapajapati, as one might expect, but Vishakha, a prominent merchant's daughter and wife who belonged to the early community and who never took the nuns' vows. Also, in the stories of outstanding nuns the focus is often on the deeds that they performed before, not after, taking the renunciant's vows. This is not true for the monks, for there are many, many Buddhist stories whose hero is a monk. Thus one cannot escape the impression that the community was more comfortable with its laywomen than with its nuns and that it probably found the latters' presence to be an embarrassment.

WHEN MODELS CONFLICT

As perplexing as the relative strength of the laywomen's position may seem, it offers an important clue to the ambivalence surrounding the nuns' role. Such ambivalence, I believe, is linked to Buddhism's attempts to reconcile two separate and somewhat contradictory understandings of sexual difference, each with its own implications for the respective roles of nuns and laywomen. The first is the more authentically Buddhist of the two and by far the more consistent with the greater body of Buddhist teachings. It perceives the difference between male and female, like other varieties of human difference, as products of humans' essentially fallen state; this is in accordance with the workings of *karma*—Buddhism's basic premise that different kinds of beings are the products of their own past desires. As one works toward spiritual perfection—essentially by learning to break the hold of desires—the consequences of fallenness, including sexual differentiation, tend to drop away. This means essentially that the process of spiritual development, in which the renunciant's vocation represents a relatively advanced step, tends to nullify sexual identifications and limitations.[22] This ideal of convergence of the sexes is re-

flected in the renunciants' identical clothes, as well as in their virtually identical spiritual paths and disciplines. It is certainly the basis as well for the triumphant song of Soma cited in the last section.

The nuns' subordination to the monks, however, as well as their uneasy status vis-à-vis the laywomen appear to draw on another model of sexual difference, which comes not from the Buddhist tradition itself but from the norms of the surrounding culture. This is the model provided by the Hindu conception of *dharma*—the vision of an all-embracing order in which everything and everyone has a place. This "place" is simultaneously a "nature" and a "role"; for being born in a particular slot means that one is at least ideally endowed with the natural capacity to fulfill that slot and has the duty to see that such a capacity is properly channeled. Failure to honor one's *dharma* invites disaster—for oneself, one's family, and ultimately the whole order. The *dharma*'s central image is that of an organism in which the various "slots" are, in effect, the equivalents of bodily members.

Now, a woman's "slot" is that of childbearer. This is also her natural capacity; hence she is the repository of a powerful generative force that seeks, above all, to put babies in the womb. Marriage and motherhood represent the proper and effective means of channeling a woman's generative drive. Her subordination to men further ensures its control—hence, the *dharma* teaching that a woman must always be subordinate to some man: in childhood, to her father; in maturity, to her husband; in old age, to her sons. In her proper place, with a living husband and surrounded by her children, a woman may achieve great honor. Out of place, she is suspect. The Hindu tradition's distrust of female ascetics is well documented, and so is its unease with other women who fail to fill their ideal role, such as the unmarried, childless, and widowed women who so often took refuge in the Buddhist community.

Buddhism was a path of enlightenment, not a revolutionary vision of renewed social order.

It made peace with the Hindu *dharma*'s precepts wherever it could, often incorporating them into its own prescriptions for ordinary human behavior and social relationships. Thus the subordination of nuns to monks can probably best be traced historically to the early community's efforts to stay at least somewhat in line with the conventional practice of the day. More important for the nuns, the Hindu *dharma*'s values percolated through into popular Buddhist expectations as well. Buddhists, like Hindus, honored fecund housewives, especially if they were also pious laywomen. We can therefore suspect that many Buddhists, like Hindus, also preferred to see women at the hearth rather than on the road or within a monastery's walls. Such preferences could easily compromise early Buddhism's rather remarkable tolerance for renunciant women.

ACCENTUATE THE POSITIVE

Given the powerful currents pulling against the nuns, I have come to wonder whether, in fact, I have not been puzzled by the wrong mystery. For it is less strange that the nuns finally came in second to the monks (and laywomen) than that they survived so well for so long. When I Ching described the poor and simple nuns of North India, their order had existed for over a thousand years. Furthermore, it continued to survive for at least two full centuries longer. Once upon a time I believed that I Ching had spoken the last word on the nuns and that they must have faded and died out shortly after his visit, yet I continue to discover traces of later nuns. A few days before completing this chapter, for example, I found another record of the nuns in a grant to a monastery of eastern India. Among the allocations for this very large establishment were ten servants for the community of nuns that was housed within the monastery's precinct. The grant is dated at

885 A.D.[23] Thus it becomes more likely that the nuns lived on until the monks' traces also vanished from Indian history.

Notes

1. Therigatha, translated with the traditional commentary by C.A.F. Rhys Davids in *Psalms of the Early Buddhists* (London: Luzac, 1964). For an excellent summary of these and other sources on the earliest nuns, see I. B. Horner, *Women under Primitive Buddhism* (London: Routledge, 1930).
2. It may seem somewhat puzzling that nuns and monks who had supposedly rejected most material possessions nonetheless had the economic resources to make donations to Buddhist building projects and monuments. In some cases relatives remaining within the lay community seem to have offered donations on the monks' or nuns' behalf. In some cases, like that of the distinguished monk-scholar Vasubandhu, the monks or nuns redirected a surplus of gifts that had been offered by laypersons for their own personal use.
3. J. J. Fleet, *Gupta Inscriptions* (Calcutta, 1988), no. 70.
4. K. J. Virji, *Ancient History of Saurashtra* (Bombay, 1955), pp. 263 and 287, no. 49.
5. As described by Richard Robinson, *Early Mādhyamika in India and China* (Madison, Wis.: University of Wisconsin Press, 1967), pp. 72–73.
6. J. Takakusu, "The Life of Vasubandhu by Paramārtha," *T'oung Pao*, ser. 2. Vol. 5 (1904), p. 286.
7. This is suggested in the romantic epic on Harsha's life, Harshacarita (8. 288), but not in historical accounts of Harsha. His sister's knowledge of Buddhist philosophy and enthusiasm for Buddhist teachings are, however, attested independently.
8. For both pilgrims' accounts, see S. Beal, *Buddhist Records of the Western World*, Vol. 1 (London: Kegan, Paul, Trench, Trübner, 1884), pp. xxxix, 181.
9. J. Takakusu, trans., *A Record of the Buddhist Religion* (London: Clarendon Press, 1896), p. 81.
10. Probably the best available source on the monastic community's structure and history is S. Dutt, *Buddhist Monks and Monasteries of India* (London: Allen & Unwin, 1962).
11. I have followed the most accessible version, the Vinayapitakam of the Southern Buddhists' Pali

Canon. For a readily available translation, see I. B. Horner, *Book of the Discipline*, Sacred Books of the Buddhists, Vols. 9–14, 20 (London: Luzac, 1949–1963).

12. Vinayapitakam, Suttavibhanga, Pātidesaniya 1.
13. See Vinayapitakam, Bhikkunīvibhanga.
14. Vinayapitakam, Cullavagga 10. 3.
15. Anguttaranikāya 1. 14. 4.
16. Sanyuttanikāya 1. 5. 2.
17. Sanyuttanikāya 16. 10.
18. Vinayapitakam, Bhikkunīvibhanga, Pācittiya 8.
19. Nandakovādasutta of the Majjhimanikāya.
20. The first version was heard and repeated by the Chinese pilgrim Fa Hsien; the second, by the later pilgrim Hsuan Tsang. For both, see Beal, *Buddhist Records*, Vol. 1, pp. xl, 204–205. The third version is translated in S. Levi, *Mahākarmavibhanga et Karmavibhangopadesa* (Paris: E. Leroux, 1932), p. 174.
21. This story has been retold many times throughout Buddhist literature. The most readily accessible version is in the Pali Vinayapitakam, Cullavagga 10. 1–3.
22. I am indebted to co-contributor Diana Paul for helping me to understand this model. See her book, *Women in Buddhism: Images of the Feminine in the Mahayana Tradition* (Berkeley, Ca.: Asian Humanities Press, 1979).
23. Reported in D. K. Barua, *Vihāras in Ancient India* (Calcutta: Indian Publications, 1969), p. 191.

Further Readings

Davids, Caroline A. F. Rhys. *Psalms of the Early Buddhists* I: *Psalms of the Sisters*. London: Henry Frowde, 1909.

Dutt, Sukumar. *Buddhist Monks and Monasteries of India: Their History and Contribution to Indian Culture*. London: George Allen and Unwin Ltd., 1962. (For background information on Buddhist monasticism; little attention to nuns.)

Horner, Ivy Baker. *Women under Primitive Buddhism: Laywomen and Almswomen*. London: G. Routledge and Sons, 1930.

Kabilsingh, Chatsumarn. *A Comparative Study of Bhikkunī Pātimokkha*. Varanasi: Chaukhambha Orientalia, 1984.

Paul, Diana Y. *Women in Buddhism: Images of the Feminine in Mahāyāna Tradition*. Berkeley, Calif.: Asian Humanities Press, 1979.

16

Evangelical Womanhood in Nineteenth-Century America: The Role of Women in Sunday Schools

ANNE M. BOYLAN

In the nineteenth-century United States, two seemingly contradictory developments shaped the lives of white, middle-class women. On the one hand, new ideals of womanhood emphasized the differences between the sexes and set women apart from men by designating a special "sphere" for them, one bounded by home and family concerns. On the other hand, women were increasingly visible in activities previously considered to be part of the public world of men. The Protestant churches in particular witnessed an extraordinary proliferation of women's organizations, most of them devoted to benevolent purposes. Through such organizations, women engaged in a wide variety of public activities, including raising funds to endow permanent institutions such as orphanages, acquiring acts of incorporation, and teaching religious doctrine.

Although historians studying these two phenomena initially assumed that they occurred sequentially, it is now clear that the development of new ideals of womanhood and the

ANNE M. BOYLAN, Assistant Professor of History and Women's Studies at the University of Delaware, received the Ph.D. from the University of Wisconsin in 1973. Her book, *Sunday School: The Formation of an American Institution, 1790–1880,* will be published by Yale University Press in 1988. She is currently writing a book on women's organizations in early nineteenth-century New York and Boston.

Editors' Note This article is reprinted, with some alterations, from *Feminist Studies,* Volume 4, Number 3 (October 1978): 62–80, by permission of the author and the publisher, Feminist Studies, Inc., c/o Women's Studies Program, University of Maryland, College Park, MD 20742.

formation of new women's groups occurred simultaneously. Women's organizations were logical extensions of emerging conceptions of womanhood; moreover, women themselves took a large role in devising both the ideology and the organizations. An analysis of women's role in the evangelical Protestant Sunday school movement demonstrates these points clearly. While women Sunday school organizers did not act with complete autonomy, neither were they mere pawns in the hands of male church leaders. In forming and running Sunday schools, they not only redefined prevailing images of women within the churches, but also constructed new arenas for women's public activity.[1]

The founding of Sunday schools in the early nineteenth century grew out of the sequence of religious revivals termed the Second Great Awakening, which lasted from about 1790 to 1835. Almost all Sunday school founders and most early teachers were either recent converts or those hopeful of experiencing conversion. Like participants in the Awakening as a whole, these individuals were generally quite young, and a majority of them were women. For them, conversion, whether actual or imminent, was a defining life experience which they commonly regarded as a "re-birth." In their new lives, they were to have recognizably different patterns of activity, characterized by exemplary behavior as well as action to evangelize others. Their search for appropriate evangelizing agencies led Protestants to create a variety of benevolent institutions, among them Sunday schools, which simultaneously met the objective needs of a society without welfare agencies and the subjective needs of energetic converts without meaningful work.[2] As the writings of Sunday school organizers reveal, a two-pronged process led women from the conversion experience to benevolent work. First, they rejected prevailing ideas about women and created new ideals rooted in evangelical Protestantism; and second, they found institutional means of enacting and promulgating their new ideals.

At the turn of the nineteenth century, the image of woman most widely disseminated in popular magazines and novels was that of the lady. These publications presented woman as a creature who cultivated fashion, charm, and the "ornamental arts," so as to enhance the reputations of the men in her life, or to acquire men who valued these accomplishments. At one extreme, the lady was also one who shunned childbearing as indelicate (and figure-ruining), viewed childrearing as boring, and regarded churchgoing primarily as a means of displaying her latest fashionable outfit. In more moderate interpretations, the lady merely delegated as many routine tasks as possible to servants, in order to have time for herself.[3]

However popular, this image was seen by many as antithetical to American values, encouraging as it did an unrepublican concern with fashion and idle devotion to the self. Vigorously protesting this "aristocratic" image of women as frivolous and fashionmongering, many commentators urged American women to devote themselves instead to cultivating the image of the "Republican Mother." Serious-minded and patriotic, the Republican Mother knew that her highest achievement lay in raising good citizens for the republic and in exemplifying those virtues—prudence, frugality, industriousness—which the country needed.[4]

The popular image of the lady was also incompatible with the tenets and social ideals of evangelical Protestantism. Echoing the republican rejection of this image, evangelical Protestant women at the turn of the century worked to create an alternative ideal of womanhood. A recurrent theme in their writings—that before conversion they had led frivolous, gay, and useless lives—points to their consciousness that conversion was inconsistent with the life of the lady. A related theme—the need to do something to signify one's conversion—reflects their concern with being useful, doing something meaningful with their lives. A third theme—the desire to save other women from the traps they had encountered—suggests their desire to develop concrete, alternative ways of life. As converted women, they must cast aside the cultural prescription of ornamental womanhood, develop a new female ideal, and take on new lives.[5]

Evangelical womanhood combined the traditional Protestant ideal of the "vertuous woman" with a new evangelical stress on action. It portrayed woman as nurturing, sensitive, pious; more aware than man of injustice, and more capable of providing comfort to those in need. Although stressing the essential differences between the sexes, this image suggested that the differences were divinely appointed for what Hannah More called the "better economy of the world," and did not imply inequalities between the sexes. Rather, men and women were complementary equals, with equally important roles to play in society. Evangelical women were to "be up and doing" and although their work differed from that of men—concerned as it was with care of children, the weak, and the oppressed—it was by no means less valuable.[6] Indeed, the exponents of this ideal came to see women's work as more important than that of men; men could be presidents, but only women could do society's most important work—rearing good children.[7]

In conjunction with this new image, women created an alternative social role: substituting a self-sacrificing dedication to others for the lady's concern with self, evangelical women designed activities for women of all ages and stations in life. A woman's central role, they knew, was that of wife and mother, and so they drew the outlines of a cult of selfless motherhood which eventually pervaded the nineteenth century. Devoting herself to husband and children, the evangelical mother sought to lead them all to salvation and useful lives. The only activity she allowed herself beyond the family circle was attendance at religious observances or membership in a maternal association (an association of mothers dedicated to improved methods of childrearing). Yet the greatest need was for meaningful work to engage young single women. With the age of first

marriage rising, and with uneven sex ratios coming to prevail in the northeastern states (especially in cities), women stayed single longer; and more women did not marry at all. Reflecting on their own experiences, evangelical women argued that it was critical for the young to have some occupation which would protect them from the seductions of a leisured life. Later they might have motherhood to employ them; now they needed other work.[8]

Evangelical womanhood, then, was a role choice whereby individuals shaped their lives around their religious convictions, forming friendships, undertaking activities, even choosing jobs that would best further their image of themselves as converted persons. The existence of this role can be seen in the biographies, autobiographies, and diaries of countless Sunday school teachers. One example will reveal the general pattern.

Harriet Lathrop, Sunday school organizer and missionary, was born into a pious family in Connecticut in 1796. At the age of 13, she experienced conversion and joined her town's Presbyterian church as its youngest member. Like other evangelicals, she interpreted her conversion as a mandate to relinquish "amusements" and "gay" friends and to attempt "to be useful to all around me." "I desire," she wrote to her mother, "to spend my life in the service of my Maker." But how? She puzzled over what "a weak, ignorant female" could do, apart from pray, in order to evangelize others, and confessed she was "almost ready to wish myself a man" that she might become a missionary. By the time she was 18, Lathrop had begun to find an answer through activities which were not only "useful" but also in keeping with her self-definition as a converted Christian. Several hours a week were devoted to a Society for the Relief of Poor Women and Children: visiting poor women in their homes or at the almshouse, praying with them and distributing tracts, soliciting donations from well-to-do Christians, and teaching poor children in a free school. One evening a week she conducted a prayer meeting which quickly metamorphosed into a missionary society, raising funds "for the education of heathen youth." Sundays were spent teaching the Sunday school which she organized in 1816. Founded upon her return from a trip to New York where she had observed the work of the New York Female Union for the Promotion of Sabbath Schools, this school involved both Sunday teaching and weekly visits to her students at home. Much of her other free time was spent in letter writing to friends and relatives on religious subjects, or in seeking out neighbors for "Christian conversation." At the age of 23, she chose her future career by marrying a minister and accompanying him to Ceylon as a missionary. Even after the move, Lathrop continued to correspond with her Sunday school, with individuals to whom she had delivered tracts, as well as with family and close friends.[9]

Lathrop's life was typical of the pattern which other evangelical women created. They considered their conversions to be the defining experience in their lives and sought ways of leading others to the same experience. Conversion marked the beginning of a life devoted to Christian growth, involving intensive self-examination about matters of daily living. Intimate friendships could be cultivated only with pious individuals, and marriage with a non-pious person was out of the question. Teaching Sunday school facilitated this quest for right living not only because it reinforced religious commitment and provided an arena for influencing others in the same direction, but also because it presented a ready source of like-minded friends. Diaries, letters, and autobiographies reveal patterns of close, exclusive, and at times intense friendships between Sunday school students and teachers, friendships which frequently traversed time and distance.[10]

Individuals such as Lathrop did not develop their lives in isolation. Rather, they existed within an intricate network of personal relationships among fellow evangelicals. Although these relationships existed primarily among converted individuals within the same community, they were also extended beyond the local level by visits and letters among evangelical friends and by new evangelical magazines such as the *Religious Intelligencer*. Lathrop, for example, learned about Sunday schools while on a visit to New York where she sought out those attractions which offered "familiar Christian communion"; as another tourist might visit Castle Garden or New York's Battery, Lathrop attended the churches with the most inspiring preachers, and sat in on a meeting of the Sunday school society. Similarly, the founding of the first Sunday school in Utica, New York, can be traced to a visit to Utica by a young woman familiar with New York City's schools. Her host on that visit, a newly converted young woman, gathered four teen-age friends with a similar commitment and founded a Sunday school.[11]

Once they had helped create the ideal and lifestyle of the evangelical woman, Sunday school workers devised ways of extending it to succeeding generations. Using a common contemporary understanding, Sunday school workers argued that "youth" (a term generally referring to age 14 and over) was "the most critical period of life" during which "the mind generally takes a decided turn, and the happiness and usefulness of the character is ensured or destroyed." Because the teenage years constituted such a crucial stage, female teachers sought ways of making their schools the central shaping force in a girl's life. Through the schools they hoped to disseminate the ideal of evangelical womanhood and secure early adherence to it among their pupils. In pursuit of this goal, they developed a rationale for Sunday school teaching, organized special classes to train adolescents to become teachers, and worked to make their own teachers significant role models in the lives of young women.[12]

Their rationale for Sunday school work stressed its long-term benefits to the young woman. It was a pious activity, they pointed out, so it maintained continuity with a youth's religious education. It was a demanding work, so it would counteract the "love of ease" which seemed to characterize youth, and the commitment it required helped to mitigate the natural tendency of the young to "indecision." Finally, it was work that existed in a growing number of locations, so that when young people moved to new areas they could, simply by offering their services to the local Sunday school, place themselves under good influences. Best of all, the experience of teaching Sunday school had been shown to promote conversion, the central experience of the evangelical life, and continuance in the work offered a sure "preservative against declension."[13]

Sunday school organizers also shaped the schools' program both to fit young people's needs and to ease the transition from childhood to youth by providing proper guidance during that "eventful and critical period." One type of guidance was personal. Envisioning the teacher as "an elder . . . sister" to her pupils, Sunday school organizers suggested that the formation of close personal and spiritual ties between teachers and their students could crucially affect the formation of the child's character. As one organizer wrote, a close relationship would give the teacher "a moral influence" over the student which would have "beneficial and enduring results," especially at adolescence when the student was choosing her future course in life. For female students, then, the female teacher was to provide a powerful model of evangelical womanhood, on which the students would want to shape their lives.[14] A second type of guidance was institutional and involved training students as future teachers. Individual teachers encouraged students who experienced conversion to bring the experience to fruition by becoming teachers. Former teacher Lydia Bacon expressed this expectation when she heard that a former student had been converted. "Tell her that I am happy to hear it," she wrote to a mutual acquaintance,

"and that I trust she will be a firm, active Christian, taking up her cross in her youth. I presume she has a class in the Sabbath school." Teachers also set up formal "Bible classes" for teenagers aimed at, among other things, training these students to become teachers.[15]

Evidence from the experiences of the first generation of Sunday school teachers suggests that these strategies did in fact meet the needs of young Protestants. Material from teachers' diaries and letters, as well as from teachers' organizations, shows that teachers and students often became close friends and that the friendships served important reciprocal functions. Visiting students in their homes was a common practice which created "strong reciprocal affections" between student and teacher. Even when separated by distance, dedicated teachers frequently carried on correspondence with their former pupils. Indeed one teacher was able to claim on the fiftieth anniversary of her first Sunday school that of the nine students in her class, six were still her correspondents. (In her case, the closeness was reinforced because she taught many of the same students in daily school.) Caroline Richards, a student and later teacher in a Canadaigua, New York, Sunday school recorded numerous instances of female teachers and students meeting socially to make quilts or other gifts for women teachers who were leaving the school. When she herself was getting married, her class of eight girls "had their ambrotypes taken with me" and made plans to "dress in white and sit on the first seat in church." These close friendships, facilitated by the generally small size of Sunday school classes, enabled teachers to pass on to succeeding generations of students the model of evangelical womanhood to which they subscribed.[16]

Bible classes and weekly teachers' meetings were also significant means of disseminating and cultivating the ideal of evangelical womanhood. In the Bible class, usually kept to between six and ten students, a young woman could meet and develop friendships with other pious young women, including the teacher. Later, when they themselves became teachers, the young women would enter a world of activities which would reinforce their commitment to evangelicalism and provide alternatives to the diversions of the world. In the teachers' meetings, which were sex-segregated for the first few decades, young women could socialize with like-minded contemporaries, share prayers and narratives of religious experiences, and initiate new teachers into the community of workers through prayer and fellowship. By engaging in decision making about matters relating to the school, they received training in organization and leadership. Later on, when teachers' meetings integrated the sexes, they provided socially acceptable opportunities for meeting potential mates: in a world in which young women were constantly warned against strange men, they could be reasonably sure that men encountered at Sunday school shared their beliefs and lifestyle.[17]

These social and psychological benefits aside, Sunday school teaching attracted succeeding generations of women because it offered them an appealing vision of themselves as useful and significant individuals. To take one example, the speeches of successive presidents of the Baltimore Female Sabbath School Society indicate that women saw Sunday school work as one of the few areas where they could influence, however indirectly, the course of society. Our "exertions," argued one president, multiply "the virtues that establish the comfort of society." Sunday school teaching, suggested another, by "fitting the present generation to act their parts upon the great stage of human action," was a powerful means of shaping the future of society. If children represented that future, then those involved in their training would perhaps help to determine whether society languished under a "torrent of vice" or benefited from "those great moral influences upon which all prosperity and happiness" were founded. It fit the "diffidence and retirement so becoming" to women, another

president proposed, that their power be exerted indirectly. "What though your names may not be emblazoned on the historical page?" asked another; your influence is as great, perhaps greater, than that of those (men) whom history does remember. You are engaged, she concluded, in "mighty operations"; "you are attending to the moral and intellectual culture of youthful immortals."[18] These sentiments expressed the belief that evangelical activities enabled women to be as important and effective as men—perhaps even more so.

The achievement of the first women Sunday school founders and teachers during the 1810s and 1820s lay in establishing their work as useful and significant, and in drawing succeeding generations into it. In doing this, they were helping to establish evangelical womanhood as an alternative role choice for nineteenth-century women, and Sunday school teaching as a key part of that role.

The definition of evangelical womanhood was never static; indeed, some of its appeal lay in its flexibility and its varying interpretations. One could select one's own level and style of commitment to the ideal, whether it be devotion to family and home, teaching Sunday school once a week, engaging in numerous benevolent activities at once, or becoming a full-time missionary. For the individual, also, a particular choice need not be a final one: many women were content to do Sunday school teaching solely, but for others teaching led into an expanding round of benevolent activities. During the 1830s and 1840s, evangelical women, many of whom began their careers as Sunday school teachers, extended the boundaries of evangelical womanhood by engaging in increasingly activist and full-time forms of benevolence. Women who saw themselves as inheritors of the mantle of evangelical womanhood became foreign missionaries, moral reformers, abolitionists, or even advocates of women's rights, all the while arguing that their activities were merely different ways of exerting female influence in the world.[19]

For some women, teaching became a stepping-stone to other more public or more time-consuming activities. Women applying to become missionaries of the American Board of Commissioners for Foreign Missions, for example, invariably used their Sunday school teaching as evidence of their suitability for the job and their general good character; letters of recommendation from their ministers echoed this view. Other women found that teaching led them into involvement in related benevolent causes. Joanna Graham Bethune, organizer of the New York Female Union for the Promotion of Sabbath Schools in 1816, extended her activities into the formation of infant schools in the 1820s and gradually developed a full-time career in benevolence. In addition, there were a large number of anonymous women teachers who shaped writing careers for themselves by feeding the seemingly insatiable appetites of Sunday school publishers for books and magazine articles.[20]

Other Sunday school teachers, especially those who were trained as common school teachers or who were married to ministers, forged careers as missionaries to the American West. Combining a willingness to teach both day and Sunday schools, these women came to frontier communities as exemplars of evangelical womanhood. They conducted school during the week, larding their instruction with heavy doses of religious teaching, and also taught Sunday school. There are numerous examples of this type of career—from the ministers' wives who did dual duty in countless American communities to the missionaries who went South during Reconstruction to teach the freed slaves—and there is good evidence that their ability to teach Sunday school made these women doubly attractive to communities seeking teachers. National Sunday school publications even appealed to "pious females in single life" during the 1830s to move to "destitute" areas of the West precisely to fill this dual function.[21]

The career of Harriet Bishop provides a good example of a Sunday school missionary. A devoted evangelical Baptist and an admirer of women missionaries, Bishop was teaching school in New York when she heard about the National Board of Popular Education, an organization founded by Catharine Beecher to recruit female teachers for Western schools. Attending a course offered by the Board in 1847, Bishop answered an appeal for a teacher in Minnesota. Organizing the first day school and the first Sunday school in St. Paul, Bishop became a missionary both of evangelical religion and of the cultural values she associated with it, in the process creating a full-time career which reflected those of hundreds of evangelical women like her.[22]

Before 1850, however, most women Sunday school teachers continued to adhere to an interpretation of evangelical womanhood which stressed invisible influence. They did not seek, or gain, access to leadership positions within Sunday schools; instead they were content to see women exerting power and influence in silent, invisible ways. Situations of overt power, such as administrative jobs, were left to male Sunday school workers. Even when women made up a large majority of teachers in a school, as was frequently the case, the superintendent and other officers were always male.[23]

Female teachers did not begin to expand their definition of evangelical womanhood and hence take more active public roles until the 1850s. During that decade, teachers' associations began electing female officers (although the superintendent's position generally remained a male preserve); and some urban Sunday school organizations began hiring women for local missionary work. The late 1850s and 1860s saw the growth of local teachers' conventions and institutes, which women attended as delegates, and at which women occasionally conducted sessions. The percentage of women delegates to the New York State Sunday School Teachers' Convention, for example, rose from 16% in 1863 to 32% in 1878. In the same way women made up 30% of the delegates to Kentucky's 1875 convention; but they were 45% of the 1878 delegates. More married women were engaging in Sunday school teaching, also; at least 45% of the women delegates to the 1867 Illinois State Sunday School Convention were married.[24]

Even though their expanded activity came more than two decades after other evangelical women had begun to assert their right to lead and to speak on religious questions, female Sunday school workers in the 1850s and 1860s encountered resistance from male leaders who invoked traditional arguments against such public activity. Women, claimed one minister in a national magazine, have special qualities which suit them to teaching but not to supervising. To another, it appeared "evident that God never intended that women should be public speakers; or that, in his church, and in related organizations, women should occupy the position of public teachers and rulers." "It would be better," he concluded, "to have a man of *very* moderate ability as superintendent, than to have a very gifted woman." At the first national Sunday school teachers' summer school in Chautauqua, New York, in 1873, the organizers barred women from addressing a mixed assembly of teachers, requiring them instead to hold separate receptions for women only.[25]

Despite such opposition, women justified their movement into more authoritative positions in much the same way as their predecessors had justified organizing and teaching the schools. They had special talents to offer as women and special work to do as evangelicals, they argued, and could best perform that work by speaking and conducting sessions at conventions. Believing that they had a "peculiar power" to do good, to take the lead in "elevating society," they confidently dismissed opposition. Thus, three years after women were denied permission to speak to the Chautauqua assembly, the barrier came down as Frances Willard addressed the mixed gathering.[26]

In the 1860s and 1870s, female Sunday school workers found two new areas of activity: promoting new teaching methods and campaigning for temperance education. Women who came to Sunday school work with normal school training brought with them an enthusiasm for new teaching techniques and a belief that these techniques could improve Sunday school teaching. Among the techniques they were instrumental in adapting to Sunday schools were those based on the philosophy of Swiss educator Johann Pestalozzi. Because Pestalozzi's system was predicated upon an understanding of the child's "nature" and the achievement of "empathy" between teacher and pupil, women claimed a special competence for teaching the system. By using arguments similar to those which had justified the employment of women for primary public school teaching, they suggested that women were best qualified to teach children.[27]

The wholesale adoption of new methods by the 1870s and the introduction of new standards of professionalism into Sunday school work brought several women to national prominence. One was Sara J. Timanus, a teacher at the Minnesota State Normal School, who developed a second career lecturing to Sunday school teachers' institutes and writing for teachers' magazines. By the early 1870s, she was also preparing a set of weekly lessons for a national periodical. After her marriage in 1874 to another Sunday school worker (whom she had met while working on a book for teachers)[28] Timanus worked her second career into a full-time one.

Another Sunday school innovation particularly associated with women was the adoption of kindergartens. Beginning in the early 1870s women such as Matilda Kriege, principal of Boston's kindergarten training school, contributed numerous articles to teachers' magazines on the principles and practices of kindergartens and their adaptation to Sunday schools. Kriege and others like her also traveled to teachers' institutes and conventions, conducting "model classroom" sessions designed to familiarize teachers with kindergartens. Through these sessions, they taught techniques associated with Pestalozzi and with Friedrich Froebel, offered practical lessons in the use of such techniques, and emphasized that only women should teach kindergarten Sunday schools. They succeeded in convincing a growing number of Sunday schools to create kindergarten divisions and established kindergarten teaching as a special area of expertise reserved for women.[29]

Temperance workers developed a different set of leadership roles for women in Sunday schools. Although temperance work had traditionally attracted evangelical women, only in the late 1860s did they begin to use Sunday school magazines to suggest that teachers could win the battle against "the rum-power" by converting children to total abstinence. From these individual efforts came lectures on the importance of instructing Sunday school pupils on temperance, and finally, meetings of women temperance workers at the first national Sunday school teachers' summer school in Chautauqua, New York, in 1873, and again in 1874. These gatherings, in turn, led to the formation of the Woman's Christian Temperance Union, which quickly established committees on Juvenile Temperance Work and Sunday Schools. The idea of using Sunday schools as the means of reaching young people came naturally to WCTU organizers, many of whom—like Jennie Fowler Willing, Emily Huntington Miller, and Frances Willard—were Sunday school teachers. During the organization's first five years, they planned and executed two successful programs: organizing Sunday school students into Juvenile Temperance Unions, complete with banners and abstinence pledges; and lobbying for the adoption of temperance lessons within each denomination's schools. The lessons, written and developed by Sunday school and temperance advocates Sara Timanus (Crafts) and Emily Huntington Miller, achieved widespread adoption by 1879.[30]

These women, although more assertive and visible than earlier generations of Sunday school teachers, were nevertheless acting within the broad outlines of evangelical womanhood drawn in the early nineteenth century. They believed as did their predecessors that women possessed certain innate qualities which suited them for particular kinds of activity. Like them, too, they used the argument for female qualities to press for special social roles for women—as teachers, temperance leaders, kindergarten workers. No longer preoccupied with defining evangelical womanhood, they expanded it to include public speaking, conducting teachers' conventions, and writing Sunday school lessons.

The concept of evangelical womanhood, as I have elaborated it in the preceding pages, helps to delineate a particular ideal and style of female behavior in the nineteenth century. Although nineteenth-century evangelical women did not use the term themselves, they recognized that their lives and social ideals, as shaped by evangelical Protestantism, were different enough to set them apart from their contemporaries. Just as evangelicalism contained an inherent critique of the values and lifestyles of the leisured classes, so too did the concept of the evangelical woman encompass a critique of "the butterflies of the *fashionable* world."[31]

In evangelicalism, women found an alternative to uselessness. They also found ideals and values which not only reflected their own view of women's nature, but also encouraged their desire to create broader educational and social opportunities for women. Hence when evangelical women developed seminaries, benevolent societies, and church groups, they were creating alternative institutions through which the evangelical ideal of woman could be developed, taught, and promulgated. Sunday schools provide only one example of this process; the discussion presented here might also by extension be applied to developments within other institutions as well. For example,

Sunday school workers' methods of transmitting the evangelical ideal, especially their use of conscious role models, were also practiced in seminaries and benevolent societies. None of these institutions existed alone; rather, their activities supported and reinforced each other, creating varied opportunities for women wishing to pursue the evangelical ideal.

This analysis also demonstrates the meaning of religious behavior for nineteenth-century women. Women had consistently made up a majority of the church members in colonial America. What was new in the nineteenth century was their redefinition of the conversion experience to mandate social action. As in the past, religious behavior offered women a means of signifying their values and goals; but now it also offered them means of shaping active, even public lives. Precisely because nineteenth-century women had fewer acceptable avenues to usefulness and activity, religious behavior became a more important means of self-expression for them than it was for men.

In arguing, as I have here, that women themselves developed the ideal of evangelical womanhood and then elaborated on the ideal through varied interpretations, I do not mean to suggest that nineteenth-century women chose this role without constraints. They did not. The constraints upon them were not, however, the simple ones of male authority. Rather, these women acted within a complex series of constraints formed by their social class, current public opinion, and the historical realities of women's subordinate status. Yet within these limits, evangelical women manifested a clear drive to take hold of their lives and shape goals and activities based on their own conception of womanhood.

Notes

1. See Barbara Welter, "The Cult of True Womanhood, 1820–1860," *American Quarterly*, 18 (1966): 151–74; Nancy F. Cott, *The Bonds of Womanhood: "Women's Sphere" in New England, 1780–1835* (New Haven: Yale University Press, 1977); Kathryn Kish Sklar, *Catharine Beecher: A Study in American Domesticity* (New Haven: Yale University Press, 1973); Keith Melder, *Beginnings of Sisterhood: The American Woman's Rights Movement, 1800–1850* (New York: Schocken, 1977); and Gerda Lerner, "The Lady and the Mill Girl: Changes in the Status of Women in the Age of Jackson," *Midcontinent American Studies Journal*, 10 (1969): 5–14.

2. Lois W. Banner, "The Protestant Crusade: Religious Missions, Benevolence, and Reform in the United States, 1790–1840" (Ph.D. dissertation, Columbia University, 1970), pp. 288–305; and "Religion and Reform in the Early Republic: The Role of Youth," *American Quarterly* 23 (1971): 677–95; Nancy F. Cott, "Young Women in the Second Great Awakening in New England," *Feminist Studies* 3 (1975): 15–29; Edwin Wilbur Rice, *The Sunday-School Movement, 1780–1917, and the American Sunday-School Union, 1817–1917* (Philadelphia: American Sunday-School Union, 1917). See also Carroll Smith-Rosenberg, *Religion and the Rise of the American City: The New York City Mission Movement, 1812–1870* (Ithaca: Cornell University Press, 1971), pp. 97–124.

3. Robert Elno McGlone, "Suffer the Children: The Emergence of Modern Middle-Class Family Life in America, 1820–1870" (Ph.D. dissertation, UCLA, 1971), chapter 1; Julia C. Spruill, *Women's Life and Work in the Southern Colonies* (Chapel Hill: University of North Carolina Press, 1938; reprinted, 1972), pp. 208–31.

4. For a good example of critiques of this image, see Thomas Branagan, *The Excellency of the Female Character Vindicated* (Philadelphia: J. Rakestraw, 1808), especially chapters 1 and 2. The concept of the "Republican Mother" is set forth in Linda K. Kerber, "The Republican Mother: Women and the Enlightenment—An American Perspective," *American Quarterly* 28 (1976): 187–205.

5. See especially Joanna Bethune, ed., *The Power of Faith: Exemplified in the Life and Writings of the Late Mrs. Isabella Graham of New York* (New York: American Tract Society, 1843).

6. On the eighteenth century, see Lonna Myers Malmsheimer, "New England Funeral Sermons and Changing Attitudes Toward Women, 1692–1792" (Ph.D. dissertation, University of Minnesota, 1973), especially chapter 4; also Laurel Thatcher Ulrich, "Vertuous Women Found: New England

Ministerial Literature, 1668–1735," *American Quarterly* 28 (1976): 20–40; and Mary Sumner Benson, *Women in Eighteenth-Century America: A Study of Opinion and Social Usage* (New York: Columbia University Press, 1935), chapters 3–4. Hannah More, a British evangelical, was very influential in the United States; see her *Strictures on the Modern System of Female Education* (London: T. Cadell & W. Davies, 1799).

7. The best explication of this ideal, as articulated by Catharine Beecher a generation later, is in Sklar, *Catharine Beecher*, especially part IV.

8. Anne L. Kuhn, *The Mother's Role in Childhood Education: New England Concepts, 1830–1860* (New Haven: Yale University Press, 1947) discusses some later manifestations of these ideas. For their origins, see especially Joanna Bethune, ed., *The Unpublished Letters and Correspondence of Mrs. Isabella Graham, From the Year 1767 to 1814* (New York: John S. Taylor, 1838), pp. 179–82, 222–24; Bethune, ed., *The Power of Faith*, pp. 82, 129–33; and *Diary of Sarah Connell Ayer* (Portland: n.p., 1910), pp. 226, 231, 358–59.

9. Miron Winslow, *Memoir of Mrs. Harriet L. Winslow, Thirteen Years a Member of the American Mission in Ceylon* (New York: American Tract Society, 1840), pp. 18, 25, 29–30, 34, 37–40, 64–66.

10. See Bethune, ed., *The Power of Faith*, pp. 167, 229–30, 235, 243, 368; J. Bethune to F. A. Packard, 4 August 1829, Gratz Collection, Historical Society of Pennsylvania, Philadelphia, Pennsylvania; B. K. Peirce, *One Talent Improved: or, The Life and Labors of Miss Susan B. Bowler, Successful Sunday-School Teacher* (New York: Carlton and Porter, 1845); *Biography of Mrs. Lydia B. Bacon* (Boston: Massachusetts Sabbath School Society, 1856).

11. Winslow, *Memoir of Mrs. Harriet L. Winslow*, pp. 54–68; First Presbyterian Church, Utica, *Semi-Centennial of the Sunday School* (Utica, N.Y.: First Presbyterian Church, 1866), pp. 39–40.

12. W. F. Lloyd, *Teacher's Manual: or, Hints to a Teacher on Being Appointed to the Charge of a Sunday School Class* (Philadelphia: American Sunday School Union, 1825), p. 82; Archibald Alexander, "Suggestions in Vindication of Sunday Schools" (Philadelphia: American Sunday School Union, 1829), p. 7; Elizabeth, New Jersey, First Presbyterian Church, Sunday School Teachers' Association Minutes, April 2, 1827, Presbyterian Historical Society,

Philadelphia, Pennsylvania; *Religious Intelligencer* 3 (July, 1818): 105; Joseph F. Kett, "Adolescence and Youth in Nineteenth-Century America," *Journal of Interdisciplinary History* 2 (1971): 283–98.

13. James Milnor, "Address to the Sunday School of St. George's Church, New York" (New York: New York Sunday School Union, 1817), p. 5; *Religious Intelligencer* 3 (December, 1818): 431; *Sabbath School Herald* 1 (May, 1829): 76–77.

14. Frederick A. Packard, *The Teacher Taught: An Humble Attempt to Make the Path of the Sunday School Teacher Straight and Plain* (Philadelphia: American Sunday School Union, 1839), pp. 87, 162.

15. Boston, Twelfth Congregational Society, "Address Delivered Before . . . the Sunday School . . . At their Sixth Anniversary, March 29, 1833. By one of the Superintendents" (Boston: Twelfth Congregational Society, 1833), p. 13; Lydia Bacon to Elizabeth C., February 15, 1832, in *Biography of Mrs. Lydia B. Bacon*, pp. 115–16; "Second Annual Report of the New Hampshire Baptist Sabbath-School Union," *American Sunday-School Magazine* 7 (1830): 318–19; New York Female Union for the Promotion of Sabbath Schools, *Third Annual Report* (1819), p. 4.

16. Peirce, *One Talent Improved*, pp. 112–15; letter of Susan Burchard Taintor, printed in First Presbyterian Church, Utica, *Semi-Centennial*, pp. 41–43; *Biography of Mrs. Lydia B. Bacon*; Caroline Cowles Richards, *Village Life in America, 1852–1872* (New York: Henry Holt and Co., 1912), p. 199.

17. Philadelphia, Spruce Street Baptist Sabbath School Society, Minutes, 1855–57, American Baptist Historical Society, Rochester, New York; Baltimore Female Sabbath School Society, Minutes, 1816–1822, Lovely Lane Methodist Museum, Baltimore, Maryland. New York Sunday School Union Society, Methodist Branch Minutes, 1816–1820, New York Public Library, New York. For a description of a Sunday school courtship, see Richards, *Village Life in America*, entry of June, 1860, pp. 132–33.

18. Baltimore Female (McKendrean) Sabbath School Society, Minutes: November 3, 1831; November 1, 1828; October 4, 1836; October 16, 1837; October 1, 1838.

19. See Melder, "Beginnings of the Women's Rights Movement," chapters 3 and 4; Alice S. Rossi, "Social Roots of the Woman's Movement in

America," in Rossi, ed., *The Feminist Papers* (New York: Bantam Books, 1974), pp. 241–81; McIntosh, "The Origins of the Feminist Movement."

20. Louise T. Knauer, "Foot Soldiers in the Kingdom of God: Backgrounds and Motivations of Single Women Missionaries" (paper delivered at the Third Berkshire Conference on the History of Women, Bryn Mawr, Pennsylvania, June 9–11, 1976); George W. Bethune, ed., *Memoirs of Mrs. Joanna Bethune* (New York: American Tract Society, 1863). The incoming correspondence in the Frederick A. Packard file, Gratz Collection, Historical Society of Pennsylvania, Philadelphia, Pennsylvania, contains letters from some of the most prolific women writers for the American Sunday School Union.

21. "An Appeal from the West," *American Sunday-School Magazine* 7 (October, 1830): 310–11; see also Ellen Harriet Thomsen, "The Interest of the Eastern Churches in Western Emigration, 1830–1839" (M.A. thesis, Columbia University, 1947), pp. 20–21; and Asa Bullard, *Fifty Years with the Sabbath Schools* (Boston: Lockwood, Brooks, and Co., 1876), p. 21.

22. See her autobiographical work, *Floral Home* (New York: Sheldon, Blakeman and Co., 1857) and the biographical essay by Winifred D. Bolin in Barbara Stuhler and Gretchen Kreuter, eds., *Women of Minnesota: Selected Biographical Essays* (St. Paul: Minnesota Historical Society Press, 1977), pp. 7–19.

23. See, for example, New York, Seventh Presbyterian Church Sunday School Teachers' Association, Minutes, 1827–1857, Presbyterian Historical Society.

24. Philadelphia Sunday School Association, *Annual Report* (1859); New York State Sunday School Teachers' Association, *Proceedings* (Troy, 1863 and Albany, 1878), appendices; Kentucky State Sunday School Association, (Lexington, 1875, 1878); Illinois State Sunday School Convention, *Proceedings of the Ninth Annual Convention* (Decatur, 1867), pp. 117–36.

25. Rev. James Pierce Root, "Woman's Work in the Sabbath School," *National Sunday School Teacher* 6 (August 1871): 281–84; J. W. Willmarth, "Women and Men in Sunday Schools," *Baptist Teacher* 5 (October, 1874): 110–11; Jesse L. Hurlbut, *The Story of Chautauqua* (New York: G. P. Putnam's Sons, 1921), p. 77.

26. National Woman's Christian Temperance Union, *Minutes of the First Convention* (Chicago, 1874), p. 6.

27. Sara J. Timanus, "Pestalozzi in Sunday School Work," *Sunday School Journal* 3 (December, 1871): 266–67; Timanus, "Object Teaching in Sunday-schools," *Sunday-School World* 5 (1865): 98; J. H. Vincent, *Sunday School Institutes and Normal Classes* (New York: Nelson and Phillips, 1872); Timanus, "Questioning," *National Sunday School Teacher* 6 (1871): 245–49; Ned Harland Dearborn, *The Oswego Movement in American Education* (New York: Teachers' College, Columbia University, 1925).

28. Sara J. Timanus, *The Infant Class: Hints on Primary Religious Instruction* (Chicago: Adams, Blackmer, and Lyon, 1870); *National Sunday School Teacher* 9 (July, 1874): 275.

29. See the articles by Matilda H. Kriege in the *National Sunday School Teacher:* 6 (February, 1871): 41–43; 6 (September, 1871): 321–22; 7 (June, 1872): 208–10. See also Lizzie L. Woolman, "The Kindergarten System in the Sunday School," *Baptist Teacher* 1 (March, 1870): 19; Jennie Fowler Willing, "Keep the Little Children in Sunday School," *Sunday School Journal* 2 (June, 1870): 194–95.

30. Jennie Fowler Willing, "Sunday-School Temperance Work," *National Sunday School Teacher* 4 (October, 1869): 293–94; Helen E. Tyler, *Where Prayer and Purpose Meet: The WCTU Story, 1874–1949* (Evanston: The Signal Press, 1949), pp. 11–28; National Woman's Christian Temperance Union, *Minutes of the Second Convention* (Chicago, 1875), pp. 66–67; *Fourth Convention* (1877), pp. 202–203; *Fifth Convention* (1878), pp. 87–89; *Sixth Convention* (1879), pp. 81–89.

31. Sarah Grimké, *Letters on the Equality of the Sexes and the Condition of Women* (Boston: Isaac Knapp, 1838), p. 86.

Further Readings

Bordin, Ruth. *Woman and Temperance: The Quest for Power and Liberty, 1873–1900.* Philadelphia: Temple University Press, 1981.

Boylan, Anne M. "Women in Groups: An Analysis of Women's Benevolent Organizations in New York and Boston, 1797–1840." *Journal of American History* 71 (1984): 497–523.

Cott, Nancy F. *The Bonds of Womanhood: "Women's Sphere" in New England, 1785–1835.* New Haven, Conn.: Yale University Press, 1977.

Hewitt, Nancy A. *Women's Activism and Social Change: Rochester, New York, 1822–1872.* Ithaca, N.Y.: Cornell University Press, 1984.

Ryan, Mary P. "A Women's Awakening: Evangelical Religion and the Families of Utica, New York, 1800–1840." *American Quarterly* 30 (1978): 602–23.

Smith-Rosenberg, Carroll. "Beauty, the Beast and the Militant Woman: A Case Study in Sex Roles and Social Stress in Jacksonian America." In *Disorderly Conduct: Visions of Gender in Victorian America.* New York: A. A. Knopf, 1986.

Welter, Barbara. "The Feminization of American Religion, 1800–1860." In *Clio's Consciousness Raised: New Perspectives on the History of Women,* ed. by Mary Hartman and Lois W. Banner. New York: Harper & Row, 1974.

17

Innovation and Tradition in a Contemporary Midwestern Jewish Congregation

MARIAN HENRIQUEZ NEUDEL

The Upstairs Minyan is a small Jewish congregation founded in 1965 at the University of Chicago Hillel Foundation. The two rabbis who have belonged to it are officially affiliated with the Conservative denomination (midway in traditional observance between Reform and Orthodox). The Minyan uses the Conservative prayerbook and regards itself, somewhat loosely, as a Conservative congregation. Its membership varies from 25 to 50 active members; a regular Saturday morning service may be attended by as few as five (especially in the summer) or as many as fifty (for bar mitzvahs and other special occasions). The membership is drawn from the university (especially graduate students and junior faculty), the neighborhood surrounding it, and, to a lesser extent, the rest of the city and its suburbs.

As a Conservative Jewish congregation, the Upstairs Minyan has operated in the context of a Jewish tradition that historically placed women on the periphery of religious ritual and organization. In the strictest practices of orthodox Judaism, women cannot be counted toward the quorum of 10 people required for public prayer, must not even be visible or audible to the male congregants in the synagogue, and are not permitted any role in public worship. They may not wear the prayer shawl and phylacteries required for men at prayer. And they may take no part in the enterprise of study, interpretation, and teaching by which Jewish religious tradition continually shapes,

MARIAN HENRIQUEZ NEUDEL A.B. Harvard 1963, M.A. (English Lit.) Roosevelt 1973, J. D. DePaul 1977, has also done extensive graduate work in sociology and history of religions at Brandeis and the University of Chicago. She is now a practicing attorney and a member of the National Association of Women Cantors.

reshapes, and transmits itself through the centuries.[1]

For the past 100 years, this definition of the position of women in Jewish ritual and religious life has been under attack from many directions, and has been eroded among the majority of Jews in the United States. Reform Judaism at its outset abolished most of the ritual functions unique to men, including the quorum for prayer, the prayer shawl and phylacteries, and the authority of traditional jurisprudence. It abolished separate seating for the sexes, abolished the *bar mitzvah* (which marked a young man's accession to the age at which ritual obligations become binding upon him), and instituted confirmation as a coming-of-age ritual for boys and girls. At least two women were ordained as rabbis in the early years of Reform (before 1940), one in Germany and one in the United States. Another woman rose to an outstanding public position in Liberal Judaism in England.[2]

Conservative Judaism adopted mixed seating, but rejected virtually all the other Reform innovations which affected the position of women. Unlike the Reform rabbinical seminaries, the Conservative seminary admitted women only for its graduate program in religious education.

When the Upstairs Minyan was founded, the current wave of feminism was just beginning, and had had virtually no impact on any major religious body in the United States. Nevertheless, the Upstairs Minyan self-consciously organized itself on the basis of six principles that, while not directly inspired by feminist thought, helped women become influential early members of the group. These six principles also made the Minyan different from any other Conservative congregation at the time. A member of the Minyan who wrote a history of the group during this era lists the six principles. First is intellectual openness on religious questions and second is respect for tradition. Affirming the legitimacy of pluralistic religious and Jewish experience is third,

while respect for the resources of nonprofessional group members is the fourth organizing principle. Concluding the list are belief that maximum self-involvement is beneficial for both individual and group, and a preference for informality and flexibility.[3] Clearly, such principles, reflecting commitment to using skills and meeting needs of members, combined with the fact that some of the Minyan's most influential early members were women, resulted in definite influence from women and increased participation by women.

The influence from and increased participation of women in the Minyan can be clearly documented in three important areas. First, one can trace women's increasing participation in liturgy. At the outset, women were confined mainly to doing English readings in the mainly-Hebrew service. Initially they began to do Hebrew readings and to be counted in the quorum required for worship; services were still led by men, however. Next, they began to lead regular Saturday morning services, to recite the blessings for reading the Torah, and to read from the Hebrew Torah scroll. Finally, women began to lead services and to read from the Torah scroll for the High Holiday services, which involved a much larger congregation composed mainly of people not familiar with the Upstairs Minyan and its innovations. A second area in which women were innovative deals with ritual accessories important to formal Jewish worship but not usually used by women. Relatively early in the Minyan's history, women began to wear the prayer shawls and skull caps typically worn by men for Sabbath worship. Thirdly, the liturgical text of the Jewish prayerbook was sometimes changed to reflect the Minyan's increased sensitivity to the exclusion of women from traditional forms and a need to include them. Less radical was the earlier inclusion of female ancestral heroes (Sarah, Rebecca, Rachel, and Leah) alongside the usual male ancestral heroes (Abraham, Isaac, and Jacob) and general references to "our Mothers" as well as to "our Fathers."

More radically and less frequently, female language has also been used to describe and address the deity.

These innovations took place over a 15-year period; like the most recently hypothesized path for biological evolution, they happened in intermittent jumps rather than a slow, steady progress. The participation of women in English readings happened almost at the outset, perhaps because, by their very nature, English readings were not perceived as part of the traditional ritual, and were therefore not off-limits to women. Women had been similarly involved in Reform services for many years, and some of the Upstairs Minyan's members have always come from the Reform tradition. At about the same time, women were also being called on to take peripheral ceremonial roles in the service for the reading of the Torah, such as calling people up to the reading and helping cover the scroll after reading.

Parallel to these developments, women were extremely prominent in another, nonritual but very important, area. The rabbis who founded the Minyan encouraged substitution of a discussion, prepared and led by various Minyan members, for the traditional sermon. Women became very active in preparing, leading, and participating in these discussions. As a result, many of those discussions focussed on the role of women in Judaism, and raised questions that the rest of the Jewish community would not be considering for at least another five years.

Almost from the outset, women were counted toward the *"minyan."* or quorum of 10, required for public prayers. This was partly a matter of logistics; it would have been impossible to hold services at all on many Saturdays if the group had had to wait for 10 *men.* The Conservative movement as a whole finally accepted the practice about 10 years later.[4]

The use of English readings in the early years of the Minyan met several needs. It was a medium of "experimental" and "interpretive" approaches to the liturgy. Many of the readings were drawn from contemporary poetry and music, but some were written by Minyan members themselves. They also served the needs of a large proportion of early Minyan members, slightly more women than men, who knew very little Hebrew. Thus the use of English readings encouraged the participation of women readers, who might otherwise have dropped out.

As time went on, the level of Hebrew knowledge in the Minyan increased considerably, for several reasons. Many of the original members, through their participation in the Minyan, learned Hebrew and other ritual skills. Some took courses at local colleges to speed up the process. The Hillel house in which the Minyan met also offered courses in Hebrew and related fields. Concurrently, the use of English readings diminished, and an increasing number of members, both female and male, took at least occasional responsibility for Hebrew readings and for leading services. In addition, typically, *incoming* members had a higher level of Jewish education since the quality of education provided by the Reform and Conservative movements had improved. At about this same time, women began to read the blessings for the reading of the Torah—again, about 10 years ahead of the Conservative movement as a whole.

As more women became comfortable with the Hebrew and developed a real sensitivity for its meaning, they—and several men in the Minyan as well—found some of the Hebrew unnecessarily exclusive of women and their experiences. The role of women in Jewish history became a particular focus of attention. Jewish history originates in a series of covenants between God and the sacred ancestors, usually listed as "Abraham, Isaac, and Jacob." The *text* of that history, in Genesis, gives much more prominence to the *female* ancestors ("Sarah, Rebecca, Leah, and Rachel") than does the language of the prayerbook.[5] A tradition is defined and laid out by its remembered beginnings; this element of Jewish origins had been, tragically and unnecessarily, lost. And it could be recaptured easily enough. The numerous places in the traditional liturgy referring to the "fathers" were rewritten to include the "fathers and the mothers." References to "Abraham, Isaac, and Jacob" were paralleled by references to "Sarah, Rebecca, Leah, and Rachel." The first blessing in the central daily prayer, which ends "Blessed are You, Lord our God, Shield of Abraham" was revised to "Shield of Abraham and Sarah." After a few months, printed inserts were placed in the prayerbook at that blessing for the use of new members and nonmembers.

The reading of the Torah scroll, in more traditional congregations, is both an honored liturgical function and an occasional logistical problem. The Torah scroll, unlike most religious Hebrew texts outside of Israel, is written without vowels (rather like speedwriting). It is generally chanted to a particular set of cantillations. Learning to read the correct vocalizations in an unvoweled text and to follow the traditional musical line requires considerable skill and study. Well-educated orthodox boys learn it as the necessary preparation for their Bar Mitzvah ceremony. But Conservative religious education was, at the time, somewhat less reliable and many Reform religious schools considered such skills minimally important. Until recently, the religious education of women in *all* Jewish denominations paid virtually no attention to these skills. Therefore, most Conservative congregations tend to rely on the rabbi, the cantor, and a few male congregants or occasional paid readers to read from the scroll. Since the Minyan had already deemphasized the role of the rabbi, had no cantor, and lacked the funds to pay outside readers, it relied for many years on the better-educated men for Torah reading. But as women members improved their Hebrew skills, Torah reading seemed to many of them a reasonable next step. They attended classes, arranged for private tutoring, or had knowledgeable men make tapes for them. Many of

these concerted efforts to produce more readers were directed at *all* members, including the men who lacked childhood training. But as a practical matter, most of the new readers were women. The Minyan's response involved no ideological shock but only considerable practical relief that a logistical problem had been solved.

At about the same time, women also began to wear the prayer shawl for services—sometimes just while reading the Torah, sometimes for the whole service. Some people—men and women—found this "jarring." It never became a universal practice, though it is universally accepted as something women can do if they choose.

Over the last eight years, a few women have been exploring the use of female language to describe and address the divinity. Experimental services have been done on several occasions; rewritten versions of the blessings have been provided as optional inserts in the prayerbook. The issue has been raised on numerous occasions and is likely to be important in many further discussions.

Usually, two or three years elapse between what the Minyan has accepted as common practice in its own Saturday morning services, and what Minyan members will do in High Holiday services for the larger community. All forms of ritual participation by women as well as liturgical changes reflecting the role of the biblical matriarchs have followed this pattern. Some of these changes are explained by the rabbi at the beginning of the holiday services in which they were introduced. Others, such as calling women to read the blessings for the Torah or to read the scroll itself, were simply left to speak for themselves. The reason for this timelag has never been made explicit but is probably a combination of two things: the need of Minyan members, especially those who lead the holiday services, to feel completely at ease with the innovation, so they do not make an error or omission due to nervousness or unfamiliarity, and the sense that the outside world was moving in the same direction on many of these issues and should be given a chance to catch up.

A few innovations have been tried, and often retried, without ever becoming the norm. The wearing of *kipot* (skullcaps) by women is one such example. Though it is commonly done in some Reform and Conservative congregations, and though married orthodox women are required to cover their hair, even the women in the Minyan who regularly wear prayer shawls rarely wear skullcaps. This may be a residue of feminist reaction against the orthodox custom, which is based on a concept of *z'niut* (modesty) offensive to some feminists.

The most significant innovation which has not so far become generally accepted is the use of "female god-language." Despite numerous efforts by members, both male and female, with respected skills, knowledge, and status, the Minyan still predominantly uses traditional male images such as "father," "king," and "lord," and masculine pronouns when talking to or about the divinity. Gender is much more intrusive in Hebrew than in English or many other languages: there is no neuter gender, verbs have gender, gender persists even in the plural forms of nouns and pronouns and in the second person. The author suspects that female god-language has not yet conquered the barrier of the sheer grammatical difficulty pursuant to changing the masculine to the feminine gender.

Jewish knowledge and its place in the system of values and relationships common to the Jewish culture in general is crucial to the success and acceptance of all these innovations, including the grammatical changes from masculine to feminine gender. That knowledge can be characterized as having three components. First is the ability to read, speak, and understand biblical and liturgical Hebrew. Knowledge of Jewish history and literature, including biblical, talmudic, and medieval writings, along with the ability to convey that knowledge to others is also important. Finally the ability

to sing and chant in traditional melodies is highly valued. Because the Minyan has always valued all of these forms of knowledge, status derives largely from such knowledge and the willingness and ability to share it with others. Because the Minyan is small and because it respects people with such knowledge, considerable attention is paid to their opinions and wishes. Members are strongly encouraged to acquire knowledge and are rewarded with status and deference for doing so.

This emphasis on skills has been important in determining women's position in the Minyan over the years. Although at the outset most of the women in the Minyan did not have the requisite knowledge and training, they all shared the Minyan's perception of itself as a place where such skills could be taught and learned. Most of them felt an obligation to acquire what learning they could. Once they acquired it, they felt both the obligation and the right to use it communally. Moreover, once they had these skills, they were in a position such that other members (of both sexes) took their opinions—including their feminism—seriously.

The Minyan thereby encouraged a self-reinforcing process in two ways. First, the emphasis on authentic liturgical skills moved the group quickly toward doing services entirely or primarily in Hebrew. This put pressure on members to acquire or improve their skills in Hebrew and discouraged new members who felt unwilling or unable to do so from remaining with the group. Thus the felt need for English readings diminished even further and even greater Hebrew and liturgical skills were demanded from even the less active members who remained. Second, as the women who remained with the Minyan acquired greater liturgical and linguistic skills, their participation became more important to the group as a whole, and their beliefs and commitments—including feminism—became more accepted by the group. As they became more central to the group, they were in a position to press for even greater openness to female participation, thereby bringing even more women into positions of status. And so on.

Let me clarify what is—and, more important, what is *not*—meant by "status" in this context. The Minyan is a voluntary organization; it owns no property, pays no salaries, and has an annual budget in three digits, raised by assessing dues and spent primarily for charity and refreshments. There is a treasurer, whose duty is to sign checks and keep the books for these purposes. There is a coordinator, whose duty is to see to it that the responsibilities for leading services, reading from the Torah scroll, bringing refreshments, and leading discussions are covered every week. Both these positions are considered obligatory burdens rather than honors. The rabbi is a member of the Minyan; at most his status may be that of *primus inter pares*; his opinions carry weight because of his learning and because as an individual he is firm in his opinions. When the Minyan is acting on behalf of Hillel, or of the local Jewish community as a whole, his position gives him more weight.

Consider a recent example: Among the responsibilities of the Minyan in planning the High Holiday services is the selection of extra, nonliturgical, readings added to the service at various points for reflection and meditation. For the past four years, the committees in charge of these selections have brought in poems by German holocaust survivors, such as Nelly Sachs, both in the original German and in English translation. Although the Minyan normally reads all non-English readings in both the original and in English, the Sachs poems and other German selections have so far been read only in English. The rabbi and a few other members feel strongly that the German language—even when used by German Jews to write about the Holocaust—cannot properly be used in a Jewish liturgy. There is strong opinion on the other side, both on the literary principle that, when available, the original—especially for poetry—should always be read along with the translation and on the political principle that no language should be abandoned to the enemies of its Jewish writers. But so far the rabbi's opinion has been the last word, primarily because the High Holiday services are not merely a Minyan function, but represent the Minyan and Hillel to the larger Jewish community. Presumably, if a member leading a Saturday morning service chose to insert a Nelly Sachs poem in the original German, that choice might lead to some heated discussion, but it would not be vetoed.

Status clearly does not derive from holding administrative office in the Minyan. Nor does it determine who holds office, except perhaps in a negative sense. A member whose skills are valued and who regularly puts those skills at the disposal of the Minyan can avoid group pressure to volunteer as coordinator or treasurer. Conversely, a person who feels ill at ease leading a service may choose to volunteer as coordinator instead, thereby fulfilling a sense of obligation to the group. Status inheres in the rabbi's position for reasons extrinsic to the Minyan and rooted in its relationship to outside groups.

Status within the group derives almost entirely from ability and willingness to lead services, read Torah, teach skills, and share Jewish knowledge. It should also be noted that while people with strong singing voices are likely to be perceived as having a high level of liturgical skills, several members are deeply involved in liturgical functions and respected for their abilities, despite a somewhat limited ability to carry a tune.

In conclusion, it is appropriate to turn from internal analyses of the Minyan to analysis of the Minyan as innovative precursor in American Judaism in general. During the 20 years of the Minyan's existence, the role of women in the Conservative movement to which the Minyan is linked has changed drastically. The pattern of change somewhat parallels the changes within the Minyan; in the Conservative movement women have progressed from being counted toward a quorum, to being called to read the blessings, to being ordained as rabbis and cantors. But in every instance, the Minyan was at least five years ahead of the Conservative movement. Furthermore, many of the changes common within the Minyan have not yet happened in the Conservative movement as a whole and may never happen. Most notably, the new Conservative prayer-book,[6] published in 1985, still includes no mention of the biblical matriarchs, much less any female god-language.

Why has the Minyan been able to transform the role of women in a way that the Conservative movement as a whole has not yet achieved? The Minyan, and especially the feminists and pro-feminists within it, have succeeded primarily by taking advantage of two elements deeply rooted in Jewish tradition.

One is the heavy emphasis on congregational autonomy, local custom, and lay leadership of the congregation.[7] Although in the last hundred years American Jewish religious organization has often sought to mimic the centralized denominational authority of American mainstream Protestant church organizations,[8] the imitations are more apparent than real. In all three Jewish denominations, the rabbi, if there is one, is hired and fired by the congregation, usually on the basis of whether the more active and prestigious members of the congregation agree with his views on ritual and on relations between the congregation and the larger community. Especially among the orthodox, it is entirely feasible for a congregation to maintain itself with no rabbi at all or to import one only for the High Holidays, leaving the liturgical functions for the rest of the year to the most learned members of the congregation.

Among the orthodox, some control is exerted over the ritual and doctrinal vagaries of local congregations by other rabbis' responses and especially by responses of the more prominent rabbinical authorities. They may say, for instance, "It is forbidden to eat in the houses of the members of such-and-such a congregation because one cannot rely on their kitchens to be *kosher*" (to serve ritually proper food). Reform congregations have a fairly strong central organization and depend on it for logistic and sometimes financial support. Furthermore, the position of a Reform rabbi often parallels that of the Protestant minister in terms of his centrality to congregational and liturgical function. Reform congregations usually do not function without a rabbi on any permanent basis.

The Conservative denomination, however, lacks both sets of denominational controls. Neither rabbis speaking for the authority of traditional Jewish law nor rabbis central to congregational existence characterize the Conservative movement. Such relatively uncontrolled congregational autonomy has enabled feminism to flourish in the Upstairs Minyan and in many congregations like it, long before the Conservative movement confronted feminism on any organized basis.

The other element of Jewish tradition which has enabled women to become so central to the Minyan is, of course, the emphasis on skills and knowledge. A group as small as the Minyan simply cannot afford to reject the skills and commitment of any member. Because of its unique orientations and its geographical distance from New York City, the Minyan cannot increase its membership significantly by drawing from the major source of learned male congregants for the Conservative movement—the disaffected orthodox. Instead, the Minyan had to develop these skills of its own members—*all* of its members who were willing and able to acquire such skills—and then had to give them the status that almost any Jewish congregation gives its most learned members. Arguably, the role of women in the Minyan was to some extent the rather common one of "reserve troops" brought in when the usual sources of manpower [sic] had failed.[9]

It is fair to ask, as Riv-Ellen Prell-Foldes does in her article on a similar group, the Westwood Free Minyan,[10] whether such groups merely allow women to take on roles traditionally appropriated by men in a system which is still fundamentally male-defined, male-oriented, and male-dominated. The failure of female god-language to become a regular part of the liturgy certainly raises that question. Two alternative explanations of that phenomenon present themselves. One, already alluded to, is the Minyan's commitment to high standards of liturgical practice, including grammatical Hebrew. The difficulty of producing a grammatically correct and literarily graceful redrafting of the liturgy using the feminine gender has so far deterred any attempts in that direction; no one wants to risk a superficial or hasty solution to such problems.

A more philosophical reason is perhaps more important. The fact that the liturgy has been revised to include references to the biblical matriarchs wherever their male counterparts are alluded to but not to include female images of deity whenever male images are used, suggests preference for historical rather than theological concerns. As one member has put it, "We know *Jews* are male and female, and always have been. We aren't willing to make such drastic statements about God, because most of us are a lot more literate historically than theologically." Furthermore, Jewish tradition, at least in this century, has strongly encouraged that orientation.

These explanations are further supported by the fact that the Minyan has used many feminist poems as readings, not only in its own Saturday morning services but in High Holiday services as well. This development, as we have seen, normally indicates complete and long-standing acceptance of the practice in question by the Minyan. Thus lack of female God-language is not the result of a rejection of feminist values, especially since for the past two years, the High Holiday readings have included an exploration of God's maternal traits in the books of the Prophets and other biblical sources. Rather these developments indicate that feminist language and thinking are introduced into the liturgy when they are consistent with the biblical and historical roots of the liturgy, and when they can be done either in literate English, when appropriate, or in grammatical Hebrew. Only if one argues that lack of female god-language radically excludes women could one argue that women are merely taking on male roles in the Minyan with its current liturgy.

The participation of women in all phases of liturgical activity has affected male participation very differently from what might have been expected. When the Conservative movement was debating whether to count women toward a *minyan*, and again when they were debating the ordination of women as rabbis, one of the more popular arguments against both innovations was that if women took on more active liturgical roles, men would drop out of them.[11] This approach ignored the fact that the dependency of many Conservative congregations on a few Jewishly well-educated men for liturgical and organizational leadership excluded less-educated *men* as much as it discriminated against women. The Minyan's emphasis on acquisition and exercise of skills by *all* members has drawn many men into more active roles than would otherwise have been possible for them. Essentially, perhaps without so intending, the Minyan has provided a new model for Jewish education for both sexes—education as part of an ongoing adult involvement, in a group with a high tolerance for errors, slipups, and awkwardness among beginners.

Again, well within the models provided by Jewish tradition, the Minyan has always placed more emphasis on practice and practical skills than on doctrine. Like many Jewish groups, it has often changed its practice first and theologized about it later, if at all. The female god-language problem has remained unresolved, in part because many perceive it to be more theological than practical. A resolution of that problem will probably have to await the highly practical remedy of a grammatically thoroughgoing revision of the prayerbook.

An informal study of 62 current and former Minyan members[12] indicates that many of them have affiliated with other Conservative congregations since leaving the Minyan's locality. Almost all who have done so characterize their current congregations as "egalitarian," though not necessarily as egalitarian as the Minyan. Many others who do not now belong to any congregation have stated that they have been unable to find any group like the Minyan in their current location. This suggests that the egalitarian values promoted by the Minyan are not a mere ephemeral "trend" among its alumni.

If this is the case, Minyan alumni may be in a position to help propel the Conservative movement in the direction of equal participation in liturgy, organization, and study. They will do it by the same quintessentially Jewish methods which have moved the Minyan in its basic direction—the slow, often irksome methods of learning, using, and sharing liturgical and linguistic skills to achieve lay leadership within individual congregations.

Because this is a slow process, it is almost certainly still incomplete, even within the Minyan. The next step may be a solution to the problem of female god-language—or it may be the beginning of a system of religious education for the children of Minyan members. But it will happen as all the previous developments have happened, by trial and error, on the most practical level possible.

In sum, to the extent that women have achieved equal involvement in the liturgical and organizational leadership of the Minyan and in other such egalitarian congregations, they have done so by using Jewish values and traditions. They have seen themselves not as imprisoned inside a web of strictures trying to get out, but as walled out of a garden of possibilities and trying to get in. And they have gained entry using a key procured from within.

Notes

1. Adler, Rachel, "The Jew Who Wasn't There," *Response*, Summer 1973.
2. Umansky, Ellen, *Lily Montague and the Advancement of Liberal Judaism*, Mellen Press, 1983.
3. Ticktin, Esther, "Exchange of Resources and the Process of Change in a Jewish Worship Group," unpubl. dissertation, Department of Education, Univ. of Chicago, 1971.
4. For the Conservative movement's own characterization of the history of women's increasing ritual involvement, see pp. 105–111 of *Conservative Judaism*, by Herbert Rosenblum, United Synagogues of America, 1983.
5. See, for instance, Linda Kuzmack, "Agadic Approaches to Biblical Women," pp. 248–256, in *The Jewish Woman: New Perspectives*, ed. Elizabeth Koltun, Schocken, 1976.
6. *Siddur Sim Shalom*, Rabbi Jules Harlow, United Synagogues of America/Rabbinical Assembly of America, 1985.
7. *American Judaism*, Nathan Glazer, Univ. of Chicago Press, 1957, p. 35.
8. Jerome Carlin and Saul Mendlovitz, "The American Rabbi" in *The Jews: Social Patterns of an American Group*, ed. Marshall Sklare, Free Press, 1958, pp. 377–414.
9. Obviously, other Jewish congregations faced with the same choice in the past—to admit women to its cadre of central personnel, or to wither and disband for lack of such personnel—have chosen the latter alternative rather than the former. The Midwest in particular is littered with the remains of Jewish congregations where today no living Jew resides.
10. Prell-Foldes, "Coming of Age in Kelton," in *Women in Ritual and Symbolic Roles*, ed. Judith Hoch-Smith and Anita Spring, Plenum Press, 1978, pp. 81–82.
11. See, for instance, Lucy Dawidowicz, "On Being a Woman in Shul," in *The Jewish Presence*, Holt, Rinehart and Winston, 1977, pp. 46–57.
12. *The Minyan Report*, Marian Neudel, unpublished but circulated to former and current Minyan members, 1985.

Further Readings

Adler, Rachel. "The Jew Who Wasn't There." *Response*, Summer, 1973.

Dawidowicz, Lucy S. *The Jewish Presence: Essays on Identity and History*. New York: Holt, Rinehart and Winston, 1977.

Glazer, Nathan. *American Judaism*. Chicago: University of Chicago Press, 1957.

Greenberg, Blu. *On Women and Judaism: A View from Tradition.* Philadelphia: Jewish Publication Society of America, 1981.

Heschel, Susannah, ed. *On Being a Jewish Feminist.* New York: Schocken, 1983.

Koltun, Elizabeth, ed. *The Jewish Woman: New Perspectives.* New York: Schocken, 1976.

Meiselman, Moshe. *Jewish Women in Jewish Law.* New York: Ktav, 1978.

Reisman, Bernard. *The Chavurah: Contemporary Jewish Experience.* New York: Union of American Hebrew Congregations, 1977.

Rosenblum, Herbert. *Conservative Judaism: A Contemporary History.* New York: United Synagogue of America, 1983.

Sklare, Marshall, ed. *The Jews: Social Patterns of an American Group.* New York: Free Press, 1958.

Umansky, Ellen. *Lily Montague and the Advancement of Liberal Judaism: From Vision to Vocation.* Lewiston, N.Y.: Edwin Mellen Press, 1983.

V

SUCCESS STORIES

Women and Men in Balance or Equality

In this section we offer a different kind of success story—different because here are examples of women who achieve eminence and satisfaction not despite their defined options but, at least in part, because of them. Each chapter describes an aspect of women's religious activity within a system that incorporates some principle of male and female balance or equality and in which, theoretically, neither sex predominates. Three possible variants of this theme are explored.

The first is exemplified in a tradition of Tantric Buddhism that developed in the final days of Buddhist history in India and then flourished for many centuries in Tibet. Here women and men who became *siddhas*, or "accomplished ones," found equal achievement and recognition in large part because gender was considered irrelevant to attaining their tradition's goals.

In the second variant, men and women are not equal in the sense that all the tradition's options are available to both; men must fit the male norm, and women, the female norm. But the men's realm and the women's are set in balance or complementarity—a pattern that is characteristic of many tribal societies. In this section we look at the impressive role of women among the North American Iroquois, tracing complex patterns of a ritual and institutional system that weaves together the women's realm and the men's realm into a seamless garment of two distinctive colors—masculine and feminine. The same complementarity is readily seen in the misfortune ritual conducted on behalf of the anthropologist observer by Rosinta, a woman diviner of the Bolivian highlands.

The third variant is perhaps least common among examples of men and women in balance and equality. The Shakers, a millenarian Christian group, had inherited Christianity's common notions of sexual heirarchy. However, they proclaimed a radically new message of salvation that stood those inherited norms on end. Christ the savior had come again in the person of a woman, Ann Lee. Her appearance abolished the old social order and required a transformed relationship between women and men. The Shakers created utopian communities in which they lived out their vision of a heavenly society activated on earth. By abolishing marriage and private property, and requiring dual male and female leadership, they came at least very close to achieving both balance and equality between the sexes.

Certain aspects of these "success stories" will, however, seem ironic to the Western reader. Tantric Buddhism itself may have been very open to women practitioners, but the surrounding millieu made it far more difficult for women than for men to take up the Tantric path. Furthermore, both men and women on this path attracted public scandal and persecution. In contrast, the prominent women of the Iroquois Longhouse religion are both respectable and influential; yet, they still do not speak formally in public assemblies. Another most ironic twist is found in the Andean tradition described in the next chapter. Here male and female ritual specialists guard and use their respective important powers, but in this division of labor and symbolism the power of men is connected with the good luck and the power of women with the bad. Finally, though Shakers self-consciously balanced women's and men's roles and authority in their communities, this balance was not the result of their belief in either the intrinsic equality of the sexes or the irrelevance of gender to achieving the final goal. Women's subordination could be ended only because Shakers had entered the millenium, the time when "all things are made new." According to Shaker teachings, women had been even more vulnerable to evil than were men in pre-millenial times and settings. Furthermore, unlike men, who gained access to perfection after the life of Jesus, women had no access to perfection until the appearance of Christ as a woman brought a redemption specific to them.

18

Accomplished Women in Tantric Buddhism of Medieval India and Tibet

REGINALD A. RAY

Vajrayana, or Tantric, Buddhism is a late development both historically and in terms of a practitioner's progress in spiritual discipline. Historically, Vajrayana Buddhism emerged in North India probably some time after 400 A.D., and it spread to Tibet after 600 A.D. Although Vajrayana Buddhism, as well as Buddhism in general, became largely extinct in India after 1200 A.D., the Vajrayana was the main form of Buddhism in Tibet until the Communist takeover in 1959. Although Tantric Buddhism may now be extinct in Tibet as well, Tibetan teachers are transmitting this form of Buddhism to Western students. These students, like Tantric practitioners of every culture and historical period, begin the practice of Vajrayana Buddhism only after thorough grounding in more preliminary forms of Buddhist discipline.

The Vajrayana is unique among Buddhist traditions in the prominence it gives both to feminine symbolism and to women practitioners. The role of women in the Vajrayana is nowhere seen more clearly than in the Tantric "biographies" of the *siddhas* ("accomplished ones" or "enlightened ones"), who lived in India roughly between the eighth and the twelfth centuries A.D. These legendary biographies[1] present a vivid and moving picture of women as Tantric students and teachers journeying on their spiritual paths and transmitting the Vajrayana from one generation to another.

However, it is also important to recognize that there were always far fewer women

DR. REGINALD A. RAY   is Associate Professor of Buddhist Studies at Naropa Institute, Boulder, Colorado, and Adjunct Professor of Religion at the University of Colorado, Boulder, Colorado.

Tantric practitioners than men and that only occasionally were major teachers female. No doubt the woman's essential role of wife and mother in ancient India and Tibet made spiritual practice only a remote option for most women. It is also likely that people of the time, influenced by prevailing cultural mores, had more difficulty accepting women than accepting men as ascetics, yogis, and Tantric practitioners. Certainly, contemporary Buddhist monastic systems were predominantly male oriented and provided more options and encouragement to men than to women. In such a situation, women probably found it much more difficult to undertake Tantric practice than did men.

Nevertheless, many "accomplished women" did exist. If the women managed to step onto the Tantric path, two elements of Tantric tradition aided them in their journey. First of all, spiritual accomplishment in the Vajrayana does not depend on monastic withdrawal as it did in earlier Buddhist traditions. The householder yogi (feminine *yogini*) who is married and has a family is as apt to become a *siddha*, or accomplished one, as the monk or nun. The extra restrictions placed on Buddhist nuns that helped precipitate the decline of the nuns' order do not apply to the householder *yogini*, nor are householders who have their own sources of income as vulnerable economically as the nuns' communities were in India.[2] Second, basic teachings of the Vajrayana insist that women and men share equally in the same fundamental human nature, including the potential for enlightenment. People have different psychological traits, which are conventionally labeled "male" and "female," but these traits can be part of both men's and women's psychological makeup.[3] In an enlightened person, whether male or female, these traits are ideally balanced.

In this chapter I will discuss some of the most important themes found in traditional life stories of female *siddhas*, particularly from the Indian period of the Vajrayana. The material to be analyzed falls naturally into four major categories: the situations of women when they first undertake Tantric practice; women as Tantric practitioners; women and men as companions on the Tantric path; and women as accomplished teachers or *siddhas*.

WOMEN AT THE BEGINNING OF THEIR TRAINING

Marriage looms at the beginning of the stories of most women *siddhas*. Parents, friends, and suitors expect that the woman will follow what they consider her destiny. Some women, confronted with the prospect of marriage, refuse to cooperate because of their spiritual aspirations. Princess Mandarava, who later became one of the main disciples of Padmasambhava (founder of a major Tantric lineage), was pressured by her father to marry. She resisted him, because she wanted to devote her life to spiritual goals. Her father, angry and unyielding, placed a heavy guard around the palace to prevent her from fulfilling her desire. She escaped from her confinement and discarded her royal clothes; she pulled her hair out and scratched her face with her fingernails, so that no suitors would want her, and began her meditation practice. Only then did her father finally relent and accept her aspirations. There is a striking parallel between this story and the story of how the Buddha abandoned his royal station and undertook an ascetic life; however, this story places far more emphasis on the woman's determination.

Other women *siddhas* are impelled into spiritual practice by the failure of a marriage or by the death of their husband. For example, we know of Ni.gu.ma, who entered into Vajrayana practice after her husband Naropa (another major Tantric teacher) announced to her that he intended to leave her and enter into religious practice. She readily agreed with his decision and, after some discussion, both of them decided to present the matter to their families as if Ni.gu.ma's inadequacies were causing insurmountable problems for the couple. After it was finally agreed that the marriage should be dissolved, both Ni.gu.ma and Naropa entered religious practice and finally became ardent and famous Tantric *siddhas*.

Yet other women marry, only to find that the marriage is incompatible with their Tantric aspirations and practice. Laksminkara was married as a young child to the son of a neighboring king. As was the custom, she continued to live with her own family until she reached puberty. During this time she was a devout student of the Tantra. When she was finally sent to her husband's palace, she immediately perceived that her new environment was incompatible with her Tantric practice. She distributed her dowry to the poor, sent her retinue of servants home, and feigned insanity. She removed her clothes, smeared her body with ashes, and refused the attentions of the doctors sent to treat her. Her husband finally abandoned her, and she subsequently became an ascetic, living off refuse and sleeping in cremation grounds.

Several themes run through these and similar stories. All the women are depicted as spiritually precocious children who, at a tender age, hear and understand the *Tantras* and are accepted by some *siddhas* as disciples. Common to all the stories is also the theme of opposition from fathers, husbands, and in-laws, who do not understand the women's callings. These biographies present an interesting evaluation of the impact of marriage and men on women's spiritual aspirations. One often finds vividly negative depictions of both. Marriage is frequently portrayed as spiritually unproductive, and men as hostile and dangerous to spiritual aspirations and completely lacking in spirituality themselves. These stories describe men in such unflattering terms not because men as a whole were regarded as antispiritual but because the particular men who occupied important roles in these women's lives happened to represent and advocate an unenlightened view. This perspective may shed some interesting light on the negative attitudes toward women

often expressed in early Buddhist literature. Do these attitudes indicate a blanket judgment of the limitations inherent in all women, or do they reflect experiences with particular women who were hostile to spiritual discipline?

Marriage, however, is not always depicted in the biographies as a spiritually neutral or negative situation for women. As we shall see, it can be a spiritually productive state, although this is generally true only if the woman's mate is another Tantric practitioner. The legends indicate that marriages with men who lack some positive relationship to Tantrism only rarely succeed.

It should also be noted that not all the women *siddhas* were involved in marriage during the early stages of their careers. Some were professional women with occupations of one sort or another, who may or may not have been married. Tilopa (founder of a major lineage) had a woman disciple who ran a liquor shop in Shravasti. She was highly successful in her trade, and her liquor was famous for its high quality and commanded a high price. Tilopa met her while drinking in her shop and accepted her as a disciple after some severe tests. Another student operated a liquor distillery for a king in Uddiyana. She is depicted as an able and perceptive woman, who knew not only her business but also the particular psychology of her employer, the king, who happened to be a non-Buddhist. Her Tantric teaching began when she told a Tantric teacher who was passing through the area exactly how to convert the king to Buddhism. The teacher was so impressed with her that he immediately gave her initiation and oral instruction.

WOMEN AS TANTRIC PRACTITIONERS

The stories about the women *siddhas* also cover the time between the women's formative experiences and their final success as fully enlightened *siddhas*. This intervening period of

Tantric training and practice was usually very long; in one case, it lasted forty years. As one might expect, the largest proportion of biographical information on the women deals with this training period. However, most details of this training period are virtually the same for men and women and the accounts are technical and repetitive, filled with endless lists of names of teachers, initiations granted, meditation practiced, places visited, and Tantric deities of particular importance to the individual. For this reason, I will briefly summarize this period and only briefly describe what I consider to be some of its more important themes.

For most of the women *siddhas*, entry into the Vajrayana marked a radical change in their external situations. Often this change was a complete break with what had formerly been most important in their lives—their social roles as actual or potential wives. From this point of view, the women's stories are quite different from the men's, who usually did not experience such a radical and total break with their pre-Tantric life, since their primary roles were occupational, not social, and they could continue in their occupations while undergoing Tantric training.

Because of the women's complete break with their pasts, the accounts of their early periods of training stress social rejection and isolation, solitude and desolation. The story of Laksminkara, who had feigned madness to escape her marriage, is typical. Her life of royal comfort and status completely behind her, she roamed alone through the back alleys, scavenging garbage heaps, sleeping in cremation grounds, and practicing in isolated caves. The motif of feigned madness as a way of extricating oneself from an impossible situation recurs frequently in these stories and further underscores the women's social isolation and solitude.

Another major theme in materials about the women's training period is that of their relationships with their gurus, both female and male. These relationships are as difficult, pain-

ful, and costly for the women as they are for the men. The highly successful and wealthy liquor saleswoman from Shravasti had her entire business destroyed by Tilopa before he accepted her as a pupil. Another woman was accepted as a pupil only after she remained fearless and resolute in the face of a horrifying spectacle. Much is asked by the teachers, and apparently little or nothing is given in return. In many of the stories the students, whether female or male, are shown practicing under a teacher's guidance for many years, without receiving so much as a nod of the head. Even after important initiations and attainments, the trainees' trials and difficulties are by no means over, as the following vivid story about an important Tibetan teacher, Ma.gcig, illustrates.

After her separation from her husband, Ma.gcig was accepted as a student by a lama. She became his Tantric consort and received from him valuable teaching and guidance. After eleven years, when she was twenty-eight, her guru consort died. During the next three years, Ma.gcig experienced intense confusion, hardship, and pain. She developed incurable infections, and her body was covered with abscesses and pustules. Her mind became so completely disoriented and ridden with passion that the Tantric deities stood aloof from her, and even animals refused her offerings. Finally she met a teacher who showed her that she had brought her sad condition on herself through her own lack of awareness, her immaturity, and her attachment. He showed her the way to overcome her confusion, and later she became one of the most renowned and accomplished teachers, male or female, in Tibet at that time.

The qualities shown by the women students are the same as those shown by the men. They are persevering and often fiercely determined. They show openness, receptivity, and intelligence. They possess courage and fortitude, and their characters are independent and uncompromising. These traits are especially interesting, because many of them do not conform to the classical Indian views of what a woman is or should be. It is important to repeat that, within the framework of Tantric Buddhism, such qualities are not regarded as the province of one sex or the other but as human traits that can be found in both women and men.

One final aspect of the *siddhas'* training deserves mention. In the course of their initiation, Tantric practitioners are confronted with deities, the Yidams, that embody the practitioners' own enlightened nature in its pure form. In the Vajrayana such deities are both masculine and feminine. Significantly, just as men and women may have either male or female gurus, so they may be especially associated with male or female deities. Such personal deities are not mentioned in the stories very often, but, when they are, we note that women have special connections with male deities as often as with female, just as men may have special connections with female deities as well as with male deities.

WOMEN AND MEN AS COMPANIONS ON THE TANTRIC PATH

In the biographies women frequently appear as solitary *siddhas*. But just as often we find them in the company of men who are also Tantric practitioners. Also, when wife and husband are interested in Tantric teachings, both partners receive instruction together from a teacher and practice together. Many stories demonstrate that the female/male relationship can be an important part of the Tantric path for both men and women. For example, at a certain point in his career, Saraha, an important Tantric teacher, felt a need to do his practice with a female companion who was also a Vajrayana practitioner. The need was brought about by Saraha's realization that he was blocked from further attainment—a realization that seems to have motivated him to search for

a companion. He journeyed to the south, where he met a woman Tantric practitioner who was an arrowsmith's daughter. Saraha worked with her, making arrows as part of his *sadhana* (the spiritual discipline assigned by one's guru). With and through her, whom he eventually married, and through his work, he gained valuable insights and attainments.

Such relationships between men and women, although they went against conventional Indian practice, were an important dimension of Tantric practice. In traditional India most intimate male/female relationships existed within the limits of caste restrictions. In the Vajrayana, however, other considerations were the basis for intimate relationships. Great importance was assigned to the capacity for insight, to the ability to see the relativity of caste structures, and to the willingness to step beyond them. Intimate associations with people from different castes would severely challenge one's own identity, both personal and social. Such associations were therefore encouraged because they would promote a breakdown of personal and social identity. Thus in the Vajrayana one often finds relationships between people of widely separated castes. For example, Princess Laksminkara worked closely with a latrine cleaner, and Princess Sankajati married a merchant. Similarly, many high-caste men were associated with women of low caste.

As one might expect, such relationships were considered as an outrage to Indian society, and stories of misunderstanding and even persecution of Tantric couples by their social environment abound. For example, one of these stories tells us that, after a certain king had received instruction from a *siddha*, he carried out his practice with a low-caste girl for twelve years. When he was finally found out, public outrage against him forced him to leave his throne in favor of his son. He and his consort went into the jungle and continued their practice there for many years. In the end, the two were put to death for their illicit relationship. Padmasambhava and Mandarava, two very important teachers, were also persecuted on account of their relationship. In one biography, their persecutors try to burn Padmasambhava to death, and Mandarava is thrown into a pit of thorns. Later both are wrapped in oil-soaked rags and burned at the stake, although once again they are able to survive because of their Tantric powers.

Some of the biographies, in spite of the opposition they describe, have a happy ending. Saraha was both a brahmin (a member of the highest caste) and an ordained monk. And yet, as we have seen, he married the daughter of a low-caste arrowsmith. Enraged at what they considered intolerable lack of propriety, a great crowd of people and the king of the region himself gathered to deride and criticize the couple. Saraha stood in front of them and said, "I am indeed a brahmin, and I live with the daughter of an arrowsmith, caste or no caste: there I do not see any distinction. I have taken the sworn vows of a monk and I wander about with a wife: there I do not see any distinction. Some may have doubts and say, 'Here is an impurity!' but they do not know . . ." At the heart of Saraha's message is the idea that social and religious distinctions have no ultimate foundation or substance and, therefore, no value. The story tells us that the king and the people accepted Saraha's view and left him and his wife alone.

One of the more interesting motifs of the male/female relationships depicted in these biographies is the degree of communication between the partners. In Tantrism communication is essential for spiritual growth, and transformed passion (total appreciation and love that expects nothing in return) is the driving force of communication. The fact that communication, which can result only from transformed passion, is considered so important in Tantrism helps us understand why relationships between women and men often play a very significant role in the ultimate success of both.

More specifically, communication between women and men is frequently used to improve each other's practice. A typical example is that of a male student who had been deeply immersed in meditation practice for many years. One day his consort interrupted his meditation because, having had an important insight into his practice, she wanted to share it with him. The interruption and her insight turned out to be decisive for his practice, and he subsequently experienced extremely high attainments. Another vivid example of the importance of communication is found in another legend about Saraha and his wife. At one point, the two went to a new locality and settled down. One day Saraha told his wife that he would like to eat radish curry. She prepared it, but when she brought it to him, she found him deeply immersed in *samadhi* (a meditative state), and she left him alone. The story tells us that Saraha stayed in that *samadhi* for twelve years without interruption and without getting up once. When he finally stirred from his meditation, he turned to his wife and asked for his radish curry. His wife replied, "You sit in *samadhi* for twelve years without getting up. And now you want your radish curry, as if it still existed. Besides, there are no radishes at this time of year." Saraha replied, "Then I will go into the mountains to meditate." And his wife said, "Simply removing your body from the world is not true renunciation. Real renunciation takes place when your mind abandons frivolous and absorbing thoughts. If you sit in meditation for twelve years and cannot even give up your desire for radish curry, what is the point of going into the mountains?" Saraha realized that his wife was right. He succeeded in his efforts to overcome unproductive thoughts and doubts and attained the highest state of self-realization.

The lively communication between men and women illustrated in these and similar Vajrayana accounts is not based on sex roles or other fixed identities, but rather on insights. One of the two practitioners has seen something significant about the other and confronts him or her with it. In both of these examples, the woman's observation challenges the man's conception of himself and his practice. Such a communication presupposes and demonstrates a point stressed above: according to the *Tantras*, men and women share the same psychological and spiritual world; they understand the workings of the mind and experience enlightenment in the same way. In these sketches, drawn not without tenderness, the women are depicted as highly insightful and intelligent, and their message is courageous and decisive. It cuts through the men's conceptual illusions about who they are and where they are, and confronts them with the reality of their situations. Here the women act as midwives to the men's own insight and to their spiritual ripening. Since these stories are told from the male practitioner's viewpoint, they stress the importance of the women's insights. But, needless to say, communication in a relationship is a two-way process that requires openness on both sides. No doubt the women would have had similar stories to tell.

Another important Tantric teacher whose story is told in the legendary biographies owes not only his accomplishments but also his initial exposure to Tantric practice to encounters with a mysterious female stranger. Abhayakaragupta, a famous scholar who came from a high-caste family in Orissa, one day was immersed in the recitation of a text when a beautiful maiden came up to him and said, "I am a Candala [a very low-caste] girl, and I would like to stay with you." Abhayakaragupta drew back and replied, "How can that be? I am from a higher caste, and I would be disgraced." The girl disappeared. A friend reprimanded him: "That was Vajrayogini (a Tantric goddess). It is too bad that you did not receive teaching from her."

Abhayakaragupta studied in Bengal, where his scholarship became more and more vast and illustrious. He knew all the *sutras* and the *Tantras* and received initiations from many masters. One day he was in the courtyard of a monastery when a young maiden came up to him dragging a chunk of raw beef dripping with blood and shoved it at him. Once again she said, "I am a Candala girl. Eat this beef that has been slaughtered for you." But Abhayakaragupta replied, "I am a pure monk. How can I eat meat that has been so blatantly prepared for me?" Again she withdrew.

Still not satisfied with his learning, Abhayakaragupta wandered everywhere to receive different teachings. For a while he stayed at Nalanda (the greatest university of his time) and became even more famous. One night a girl who looked exactly like the servant girl who drew his guru's water came to him. She carried the ritual implements for a *ganacakra* (a Tantric ceremony involving drinking, singing and dancing together) in a small basket. "I have been sent by your teacher to perform with you a *ganacakra*, which, up to now, you have not been willing to enter into. Now is the time to do so!" When his misgivings won out and he refused her, she said, "You know three hundred *Tantras*, and you have intellectually mastered all of their teachings, right up to the end. How can you possibly justify these reservations about the actual practice of the *Tantras*?" Then she picked up her basket of *ganacakra* implements and went away. Next morning Abhayakaragupta's guru said, "You have excessive scruples. You had the opportunity to receive 'accomplishment' (*siddha*) from Vajrayogini, and you refused!"

Abhayakaragupta fell into deep despair and for seven days spent his time in prayer and refused all food. In the night of the seventh day, he saw an old woman in a dream. He recognized her as Vajrayogini and confessed and prayed to her. Although he finally recognized her and, letting go of his hesitation, opened himself up to her, she reminded him of his constant unwillingness to communicate with her and implied that his refusals had injured their relationship. In spite of the goddess' reproaches, the dream was the turning point of Abhayakaragupta's quest for knowledge. He had finally seen Vajrayogini, she had accepted him, and he had received valuable teaching from her. So he went on to become accomplished in practice as well as in scholarship.

This story illustrates the pitfalls of dwelling on one's own conceptions of oneself rather than being open to communication. The story also contains another, and even more important, theme. Constant ambiguity about the maidens' identity is obvious. When they appear to Abhayakaragupta, one does not know whether they are ordinary women or Tantric deities. Although they appear as human beings, there is something special about them that leaves Abhayakaragupta constantly in doubt. In fact, the ambiguity cannot be resolved. They appear as human women, but as women who represent enlightened and unusual points of view. They speak with the voice of insight and, in expressing pure intelligence, they assume a transcendent form, which is the form of the Tantric deities. It should be remembered that in Tantrism the deities are the forms humans take on when they have shed the impurities of an ego-centered mind. The question about whether women and men, when they communicate purely and truly with each other, transcend their human natures underlies much of the interaction of men and women in the Vajrayana.

WOMEN AS FULLY ENLIGHTENED SIDDHAS

When the women's training period comes to an end, they are called *siddhas* and they become teachers themselves, with their own disciples. Much can be said about the images of enlightened teachers in Tantric literature—images that are remarkably consistent for both men and women. Two characteristics stand out as typical of the fully accomplished *siddha*: personal wisdom and effectiveness in working with others.

Female *siddhas* are often regarded as the foremost, or among the foremost, disciples of their teachers. Many of them became specialists in their traditions, and Tantric practitioners, both male and female, would travel great distances to receive teaching from these women. These *siddhas* were renowned for their attainments in both the scholarly and the yogic (meditative or practicing) aspects of their discipline. A typical, if unusually detailed, example is provided by the story of the *siddha* Dinakara. Her biography credits her with a remarkably sharp and penetrating intellect and tells us that she mastered much of the scholarly literature of the day, both secular and religious. In addition to her intellectual achievements, she was a renowned *yogini*, who understood the innermost essence of the *Tantras*, possessed extraordinary vision, and was unequaled in the *siddhis* (extraordinary powers).

Perhaps the women *siddhas'* greatest accomplishment was their role as teachers—a role that is emphasized in many of the stories about them. For countless other *siddhas*, the encounter with these women marked a decisive turning point in their careers, as illustrated by the following story. One day Luhipa knocked at the door of a house of prostitution, begging for food. The head of the house, an unnamed but obviously "enlightened" woman, filled his bowl with rotten food. When Luhipa threw the offering away in disgust, she angrily asked him how it was that he, a *yogi*, still saw distinctions in the food he ate. Thanks to this observation, Luhipa realized the impurity of his conceptual mind, which still discriminated and made judgments. Thereafter, in order to purify and transcend his mind, he lived for twelve years on the banks of the Ganges eating only the innards of fish discarded by the fishermen.

A particularly interesting story concerns the *siddha* Khambhala, who received his Tantric training from his mother. The son of a king, Khambhala inherited the throne when his father died. When his mother expressed grief because his involvement in government detracted from his spiritual development, the young king took her words to heart and suggested that he might become a Buddhist monk. His mother assented. Later, after he was ordained as a monk, his mother expressed sorrow because his life of wealth and status in the monastery distracted him from higher spiritual development. Again he took her words to heart and left his monastic setting to live as an ascetic in the jungle. Once again his mother expressed sadness at the way he was living; this time she observed that he lived in one place, comfortable with his few possessions, at the expense of higher development. And once again her son listened to her and adopted the life of a wandering *yogi* practicing Tantrism. Then his mother gave him important secret initiations and teachings. After he had become a *siddha* endowed with magical powers, she appeared to him once more to convince him to stay on earth to help others.

Another story concerns a woman *siddha* who taught the Vajrayana in her town after a somewhat unusual training period. Manibhadra was married at the age of thirteen to a man of corresponding caste but still lived with her parents. During this period she received Tantric teachings from a *siddha*. One day she disappeared from her house and spent a week meditating with the *siddha* in the town's cremation ground, receiving initiations and oral instruction. When she returned to her house, her parents were extremely angry and beat her, because her behavior would, if known, bring disgrace to the family and be grounds for the dissolution of the marriage. Yet for the next year she did nothing but practice her assigned spiritual discipline. Then she went to live with her husband's family. Apparently he did not know about, or was not particularly interested in, her special connection with the Vajrayana. She was the ideal Indian housewife, performing her duties competently, showing proper respect toward her husband, and giving birth to a son and two daughters. Eleven years

passed, and apparently during this time she continued with her Tantric meditation. One day, as she returned in the early morning from the village well carrying the water for the day's needs, she tripped over a root, and fell down. Her water pot was smashed to pieces, and Manibhadra attained enlightenment. From that time on, she devoted herself to the teaching of the Vajrayana in her town.

CONCLUSIONS

The preceding discussion permits us to draw several generalizations about women in the Vajrayana. First of all, the Vajrayana very strongly defines itself as a tradition for both women and men, even though, in sheer numbers, men practitioners and *siddhas* always outnumbered female practitioners and *siddhas*. Much of the Vajrayana's openness to women may be due to its complex and sophisticated psychology, which sees the human traits defined by other traditions and cultures as "masculine" or "feminine" as part of both men's and women's psychological makeup. Therefore, women and men have the same inherent obstacles to overcome and the same inherent potential for spiritual discipline and enlightenment. All in all, the image of women *siddhas* presented in the traditional literature is highly positive; they are depicted as insightful, dignified, courageous, independent, powerful, and creative—the same qualities that are displayed by male *siddhas*. In brief, Tantrism is a tradition that ennobles both women and men who can overcome great obstacles and regards them as capable of the same accomplishments.

Notes

1. The main texts referred to are the "Lives of the 84 Siddhas" (ca. eleventh century) by Abhayadatta and the "Seven Revelations" (ca. fourteenth century) by Taranatha. We also draw on some other Tibetan histories, mainly Gos.lo.tsa.ba's *Blue*

Annals, Buston's *History of Buddhism*, and Padma-karpo's *History of Buddhism*.

2. See Nancy Auer Falk, "The Case of The Vanishing Nuns," in this volume.

3. These are summarized in the so-called five buddha families. The *Vajra* family (Diamond family) is intellectual sharpness and precision and critical clarity. The *Ratna* family (Jewel family) embodies personal color, warmth and richness, and the ability to fully appreciate and enjoy life. The *Padma* family (Lotus family) expresses concern for love, communication, and interpersonal relationships. The *Karma* family (Action family) manifests efficiency, directness of action, and creativity—all combined to produce concrete results. The *Buddha* family (Awake family) embodies a basic openness, accommodation, and non-judgmental acceptance of what occurs in one's life. Although cultures characteristically divide these types of intelligence into "male" and "female," the Vajrayana sees them as available to both men and women.

Further Readings

Dowman, Keith, tr. *Sky Dancer: The Secret Life of the Lady Yeshe Tsogyel*. London: Routledge and Kegan Paul, 1984.

Gross, Rita M. "Yeshe Tsogyel: Enlightened Consort, Great Teacher, Female Role Model." *Tibet Journal*. Winter 1987.

Ray, Reginald A. "Mahasiddhas." *The Encyclopedia of Religion*. New York: Macmillan, 1987.

——————. "Marpa." *The Encyclopedia of Religion*. New York: Macmillan, 1987.

——————. "Milaraspa." *The Encyclopedia of Religion*. New York: Macmillan, 1987.

——————. "Naropa." *The Encyclopedia of Religion*. New York: Macmillan, 1987.

——————. "Some Aspects of Tulka Tradition in Tibet." *Tibet Journal*. Winter 1986.

——————. "Tilopa." *The Encyclopedia of Religion*. New York: Macmillan, 1987.

19

Women of Influence and Prestige among the Native American Iroquois

ANNEMARIE SHIMONY

The Iroquois tribes of eastern North America have often been called "matriarchal"—implying that, among the Iroquois, women were dominant socially and politically. Careful study of contemporary Iroquois society and of historical records shows that the claim of an Iroquois "matriarchy" is misleading. Nevertheless, women have played a number of important roles in Iroquois life, and they continue to do so, notably in the traditional Longhouse religion. This chapter will describe some of these roles and thereby try to clarify the issue of Iroquois women's significance.

The Iroquois Indians are among the best known of the Native American populations both because they played an important role in the history of the continent and because they have been described from earliest times by competent ethnographers. Historically the Iroquois were wooed by the French, Dutch, and British colonial powers either as trade partners in furs or as intermediaries for the more westerly fur trade. They contributed to a British victory in the French-Indian Wars, and they were a considerable factor in the American Revolution. Prior to this time the League of Five Nations (the Mohawk, Oneida, Onondaga, Cayuga, and Seneca) had had a long-standing rule that all decisions must be arrived

DR. ANNEMARIE SHIMONY is Professor of Anthropology and Chairman of the Anthropology Department at Wellesley College. She received her Ph.D. from Yale University and has done field work among the Iroquois of Canada and the United States for many years. She has also worked in West Africa. Currently, she is engaged in a study of the succession of the hereditary peace chiefs in Canada. She is also engaged in research on urban Iroquois, documenting their reliance upon a reservation religious center.

at unanimously in a council of the tribes. This rule was broken during the Revolution, largely because of the influence of pro-Revolutionary missionaries among the Oneida; thus, a split of the tribes occurred. Some of the tribes sided with the colonies, while others, led by Joseph Brant of the Mohawk tribe, fought for the British. Subsequently these "loyalists" were granted a tract along the Grand River in Ontario and emigrated with their leader and their families. There they established a duplicate league and preserved their traditions until this day. The offspring of the once powerful political confederation are now resident mainly in New York State and Ontario, although notable communities of Iroquois also exist in Quebec, Wisconsin, Oklahoma, and in the state of Washington.

Our best-known accounts of the Iroquois before their subjugation by the European colonists derive from the Jesuit Relations, those remarkable diaries and reports of the French missionaries to Canada in the seventeenth century; from the writings of Lafitau, published in the early eighteenth century; and from Lewis Henry Morgan's classic description of the New York State Iroquois, known as the *League of the Ho-De-No-Sau-Nee or Iroquois*, in the nineteenth century. This latter account, together with comments on the Iroquois in Morgan's other work, *Ancient Society*, is probably most responsible for later popular ideas about Iroquois women's dominant role.

Morgan described the matrilineal social organization of the Iroquois, whereby a child was counted a member of a group of individuals who can trace a common ancestry through uterine links—that is, a line of mothers. Thus an Iroquois "belonged" to his or her mother's lineage and clan group and was named after a deceased relative from that group of his or her own sex. Since the names were exclusive to the kin group—that is, no other lineage or clan could use them—one could quickly identify the group to which a person belonged. But membership in a particular group was not just

a matter of acquiring a name. For the matrilineal clans (which Morgan called "gentes") were important also as economic, social, and political units. Thus, according to Morgan, they owned property in common with mutual rights of inheritance from deceased members; they were exogamous (that is, members had to find marriage partners outside their own clan); they had reciprocal obligations of help, defense, and redress of injuries; they had the right to adopt strangers into their own groups; they shared some common religious responsibilities; they governed their own internal affairs through clan councils; and they had the right to elect and depose a "peace chief" (a delegate to the central Iroquois chiefs' council) if such a chieftain's title resided in the clan.

It was easy to conclude from such a description that the women through whom the members of a clan reckoned their relationship must have had unusual significance throughout Iroquois life. And in fact scattered information seemed to confirm this inference. Morgan noted, for example, that women "owned" their children, taking them along without challenge in the event of a divorce, and that they had exclusive say in arranging their offsprings' marriages. Furthermore, they played an important role in ritual life by holding the religious office of "faithkeeper."

The reliability of Morgan's conclusions about the role of women is diminished, however, by the fact that they are more dependent on his theory of social evolution than on observations of Iroquois women. Morgan interpreted the Iroquois as the prime example of a people whose political institutions were based on their social system, a condition that he called a "kinship state." He also thought that a "kinship state" based on matriliny prevailed because the Iroquois were in a state of barbarism, beneath full civilization. Thus, subsequent commentators who would like to utilize the Iroquois, as interpreted by Morgan, as an early example of women's liberation tend to misinterpret Morgan's conception. Ironically,

Morgan himself believed that Iroquois women considered themselves inferior.

What, then, is the position of women among the Iroquois? To what extent are women leaders of the social, political, and religious institutions? And how is their role as matriarchs to be understood? It is difficult to answer these questions for the Iroquois of the pre-Columbian period, or even for the Colonial and post-Revolutionary periods, but fortunately it is possible to observe contemporary communities that have retained a remarkable number of the cultural prescriptions of their ancestors,[1] and to make some reasonable inferences. The single largest and most conservative community today is the one founded by Joseph Brant and located around Ohsweken, Ontario. Called Six Nations, this community will be described in this chapter, although many of its traditions and practices are identical or very similar to those of the Iroquois of New York State.

Despite changes in patterns of property ownership and inheritance introduced by Canadian law, conservative and traditional Iroquois today experience their social organization as basically matrilineal. At least it is matrilineal in the sense that, with some slight alterations, an Iroquois will still identify his or her mother's uterine line as the "main," "own," or "real" family.[2] Furthermore, a child acquires the lineage and clan designations of his or her mother. If the mother belongs to the Bear clan, so does her child; this in turn means that the child belongs to the mother's tribe and moiety division as well.

However, contrary to many of our own popular assumptions, this matrilineal reckoning does not necessarily in and of itself give to women any extra measure of respect, freedom, or power. Rather, it is merely a way of defining and regularizing certain rights and duties within the tribe. It would be interesting to ask an Iroquois whether the fact that one belongs to the mother's family implies that women are superior to men. If the question made any sense at all, I am reasonably sure that the an-

swer would be no. Nor does the older literature give a different impression. It is true that murdering a woman once brought higher penalties than murdering a man. But the Jesuits reported that this was motivated by the very practical recognition that women were needed to people the land and not by any superior regard for women themselves.[3]

An illuminating index to the Iroquois perception of women's status is found in the way in which ceremonial speeches conventionally list the population. These lists always follow an order of respect. A commonly used list cites the following hierarchy of offices: chiefs, faithkeepers, other adults (i.e., those without office), and children—with descending order of respect. A second list enumerates the Iroquois classes of society, this time in ascending order: children, women (or "our mothers"), warriors, and old people. The high-placed "chief" and "warrior" groups are both exclusively male, while "women" are entered in a conspicuously lower position. On the other hand, such lists do not imply denigration of women, for female faithkeepers are equivalent to male faithkeepers, and old women (those past menopause) may assume ritual positions denied to younger women.[4] As in the case of men, respect follows roles. Some women achieve special status among the Iroquois because they are able to fill certain important roles.

One striking role that many commentators have singled out as the mainspring of Iroquois women's power is that of the so-called chief's matron. Some of the Iroquois lineages and clans still maintain the hereditary right to choose a "peace chief." In pre-Colonial days the hereditary council of peace chiefs was the Iroquois' major coordinating body for peacetime affairs; at Six Nations it remained the Iroquois' major instrument for internal governance until 1924, when the Canadian government imposed an elected tribal council. To this day, at Six Nations the chief's council continues to meet as a center of protest against government interference; however, a number of chiefs' offices have remained unfilled, as older chiefs have died and younger men have been unwilling to accept a demanding position that by now entails very little real power.

Women were never peace chiefs themselves, but the woman called "chief's matron" held the set of wampum beads that validated a chief's position. This woman was a matron of the matrilineal family—not necessarily the most senior, but one chosen for her character and knowledge of traditional practice. When a chief died, the woman who held his wampum appointed the new chief. In cases where additional personnel were traditionally selected to accompany the chief, the matron designated them as well.

Thus, in a sense, these matrons were "king makers." Nonetheless, their power was subject to a number of checks. In modern times, at least, the matron's choice was subject to approval by the council of chiefs; if they rejected her candidate for any reason, she would be expected to propose another. Consequently, in the final analysis, men held a possible veto over the women's choice. Still another limit was placed on a matron's range of selection by the expectation that she must serve a higher principle than favoritism to a son or nephew. Case histories show that chiefs' matrons have in fact at times bypassed their own children in favor of other candidates thought more meritorious, although accusations of favoritism have also been made.

As holder of the chief's wampum, the matron held the power to depose as well as install her chief; a few cases on record show that matrons have done this. The matron was also entitled to "borrow" a candidate from another family or clan if none of her own proved suitable. Hence, the political influence of the chiefs' matrons, although indirect, must at one time have been considerable. Furthermore, although women in general did not attend council meetings, chiefs' matrons at Six Nations had the right to attend and to speak their minds. Many were, in fact, forceful speakers

who could and did sway the decisions of their appointed councillors.

In modern times chiefs' matrons have been chosen largely on the basis of their knowledge of Iroquois traditions and their willingness to "keep things going." These same characteristics have meant that, in addition to having political roles, they are often sought out as traditional authorities in a broad variety of nonpolitical contexts. Thus a matron may be asked to provide a name for the newborn tribal member from the stock of lineage and/or clan names in her memory. Furthermore, if family problems must be solved, or commemorative feasts given, or medicinal rituals performed, men and women of the matron's lineage commonly seek her advice. Thus the prestige deriving from her political role is converted into social and religious authority also, although a particular matron's personality is an important factor here as well.

A second traditional Iroquois personage, who plays a very different kind of advisory role, is the fortuneteller. Both men and women can be fortunetellers, but the majority are women. To appreciate the fortuneteller's significance in Iroquois life, one must recognize the contemporary Iroquois' preoccupation with maintaining health and personal well-being. A number of traditional religious rites are customarily adapted as curing rites. These may be sponsored by individual Iroquois either during special days set aside for them as part of the yearly cycle of ceremonies at the Longhouse or for special performances in the home. In addition, at Six Nations there are about a dozen societies, with rites of their own, that concern themselves with curing individuals, keeping them from harm, and placating the forces of nature and the dead so that the living may have peace of mind.

At the onset of illness, or in response to a threatening dream or omen, the conservative Iroquois will approach a fortuneteller for advice. The fortuneteller may work with a number of methods: some read tea, some use cards, some interpret dreams. If witchcraft is suspected, the fortuneteller may use an old method of interpreting the movements of a special root that is floated in a saucer of water. She or he may then prescribe an herbal cure, a visit to a White doctor, and/or one or more of the special ritual performances cited above. Every traditionally minded Iroquois knows that illness and death follow the neglect of a fortuneteller's prescription; the sanctions supporting fortunetllers are so personal and so deep that it is very difficult to ignore them short of total acculturation to White society. Consequently these few people, mostly women, have come to have a disproportionate amount of influence, especially in perpetuating aspects of ritual practice that might otherwise be lost in a modern setting.

In a sense, both the chief's matron and the fortuneteller can be considered "religious" figures. For each is believed to be endowed by the Great Creator with a special gift for "seeing." Thus it is said that the matron's ability to recognize the "best" candidate for the chief's position is supernaturally ordained. The fortuneteller's powers are likewise endowed by birth, while their advice is inspired and directed by the Creator himself or by a tutelary spirit, such as the Otter or the Bear Spirit.

In the arena of the Longhouse religion per se, however, women's roles and influence are most richly elaborated. Conservative Iroquois in both Canada and the United States adhere to a doctrine known as *kaiwiyoh* ("Good Message," or "The Code of Handsome Lake"). This religion, still practiced by about one-third of the Six Nations residents, is an amalgam of aboriginal Iroquois rituals—calendric agricultural ceremonies, elements from the dreamguessing and curing rites, and the war complex—and the teachings of a Seneca prophet, Handsome Lake, who preached his doctrine at the turn of the nineteenth century. Four Longhouse congregations (often referred to as "Longhouse" or "Longhouse people," after

the building in which they worship, which is also called the "Longhouse") are currently functioning at the Six Nations reserve, and other Iroquois reservations have Longhouse congregations as well. Each congregation has its own personnel, and women can achieve considerable prestige and power in the organization and activities of these Longhouse communities.

To understand the roles of women within the Longhouse practice and organization, we must first explore briefly some important aspects of the Longhouse religion. Longhouse practice in general reveals an emphasis on dichotomies, two of which are especially important. One is the interplay of moieties, or tribal "halves," that is characteristic also of many other Native American peoples. The second is the dichotomy of male and female. At different points in the ritual cycle, various aspects of these divisions may be emphasized. This is most clearly seen in the Longhouse's spatial organization. For certain ceremonies, the Longhouse is organized by moieties, with a door, a side, and a stove designated for each of the two divisions. For others—in fact, for the majority—the spatial layout is organized by sex. Thus members say that they enter by the men's or women's door and sit on the men's or women's side. During the rites themselves, action is reciprocal between the two domains, and much of the service consists of dialogue between the opposing units. Thus, on the whole, a balance is struck, and the efficacy of a ceremony depends on the combined efforts of whatever divisions are in play.

Furthermore, many rituals of the ceremonial cycle are themselves designated as "women's" or "men's" observances. Falling into the women's sphere are a number of rites that thank the Great Creator for his "works" and beseech him for their continuation—especially rites involving the spirits of food plants. Women today, as in the past, have special associations with "Our Life Supporters" (corn, beans, and squash). By extension, each time a

Food Spirit is addressed, the ceremony will include some of the special series of dances, songs, and other observances that have been traditionally associated with women. In addition, whenever one of these special women's observances is incorporated into one of the more complex ceremonial events, the larger ceremony itself is marked as falling into the women's domain.

A set of *tyohekoh* (literally, "what we live on") dances—the Women's Shuffle Dance, Standing Quiver Dance, Corn Dance, Squash Dance, and sometimes the Bottle Dance—is the most notable example of such women's observances. This set of dances is a major component of seven different Longhouse events: the Seed Planting, Corn Sprouting, Raspberry, Green Beans, Corn Testing, Our Sustenance, and Harvest ceremonies. Certain sections of the set are also performed during the ceremony honoring the spirits of bushes and trees that is called the Bush Dance. Specific women's songs also accompany the Seed Planting, Moon, and Harvest ceremonies; they are sung by individual women and followed by their prayers. Not long ago the Sour Springs Longhouse even had a special Women's Society that was responsible for the turtle-rattle instruments peculiar to these songs. The songs utilized in these ceremonies may be inherited and are "owned" by their female singers. They are comparable to men's *atonwe* songs, also individually owned, which are given to them at their naming ceremonies. As a woman sings her song at the Seed Planting and Harvest festivals in anticipation of and gratitude for the year's crops, so the man may substitute his *atonwe* chant; but the ceremony would be incomplete—in truth, inconceivable—without the women's participation.

Another prominent feature of the Seed Planting ceremony, which again emphasizes its feminine component, is a shortened version of the commonly used Sacred Bowl Game. This gambling game is said to be one of the Four Sacred Rituals prescribed by the Great Creator

himself; in its more common, long form, it is played between the moieties to amuse the Great Creator. But it has also been adapted to please the Food Spirits at the time of planting. Packets of seeds are collected by a man from all the males of the congregation and by a woman from the females. Then these packets are paired as stakes to be gained by the winner. Women contend against men, playing at the imaginary line that divides the Longhouse into the women's and the men's sides. A head deaconess is always the first player. The game is characterized by a friendly sex rivalry, and the results are discussed throughout the year. If men win, they should cultivate the gardens for the entire year, but it is predicted that the gardens will then be weedy; at least this is the women's version. The men claim that, if the women win, then there will be no corn, for the women will not plant it. Both sexes agree, however, that if the men win, the harvest will be generally poor, and that, if the women win, it will be good. This male/female version of the Bowl Game is also performed at the Bush festival and during the Moon festival; for the Moon has been traditionally associated with conception and the auspicious initiation of growth. It should be stressed that, the exchange of jokes notwithstanding, the principle behind the sexually competitive Bowl Game is that the sexes are equal and both are needed to entertain the Food Spirits. The cooperative and essentially complementary character of the participants is pleasing and efficacious.[5]

Unlike the religious festivals of many other cultures, the ceremonial cycle of the Longhouse does not follow a fixed schedule of dates. There is a customary seasonal cycle, but specific dates for each celebration must be set by the individual Longhouse congregations. Here again one sees the interplay of men's and women's spheres; for some ceremonies must be "set" by men, while women are responsible for the others. There is some variation among congregations, but usually women schedule ceremonials dedicated to the Food Spirits and associated with gardening and the first fruits offerings. At Sour Springs, one of the two Cayuga Longhouses at Six Nations, the male faithkeepers set the comparatively minor Sun and Moon and Thunder ceremonies as well as the two most important yearly events, the Midwinter ceremony and the Green Corn Dance. The False Face ceremony, which is largely directed toward keeping away both human diseases and afflictions of the crops, is also set by men. Because, to an Iroquois, a ceremony becomes somewhat more "masculine" or "feminine" depending on who has scheduled it, these latter events are considered "male festivals," while the rest are considered "female festivals."

Over the years the female dimension of Longhouse religion has actually increased as the Longhouse ceremonies themselves have become increasingly oriented toward the agricultural cycle. The traces of this reorientation are clearly seen in the rites themselves. Rituals once associated with the exclusively male spheres of hunting and war activities are now said to further agricultural aims. As symbolic associations with the crops are developed, women and feminine symbols acquire new roles within men's rites. A good example is the Thunder ceremony. The ceremony's traditional lacrosse game and war dance, as well as the prayers and speeches that have been reframed from the original boasting recitals, are now directed toward Our Grandfathers, the Thunderers, to implore them to control winds and pests and to bring the rain. The Thunder ceremony's principal performers are still men. But after the war dance, women sprinkle men with water from pails that they hold, and men enter the Longhouse via the women's door immediately thereafter. Needless to say, the rain thus anticipated invariably follows. At Sour Springs, it is said that in the past women scheduled this nominally male event when they felt that a drought had to be broken. Yet, historically, the entire complex was more likely related to the war path.

In one sense, of course, it is easy to understand how such shifts have occurred. Iroquois men are no longer hunters and warriors, and it is not surprising that the men's rites would be reinterpreted to fit other purposes. But, ironically, this reinterpretation has occurred while both men and women are shifting away from their traditional roles. Once upon a time the women were in fact the major food-crop producers; their ritual association with plant foods reflects this former economic reality. But at present women actually contribute less and less to the congregation's sustenance, for economically all the Iroquois now participate in a modern world. Women do still plant the ritual tobacco and the food crops required at the Longhouse or for the medicine societies' "doings." Many of the women also plant gardens for home use, but the Iroquois no longer rely on the women's gardens for nonmeat foods as they did in the past.

One can easily see why Iroquois women have been able to assume important roles of religious leadership throughout their recorded history. The Longhouse religion has no professional personnel in the sense in which a Christian church may have a full-time priest or minister. Holding an office in the congregation of *kaiwiyoh* followers is only one of the roles of an ordinary Iroquois citizen, who may also be a farmer, a laborer, a housewife, or a professional. All offices are unpaid, and even the concept of remuneration for expertise in the Longhouse is ludicrous, if not sinful, to an Iroquois. Longhouse officers fall into two major categories. One category includes ritual specialists of one variety or another, such as the "speakers," who recite the traditional addresses and prayers, the "singers," who may retain whole cycles of ceremonial songs, and the itinerant "preachers," who commit to memory and recite the long Code of Handsome Lake. Here men are most conspicuous. Women do not "speak" formally in the Longhouse; hence there are no women speakers or preachers. However, women are prominent as "faithkeepers" or "deaconesses," officers who perform a different kind of service. They are in effect organizational leaders, and much of the practical responsibility for Longhouse affairs falls on their shoulders. It is almost impossible to conceive a Longhouse congregation functioning without these leaders; for not only do they set dates, organize the rituals, and prepare feast foods, but they transmit all the needs of the people to the appropriate speakers, singers, and performers.

Under ordinary circumstances, every congregation has one male and one female head deacon from each moiety; they are aided by a varying numer of assistants. The head deacons and deaconesses take the initiative in scheduling Longhouse ceremonies. When a "women's" ceremony must be set, for example, the two head deaconesses consult with each other, and they check with their male counterparts to coordinate plans. Wherever the original initiative comes from, the men and women are charged to cooperate. But, unlike the situation in political affairs, in which the chiefs can override a matron's recommendation, the Longhouse women always retain the right to make a final decision on matters that fall into their own sphere.

This principle also holds true in the arrangement of other aspects of the rituals. Here again deacons and deaconesses have exclusive responsibility for performances that fall into their own male and female spheres. They choose the speakers and singers and dancers. They supervise food preparation; the women take charge of the various plant dishes that are commonly distributed during the women's customary rites while the men prepare the sides of beef now substituted for the results of the hunt that were formerly served in connection with the men's performances. When performances require participants of both sexes, the deacons and deaconesses negotiate to assemble the necessary expertise. This is especially important when an individual Iroquois sponsors one of the curing performances mentioned earlier, or a special rite of passage, or a commemorative celebration for the dead. If, for example, a woman wants to sponsor a ceremony that requires the services of a male speaker or singer, she usually will ask her deaconess to make the arrangements for her. The Iroquois customarily observe a mild sex taboo; thus members of one sex hesitate to ask members of the opposite sex directly for services or advice. The deacons and deaconesses are, however, exempt from this taboo; hence they move quite freely between the sexual divisions. This aspect of their activity can be seen most clearly on the so-called Pass Dance days that are set aside during some of the great festivals for individually sponsored performances. Pass Dances are usually organized on the spot rather than in advance. On Pass Dance days, the deacons and deaconesses move constantly across the floor collecting the necessary dancers, speakers, and singers, giving instructions, and making sure that the special foods contributed are being properly prepared for the performances that demand them.

We must again remember that the Longhouse ceremonies have been brought increasingly into the women's sphere. Thus the power of the head deaconesses has effectively increased also; and the head deaconesses have come to bear a major burden of responsibility for the congregation's functioning. This may be why these central congregational leaders have also acquired a number of important peripheral functions. If an individual, especially a woman, wants to be adopted into the Longhouse congregation, the head deaconess makes the decision to accept (or reject) the new Longhouse member. Some deaconesses may be so trusted that they are appointed keepers for some of the Longhouse wampum, as was the case at Sour Springs. As the chiefs, and consequently their matrons, have lost their power, the deaconesses have also come to assume many of the functions that were once exercised by these political figures. Thus the deaconess, like the chief's matron, also keeps names; furthermore, she may now settle a quarrel that would once have been referred to a chief. The prestige and authority that the deaconess acquires through her religious activities (like those that the chief's matron acquires from her political activities) are transferred to the everyday realm; thus a deaconess is frequently consulted for problem solving in ordinary life. Furthermore, the Iroquois have some feeling that obtaining the aid of a deacon or deaconess makes a particular rite or action "better," since the goodness and righteousness of the helper are incorporated into the action that is taken.

Who are these influential and prestigious women? Some deaconesses acquire their positions through inheritance, with the privilege of access to the office carried, as in the chiefs' case, through the matrilineal line. Others are elected by their colleagues. In a congregation such as Sour Springs, where the head deaconesses are chosen by their women colleagues in each moiety, any responsible and religious woman can gain much influence.

One last significant function of the Longhouse women should be mentioned. Iroquois women, like women in many other traditional societies, play a very prominent role in observances for the dead. As noted earlier, each Longhouse relies on a number of societies that serve special functions. One such society found at every Longhouse is charged with scheduling and executing the semiannual commemorative ceremonies. Under the direction of a head woman from each moiety, this society cleans the cemetery on the day of the *ohkiweh* (Feast of the Dead) and then makes sure that the ceremony will be observed respectfully. Otherwise the dead will feel neglected, and they may even harm the living in revenge. As in the case of other Longhouse events, the community must actively "unite their minds" for this observance, and then all will "sleep well and feel well." To an outsider, men may seem to play a larger role during the Feast of the Dead because men speak and render the tobacco invocation (they do so, incidentally, at the women's stove). But, organizationally, the "care of the dead" is considered to lie within the women's realm. For women collect the necessary

offerings of cloth (perhaps a substitute for the presents once so prominently associated with funerary practice). Women direct their male helper to "go around" and announce the date that women have designated for the ceremony. And women prepare the midnight and morning feasts.

What kind of conclusions can we draw from these materials? First, it seems clear that women do not dominate conservative Iroquois life. Many important and powerful roles are assigned to men—witness the all-male chiefs and Longhouse speakers and preachers, together with the deacons who head the men's moiety and the largely male membership and leadership in some Longhouse societies. The possibility of female domination in the past is even more remote, for, as we have noted, the role of women in the Longhouse is expanding, not contracting, as the old cycle of men's ceremonies is readapted to the more traditionally feminine agricultural sphere.

Second, it is equally apparent that women have great power and influence in their own traditional realm. This is not unusual, of course; similar patterns have been documented among many traditional peoples. What *is* unusual is that the women's realm as a whole is not subjected to the men's, as one may find in the great civilizations and so-called world religions. Instead, the worlds of women and of men are woven together in an intricate system of balance and mutual interdependence.

For this reason, the habitual attempts of scholars and feminists to discover who is superior and who is inferior, who is dominant and who is subordinate become, more than anything else, irrelevant. The same can be said for considerations of equality. Iroquois men and women are not equal—at least not in the sense of having access to the same roles and the same kinds of power. It is more appropriate to say that they are complementary, with each of their worlds and works being essential to life as a whole.

One important question remains and that is whether the delicate patterning of balance and complementarity that we find in the traditional ideal Iroquois culture has any broad-range impact on the lives of ordinary women. If some women hold prestigious and powerful roles, if women's performances and initiatives are essential to many segments of ritual life, if women occupy equal portions of Longhouse space and have leaders whose authority cannot be overridden by their male counterparts—does this mean that a woman who participates in the conservative Iroquois religion will be treated any differently when she goes home to face her husband and brothers and sons? Unfortunately, this question has no clear answer. Today even the most traditional Iroquois are thoroughly steeped in the surrounding White culture and its attitudes and values. Iroquois go to school with children from the surrounding areas (at Six Nations, after elementary school), they are exposed to the same media as the population in general, and they are exposed to the same propaganda about, and resistance to, women's liberation as any working class group. I did not find that Iroquois attitudes towards women were strikingly different from those of the Canadian or American public at large. Instead, as in American culture, the relationships between men and women varied considerably from family to family. One can, however, suspect that, because of the constant exposure to and reiteration of the traditional ideals, men may feel some pressure to regard women more highly than might have been the case otherwise. One can also reasonably expect that this same constant exposure contributes to women's own self-image and enhances their morale. Such suppositions are difficult if not impossible to prove; but they are more likely to be true than romantic visions of Iroquois women's supremacy.

Notes

1. To verify similarities between ethnographic data for the Iroquois of more recent times and the relatively unacculturated Iroquoian-speaking Huron (a people very closely related to the Five Nations), it is helpful to consult the excellent comparison of data by Elizabeth Tooker in *An Ethnography of the Huron Indians, 1615–1649*, Bureau of American Ethnology Bulletin, no. 180. (Washington: United States Government Printing Office, 1964).

2. Today some informants also include the mother's father and some of his kin in this "real" family; at some reservations people may also include the father and other paternal relatives with whom they reside.

3. Cf. *Jesuit Relations* and *Allied Documents: The Travels and Explorations of the Jesuit Missionaries in New France, 1610–1791*, ed. R. G. Thwaites (Totowa, N.J.: Rownian and Littlefield, 1959), Vol. 33:243: Tooker, *An Ethnography of the Huron Indians*, pp. 52–53, and her quotations from Hewitt.

4. Like many other peoples, the Iroquois feel that a menstruating woman is a source of danger; thus, she is expected to stay away from ceremonies. The menstrual taboo is not interpreted as a form of discrimination but as a practical recognition of a possible source of contamination. Popular belief holds that all women menstruate at the same time, during the five days that include and follow the date of the new moon. It is interesting to note that the Iroquois ideally schedule their Midwinter ceremonies five days after the new moon.

5. For further details concerning the Iroquois ceremonials, cf. F. Speck, *Midwinter Rites of the Cayuga Long House* (Philadelphia: University of Pennsylvania, 1949), and A. Shimony, *Conservatism among the Iroquois at the Six Nations Reserve*, Yale University Publications in Anthropology, no. 65 (New Haven: Department of Anthropology, Yale University, 1961).

Further Readings

Fenton, William N. *The False Faces of the Iroquois.* Norman, Okla. and London: University of Oklahoma Press (published in cooperation with the Museum of the American Indian—Heye Foundation), 1987.

_____. "The Iroquois in History." *North American Indians in Historical Perspective*, ed. by Eleanor B. Leacock and Nancy O. Lurie, 129–68. New York: Random House, 1971.

Morgan, Lewis H. *League of the Ho-dé-no-sau-nee or Iroquois.* Rochester, N.Y.: Sage; New York: M. H. Newman, 1851 (reprinted as *League of the Iroquois*, New York: Corinth Books, 1962).

Randle, Martha C. "Iroquois Women, Then and Now." *Symposium on Local Diversity in Iroquois Culture*, ed. by William N. Fenton, 167–80. Bureau of American Ethnology, Bulletin 149. Washington, D.C.: U.S. Government Printing Office, 1951.

Shimony, Annemarie. "Iroquois Religion and Women in Historical Perspective." *Women, Religion, and Social Change*, ed. by Yvonne Y. Haddad and Ellison B. Findly, 397–418. Albany, N.Y.: State University of New York Press, 1985.

——————. "Conflict and Continuity: An Analysis of an Iroquois Uprising." In *Extending the Rafters: Interdisciplinary Approaches to Iroquoian Studies*, ed. by Michael K. Foster, Jack Campisi, and Marianne Mithun, 153–64. Albany, N.Y.: State University of New York Press, 1984.

——————. "Alexander General, Deskahe, Cayuga-Oneida, 1889–1965." In *American Indian Intellectuals*, ed. by Margot Liberty, 159–75. 1976 Proceedings of the American Ethnological Society. St. Paul, Minn.: West Publishing Co., 1978.

——————. "Iroquois Witchcraft at Six Nations." In *Systems of North American Witchcraft and Sorcery*, ed. by Deward E. Walker, Jr., 239–65. Anthropological Monographs of the University of Idaho, No. 1. Moscow, Idaho: University of Idaho, 1970.

——————. "The Iroquois Fortunetellers and Their Conservative Influence." *Symposium on Cherokee and Iroquois Culture*, ed. by William N. Fenton and John Gulick, 205–11. Bureau of American Ethnology, Bulletin 180. Washington, D.C.: U.S. Government Printing Office, 1961.

——————. *Conservatism among the Iroquois at Six Nations Reserve*. Yale University Publications in Anthropology, No. 65. New Haven, Conn.: 1961.

Sturtevant, William C., general ed. and Bruce Trigger, volume ed. *Handbook of North American Indians*, vol. 15. Smithsonian Institution, Washington, D.C.: U.S. Government Printing Office, 1978.

Trigger, Bruce. *The Children of Aataentsic: A History of the Huron People to 1660.* 2 vols. Montreal: McGill-Queen's University Press, 1976.

——————. *The Huron: Farmers of the North.* New York: Holt, Rhinehart, and Winston, 1969.

Wallace, Anthony F. C., *The Death and Rebirth of the Seneca*. New York: Alfred A. Knopf, 1969.

20

Rosinta, Rats, and the River: Bad Luck Is Banished in Andean Bolivia

JOSEPH W. BASTIEN

A distinctive mark of Andean religion is its highly specialized rituals and ritual experts. In Andean regions, the state, the territory, the community, the lineage, and the family all have separate and distinctive shrines, rituals, and ritualists. Each territory, for example, has its own pattern of place shrines, with territorial ritualists who know their names and locations. The various economic activities connected with different ecological zones also have their own rites and ritual specialists. Thus highland herders have rites for alpacas, llamas, and sheep; people of the mountain's central slopes have potato rituals; and people of the lowlands perform rites for corn. Because the rites are so specialized, there are many ritualists and a great variety of ritual roles.

This system of ritual specialization is itself quite old, being evidenced as far back as the Spanish Conquest. One feature of the system that is prominent now, however, seems to have

JOSEPH W. BASTIEN   received a Ph.D. in Cultural Anthropology from Cornell University in 1973. As Professor of Anthropology at the University of Texas at Arlington, Dr. Bastien has studied among the Bolivian natives since 1963 and as recently as June 1987. His most famous publication is *Mountain of the Condor: Metaphor and Ritual in Andean Ayllu*. His most recent work is titled *Healers of the Andes: Kallawaya Herbalists and Their Medicinal Plants*.

Author's Note   I spent the 1976–1977 academic year as a National Endowment of the Humanities Postdoctoral Fellow at Tulane University. I would like to thank the N.E.H. for providing me with the opportunity to study with Professors Arden King and Donald Robertson of Tulane University, who assisted me with this article.

been less sharply defined in ancient times. This is the distinction of rituals by sex, with the belief that only men or women can perform certain crucial functions. This chapter will investigate one such sex-specific ritual and the woman diviner who performed it. My wife Judy and I were both subjects and observers of this ritual in 1972, during a year of fieldwork in the Bolivian Andes.

MEN AND WOMEN, MOUNTAIN AND RIVER

In midwestern Bolivia, northeast of Lake Titicaca, stands Kaata, a sacred mountain. On its central slopes is a community, also called Kaata, that is renowned throughout the central Andes for its diviners. Among its approximately one thousand inhabitants, forty-six men are diviners (*qari yachaj*), while no less than sixty-one women are *warmi yachaj*, women diviners. Together, these make up a full 25 percent of the adult population.

One reason for the Kaatan diviners' special fame is their linkage to an ancient Andean religious tradition handed down by the Qollahuaya Indians. These renowned ritualists of the Andes, who travel from Columbia to Chile, are a special cultural subgroup of the Aymara. Purveyors of a tradition of curing and divination, the Qollahuayas of Mount Kaata performed brain surgery as early as 700 A.D. and carried the Inca emperor's chair in the fifteenth century (the emperor was considered a descendant of the sun, and we can assume that only very sacred people could carry him). An early ethnographer in South America, Bandelier, described the Qollahuayas as "Wizards of the Andes."[1] He thought that an analysis of their rituals would provide the key to understanding Andean religion. Because Kaatan diviners draw on symbols of the Qollahuaya heritage, the rites that they perform today still offer a

unique mode of entry into the traditional Andean religious world.

The special import of women diviners in Kaata is due in large part to their role in a complex of rituals concerned with good and bad fortune. Men diviners perform good-fortune rituals to set in motion a series of favorable events, such as a good harvest or the renewed health of a sick person. Women diviners perform misfortune rituals to remove bodily or social disintegration. This contrast between male and female ritualists is in turn part of a very complex local symbolic system. This system clusters together men, stability, and the mountain and contrasts them to women, the river, and a natural and social cycle of dissolution and renewal.

Let us examine these important sets of associations more closely. Kaatans equate their mountain symbolically to a human body and draw fairly detailed parallels between areas of the mountain and parts of the body. Thus Apacheta, the highland community of herders, is the mountain's head; Kaata, the central community of potato growers, is its heart and bowels; and Niñokorin, the lowland community of corn producers, is its legs. Men seem best fitted to preserve this mountain body because of their inherent stability, for, just as the mountain is stable within the Bolivian landscape, so the men are stable within the Kaatan social system. Kaatans practice virilocality and exogamy; that is, sons always remain at the place on the mountain where their fathers and mothers lived and worked the land, and their wives come to join them there. Daughters, instead, must always move away to marry and live with a husband from one of the adjacent levels.

Thus men diviners, fixing good fortune, offer highland symbols of llama fat and foetuses to all thirteen earth shrines of Mount Kaata in a yearly cycle of ritual performances. They feed all the levels of the mountain in a meal that symbolizes both the community's unity and its bodily integrity. Women diviners, instead, offer lowland symbols of pig fat and dead rats to wind, river, and landslide—the mountain's erosive elements. These women work especially with the river, which flows down the mountain, linking its different levels but also causing destruction through erosion, floods, and landslides. The latter often bring death, especially to people who live in the lowlands. Hence Kaatans associate the river with personal calamity—not only the death that the landslides bring, but also the sickness that destroys the human body as the river dissolves the mountainside.

Women belong with the river in part because they flow like it and experience losses from their body through the menstrual cycle. Because of menstruation, it is said, women are better able than men to get rid of bad things. The flow of blood cleanses women of misfortune, such as infertility. It also helps to prepare the woman for conception.

But women also flow in other ways— through the marriage system, passing from level to level, just as the river passes down the mountainside. Furthermore, like the flow of the river and that of the menstrual blood, the flow of women in marriage also carries a promise of cleansing and renewal. Kaatan legend says that, after flowing down the mountain, the river circles underground to return to its source. This is the *uma pacha*, the mountain's summit and, according to Kaatan myth, the original source of llamas and people. The dead return with the river to the highland lakes, and so do the organs destroyed by sickness and the land lost through theft; therefore the river can restore them. Permanent misfortune occurs only when such bad luck is not given to the river so that it can complete its restorative cycle. Similarly, the Kaatan social cycle finally restores the women to their families. For Kaatans also practice bilateral inheritance, which means that women as well as their brothers inherit access to their parents' land. Of course, women themselves cannot work it when they move away to marry. But women come back in the next generation. Land rights passed on

to the daughters entice the daughters to return to and marry men from the level of their mothers' birthplace.

Thus ultimately both women and river have the power to transform bad luck into good fortune. Note, incidentally, that despite the difference between symbols and practice, both men and women protect the mountain. Men feed the entire mountain body and thereby protect its future wholeness. Women divine and remove misfortune and thereby help the person, society, and community to become whole once again.

ROSINTA

Sex not only distinguishes the Kaatan diviners' functions but also determines how the diviners' roles will be inherited. Male and female diviner roles are passed along, respectively, through the father's and mother's lineage. Thus the renowned male diviner Sarito Quispe learned to set up good fortune tables from his father's father, whereas the equally famous Rosinta Garcia learned her ritual role by serving as apprentice to her mother's sister, who was a very powerful ritualist. Aspiring diviners master all the rituals' intricacies only after years of apprenticeship. One day, after some natural manifestation—such as lightning for the male diviner or a landslide for the female—they announce to the community, "The ancestors have chosen me to divine. I know!"

Like diviners of many other cultures, Kaatan diviners may make use of a trance induced by chewing coca (cocaine), to help them see into the future. Her clairvoyance has made Rosinta Garcia especially successful. Many Andeans, who are quite poor, travel from afar to the Qollahuaya region where Rosinta lives and offer her a month's supply of food in return for divination. They seek out Rosinta because she is powerful; and, indeed, many of Rosinta's predictions have been fulfilled. Andeans believe Rosinta's evil eye has caused the death of seven people, and they may solicit her to send bad luck as well as to remove it. Rosinta bewitches Andeans by sticking pig fat and the victim's hair (called a *chije*, or misfortune) inside a cat's and a dog's skull, putting them together as if they were fighting with each other. If the victim discovers the *chije*, he or she can either throw it in the river or retaliate by soliciting another sorceress, who then engages in a mystical war with Rosinta. If either sorceress is caught in the act, she is taken to the sheriff, who fines her a month's salary and makes her promise on the cross never to bewitch again. The sheriff, however, fears Rosinta, so she is never arrested.

BAD LUCK

Rosinta was called upon when a string of misfortunes fell upon the Yanahuaya family, with whom Judy and I were living. The first misfortune was a long-standing complaint. Carmen's husband, Marcelino Yanahuaya, blamed Carmen for her failure to give him a living son. Carmen had borne two sons, but they both died shortly after birth. Consequently, Marcelino had no male heir to help him work his land and take it over as he grew old. Instead, Carmen's five daughters—Elsa, Celia, Gloria, Sophia, and Valentina—had survived, and now they were marrying away from his extensive landholdings in the central hamlet of Qollahuaya. Furthermore, Marcelino was upset with his oldest daughter, Elsa. Because Elsa had been herding when a landslide killed two of her father's sheep, he thought she had lost her competence as a herder. He blamed this loss on the fact that she had lived for two years as a bread seller in La Paz, where her maternal uncle had mistreated her badly. She returned in ill health.

The next disaster occurred when the couple's beloved granddaughter Erminia got sick with chronic diarrhea and vomiting. Erminia's parents were Carmen's daughter Celia and her husband Martín Mejía, who lived in Chaqahuaya, a lowland hamlet. When Erminia could not retain the pills I gave her, a male diviner was called in to restore her health, a function within the sphere of male ritualists. The diviner assured the parents that Erminia would soon be cured. The child showed some temporary signs of recovery. But a month after his divination, she was dead. Soon after, Marcelino's sister died of the same disease, now diagnosed as typhoid. Erminia's death increased the already existing hostility between Celia and her husband Martín's lineage. When her mother-in-law accused Celia of causing Erminia's death, Celia struck her in the eye and blackened it. On behalf of the mother-in-law, I reprimanded Celia, who then avoided me for three weeks.

The final misfortune struck when Martín's collarbone was fractured soon after Erminia's funeral. A woman smashed his collarbone with a rock and broke it while Martín was fighting with her husband in a drunken brawl. If it was not cured, a crippled collarbone would permanently prevent Martín from using his hand plow.

The broken collarbone stopped the feuding between the Mejías and the Yanahuayas, for both families realized that another person would be lost if they did not help each other. In a gesture of reconciliation, Marcelino called another male diviner to cure his son-in-law. The diviner applied a compress of dried frog skins and herbs to the front and back of the broken bone. Several elders also visited Martín, and they recalled that someone had died the year before, after his broken bone had protruded and became infected from the herb medicine. This time the herbs failed, and Marcelino asked me to cure Martín. Martín, bedridden with pain, cried as he showed me his deformed collarbone; it was setting in its broken position. Celia begged me to do something, so I sent Martín, accompanied by

Marcelino, to La Paz to have the bone set. When Marcelino and Martín returned, they were very happy, not so much because Martín was on his way to recovery, but because they had the legal papers to sue the woman who had hit Martín. A common enemy had united two families. I was glad that I had been able to help Martín recover; my good feelings, however, suffered a blow when one morning I saw him cross the patio carrying a one-hundred-pound sack, wearing no cast. It turned out that he had chipped the cast off because it bothered him. Carmen and Marcelino were disgusted with Martín for removing the cast, and they called him an ass.

Then Judy and I became ill with typhoid. The Yanahuayas thought that their bad luck would never end. Marcelino, representing "male" interests, blamed his bad luck on the women and his wife's relatives. He contended that the misfortunes had begun when his daughters had left home to live in other communities, where they were mistreated. If his daughters had been able to stay with him, this ill treatment would not have occurred. Incidentally, this would have been, of course, impossible, since in Kaata it is women's lot to move away when they marry.

Carmen had her own "female" set of interpretations. She said that the landslide, which had killed the two sheep, had been caused by Marcelino's disrespect toward her people. She also had an explanation for Martín's injury; she complained that Martín had not set up a table for Erminia, their dead granddaughter, during the Feast of the Dead and that he had avoided her gravesite. During the feast, Celia had sat alone in front of Erminia's grave and had given bread, bananas, and oranges to those who prayed for her daughter. Carmen was certain the ancestral spirits were punishing Martín for his blatant disrespect toward the dead.

One evening, as the two were arguing again, Carmen insisted in a high-pitched, whining voice that women were not the only causes of

misfortune and that men were also to blame. Carmen then invited Rosinta Garcia to divine the "masculine" causes of their bad luck.

BAD LUCK IS BANISHED

Rosinta performed her ritual on Tuesday, December 12. (She had previously discovered during a trance that I was the target of sorcery and the cause of bad luck.) Eight people participated: myself and Judy, Carmen and Marcelino, and their daughters Celia, Elsa, Sophia, and Valentina. The absent daughter, Gloria, and the dead sons, Sabino and Roberto, were represented by symbols.

It was dark when Rosinta arrived through the back gate of Marcelino's house. Her wrinkled and leathery face reflected her supernatural powers. She quickly unpacked her ritual paraphernalia inside the supply house; Carmen was thrilled to see the dead rat that Rosinta had strangled for the occasion. Marcelino nervously prodded Rosinta to move more quickly, but from the start she set her own pace. Methodically and confidently, she began removing the misfortunes. Cupping a bowl in front of her mouth, Rosinta blew puffs of incense around our heads and feet; then she balanced a cup of alcohol on our heads and then threw it to our earthshrines. She explained that the aspersions were to ask permission of the spirits of the patio and kitchen, as well as of the spirits of the various levels of the mountain. She needed their approval to perform this ritual for the river.

After Rosinta had purified the participants, she asked for the wind's permission as well, by throwing alcohol into the air so that the wind could carry it "where the wind blows." That same wind had also brought the present misfortunes to the Yanahuayas. In retaliation, Rosinta poured another cup of alcohol for the wind; she passed this cup over our heads and went into the patio to throw it more directly into the wind. This gesture was meant to ensure that the wind would parch the land of those who had cursed the Yanahuayas.

In these opening rites, the wind's significance and function parallel those of the river that would later in the ceremony become paramount, for the wind, too, both destroys and restores. On the one hand, the wind parches the earth, and Kaatans use it as an instrument for cursing people. But, on the other hand, the wind brings the rain clouds and blows away misfortune. Furthermore, both wind and river, through their natural changeability, prefigure the change in luck that the ritualist hopes to achieve. Thus both wind and river are fed the symbols of misfortune: rats, moss, and cacti. Rats eat valuable supplies, moss cracks the foundations of homes and fences, and cacti are harmful to animals and difficult to remove from the fields.

Sharing the meal with the wind and the river in our ritual performance were the dead ancestors of Marcelino's patrilineage, the patron spirit of the patio, the matron spirit of Carmen's kitchen, and Mount Kaata. For these guests, Rosinta served six cotton wads of coca, llama fat, carnations, and incense into the shrine alongside the supply house. The wads were thrown in the fire that burned within the shrine. Rosinta set aside another six wads to be burned and fed into the river. We were admiring Rosinta's skill, when she asked each of us to name two of our enemies, so she could send them a calamity. I could not hear whom the others specified as their enemies, but, when Rosinta asked me, they all listened intently as I named Lionel Alvarez of Charazani. Alvarez was the owner of a truck. Over and over again, after my wife and I had reserved the cabin of his truck for our twenty-hour trip to La Paz, he would inform us that the cabin was no longer available. We knew that he had sold the seats to someone else for more money. When I named Alvarez as my

enemy, Carmen and Marcelino smiled; they, too, disliked the mestizo, because he exploited the Indians, crowding them into the back of his truck and charging them high rates.

Midnight marked a shift in both the sites and the ritual foods of our misfortune ritual. Before midnight our spiritual "guests" were fed llama fat and cotton in Marcelino's patio. After midnight, they ate pig fat and black llama wool at the Kunochayuh River. The pig traditionally comes from the lower mountain levels, and its fat symbolizes negative power from that area. The llama is native to the highlands, but its dark wool symbolizes death. Both symbols together suggest that the negative forces of death and decay from the lower levels are restored by the highlands' positive forces. Although land and people erode and die on their journey down the levels toward the lowlands, they will return to the highlands and regenerate when they die.

After midnight Tuesday morning, Rosinta began preparing the meal for the river by divining with a gray guinea pig, which she had first touched to everyone's forehead. She opened its viscera with her fingernails and poured its blood into a cup with wine, eggs, and corn. After removing the ribcage, she examined the protrusion in the front, which formed a small half-moon. She said it looked fine. On the guinea pig's pancreas she spotted two incisions, which she said were two mouths. They represented enemies who were bewitching us, she explained. Marcelino identified one mouth as that of Dominga Ari. Dominga had become impoverished after the death of her husband, who, twenty years earlier, had usurped Marcelino's land. Marcelino said that Dominga's blindness and poverty were punishments from Marcelino's ancestors, but Dominga accused Marcelino of soliciting a sorceress to send these misfortunes. When two hostile Andean families suffer calamities, an exchange of sorcery is invariably suspected.

Josefa Waque, identified as the second

mouth, was suspected of cursing me. This tough seventy-year-old woman had been trampled by horses, severely damaging her skull. She was dying when they brought her to me to be cured. After I shaved her head, I cleansed and bound the bone together with a bandage. She recovered in a month and came to me asking for her hair. When I explained that I had burned it, she suspected me of using her hair in witchcraft against her. At the same time, Dominga and Josefa became close friends, further arousing Carmen's suspicions about them.

At 2:30 A.M., Rosinta began to prepare servings for the river. She laid the rat at the head of the ritual cloth and sorted out twenty wads of dark llama wool. Earlier Carmen had secretly snatched some coca leaves from various shrines in the community, and Rosinta placed twelve of these leaves on each wad. She put slivers of pig fat on the coca, and then daisies, seeds, herb clumps, and moss. Once Rosinta had laid the food out, she wrapped the dark wool tightly around it. She tied one wad to the rat's back and gave two to each participant, setting one beneath a man's hat or woman's headband, and the other between the left big toe and sandal. She then stuffed two wads into the corners of each main room in the house as well as in the sheep, horse, and burro corrals. While the wads were drawing evil forces from these areas, we rested and ate to prepare for our journey to the river.

Then Rosinta gathered the wads from their different places, each time passing a llama thread from a spindle across the threshold of the room's door or around the legs of the animals in the corrals and then breaking the string. Marcelino hurried everyone along, fearing that Josefa or Dominga would hear us if they were awake when we passed their homes. Rosinta finally collected all the wads, and we were ready to go; but then she could not find her coca cloth. Carmen raced around looking for it, and finally gave her another one. We filed out the front gate into the mud and rain.

Each of us carried a large bag of dirty clothes, which we would wash in the river just as we washed our bodies. We stumbled along in the dark, Marcelino leading, and Rosinta in the rear. The trail cut across the side of the mountain and over a landslide, where the going was very dangerous because of the rocks and slippery clay. Several times Marcelino told me to help the elderly Rosinta, who hobbled along loaded with a large sack of dried food, which had been the payment for her night's work. However, in spite of her seventy years and the heavy load she was carrying, she needed little help and kept pace with everyone.

Somewhere I lost the misfortune wad that was stuck between my foot and my sandal. I dreaded what Carmen and Marcelino would say if they found out that it had been left behind, so I removed the wad from my hat and divided it into two. It was a very dark night, and no one noticed. Two hours later, we arrived at the bridge crossing the Kunochayuh River and climbed another steep path three hundred yards up the mountain. Then we entered a cave alongside the river. We crouched inside the grotto, the women deep within and Marcelino and I by the entrance. Rosinta threw an offering of coca to the Lord of the River, and prayed that our sorrows and misfortunes would go away. Carmen served us hot potatoes and coca, and we talked about the river.

The Kunochayuh flowed rapidly in front of the grotto, descending twenty feet in about twenty-five yards. The river was about fifteen feet across, winding in and out of the gorges cut into the mountainside and flowing around and over large rocks pushed down by its swift current. Owing to the steep slope, the river descended in a series of stepped waterfalls that resembled the terraces of the land. Marcelino told us how he had played on the rocks of the river when he was a boy. He pointed out places where he used to sit and which were now washed away, and ponds, now filled with boulders, where he once swam.

Marcelino gathered dry straw and wood to build a small fire inside the grotto. Rosinta placed one cotton wad in each of our hands. We presented the offerings to the lords of the mountain and the river, and prayed that our enemies would let us alone. Rosinta burned all the wads and threw the ashes into the river. Then Carmen gave Rosinta a large black-and-white guinea pig, which she dissected to examine its viscera. The still-beating heart predicted good health. Everyone crowded around as she showed us the two pancreases, dark red with white tips. She said that this sign indicated lack of life in the Yanahuaya household and that the household had not been feeding the ancestral shrines for its lineage. If the family wanted life to grow, they should begin to offer more rituals. Marcelino and Carmen immediately promised to do so.

We knelt facing the river's descent. Rosinta threw the yolk and white from a chicken egg into the waters, and then she removed the black wads from our hats, headbands, and sandals. As she had done when she took them from the house and the animals, she once again passed a llama wool thread, this time around our hands and feet, and then broke it. She put the black wads into an old coca cloth with the guinea pigs, rat, coca quids, cigarette butts, and ashes. Everyone looked away as Rosinta flung the cloth into the river, saying, "Begone, misfortunes!"

Rosinta was anxious to return home. She bade everyone good-bye as she crossed the river; for an instant she entered its icy waters, holding her skirt in her right hand and her sandals in her left. The water rushed around the woman diviner as she took one final step into the whirling pool and then stepped out again. She rapidly ascended the zigzag path, rising into a cloud, and disappeared into the darkness just as she had come out of it earlier that evening when she came to our house.

Our physical bodies also needed cleansing; so Marcelino and Carmen began brewing a concoction of cacti, thorny weeds, and water.

Carmen and her daughters took the spiny water to the shores of the river. After gargling with it, they stripped naked and thoroughly washed each other with the spiny water, making sure that they didn't miss any part of the body. Marcelino and I stayed out of sight in the cave, as Kaatan women are very shy, even during rituals. After they had finished, Marcelino and I also washed. The earthen pot and washbasin were then floated down the river.

Carmen and Marcelino removed every trace of our presence; even the ashes were thrown into the waters, and the place appeared as if no one had ever been there. We returned to Kaata by a higher path. I had been warned by Marcelino and Elsa, "Once we have left the river, you may look only in front of you—not to the right, nor to the left, nor behind you." Carmen and Elsa were always more careful to observe the ritual's details, but Marcelino soon forgot the taboo as we climbed up the steep incline and began to talk about the river and the old irrigation canal whose route our path was following. After an hour's journey we could see Kaata. Marcelino and Elsa told me not to look down at the path over which we had traveled to the river earlier that morning. I didn't. Eventually we arrived behind Marcelino's house and climbed over the fence just as a traveler came around the side of the house. Marcelino said that we had been very lucky not to meet anyone while we were going or returning. Our travels had made a large circle. We had taken a low route when we were going to remove our misfortunes by the river; by taking the upper road across the highlands on our way back, we had compensated for our losses. In short, like the river and the women in their marriage cycle, our route had joined together the mountain's different levels.

Once inside the patio we passed our hands and feet through the smoke of a fire to dispel, Carmen said, any of the grief remaining from the misfortunes. Celia brought us large plates of pig-head soup, which we ate heartily after eleven hours of ritual activity. I found the black wad that I had carelessly left behind. Marcelino was startled when I showed it to him; he quickly told me to burn it without letting Carmen see it.

Shortly before noon, Josefa Waque came into the patio to beg for food. Carmen angrily chased her away, disturbed that one of the bewitchers had arrived so soon after we had got rid of the misfortunes. Carmen and Marcelino began to question the efficacy of the misfortune ritual, until they saw visible effects of Rosinta's powers that same afternoon. Dominga Ari and her son, Julian, began screaming at each other toward suppertime, and at one point Dominga struck Julian. Marcelino smiled, and Carmen was smug with glee. Later Carmen explained that Rosinta's sorcery had been effective against Dominga. Dominga had collected strands of her son's hair with the intent of bewitching him. When Julian heard about it, he took his mother to the sheriff, who severely reprimanded her. Carmen complimented Rosinta's powers by saying, "*Yachan.* She's a prophet!"

CONCLUSION

In this chapter I have tried to show how a female ritualist exercises her distinctively female powers to end misfortune by using symbols intimately associated with femaleness. Rosinta effectively divined the sources of misfortune. Using the power and the associations evoked by the river, she was able to symbolically remove our misfortune. But, in doing so, she also answered Marcelino's original complaint, for she had pointed to the river, which, like the Kaatan women, flows away only to return once again to its source. Although Marcelino's daughters must marry away from his land, his granddaughters will return again. Thus she had successfully protected on all levels the interests of Carmen, who hired her to do so.

Perhaps this is ultimately the key to

understanding the distinct importance of the Kaatan woman ritualist. By evoking women's fluid mode of existence through their rituals and symbols, the ritualist recalls and affirms the significance of women's role. Men and women together are needed to make a complete and successful world, just as both the mountain and the river, and both the ability to attract good luck and the ability to control misfortune are necessary to the Kaatan universe.

Notes

1. Adolph F. Bandelier, *The Islands of Titicaca and Kaati* (New York: The Hispanic Society of America, 1910), p. 13.

Further Readings

Allen, Catherine J. "Body and Soul in Quechua Thought." *Journal of Latin American Lore* 8 (1982): 179–95.

Arguedas, José María. *Deep Rivers,* tr. by Frances Horning Barraclough. Austin: University of Texas Press, 1978.

Arrieaga, Pablo Joseph de. *The Extirpation of Idolatry in Peru* (1621), trans. Horacio Urteaga. Lima, Peru, 1920; also trans. and ed. by L. Clark Keating, Lexington, Ky.: University of Kentucky Press, 1968.

Bastien, Joseph W. *Qollahuaya Rituals: An Ethnographic Account of the Symbolic Relations of Man and Land in an Andean Village.* Ithaca, N.Y.: Cornell University Dissertation Series, no. 56, 1973.

——————. *Mountain of the Condor: Metaphor and Ritual in an Andean Ayllu.* Prospect Heights, Ill.: Waveland Press, 1985.

——————. *Healers of the Andes: Kallawaya Herbalists and Their Medicinal Plants.* Salt Lake City: University of Utah Press, 1987.

Isbell, Billie Jean. *To Defend Ourselves: Ecology and Ritual in An Andean Village.* Prospect Heights, Ill.: Waveland Press, 1985.

Sharon, Douglas. *Wizard of the Four Winds: A Shaman's Story.* New York: Free Press, 1978.

Urton, Gary. *At the Crossroads of Earth and Sky: An Andean Cosmology.* Austin: University of Texas Press, 1981.

21

When Christ Is a Woman: Theology and Practice in the Shaker Tradition

SUSAN M. SETTA

On the eve of the American Revolution, Ann Lee and a small band of followers left England and set sail to establish a heavenly kingdom in the American colonies. They called themselves the United Society of Believers in Christ's Second Appearing. Only a few of the original Shakers accompanied Lee; the rest remained in England with John and Jane Wardley, who had originally founded the group as an offshoot of the Society of Friends. Within 75 years of its journey west, the United Society had 5,000 fully covenanted members, and probably three times as many devotees who, for personal reasons, could not live with their Shaker brothers and sisters. The religious system of the United Society of Believers in Christ's Second Appearing is unique in human history. It proclaimed the Motherhood and Fatherhood of God, asserted that the second coming of Christ had occurred in the woman Ann Lee, fostered a social and political structure of both male and female leadership, and prohibited both marriage and private ownership of property.

By insisting that Ann Lee was the Christ and that God was both male and female, the Shakers undercut the patriarchal bias of eighteenth- and nineteenth-century Christianity. Because both men and women had been created in the image of God, and because the female Christ had explicitly brought redemption for women, Shakers believed that women as well as men should have full access to all forms of religious practice and leadership. Living in their own version of the Kingdom of

SUSAN M. SETTA, Ph.D., is Associate Professor of Philosophy and Religion at Northeastern University, Boston, Massachusetts. She is a former Chair of the Women and Religion Section of the American Academy of Religion.

221

God on Earth, Shaker women and men had a rare opportunity to live in full accordance with this conviction.

ANN LEE AND THE EARLY SHAKER COMMUNITIES

Shaker sources consistently trace Shaker origins to 1747, when Jane and John Wardley formulated a group based loosely on the ideas of the Society of Friends. A group that emphasized ecstatic religious experience, they came to be known as Shakers because they both quaked and shook during their worship services. One striking feature of the Wardleys' teachings was the expectation that Christ would come soon, probably in female form. In 1758, Ann Lee and her husband Abraham Stanley were drawn to the group. At first Ann was merely a follower of the Wardleys. But eventually she would proclaim herself the second Christ and become a source of divisive controversy.

It is as difficult to uncover the life of the historical Ann Lee as it is to find the historical Jesus. Because Lee was illiterate, the reconstruction of her life, work, and ideas depends upon both the writings of those who knew her and later interpretations of the original accounts. Stories and sayings attributed to her often vary according to the prevailing theology of the time period in which they occur. Despite the difficulties in presenting her biography, several facts about Lee's life are clear. Lee was born to indigent parents in Manchester, England in 1736, five years before the Great Awakening was to sweep New England in the American colonies. Lee married Abraham Stanley in 1756. They had four children, all of whom died at birth or in early childhood. Lee and her parents had been members of the Anglican church, but in the year of their marriage, Lee and Stanley joined the Wardley community.

The loss of her children was very painful for Lee, and during the late 1760s she underwent a period of spiritual crisis. She became extremely troubled by day and unable to sleep by night; she prayed constantly for deliverance. Spiritual and physical agonies plagued her until, as her biographers claim, she perspired blood. Meanwhile, the Wardleys' small association was being persecuted by civil and church authorities for such infractions as Sabbath breaking and blasphemy. While Lee was imprisoned for Sabbath breaking in 1770, she claimed to have a revelation informing her that she herself had been chosen to be the final incarnation of Christ. When Lee was released from prison, returned to the group, and related her vision, other Shakers experienced the same revelation and hence accepted the truth of her claim. From that time on, Lee's vision became a central focus of Shaker teachings. However, in addition to her claim to be the Second Appearance of Christ, Lee claimed God had revealed to her that the root of all sin was lust, which in turn prompted all sexual relations. Thus Lee taught her followers to abandon sex and take up celibacy as a central feature of their spiritual practice. This, together with Lee's increasing prominence in the group, ultimately led to a break with the Wardleys.

In 1774, Lee had another revelation, telling her to take her gospel message to America and to create God's kingdom on earth in the colonies. Together with a small group of followers, who were mostly her relatives, Lee set sail for the Shakers' new home. The trip was difficult: a storm threatened the very lives of the Shakers; their vessel was damaged and came perilously close to sinking. Lee, however, was not daunted by the danger and, according to her companions, she controlled the forces of nature so that a wave mended the ship. This action further convinced an already devoted group that Lee shared in the power of God.

Landing in New York City, the American Shakers soon moved to a rural area in upstate New York. Despite considerable economic difficulty, the small group of believers proselytized actively, caught the attention of many clergy in the area, and began to attract new members. However, at the same time, many of their new neighbors were eying them with considerable suspicion. For one thing, it was the eve of the American revolution and these English women and men were preaching that a new kingdom was about to be established on earth. At one point Lee was even arrested for treason. But she was released after informing the judge that God had told her he was on the colonies' side. The novel, albeit heretical, religious ideas of the Shakers were scorned by many in the surrounding community. This scorn ranged from derogatory sermons to physical persecution. Lee herself died in 1784 from injuries inflicted by an angry mob.

Lee's death precipitated a crisis for her followers. Although Lee had never claimed to be immortal, some of her followers apparently believed that Christ's Second Coming could not die. Before her death, Lee had named as her successor James Whittaker, one of the original English Shakers; Whittaker led the group until his death just three years later, in 1787. As a result of the uncertainties provoked by Lee's death, Whittaker concentrated on clarifying Shaker doctrine, and the group survived its founder's passing. An American convert, Joseph Meacham, replaced Whittaker and led the group until 1796. Prior to her death, Lee had called Meacham her "first born son in America." Under Meacham's leadership, the Shaker community organized a system of spiritual and temporal governance that has continued until the twentieth century. Lee had set a precedent for dual male and female leadership when she appointed Lucy Wright, another American-born member, to oversee women's affairs in the community. Meacham formalized Wright's position in the group, and she became known as Mother Lucy. After Meacham's death, Mother Lucy became the Shakers' leader. Under her tenure, the original small group developed into a successful utopian community and began several missionary ventures westward.

The leadership that followed was never as dynamic nor as successful as that of Whittaker, Meacham, and Wright. Those three had been chosen by Lee herself; later individuals rose to leadership roles primarily because of seniority within the group. Times were especially difficult from the mid-1820s until the 1840s. Financial hardship, coupled with a conservative leadership that had never known the foundress, led to low morale and strained relationships.

During the 1840s, the community's fortunes rose again, as the result of an innovative revival called "Mother's Work." At this time, the spirits of Ann Lee and other historical or spiritual figures began appearing regularly through human "instruments," or mediums, who transmitted to the community their messages, paintings, poems, hymns, and new laws. Lasting until about 1847, this interval of dramatic spiritual activity brought renewed financial prosperity, increased membership, and missionary expansion. By the end of the 1860s, however, the Shaker communities again were in decline; individual societies were closed, members began to leave, and new converts became rare. The membership, once almost equally divided between men and women, now became predominantly female.

The decline and transformation of the Shaker communities cannot be attributed to any one factor. Ironically, financial success contributed to the decline because the group's prosperity attracted members seeking an escape from poverty rather than responding to a spiritual calling. In addition, to gain more converts, Shakers accommodated their theology to American Protestantism and hence became less distinctive. The fervent, innovative, and ecstatic worship that had once been a hallmark of the Shaker tradition now also became more restrained and traditional. Today, only a handful of practicing Shakers remain.

SHAKER TEACHINGS: ANN THE CHRIST

One striking example of increasing conservatism in Shaker teachings was a withdrawal from their initial understanding of Ann herself. The earliest Shaker communities, dating from 1770–1830, contended that Lee and Jesus were co-saviors. To support their claim that Lee had been a second savior, early Shakers reinterpreted the traditional Christian view of Christ. They saw Christ not as Jesus, but as a principle—the "Unity of Divine Male and Female."[1] This had first appeared in Jesus and then finally, and necessarily, in Ann Lee. Christ had to come in both male and female forms, they argued, because God was both male and female. Hence they sometimes called Ann Lee their Mother in Christ because she represented the female aspect of God.

The original Shakers had described the second coming of Christ in terms parallel to those that other Christians had used to refer to the first appearance in Jesus. Hence they also called Lee "the Second Eve," "Ann Christ," and "Ann the Daughter." After Lee's death, Mother Sarah Kendall wrote that she knew Lee was

> the Lord's anointed, the Bride, the Lamb's Wife spoken of in ancient days by holy inspiration; for she did the same work and performed miracles in the same spirit that Christ did while on earth.[2]

Despite the danger of making such heretical statements, Kendall affirmed the strength of her conviction by adding:

> As soon would I dispute that Christ made his first appearance in the person of Jesus of Nazareth as I would that he made his second appearance in the person of Ann Lee.[3]

Lee's earliest biographers tell of Lee's powers, her ability to heal the sick, and her capacity to search a soul merely by looking into someone's eyes. One such account comes from Hannah Cogswell:

> I know of a certainty, that Mother Ann had the gift of prophecy and the revelation of God, by which she was able to search the hearts of those who came to see her; for I have myself been an eye and ear witness of it. I have known some to come to her under a cloak of deception, thinking to conceal their sins in her presence; and I have seen her expose them by the searching power of truth, and to acknowledge that the light and revelation of God was in her.[4]

Rebecca Jackson, who founded the predominantly black community of Philadelphia Shakers, spoke of Jesus and Ann in identical terms. Jackson claimed that Jesus and Ann "lived on earth as angels do in heaven, living angel lives in earthly bodies."[5] Speaking of her vision of the new creation, Jackson said that both Lee and Jesus had existed before the world was made. According to Jackson, Lee had restored four spirits in one: the Mother, the Father, the Daughter, and the Son; by completing this divine quartet, Lee had saved the world.[6] Others argued that when Jesus said "I go to prepare a place for you," he was referring to the completion of God's plan of salvation that had occurred through the appearance of Lee. Lee and Jesus together are the saving pair who come to redeem the world; but it is Ann, not Jesus, who completes the purpose of salvation history.

However, early Shaker writers did not simply add the concept of a female savior to Christian teachings; they rather reinterpreted the entire Bible within the context of Lee's revelation. They used for this purpose a special approach to scripture that was common in the eighteenth and nineteenth century. According to this "typological" method of Biblical interpretation, certain figures or actions called "types" anticipate and point to the final act of salvation. But the significance of any such "type" is not apparent until its fulfillment. Using this approach, the Shakers tried to show that all of salvation history had been moving towards completion of the Christ principle in the woman Ann Lee. When Shaker writers looked to the Bible with the idea of a female Christ in mind, they saw the women of the Bible in a new and more important light. Many Biblical women became "types" of Ann, who pointed to God's redemption of the world through her. For example, the mother of Moses became a "type" of Ann, for Ann "is the true figure of the final deliverance of the people of God though the woman."[7] Of course, Jesus himself was also understood to be a "type." As Son of God and Anointing Spirit, he pointed to the divine Daughter, Ann.

Although early Shaker sources portrayed Lee and Jesus as equals, later Shaker theology downplayed the similarity between them. In a 1904 Shaker publication, the Shaker sisters Leila S. Taylor and Anna White claimed that Shakers had never believed that Ann was Christ.[8] Frederick Evans, who became an elder at the end of the nineteenth century, reiterated this claim. A Shaker sister interviewed more recently, in 1974, asserted that Lee demonstrated the light of Christ that lies within every human being, but Lee herself was not the Christ. To these later writers, Lee became an exemplary prophet, a model for the true Christian. Although Lee's spiritual maturity had been without earthly parallel, she was not considered equal to Jesus. Rather than insisting on a female incarnation of Christ, later Shakers turned to the image of God as Mother to develop their concept of a female aspect of divinity.

GOD AS FATHER AND MOTHER

Whereas Shaker views of the nature of Lee changed over time, their vision of God as male and female, father and mother, remained constant. Taking the first chapter of Genesis as their starting point, they contended that God's statement "Let *Us* create man in *Our* image. . . ." must be taken to mean that God was both male and female. Ridiculing the then-standard interpretation of this passage, which claimed that God was speaking to Jesus in this passage, the Shakers asked:

> Was it to the Son, the Father spoke, as the divines have long taught? How then came man to be created male and female? *Father* and *Son* are not male and female; but *father* and *mother* are male and female, as likewise are *son* and *daughter*. . . .

> And without this relationship there can exist no order in creation! Without a father and mother we can have no existence.[9]

In the Shakers' opinion, the truth about the motherhood of God had been suppressed by 2,000 years of Christian teaching. In order for humanity to become perfect and to live in a Heaven on Earth, both the motherhood and the fatherhood of God had to be acknowledged.

The period of Shaker history known as "Mother's Work" saw an important development in the concept of the motherhood of God. During this time a figure called Holy Mother Wisdom began to speak through the Shaker mediums; the first to receive her were a group of male and female children, but later she appeared mostly through female instruments. Holy Mother Wisdom was believed to be a manifestation of the female in God. She was not Ann Lee, but was Ann's and everyone else's Mother in Creation. According to one recorded manifestation, Wisdom had come "to set my house in order to complete and fortify the walls of my Zion."[10] Eternal Wisdom stood with the Eternal Father when she proclaimed:

> Bow down, obey, all ye who hear my Word, both ye who dwell on Zion, and ye who dwell in distant lands, say I Eternal Wisdom. . . . In word of solemn warning I sound my trumpet of wisdom unto you. . . .

> Know ye that I am Wisdom, Eternal and Unchangeable Wisdom: one with God I am, and always shall be; even as he is your Eternal Father, so do I Eternal Wisdom, stand as your everlasting Mother with Him.

I sound forth mercy, with Him Judgment proclaim; We stand as one, and work but as one alone; . . .[11]

Often, as in the above passage, Mother Wisdom is portrayed as a Warrior working to complete the creation. But at other times, Wisdom seems almost timid. Paulina Bates's long book titled *The Divine Book of Holy and Eternal Wisdom*[12] recorded revelations of Mother Wisdom in which this female aspect of God was often humble and meek and possessed many attributes considered valuable for the nineteenth-century gentlewoman. According to this view, Holy Mother Wisdom had not made herself known in the past because the world was not safe enough for her appearance. But whether her image was fierce or gentle, Mother Wisdom stood on equal footing with God and gave Shakers a complex image of God as female.

WHY WOMEN NEED A SPECIAL SAVIOR

The images of Mother God as Warrior, Gentlewoman, and Wise Woman, together with the belief in Ann Lee as completion of Christ, offered the Shakers a full reflection of woman in the deity. Furthermore, the Shaker conception of the fourfold nature of God profoundly affected Shaker attitudes towards women and Shaker social institutions. Thus, Shaker theology offered to women a means by which many Shaker sisters could become freer than women who were their contemporaries in United States society.

According to the Shaker view, women were equal to men in their original nature because the two genders had been created in the likeness of a God who was both male and female. Nevertheless, Shakers agreed with mainstream Christianity of the time on two important points of biblical interpretation. First, they agreed that men and women had sinned

through Adam and Eve and hence had lost the possibilities of this original condition. Second, the Shakers, along with most Christian interpreters, agreed that women had then become subordinated to men because Eve had brought about humanity's fall. Unlike most other Christian interpreters, however, the Shakers claimed that female subordination was not final. Because the Millenium had arrived through the coming of Ann Lee, male domination had been overcome, and the true equality of men and women could be restored.

Moreover, Shaker writers asserted that women could be redeemed *only* through a female savior. An early Shaker theological compendium noted:

It was therefore indispensably necessary, for the final restoration of man to eternal life, that the spirit should be revealed *in that sex where sin first began*; and there destroy that enchanting influence which the woman received from the serpent, that alluring power by which the natural man is led, and through which the fall of man was first produced. [Emphasis added.][13]

Note this text's presupposition that sin "first began" with the female sex. The writer assumes that women are even more vulnerable to evil than males. He goes on to say that women therefore had to be raised from "the lowest state of the fall" in order to be "made a fit temple for the Holy Spirit to dwell in." Thus, the Shakers' very positive view of women's potentialities was based on an initially negative assessment.

Until the Second Coming of Christ, women and men had not shared a similar capacity for perfection. Instead, since the fall women and men had had a completely different moral makeup. The female nature was most evident in the character of the first woman, Eve. Like most Christian interpreters of the day, Shaker theology located the origin of the world's evil in Eve's inclination towards what they called "animal sensations." While Adam was somewhat responsible for his own actions, Eve was plainly responsible for the downfall of both human ancestors. Instead of rejecting Eve's role, as one might expect, Shaker writers never questioned this notion. Instead they tried to show why it had been necessary for evil to enter the world through a woman. The Shakers argued that since all humanity had entered the world through women, evil must have arisen out of the same source. Eve's communication with the devil had excited her "animal sensations," and lust, which gave rise to sin, had thus been born. Through the interaction of Adam and Eve, the male had also fallen prey to these sensations. Adam and Eve participated "in the act of sexual coition; and thus partook of the forbidden fruit."[14]

Before the Second Coming, women had been weak, and hence were easily led astray. Like all creatures, Eve had the ability to refuse temptation; but she instead gave in to her fleshly nature. Because of this, the animal nature became humanity's reigning principle. Only by intervention of God's Spirit could humanity be restored to its true spiritual nature. Jesus, a male, had brought redemption for men. However, women required a different plan of salvation, because women's moral quality differed from that of men. Before Ann Lee, women had no savior. Thus, in the Shaker view, men had gained access to perfection almost two thousand years before women had done so. Clearly, the sin of the female was grave, for it took two separate appearances of Christ to eradicate women's sinful tendencies. But women had finally been redeemed, and a new, egalitarian "Heaven on Earth" had now become possible.

WOMEN IN GOD'S KINGDOM ON EARTH

Perhaps the most exciting aspect of Shaker practice was the fact that Shakers actually tried to design and live in such an egalitarian "Heaven." From the time of their beginnings in New York, the Shakers were millenarians;

they believed that they were living representatives of the Kingdom of God on earth. Their pattern of daily life could therefore not be ordered by the laws and customs of the fallen, secular, imperfect world. Their own rules of governance and day-to-day activity had to mirror the ways of heaven. To live in the way that they felt the redeemed ought to live, the Shakers founded alternative communities. Situated mostly in rural areas that at the time of founding were part of the American frontier, these communities owned their own land, designed and built their own buildings, and produced most of their own food, clothing, furniture, and even machinery. Being self-sufficient and unobtrusive, they were usually left alone by the new U.S. government and by their neighbors. Hence they were also able to shape their own social and political life-style. Three central components of this life-style held important implications for Shaker women: celibacy, communal property, and the Shaker form of community organization and governance.

From the time of Lee's vision to the present, a central Shaker practice has been celibacy—that is to say, total abstinence from sex and marriage. Like other Shaker teachings, Shaker justifications for celibacy changed during the course of Shaker history. Lee herself set the tone for the early Shaker abhorrence of sexual intercourse when she stated:

> Those who choose to live after the flesh, can do so; but I know, by the revelation of God, that those who live in the gratification of their lusts will suffer in proportion as they have violated the law of God in nature.[15]

Early Shaker sources, following Lee's own teachings, generally charged that sexual relations are the primary cause of sin in the world. Later sources were less likely to stress the evils of sexuality itself. But they still viewed celibacy as an important way to protect the unity of the millenial community. Sexuality leads to marriage, and married persons tend to look to their spouses' and children's needs rather than committing themselves fully to their spiritual families. Most Shaker defences of the celibate life furthermore emphasized that marriage places women in a subordinate role.[16]

The Shaker practice of celibacy is often misunderstood. Although Shakers preferred a celibate life-style and required celibacy before a person could take up residence in one of the Shakers' own settlements, not all Shakers lived within the celibate communities. Noncelibate Shakers, sometimes called "householders," often remained with their worldly families. In all probability, most of these "householders" were women. Eighteenth- and nineteenth-century laws invariably granted custody of children to a father if one of the parents left the household. A woman who joined a celibate Shaker community without her husband would lose all claim to her children and be unable to see them. In contrast, a man who left his wife to join would take his children along with him. Mary Dyer, a woman of the early nineteenth century who published scathing attacks on the United Society, published her exposé, *A Portrait of Shakerism*, as part of her efforts to win custody of her children from her Shaker husband.[17]

Moreover, Shakers at times questioned their own celibate practice. Near the close of the nineteenth century, when their population was dwindling, some Shakers even for a time considered starting a "generative order"; this would be for those who found celibacy too difficult a cross to bear. However, other members disputed this idea, and the noncelibate order was never founded.

In contrast, Shakers never challenged their second major departure from mainstream American practice—the abolition of private ownership. The Shaker belief that members should hold all lands and goods in common was based on Lee's revelation that "Christianity did not admit to private property." This practice was closely linked to the celibate ideal, for *any* interest in the material world was considered to be an expression of lust. All carnality—all desire for worldly things—had to be

eradicated in the New Kingdom. This included both the desire for sexual union and the desire for material wealth.

The practice of sharing property was already on record in 1782; in that year, Benjamin Barnes gave all of his land to the settlement which survives today as Sabbathday Lake. From these early beginnings it swiftly became the norm for all fully covenanted members to donate all their property to the community. By the 1820s, Lucy Wright was asserting that the Union was the Gift. That is to say, Union, the united effort of the believers, depended on the sharing of Shaker resources. Shakers argued that private ownership was a barrier to spiritual and temporal equality. Property served to divide rather than unite a community. It led to the subjection of women, to slavery, and even to war.

In fact, the ability to give up property, rather than the practice of celibacy, was the ultimate test of commitment to Shaker teachings. A person living at a Shaker settlement could lead a celibate life and still not be considered fully in Union. Union was reserved for those who signed the Covenant, a document that transferred permanent ownership of the signer's property to the community. Shakers did not do this immediately upon joining; in 1799, Mother Lucy Wright created a "Gathering Order"—a kind of novitiate—that lived exactly like other Shakers and practiced celibacy. But these new members retained their right to retrieve their property if they decided to leave the community. In contrast, if fully covenanted members left, their property remained with the Shaker community. Because Shaker property was jointly held, it was considered to be wholly devoted to God. It could not be used to benefit individual members, even in cases where members retained some right to reclaim it. The Shakers adamantly upheld this position even from the time of the first written covenant.

The Shaker practice of sharing property,

like the practice of celibacy, had important implications for Shaker women; for both tended to equalize the relationship between men and women. Nineteenth-century thinkers were well aware of the close correlation between private ownership and the subjection of women. At the time when Shaker communities were enjoying their largest membership and prosperity, Friedrich Engels was writing his *Origins of the Family, Private Property, and the State.* Monogamous marriage, Engels contended, was a means of extending property and insuring its transference to male heirs. This kind of relationship was "the first form of the family to be based, not on natural but on economic conditions, on the victory of private property over primitive natural communal property."[18] Engels argued that the male's ownership of property and consequent economic superiority over the female led to male supremacy in the marriage relationship. Therefore the marriage relationship was not mutual. Instead, in his view, "the modern individual family is founded on the open or concealed domestic slavery of the woman."[19]

Comments remarkably similar to those of Engels on the inequality of the marriage relationship and women's dependent status appear frequently in the writings of Shaker sisters. For example, Paulina Bates commented on the status of the married woman:

> Hence ariseth the belief in many that the female is not in possession of a living soul; but [is] merely a machine for the use and benefit of man in his terrestrial state of existence.[20]

Yet another woman echoed Engels's own words when she wrote, in 1882: "Woman's condition is little superior to slave."[21]

Both Engels and the Shaker writers of course presupposed the economic structure of eighteenth- and nineteenth-century marriage. In America of that time, as in Engels's Europe, ownership of property was allotted almost exclusively to men. American women were sub-

jected to the principle of coverature, which the United States had taken over from English common law. In marriage, according to this legal standard, "the husband and wife were one person—the husband."[22] Because of coverature, married women had no rights of ownership; during the eighteenth and early nineteenth centuries women could hold property only if they were single or widowed. The Married Women's Laws, passed during the 1860s, altered this principle slightly, but they protected only the property that a woman brought to her marriage. Anything acquired by the woman during the marriage was still owned by her husband. Hence within a typical family structure, women became totally dependent upon men; for men controlled their means of financial support. When a woman married she ran the risk of becoming yet another possession, because she had no financial autonomy. And yet for most women of the time, marriage was the only viable option for women; they had no other means of making a living.

Both Shaker celibacy and the Shaker system of community property undercut this system at its foundation. Shaker men did not hold property; nor could they use community property for their own benefit; therefore they could not use it to exercise power over women. Women had equal access to the Shaker community property; therefore they were no longer economically dependent on men. Shaker celibacy meant that men and women did not marry; even if a Shaker couple had been previously married, they did not live together, and their marriage was not recognized by the community. Hence even the habit of wives submitting to their husbands could not carry over into the redeemed community.

But perhaps even more importantly, by doing away with households founded on marriage and individual ownership, the Shakers gained an opportunity to create a whole new style of human society. People in the Shaker community were joined by faith, not by marriage or blood relationships. They lived in Spiritual Families as children of Heavenly Parents. "Families," or living groups of from 30 to 100 men and women, made up a "Community." They were designated by location—for example, they were called "South Family" or "North Family." Several "Communities" were in turn gathered into a "Bishopric"; and the "Bishoprics," in turn, comprised the United Society.

Moreover, at each organization level, the Shakers had multiple leaders. They separated "spiritual" from "temporal" office. The Lead Ministry, consisting of Elders and Eldresses, provided spiritual leadership; Deacons, Deaconesses, and Trustees directed temporal matters. Spiritual leadership was patterned after the heavenly rule of the Father/Son and Mother/Daughter; therefore two men and two women directed spiritual affairs in each administrative unit. The four Shakers in the Lead Ministry were referred to as "Mother" and "Father." They headed the United Society from New Lebanon, New York. Each Bishopric was directed by a "Ministry," consisting, again, of two men and two women. Two Elders and two Eldresses led each "Family." Deacons and Deaconesses, as temporal leaders, did not govern, but rather supervised particular tasks. There were, for example, Farm Deacons and Kitchen Deaconesses. Trustees were in charge of financial matters and controlled the Shaker communal property.

Because this complex governmental structure required leaders at each level, women had much greater access to leadership roles than they did in the greater American society. About one in fifty Shaker sisters would fill a leadership position during her life in the United Society.[23] Moreover, the woman leaders were no mere figureheads; especially those in the Lead Ministry held considerable responsibility. Lucy Wright, the most important Eldress in Shaker history, made final decisions concerning construction of new buildings, mis-

sionary expansion, and publications. Wright's opinion prevailed even when her views were controversial. Although later Eldresses were somewhat less visible than Wright, they travelled on missionary ventures, visited the Western societies, and directed spiritual matters. Even in cases where male leaders seemed more prominent than the women, the women still held more power than non-Shaker counterparts.

Lesser ministerial roles of men and women within the community were similar. Confession of sins was a requirement for union. Women heard women's confessions; men were confessors to men. In addition, women taught and produced spiritual sayings that were passed down and revered for generations. Work roles had male and female supervisors; Deaconesses supervised women's work; deacons supervised the work of men.

Still the Shakers made some discrimination between the tasks of men and the tasks of women. Early records indicate that Mary Whitcher was a trustee in 1792,[24] but by 1800 women no longer functioned in this capacity. Although Shaker records do not indicate a reason for this change, women trustees would clearly have endangered the community because of existing U.S. property laws. Any Shaker property held in the name of a female would have been subject to these laws. Although married couples lived separately after joining the communities, the states continued to recognize their marriages. If the former husband of a trustee had left the community, he could have claimed all of her property, including any that the United Society held in her name.

Moreover, with few exceptions, the daily tasks of men and women were assigned along conventional gender lines: women worked within the Shaker kitchens and dormitories, while men worked in the fields and outbuildings. Despite these stereotypical roles, the Shaker division of labor held different implications from the standard practice of the nation. For one thing, in the Shaker community, women's work was not considered to be of lesser value than the work of men. All work was equally sacred because it contributed to God's new creation on earth. Furthermore, the women's work was economically vital to the community. Shakers were farmers; the crops they produced had to be processed and preserved so that the community could use them. Food preservation was especially important; preservation kept food through the winter, and sale of surpluses brought income for necessities. Finally, Shaker work was communal; women worked by the side of other women. This meant that women's "inside" tasks never isolated Shaker women as they isolated other American women within their nuclear homes.

One striking final distinction between Shaker male and female activity is harder to account for or justify. Despite the Shakers' commitment to the sharing of spiritual power, men almost totally dominated the development of Shaker theology. With only one exception,[25] the Brothers edited and authored all theological works until the end of the nineteenth century. On the other hand, during the era of "Mother's Work," women were the primary "instruments," the mediums, through whom Holy Mother Wisdom and other spirits spoke. Hence the Shakers seem to have maintained the frequent human division between men as scholars and thinkers and women as vehicles for religious experience. This distinction has no basis in Shaker theology. Moreover, it did correspond to a difference in power. Those who produced the approved theological writings were senior males of the society; and their writing itself was powerful because it told Shakers and others what Shakers thought about themselves. The mediums in "Mother's Work," however, were often people with little seniority; and because they served as instruments only, their roles brought them virtually no power in the group.[26] Ironically, however,

the products of these women who channeled "Mother's Work" are now the best-known aspect of Shaker creativity. Most Americans now know Shakers, if at all, primarily through the mediums' spirit drawings, poetry, and hymns.

CONCLUSION

The Shaker vision of Christianity brought to women a degree of equality and control of their lives that is unparalleled elsewhere in Christian history. Responding to an image of God as male and female, a belief in separate but full redemption for men and women, and a conviction that God's Kingdom could be established on earth, the Shakers founded a society in which men and women shared in power and spiritual authority. Although they failed to solve all of the problems created by gender distinctions, they nonetheless provide us today with a vision of what a truly egalitarian society might be like. Their solution was quite radical: doing away with property, sexuality, and marriage is a sacrifice that few contemporary men or women would be willing to make. Nonetheless, their effort still inspires us, while their view of God as female Savior, Wisdom, Warrior, and Mother offers a positive, empowering vision of all that women can be.

Notes

1. Benjamin Youngs, *Christ's Second Appearing* (n.p.: The United Society, 1808), p. 12.
2. Mother Sarah Kendall, quoted in Roxalana Grosvenor, ed., *Sayings*, p. 9, as quoted in Robley Whitson, ed., *The Shakers: Two Centuries of Spiritual Reflection* (New York: Paulist Press, 1983).
3. *Ibid.*
4. Hannah Cogswell, quoted in Seth Wells, ed., *Testimonies Concerning the Character and Ministry of Mother Ann Lee* (Albany, N.Y.: Packard and Van Benthuysen, 1827), p. 31.

232 Susan M. Setta

5. Jean McMohan Humez, *Gifts of Power: the Writings of Rebecca Jackson, Black Visionary, Shaker Eldress* (Amherst, Mass.: University of Massachusetts Press, 1981), p. 287.

6. *Ibid.*, p. 282.

7. Youngs, *Christ's Second Appearing*, p. 52.

8. *Shakerism, Its Meaning and Message* (Columbus, Ohio: Fred J. Heer, 1904).

9. Youngs, *Christ's Second Appearing*, pp. 503–4.

10. Philemon Stewart, *A Holy, Sacred and Divine Roll and Book*, vol. 2 (Canterbury, N.H.: The United Society, 1843), p. 262.

11. *Ibid.*

12. Canterbury, N.H.: The United Society, 1849.

13. Calvin Green, *A Summary View of the Millenial Church* (Albany, N.Y.: Packard and Van Benthuysen, 1823), p. 230.

14. *Ibid.*, p. 130.

15. Whitson, *The Shakers*, p. 163; quoting Daniel Mosely who is quoting Ann Lee.

16. *Ibid.*, p. 158. Contrary to popular opinion, celibacy was not the reason for the Shakers' decline. In fact, the practice of celibacy probably contributed to the Shaker community's success in comparison with other utopian communities, which could not handle the economic or ideological stress of having to raise and indoctrinate a second generation.

17. (Concord, N.H.: For the Author, 1822).

18. Alice Rossi, ed. *The Feminist Papers: From Adams to de Beauvoir* (New York: Bantam Books, 1974), p. 142, quoting Engels, n.p.

19. *Ibid.*, p. 480.

20. Paulina Bates, *The Divine Book of Holy and Eternal Wisdom* (Canterbury, N.H.: The United Society, 1849), p. 505.

21. Ruth Webster, *The Shaker Manifesto*, XII, No. 4 (1882), p. 82.

22. Norma Beach, *In the Eyes of the Law* (Ithaca, N.Y.: Cornell University Press, 1982), p. 17.

23. Marjorie Procter-Smith, *Women in Shaker Community and Worship* (Lewiston, N.Y.: Edwin Mellen Press, 1985).

24. *The Shaker Quarterly*, III, No. 4 (Winter 1963), p. 92.

25. Bates, *Divine Book of Holy and Eternal Wisdom.*

26. See Priscilla Brewer, *Shaker Communities, Shaker Lives* (Hanover, N.H.: University Press of New England, 1986), Chapter 7.

Further Readings

Brewer, Priscilla J. *Shaker Communities, Shaker Lives.* Hanover, N.H.: University Press of New England, 1986.

Proctor-Smith, Marjorie. *Women in Shaker Community and Worship.* Lewiston, N.Y.: Edwin Mellen Press, 1985.

Setta, Susan M. *Woman of the Apocalypse: The Second Coming of Christ in Ann Lee.* Ann Arbor, Mich.: University Microfilms, 1979.

——————. "The Appropriation of Biblical Hermeneutics to Biographical Criticism." *Historical Methods* 16, no. 3 (Summer 1983).

Wells, Seth. *Testimonies Concerning the Character and Ministry of Mother Ann Lee and the First Witnesses of Christ's Second Appearing.* Albany, N.Y.: Packard and VanBenthuysen, 1827.

Whitson, Robley Edward. *The Shakers, Two Centuries of Spiritual Reflection.* New York: Paulist Press, 1983.

VI

WOMEN'S POWER

Mythical Models and Sacred Sources

To modern feminists, the women whose lives we have studied in this volume often appear to have little power, despite our attempts to portray them vividly and empathetically. Why? Women's power, in most traditional societies, was not equivalent to legal, economic, political, social, or religious equality. As we understand it in the modern West, the phrase "equality between women and men" really means overcoming, or at least minimizing, traditional gender roles. The dissolving of gender roles is not the basis of women's power in most of the instances explored in this volume. However, women almost always find avenues to affirm self-worth and to take some control over their lives and their worlds. This volume has surveyed many different methods by which women take such power. Sometimes they bond together. Sometimes they ritually control their environment. Sometimes they live in clear patterns of balance and equality with men.

In our final section, we explore another important method by which women may achieve power. When women *have* powerful or provocative myth-models with which they can identify, or when women *are* exemplary sacred sources, they feel powerful and they are powerful. This power of psychological worth may not translate directly into social, political, or even religious equality. Nevertheless, the power women derive from identifying with female myth-models and the power they manifest as sacred sources should not be overlooked as "merely symbolic."

Chapter 22 examines the relationship between two female spirits of Haitian Vodou and a mother and daughter who serve them as priestess and apprentice in New York City. Author Karen McCarthy Brown points to a close "fit" between the spirits' imagery and personality and the lives of the women who serve them— a "fit" which allows the spirits to bring solace and to "pick up dreams and give them shape." Drawing on personal experience, author Inés Talamantez traces in Chapter 23 the complex response of the Mescalero Apache people to an awesome Mother Goddess called Isanaklesh. Mescalero women become Isanaklesh during the ceremony that allows a girl to make her passage into womanhood; hence through the ceremony the goddess comes to be ingrained in Mescalero Apache consciousness. This particular article focuses mainly on the implications of Isanaklesh for women; still it is clear that she brings power to all Mescalero—males included.

The concluding article, by co-editor Rita M. Gross, does not focus on the power of female mythical models, but on the power of women themselves to be a sacred source and paradigm. Aboriginal women of Australia experience themselves as reserves of sacred power that is manifested in their own bodies and physiological processes. Women ritualize these sacred processes; men imitate them, utilizing the powerful image of giving birth in their own most potent and elaborate rituals. In fact, it seems almost as though the men manifest a case of "womb envy."

These chapters, particularly the final chapter, also bring us full circle to our opening critique of Western scholarship and its habitual blindness to women's religious lives. Previous scholarship about Australian religions often contended that only men were sacred or had religious lives; women were said to be both profane and without a significant religious life. However, when the scholar attends to women's religious lives and presumes that women are as interesting and as worthy of study as are men, then such interpretations become unlikely. Gross not only demonstrates clearly that Australian women *have* religious lives; she shows that these are important, both in their own right and for the perspective they lend us on the whole of native Australian culture.

22

Mama Lola and the Ezilis: Themes of Mothering and Loving in Haitian Vodou

KAREN McCARTHY BROWN

Mama Lola is a Haitian woman in her mid-fifties who lives in Brooklyn, where she works as a Vodou priestess. This essay concerns her relationship with two female *lwa*, Vodou spirits whom she "serves." By means of trance states, these spirits periodically speak and act through her during community ceremonies and private healing sessions. Mama Lola's story will serve as a case study of how the Vodou spirits closely reflect the lives of those who honor them. While women and men routinely and meaningfully serve both male and female spirits in Vodou, I will focus here on only one strand of the complex web of relations between the "living" and the Vodou spirits, the strand that

connects women and female spirits. Specifically I will demonstrate how female spirits, in their iconography and possession-performance, mirror the lives of contemporary Haitian women with remarkable specificity. Some general discussion of Haiti and of Vodou is necessary before moving to the specifics of Mama Lola's story.

Vodou is the religion of 80% of the population of Haiti. It arose during the eighteenth century on the giant sugar plantations of the French colony of Saint Domingue, then known as the Pearl of the Antilles. The latter name was earned through the colony's veneer of French culture, the reknowned beauty of its Creole women, and most of all, the

---

KAREN McCARTHY BROWN is Professor of the Sociology and Anthropology of Religion in the Graduate and Theological Schools at Drew University. She began research on Vodou in Haiti in 1973 and among Haitian immigrants in New York in 1978. She has written several articles on Vodou as a resource for North American feminists. Brown is currently at work on a manuscript, *Mama Lola: A Vodou Priestess in Brooklyn*.

productivity of its huge slave plantations. Haiti is now a different place (it is the poorest country in the Western hemisphere) and Vodou, undoubtedly, a different religion from the one or ones practiced by the predominantly Dahomean, Yoruba, and Kongo slaves originally brought there. The only shared language among these different groups of slaves was French Creole, yet they managed before the end of the eighteenth century to band together (most likely through religious means) to launch the only successful slave revolution during this immoral epoch. As contemporary Haitian history has made amply clear, a successful revolution did not lead to a free and humane life for the Haitian people. Slave masters were quickly replaced by a succession of dictators from both the mulatto and black populations.

Haitians started coming to the United States in large numbers after Francois Duvalier took control of the country in the late 1950s. The first wave of immigrants was made up of educated, professional people. These were followed by the urban poor and, most recently, the rural poor. All were fleeing dead-end lives in a society drenched in corruption, violence, poverty, and disease. There are now well over one-half million Haitians living in the U.S.

Alourdes, the name by which I usually address Mama Lola, came to New York in 1963 from Port-au-Prince, the capital of Haiti and a city of squalor and hopelessness where she had at times resorted to prostitution to feed three small children. Today, twenty-five years later, Alourdes owns her own home, a three-story rowhouse in the Fort Greene section of Brooklyn. There she and her daughter Maggie run a complex and lively household that varies in size from six people (the core family, consisting of Alourdes, Maggie, and both their children) to as many as a dozen. The final tally depends on how many others are living with them at any given time. These may be recent arrivals from Haiti, down-on-their-luck friends and members of the extended family, or clients of Alourdes's Vodou healing practice.

Maggie, now in her thirties, has been in the United States since early adolescence and consequently is much more Americanized than her mother. She is the adult in the family who deals with the outside world. Maggie does the paperwork which life in New York requires and negotiates with teachers, plumbers, electricians, and an array of creditors. She has a degree from a community college and currently works as a nurse's aide at a New York hospital.

Most of the time Alourdes stays at home where she cares for the small children and carries on her practice as a *manbo*, a Vodou priestess. Many Haitians and a few others such as Trinidadians, Jamaicans, and Dominicans come to her with work, health, family, and love problems. For diagnostic purposes, Alourdes first "reads the cards." Then she carries out healing "work" appropriate to the nature and severity of the problem. This may include: counseling the client, a process in which she calls on her own life experience and the shared values of the Haitian community as well as intuitive skills bordering on extrasensory perception; administering baths and other herbal treatments; manufacturing talismans; and summoning the Vodou spirits to "ride" her through trance-possession in order that spiritual insight and wisdom may be brought to bear on the problem.

Vodou spirits (Haitians never call them gods or goddesses) are quite different from deities, or even saints, in the way that we in North America usually use those terms. They are not moral exemplars, nor are their stories characterized by deeds of cosmic or even heroic proportion. Their scale (what makes them larger than life though not other than it) comes, on the one hand, from the key existential paradoxes they contain and, on the other, from the caricature-like clarity with which they portray those pressure points in life. The *lwa* are full-blown personalities who preside over some particular social arena, and the roles they exemplify contain, as they do for the living who must fill them, both positive and negative possibilities.

Trance-possession within Vodou is

somewhat like improvisational theater.[1] It is a delicate balancing act between traditional words and gestures which make the spirits recognizable and innovations which make them relevant. In other words, while the character types of the *lwa* are ancient and familiar, the specific things they say or do in a Vodou ritual unfold in response to the people who call them. Because the Vodou spirits are so flexible and responsive, the same spirit will manifest in different ways in the north and in the south of Haiti, in the countryside and in the cities, in Haiti and among the immigrants in New York. There are even significant differences from family to family. Here we are considering two female spirits as they manifest through a heterosexual Haitian woman who has lived in an urban context all her life and who has resided outside of Haiti for a quarter of a century. While most of what is said about these spirits would apply wherever Vodou is practiced, some of the emphases and details are peculiar to this woman and her location.

Vodou is a combination of several distinct African religious traditions. Also, from the beginning, the slaves included Catholicism in the religious blend they used to cope with their difficult lives. Among the most obvious borrowings were the identifications of African spirits with Catholic saints. The reasons why African slaves took on Catholicism are complex. On one level it was a matter of habit. The African cultures from which the slaves were drawn had traditionally been open to the religious systems they encountered through trade and war and had routinely borrowed from them. On another level it was a matter of strategy. A Catholic veneer placed over their own religious practices was a convenient cover for the perpetuation of these frequently outlawed rites. Yet this often cited and too often politicized explanation points to only one level of the strategic value of Catholicism. There was something deep in the slaves' religious traditions that very likely shaped their response to Catholicism. The Africans in Haiti took on the religion of the slave master, brought it into their holy places, incorporated its rites into theirs, adopted the images of Catholic saints as pictures of their own traditional spirits and the Catholic calendar as descriptive of the year's holy rhythms, and in general practiced a kind of cultural judo with Catholicism. They did this because, in the African ethos, imitation is not the sincerest form of flattery but the most efficient and direct way to gain understanding and leverage.

This epistemological style, exercised also on secular colonial culture, was clearly illustrated when I attended Vodou secret society[2] ceremonies in the interior of Haiti during the 1983 Christmas season. A long night of thoroughly African drumming and dancing included a surprising episode in which the drums went silent, home-made fiddles and brass instruments emerged, and a male and female dancer in eighteenth-century costume performed a slow and fastidious *contradans*. So eighteenth-century slaves in well-hidden places on the vast sugar plantations must have incorporated mimicry of their masters into their traditional worship as a way of appropriating the masters' power.

I want to suggest that this impulse toward imitation lies behind the adoption of Catholicism by African slaves. Yet I do not want to reduce sacred imitation to a political maneuver. On a broader canvas this way of getting to know the powers that be by imitating them is a pervasive and general characteristic of all the African-based religions in the New World. Grasping this important aspect of the way Vodou relates to the world will provide a key for understanding the nature of the relationship between Alourdes and her female spirits. When possessed by her woman spirits, Alourdes acts out the social and psychological forces that define, and often confine, the lives of contemporary Haitian women. She appropriates these forces through imitation. In the drama of possession-performance, she clarifies the lives of women and thereby empowers them to make the best of the choices and roles available to them.

Sacred imitation is a technique drawn from the African homeland, but the kinds of powers subject to imitation shifted as a result of the experience of slavery. The African religions that fed into Haitian Vodou addressed a full array of cosmic, natural, and social forces. Among the African spirits were those primarily defined by association with natural phenomena such as wind, lightning, and thunder. As a result of the shock of slavery, the lens of African religious wisdom narrowed to focus in exquisite detail on the crucial arena of social interaction. Thunder and lightning, drought and pestilence became pale, second-order threats compared with those posed by human beings. During the nearly 200 years since their liberation from slavery, circumstances in Haiti have forced Haitians to stay focused on the social arena. As a result, the Vodou spirits have also retained the strong social emphasis gained during the colonial period. Keeping these points in view, I now turn to Alourdes and two female Vodou spirits she serves. They both go by the name Ezili.

The Haitian Ezili's African roots are multiple.[3] Among them is Mammy Water, a powerful mother of the waters whose shrines are found throughout West Africa. Like moving water, Ezili can be sudden, fickle, and violent, but she is also deep, beautiful, moving, creative, nurturing, and powerful. In Haiti Ezili was recognized in images of the Virgin Mary and subsequently conflated with her. The various manifestations of the Virgin pictured in the inexpensive and colorful lithographs available throughout the Catholic world eventually provided receptacles for several different Ezilis as the spirit subdivided in the New World in order to articulate the different directions in which women's power flowed.

Alourdes, like all Vodou priests or priestesses, has a small number of spirits who manifest routinely through her. This spiritual coterie, which differs from person to person, both defines the character of the healer and sets the tone of his or her "temple." Ezili Dan-

tor is Alourdes's major female spirit, and she is conflated with Mater Salvatoris, a black Virgin pictured holding the Christ child. The child that Dantor holds (Haitians usually identify it as a daughter!) is her most important iconographic detail, for Ezili Dantor is above all else the woman who bears children, the mother par excellence.

Haitians say that Ezili Dantor fought fiercely beside her "children" in the slave revolution. She was wounded, they say, and they point to the parallel scars that appear on the right cheek of the Mater Salvatoris image as evidence for this. Details of Ezili Dantor's possession-performance extend the story. Ezili Dantor also lost her tongue during the revolution. Thus Dantor does not speak when she possesses someone. The only sound the spirit can utter is a uniform "de-de-de." In a Vodou ceremony. Dantor's mute "de-de-de" becomes articulate only through her body language and the interpretive efforts of the gathered community. Her appearances are thus reminiscent of a somber game of charades. Ezili Dantor's fighting spirit is reinforced by her identification as a member of the Petro pantheon of Vodou spirits, and as such she is associated with what is hot, fiery, and strong. As a Petro spirit Dantor is handled with care. Fear and caution are always somewhere in the mix of attitudes that people hold toward the various Petro spirits.

Those, such as Alourdes, who serve Ezili Dantor become her children and, like children in the traditional Haitian family, they owe their mother high respect and unfailing loyalty. In return, this spiritual mother, like the ideal human mother, will exhaust her strength and resources to care for her children. It is important to note here that the sacrifice of a mother for her children will never be seen by Haitians in purely sentimental or altruistic terms. For Haitian women, even for those now living in New York, children represent the main hope for an economically viable household and the closest thing there is to a guarantee of care in old age.

The mother-child relationship among Haitians is thus strong, essential, and in a not unrelated way, potentially volatile. In the countryside, children's labor is necessary for family survival. Children begin to work at an early age, and physical punishment is often swift and severe if they are irresponsible or disrespectful. Although in the cities children stay in school longer and begin to contribute to the welfare of the family at a later age, similar attitudes toward childrearing prevail.

In woman-headed households, the bond between mother and daughter is the most charged and the most enduring. Women and their children form three- and sometimes four-generation networks in which gifts and services circulate according to the needs and abilities of each. These tight family relationships create a safety net in a society where hunger is a common experience for the majority of people. The strength of the mother-daughter bond explains why Haitians identify the child in Ezili Dantor's arms as a daughter. And the importance and precariousness of that bond explain Dantor's fighting spirit and fiery temper.

In possession-performance, Ezili Dantor explores the full range of possibilities inherent in the mother-child bond. Should Dantor's "children" betray her or trifle with her dignity, the spirit's anger can be sudden, fierce, and uncompromising. In such situations her characteristic "de-de-de" becomes a powerful rendering of women's mute but devastating rage. A gentle rainfall during the festivities at Saut d'Eau, a mountainous pilgrimage site for Dantor, is readily interpreted as a sign of her presence but so is a sudden deluge resulting in mudslides and traffic accidents. Ezili's African water roots thus flow into the most essential of social bonds, that between mother and child, where they carve out a web of channels through which can flow a mother's rage as well as her love.

Alourdes, like Ezili Dantor, is a proud and hard-working woman who will not tolerate disrespect or indolence in her children. While her anger is never directed at Maggie, who is now an adult and Alourdes' partner in running the household, it can sometimes sweep the smaller children off their feet. I have never seen Alourdes strike a child, but her wrath can be sudden and the punishments meted out severe. Although the suffering is different in kind, there is a good measure of it in both Haiti and New York, and the lessons have carried from one to the other. Once, after Alourdes disciplined her ten-year-old, she turned to me and said: "The world is evil. . . . You got to make them tough!"

Ezili Dantor is not only Alourdes's main female spirit, she is also the spirit who first called Alourdes to her role as priestess. One of the central functions of Vodou in Haiti, and among Haitian emigrants, is that of reinforcing social bonds. Because obligations to the Vodou spirits are inherited within families, Alourdes's decision to take on the heavy responsibility of serving the spirits was also a decision to opt for her extended family (and her Haitian identity) as her main survival strategy.

It was not always clear that this was the decision she would make. Before Alourdes came to the United States, she had shown little interest in her mother's religious practice, even though an appearance by Ezili Dantor at a family ceremony had marked her for the priesthood when she was only five or six years old. By the time Alourdes left Haiti she was in her late twenties and the memory of that message from Dantor had either disappeared or ceased to feel relevant. When Alourdes left Haiti, she felt she was leaving the spirits behind along with a life marked by struggle and suffering. But the spirits sought her out in New York. Messages from Ezili and other spirits came in the form of a debilitating illness that prevented her from working. It was only after she returned to Haiti for initiation into the priesthood and thus acknowledged the spirits' claim on her that Alourdes's life in the U.S. began to run smoothly.

Over the ten years I have known this family,

I have watched a similar process at work with her daughter Maggie. Choosing the life of a Vodou priestess in New York is much more difficult for Maggie than it was for her mother. To this day, I have yet to see Maggie move all the way into a trance state. Possession threatens and Maggie struggles mightily; her body falls to the floor as if paralyzed, but she fights off the descending darkness that marks the onset of trance. Afterwards, she is angry and afraid. Yet these feelings finally did not prohibit Maggie from making a commitment to the *manbo's* role. She was initiated to the priesthood in the summer of 1982 in a small temple on the outskirts of Port-au-Prince. Alourdes presided at these rituals. Maggie's commitment to Vodou came after disturbing dreams and a mysterious illness not unlike the one that plagued Alourdes shortly after she came to the United States. The accelerated harassment of the spirits also started around the time when a love affair brought Maggie face to face with the choice of living with someone other than her mother. Within a short period of time, the love affair ended, the illness arrived, and Maggie had a portentous dream in which the spirits threatened to block her life path until she promised to undergo initiation. Now it is widely acknowledged that Maggie is the heir to Alourdes's successful healing practice.

Yet this spiritual bond between Alourdes and Maggie cannot be separated form the social, economic, and emotional forces that hold them together. It is clear that Alourdes and Maggie depend on one another in myriad ways. Without the child care Alourdes provides, Maggie could not work. Without the check Maggie brings in every week, Alourdes would have only the modest and erratic income she brings in from her healing work. These practical issues were also at stake in Maggie's decision about the Vodou priesthood, for a decision to become a *manbo* was also a decision to cast her lot with her mother. This should not be interpreted to mean that Alourdes uses religion to hold Maggie against her will. The affection between them is genuine and strong. Alourdes and Maggie are each other's best friend and most trusted ally. In Maggie's own words: "We have a beautiful relationship . . . it's more than a twin, it's like a Siamese twin. . . . She is my soul." And in Alourdes's: "If she not near me, I feel something inside me disconnected."

Maggie reports that when she has problems, Ezili Dantor often appears to her in dreams. Once, shortly after her arrival in the United States, Maggie had a waking vision of Dantor. The spirit, clearly recognizable in her gold-edged blue veil, drifted into her bedroom window. Her new classmates were cruelly teasing her, and the twelve-year-old Maggie was in despair. Dantor gave her a maternal backrub and drifted out the window, where the spirit's glow was soon lost in that of a corner streetlamp. These days, when she is in trouble and Dantor does not appear of her own accord, Maggie goes seeking the spirit. "She don't have to talk to me in my dream. Sometime I go inside the altar, just look at her statue . . . she says a few things to me." The image with which Maggie converses is, of course, Mater Salvatoris, the black virgin, holding in her arms her favored girl child, Anaise.

It is not only in her relationship with her daughter that Alourdes finds her life mirrored in the image of Ezili Dantor. Ezili Dantor is also the mother raising children on her own, the woman who will take lovers but will not marry. In many ways, it is this aspect of Dantor's story that most clearly mirrors and maps the lives of Haitian women.

In former days (and still in some rural areas) the patriarchal, multigenerational extended family held sway in Haiti. In these families men could form unions with more than one woman. Each woman had her own household in which she bore and raised the children from that union. The men moved from household to household, often continuing to rely on their mothers as well as their women to feed and lodge them. When the big extended families began to break up under the combined pressures of depleted soil, overpopulation, and corrupt politics, large numbers of rural people moved to the cities.

Generally speaking, Haitian women fared better than men in the shift from rural to urban life. In the cities the family shrank to the size of the individual household unit, an arena in which women had traditionally been in charge. Furthermore, their skill at small-scale commerce, an aptitude passed on through generations of rural market women, allowed them to adapt to life in urban Haiti, where the income of a household must often be patched together from several small and sporadic sources. Urban women sell bread, candy, and herbal teas which they make themselves. They also buy and re-sell food, clothing, and household goods. Often their entire inventory is balanced on their heads or spread on outstretched arms as they roam through the streets seeking customers. When desperate enough, women also sell sex. They jokingly refer to their genitals as their "land." The employment situation in urban Haiti, meager though it is, also favors women. Foreign companies tend to prefer them for the piecework that accounts for a large percentage of the jobs available to the poor urban majority.

By contrast, unemployment among young urban males may well be as high as 80%. Many men in the city circulate among the households of their girlfriends and mothers. In this way they are usually fed, enjoy some intimacy, and get their laundry done. But life is hard and resources scarce. With the land gone, it is no longer so clear that men are essential to the survival of women and children. As a result, relationships between urban men and women have become brittle and often violent. And this is so in spite of a romantic ideology not found in the countryside. Men are caught in a double bind. They are still reared to expect to have power and to exercise authority, and yet they have few resources to do so. Consequently,

when their expectations run up against a wall of social impossibility, they often veer off in unproductive directions. The least harmful of these is manifest in a national preoccupation with soccer; the most damaging is the military, the domestic police force of Haiti, which provides the one open road toward upward social mobility for poor young men. Somewhere in the middle of this spectrum lie the drinking and gambling engaged in by large numbers of poor men.

Ezili Dantor's lover is Ogou, a soldier spirit sometimes pictured as a hero, a breathtakingly handsome and dedicated soldier. But just as often Ogou is portrayed as vain and swaggering, untrustworthy and self-destructive. In one of his manifestations Ogou is a drunk. This is the man Ezili Dantor will take into her bed but would never depend on. Their relationship thus takes up and comments on much of the actual life experience of poor urban women.

Ezili Dantor also mirrors many of the specifics of Alourdes's own life. Gran Philo, Alourdes's mother, was the first of her family to live in the city. She worked there as a *manbo*. Although she bore four children, she never formed a long-term union with a man. She lived in Santo Domingo, in the Dominican Republic, for the first years of her adult life. There she had her first two babies. But her lover proved irrational, jealous, and possessive. Since she was working as hard or harder than he, Philo soon decided to leave him. Back in Port-au-Prince, she had two more children, but in neither case did the father participate in the rearing of the children. Alourdes, who is the youngest, did not know who her father was until she was grown. And when she found out, it still took time for him to acknowledge paternity.

In her late teens, Alourdes's fine singing voice won her a coveted position with the Troupe Folklorique, a song and dance group that drew much of its repertoire from Vodou. During that period Alourdes attracted the attention of an older man who had a secure job with the Bureau of Taxation. During their brief marriage Alourdes lived a life that was the dream of most poor Haitian women. She had a house and two servants. She did not have to work. But this husband, like the first man in Philo's life, needed to control her every move. His jealousy was so great that Alourdes was not even allowed to visit her mother without supervision. (The man should have known better than to threaten that vital bond!) Alourdes and her husband fought often and, after less than two years, she left. In the years that followed, there were times when Alourdes had no food and times when she could not pay her modest rent but, with pride like Ezili Dantor's, Alourdes never returned to her husband and never asked him for money. During one especially difficult period Alourdes began to operate as a Marie-Jacques, a prostitute, although not the kind who hawk their wares on the street. Each day she would dress up and go from business to business in downtown Port-au-Prince looking for someone who would ask her for a "date." When the date was over she would take what these men offered (everyone knew the rules), but she never asked for money. Alourdes had three children in Haiti, by three different men. She fed them and provided shelter by juggling several income sources. Her mother helped when she could. So did friends when they heard she was in need. For a while, Alourdes held a job as a tobacco inspector for the government. And she also dressed up and went out looking for dates.

Maggie, like Alourdes, was married once. Her husband drank too much and one evening, he hit her. Once was enough. Maggie packed up her infant son and returned to her mother's house. She never looked back. When Maggie talks about this marriage, now over for nearly a decade, she says he was a good man but alcohol changed him. "When he drink, forget it!" She would not take the chance that he might hit her again or, worse, take his anger and frustration out on their son.

Ezili Dantor is the mother—fierce, proud, hard-working, and independent. As a religious figure, Dantor's honest portrayal of the ambivalent emotions a woman can feel toward her lovers and a mother can feel toward her children stands in striking contrast to the idealized attitude of calm, nurture, and acceptance represented by more standard interpretations of the Holy Mother Mary, a woman for whom rage would be unthinkable. Through her iconography and possession-performances, Ezili Dantor works in subtle ways with the concrete life circumstances of Haitian women such as Alourdes and Maggie. She takes up their lives, clarifies the issues at stake in them, and gives them permission to follow the sanest and most humane paths. Both Alourdes and Maggie refer to Ezili Dantor as "my mother."

Vodou is a religion born of slavery, of wrenching change and deep pain. Its genius can be traced to long experience in using the first (change) to deal with the second (pain). Vodou is a religion in motion, one without canon, creed, or pope. In Vodou the ancient African wisdom is preserved by undergoing constant transformation in response to specific life circumstances. One of the things which keeps Vodou agile is its plethora of spirits. Each person who serves the spirits has his or her own coterie of favorites. And no single spirit within that group can take over and lay down the law for the one who serves. There are always other spirits to consult, other spirit energies to take into account. Along with Ezili Dantor, Alourdes also serves her sister, Ezili Freda.

Ezili Freda is a white spirit from the Rada pantheon, a group characterized by sweetness and even tempers. Where Dantor acts out women's sexuality in its childbearing mode, Freda, the flirt, concerns herself with love and romance. Like the famous Creole mistresses who lent charm and glamour to colonial Haiti, Ezili Freda takes her identity and worth from her relationship with men. Like the mulatto elite in contemporary Haiti who are the heirs of those Creole women, Freda loves fine clothes and jewelry. In her possession-performances, Freda is decked out in satin and lace. She is given powder and perfume, sweet smelling soaps and rich creams. The one possessed by her moves through the gathered community, embracing one and then another and then another. Something in her searches and is never satisfied. Her visits often end in tears and frustration.[4]

Different stories are told about Freda and children. Some say she is barren. Others say she has a child but wishes to hide that fact in order to appear fresher, younger, and more desirable to men. Those who hold the latter view are fond of pointing out the portrait of a young boy that is tucked behind the left elbow of the crowned Virgin in the image of Maria Dolorosa with whom Freda is conflated. In this intimate biographical detail, Freda picks up a fragment from Alourdes's life that hints at larger connections between the two. When Alourdes was married she already had two children by two different men. She wanted a church wedding and a respectable life, so she hid the children from her prospective in-laws. It was only at the wedding itself, when they asked about the little boy and girl seated in the front row, that they found out the woman standing before the altar with their son already had children.

Alourdes does not have her life all sewn up in neat packages. She does not have all the questions answered and all the tensions resolved. Most of the time when she tells the story of her marriage, Alourdes says flatly: "He too jealous. That man crazy!" But on at least one occasion she said: "I was too young. If I was with Antoine now, I never going to leave him!" When Alourdes married Antoine Lovinsky she was a poor teenager living in Port-au-Prince, a city where less than 10% of the people are not alarmingly poor. Women of the elite class nevertheless structure the dreams of poor young women. These are the light-skinned women, who marry in white dresses in big Catholic churches and return to homes that have bedroom sets and dining room furniture and servants. These are the women who never have to work. They spend their days resting and visiting with friends and emerge at night on the arms of their men dressed like elegant peacocks and affecting an air of haughty boredom. Although Alourdes's tax collector could not be said to be a member of the elite, he provided her with a facsimile of the dream. It stifled her and confined her, but she has still not entirely let go of the fantasy. She still loves jewelry and clothes and, in her home, manages to create the impression, if not the fact, of wealth by piling together satin furniture, velvet paintings, and endless bric-a-brac.

Alourdes also has times when she is very lonely and she longs for male companionship. She gets tired of living at the edge of poverty and being the one in charge of such a big and ungainly household. She feels the pull of the images of domesticity and nuclear family life that she sees everyday on the television in New York. Twice since I have known her, Alourdes has fallen in love. She is a deeply sensual woman and this comes strongly to the fore during these times. She dresses up, becomes coquettish, and caters to her man. Yet when describing his lovable traits, she always says first: "He help me so much. Every month, he pay the electric bill," and so forth. Once again the practical and the emotional issues cannot be separated. In a way, this is just another version of the poor woman selling her "land." And in another way it is not, for here the finances of love are wound round and round with longing and dreams.

Poor Haitian women, Alourdes included, are a delight to listen to when their ironic wit turns on what we would label as the racism, sexism, and colonial pretense of the upper-class women Freda mirrors. Yet these are the values with power behind them both in Haiti and in New York, and poor women are not immune to the attraction of such a vision. Ezili Freda is thus an image poor Haitian women live toward. She picks up their dreams and gives them shape, but these women are mostly too experienced to think they can live on or in dreams. Alourdes is not atypical. She serves Freda but much less frequently than Dantor. Ezili Dantor is the one for whom she lights a candle every day; she is the one Alourdes turns to when there is real trouble. She is, in Alourdes' words, "my mother." Yet I think it is fair to say that it is the tension between Dantor and Freda that keeps both relevant to the lives of Haitian women.

There is a story about conflict between the two Ezilis. Most people, most of the time, will say that the scars on Ezili Dantor's cheek come from war wounds, but there is an alternative explanation. Sometimes it is said that because Dantor was sleeping with her man, Maria Dolorosa took the sword from her heart and slashed the cheek of her rival.

A flesh and blood woman, living in the real world, cannot make a final choice between Ezili Dantor and Ezili Freda. It is only when reality is spiced with dreams, when survival skills are larded with sensuality and play, that life moves forward. Dreams and play alone lead to endless and fruitless searching. And a whole life geared toward survival becomes brittle and threatened by inner rage. Alourdes lives at the nexus of several spirit energies. Freda and Dantor are only two of them, the two who help her most to see herself clearly as a woman.

To summarize the above discussion: The Vodou spirits are not idealized beings removed from the complexity and particularity of life. On the contrary, the responsive and flexible nature of Vodou allows the spirits to change over space and time in order to mirror people's life circumstances in considerable detail. Vodou spirits are transparent to their African origins and yet they are other than African spir-

its. Ancient nature connections have been buried deep in their iconographies while social domains have risen to the top, where they have developed in direct response to the history and social circumstances of the Haitian people. The Vodou spirits make sense of the powers that shape and control life by imitating them. They act out both the dangers and the possibilities inherent in problematic life situations. Thus, the moral pull of Vodou comes from clarification. The Vodou spirits do not tell the people what should be; they illustrate what is.

Perhaps Vodou has these qualities because it is a religion of an oppressed people. Whether or not that is true, it seems to be a type of spirituality with some advantages for women. The openness and flexibility of the religion, the multiplicity of its spirits, and the detail in which those spirits mirror the lives of the faithful makes women's lives visible in ways they are not in the so-called great religious traditions. This visibility can give women a way of working realistically and creatively with the forces that define and confine them.

Notes

1. I use terms such as possession-performance and theater analogies in order to point to certain aspects of the spirits' self-presentation and interaction with devotees. The terms should not be taken as indicating that priestesses and priests simply pretend to be spirits during Vodou ceremonies. The trance states they enter are genuine, and they themselves will condemn the occasional imposter among them.
2. In an otherwise flawed book, E. Wade Davis does a very good job of uncovering and describing the nature and function of the Vodou secret societies. See *The Serpent and the Rainbow* (New York: Simon and Schuster, 1985).
3. Robert Farris Thompson traces Ezili to a Dahomean "goddess of lovers." *Flash of the Spirit: African and Afro-American Art and Philosophy* (New York: Random House, 1983), p. 191.
4. Maya Deren has drawn a powerful portrait of

this aspect of Ezili Freda in *The Divine Horsemen: The Living Gods of Haiti* (New Paltz, N.Y.: Documentext, McPherson and Co., 1983), pp. 137–45.

Further Readings

Brown, Karen McCarthy. "The Center and the Edges: God and Person in Haitian Vodou." *The Journal of the Interdenominational Theological Center* 7, no. 1 (Fall 1979).

——————. "Olina and Erzulie: A Woman and a Goddess in Haitian Vodou." *Anima*, Spring 1979.

——————. "Systematic Forgetting, Systematic Remembering: Ogou in Haiti." In *Africa's Ogun: Old World and New.* ed. by Sandra T. Barnes. Bloomington, Ind.: University of Indiana Press, 1988.

——————. "Alourdes: A Case Study of Moral Leadership in Haitian Vodou." In *Saints and Virtues*, ed. by John S. Hawley. Berkeley, Calif.: University of California Press, 1987.

——————. "Afro-Caribbean Spirituality." In *Caring and Curing: Health and Medicine in the Western Religious Traditions*, ed. by Lawrence Eugene Sullivan. New York: Macmillan Press, 1988.

——————. "The Power to Heal: Reflections on Women, Religion and Medicine." In *Shaping New Vision: Gender and Values in American Culture*. Ann Arbor, Mich.: UMI Press, 1987.

Deren, Maya. *Divine Horsemen: The Living Gods of Haiti*. New Paltz, N.Y.: Documentext, McPherson and Co., 1983.

Metraux, Alfred. *Voodoo in Haiti*. New York: Schocken Books, 1972.

Thompson, Robert Farris. *Flash of the Spirit: African and Afro-American Art and Philosophy*. New York: Random House, 1983.

23

The Presence of Isanaklesh: A Native American Goddess and the Path of Pollen

INÉS TALAMANTEZ

I dreamed of the goddess Isanaklesh about ten years ago during a ceremony held for the daughter of a friend on the Mescalero Apache reservation in New Mexico. I had worked during the day before my dream, helping the women in the cooking arbor to prepare food for the guests. For many hours I listened silently as the women told of their own ceremonies and those of their daughters and granddaughters. That evening, my friend, the initiate's mother, invited me to sleep with the girl's female relatives in the family's tipi. Gazing up the smoke hole, I could see the night sky, clear and filled with thousands of stars. Although we were all very tired after a long day of work, we talked on, perhaps for several hours. Then I fell asleep. During that peaceful night, the dream began. The images are so sharply imprinted on my memory that it seems as though everything were happening today . . .

INÉS TALAMANTEZ   is Associate Professor in the Department of Religious Studies of the University of California, Santa Barbara. She has published a series of articles on Native American themes and two books of translations of ritual texts, and currently serves as managing editor of the journal *New Scholar: An Americanist Review*. Her awards include a Mary Ingraham Bunting Fellowship at Radcliffe College (1978), an Andrew W. Mellon Fellowship at Harvard University (1981), and a recent FIPSE grant to pursue her research on the relationship between Native American religious traditions, ecological concerns, and the documentation of sacred space.

246

THE DREAM

I am walking near the river, towards the very center of Mescalero, following an old animal path. Slowly a female figure approaches, stirring the pollen dust on the path with each gracefully placed step. I sense that she wants something from me. I wonder who she is and why she is here. The air has become so quiet that only the rippling river can be heard. The green meadows disappearing behind me as I pass are covered thickly with grasses, fragrant wild onions, and ferns. Fresh-smelling blue flowers are scattered here and there, and dropped evergreen needles make the ground soft underfoot. The entire landscape spread out before me is suffused with yellow pollen. Pollen falls like a soft rain from heavy boughs of nearby evergreen trees; the wet meadow grass shimmers, mirage-like with the yellow dust. The sunlight filtering under the pollinating trees, the forested mountains and misty passes under the slow-moving clouds all appear undisturbed, as they were at the world's beginning.

I know I am dreaming. Feelings and memories fuse together. I know why I am here; yet everything I see appears to be mysterious, veiled, hidden. Yet as I approach, the mask pulls away, and I see what is actually there. Am I seeing the essence of the trees and grasses and wildflowers? Or am I remembering what I once knew—what I was always told?

Within minutes I am in a pine forest. I suddenly feel alone and anxious, disturbed without knowing why. The path ahead is clearly marked and the sunlight that filters through the trees has become quite bright; my shadow moves along beside me. The trees shimmer with yellow pollen that gently falls in the breeze. Suddenly I see Her again, walking towards me. All at once she is standing in front of me, tall and dark-skinned, with smooth black hair flowing to the ground. It too is covered with pollen. Her deerskin dress is carefully stained the same green as the evergreen pines. Hanging from her neck is an abalone shell that contains the pollen of the ocean floor. Her eyes are like shining obsidian, and her beads sparkle, catching the sun. I look down at her moccasins, beaded with crystals, and covered with small pieces of turquoise. At first I cannot speak; I take a deep breath and raise my head slowly. She is still looking at me. I wonder what I should say. I hear my own words, coming as if from a distance:

"What are you doing here?"

"I've come to do a ceremony for you."

She turns and points with her lips in the Apache way, beckoning me to follow. As she walks away, I see pollen flowing from the fringes of her dress. Slowly she walks further and further away. I know that this is Isanaklesh, Mother Earth, the woman who never grows old, she who is born over and over again in our ceremony, she who witnessed the creation and gives us what we need for life. I feel awed, yet balanced and peaceful, fearless, protected by a power that no outer source can penetrate. I have reached the place of meeting on the pollen path.

In Mescalero Apache culture, to dream the goddess Isanaklesh is to be ritually bound to her just as her myth is bound to the ceremony that initiates young Mescalero girls into womanhood. Whomever the goddess enriches through a yellow cattail pollen vision or dream must always work for her, for she is asking for something, she wants something from the dreamer. Her power and beauty, utterly beyond that of all earthly women, compel the dreamer to search always for the meaning of this wondrous vision.

I therefore told my dream to several spiritual advisors, for Apaches feel that seeking such advice is proper when one has experienced such a powerful dream. One elder woman respected for her knowledge explained the general significance of dreams to me. She told me that understanding our dreams helps us to understand the world around us. Dreams, she said, reveal the many things that we do not apprehend during our waking lives. By reflecting on our dreams and their meaning, we learn to develop our senses and heed spiritual signs. Apache elders use this method of dream interpretation to see and study the world more carefully, and especially to locate links between the natural and supernatural realms. Dreams full of color, like mine, are said to reveal nature and the spirit world. Others may lead one to understand a certain person or object, or they may yield sacred traditional knowledge about plants or animals.

In my dream, Isanaklesh showed herself amidst yellow pollen. Cattail pollen, *tadidine*, is the essence of *diye*, supernatural power. The quest for *diye* is at the very heart of the Apache religious system. Most traditional Apaches seek *diye* for protection, healing, and spiritual knowledge. *Diye* assures one of a long and fruitful life. A second advisor and old friend interpreted my dream's imagery in the following way:

All that pollen, the fir trees must be in their fourth year; that is, when they drop their pollen. The bright light means summer is coming and you have to be alert and ready. If you look closely at everything, if you look inside, you can see what's going to happen ahead of you. For the next four years you must think about this dream. The more you pray about it the better it comes every time. It will stick with you because it is important. You were up about 10,000 feet in the forest; if you were walking on softness, you were among the clouds. These are the springtime clouds pushing under your feet. The breeze is behind you so you are going down canyon as the pollen falls from the trees and all around you. Walking towards the center means any place where you go it is with you. It is a good day when you see all of these things around you. That good strong feeling means you will be around for a long time. There is a lot of motion, a lot of feeling, as I have told you

before; a good day is when you move around, when you accomplish something.

Still another spiritual advisor, a woman at Mescalero, told me about Isanaklesh:

We must always remember Isanaklesh, her name means "our mother," she is sacred Mother Earth. We depend on her for all of our needs. We ask her for our food both from the plant world and the animal world, as well as for shelter and healing. Because of her power, we have been given life, we are shaped and molded by her. All of our life we are protected by her; we experience her as we see with our eyes, hear with our ears, smell with our nose, as we touch, as we grow old and become wise like her. If she appeared to you she wants you to work for her, you must do this or things could go wrong for you. Now you are tied to her. You must pray to her for *diye* which will protect you and keep you to a healthy old age.

The Mescalero Apache preserve an extensive mythology about Isanaklesh. She is a living reality, as well as the creative Earth Mother. She *is* the earth; her name literally means "Woman (*isana*) of Earth or Clay (*klesh*)." She wears the earth's white clay on her face when she is seasonally painted with it during the Isanaklesh Gotal ceremony. Because of our belief in her, and because the ceremony again and again renews her, Isanaklesh, the Woman of Earth, never grows old.

THE MYTH OF ISANAKLESH

In Mescalero Apache sacred stories about the beginning of the world, Isanaklesh is said to be one of the five great deities who were present when the world was made. The bottom half of her face was painted with white earth clay and her body was completely covered with yellow cattail pollen. Wearing a necklace of abalone shell on her chest, she watched over all things growing on earth. She used her *diye* to ripen trees and fruits, flowers of the fields, all plants and herbs. Her compassion and creative wisdom as healer gave aid from the beginning of time to those who suffered from distress, injury, or disease.

An older woman friend told her clan's version of this myth to me; (I recorded it in Apache, and then together we translated it into English). She took about five hours to explain the following portion of the myth to me. This depicts Isanaklesh as the mother of the culture hero and as the one responsible for our knowledge of healing.

Isanaklesh hid her son, Tobaschinine, Child of the Water, and raised him with great care so Giant would not find him. When he was old enough, she made four sacred arrows for him and he went out to find Giant. Giant, as it is said, had a coat of hair that was four layers thick, and for that reason he was not afraid of anything. Child of the Water finally came upon Giant. He took aim and quickly shot the first sacred arrow at him and the outer layer of Giant's thick coat first came off. Child of the Water then took aim again and the second arrow took off his second coat. The third sacred arrow took off his third coat and left his heart still beating. Child of the Water then shot the fourth sacred arrow and it pierced Giant's heart. After this, the Earth became safe and Isanaklesh and Tobaschinine taught Apaches how to live on this earth. This all happened on Sierra Blanca at the time of Creation.

Child of the Water spoke in sacred language while he was creating all of the things that we need for life. But at one point in the story he stopped and asked his father Life Giver to look at all he had made for the people, and to tell him of anything that might still be needed. His father approved of what he saw around him, but said that the people would be exposed to disease; therefore, they must have something that they can prepare to cure it. Child of the

Water said that he would ask his mother Isanaklesh for this. Isanaklesh then appeared and told him how to create the many herbs and minerals that would cure diseases. She gave him the names for the sacred plants and taught him how to use them properly, explaining that:

> some they will have to gather and then boil them, some they will chew and swallow, some they will ceremonially paint on their bodies in very special ways, some they will burn and use for their healing smoke and ashes that will be used to heal the skin, some they will drink as medicine, and some they will breathe in for their healing vapors.

Medicine from all the herbs that we know will be used to cure if it is breathed in four times in a ceremonial manner. Among Apaches, as among many other Native American peoples, things of a sacred or ceremonial nature, for example blessings or healings, are usually repeated four times, facing in each of the four directions. One starts with the east, where the sun rises, then turns to the south, where the sun travels, then to the west, where it sets, then to the north where it does not appear at all until it rises again in the east.

Isanaklesh then gave the ritual prescriptions for the use of cattail pollen, also known as the "pollen of the earth," which symbolizes the earth's life-giving powers as these powers go out to the four directions to bless all people. To live "in the pollen way" means to live in balance and harmony, like the balance and harmony that we see in nature. In this way, one will live to be old. If anything is even mixed with pollen, then Isanaklesh will give the added substance the power to heal.

Thus Isanaklesh spoke of all the herbs, trees, and minerals that are sacred to the Mescalero—everything needed to sustain life and heal humankind, so that people can live in a peaceful, harmonious way. In this version of the creation myth, she also gives the Isanaklesh Gotal ceremony to counteract the diseases and imbalances that provoke disharmony and suffering for women and all of humanity. This ceremonial gift, focused on the life of the Mescalero girl who is passing through puberty, is the ritual that Apaches still celebrate. By honoring each young girl with these rites, Apaches honor Isanaklesh as well. They hence win for themselves a long full life by drawing upon Isanaklesh's healing power.

THE CEREMONY

In southern New Mexico, east of the great White Sands, stands Dzil gais'ani, or Sierra Blanca. This 12,000 foot sacred mountain is the home of Isanaklesh, who has been revered as a powerful female deity since oldest Apache memory. At the time of creation, after the world was made safe for people, Apaches gathered together in small bands to receive *diye* and to learn the traditions. Isanaklesh then spoke and proclaimed her special ceremony:

> We will have a feast for the young girls when they have their first flow. Many songs will be sung for them, so that they will grow strong and live a long life.

This eight-day ceremony, called Isanaklesh Gotal, is celebrated in recognition of the significance of a young Apache girl's first menses. According to Apache myth, the ceremony was founded by Isanaklesh as a means through which the girl might temporarily experience herself as a manifestation of the goddess and be honored as such by the people. The first four days of the ceremony are marked with elaborate ritual detail and festive social activities. The ceremony's songs, stories, and images combine to leave a powerful imprint of Isanaklesh both on the girl herself and on the relatives, friends, and family members who attend. Throughout the final four days the girl secludes herself to reflect on her ritual experiences.

The name given to this ceremony, Isanaklesh Gotal, literally means "Ceremonial Sing for Isanaklesh." The Apache term *gotal*, "ceremonial sing," suggests not only a festive celebration, but also a raising of supernatural power to accomplish the many moments of transformation that the young girl experiences. Not only is the girl temporarily transformed into the goddess during this rite of passage; she is also permanently transformed into a mature Apache woman by the end of the ritual.

This transformation into womanhood is accomplished by ceremonially awakening the initiate to the world around her. For some girls, the ceremony is said to calm their adolescent imbalances. The Mescalero conceive of "fixing" the young initiate, ridding her of her baby ways and helping her through the door of adolescence, for at this young age the girls are said to be soft and moldable, capable of being conditioned and influenced by their female kin and others around them. Timid girls may need to be awakened to their powerful female identities; others may need to be taught to settle down and be more sensible and feminine. This sense of awakening female potential is expressed in the words of a twelve-year-old, recalling her ceremony:

> While we were at my sponsor's house, she told us about how the feast would help me to be good, healthy, and keep the Apache tradition in its full swing. On Friday, she washed my hair in the soap suds of a yucca plant. Before she did, she blessed it with pollen. She prayed in Indian while she washed. She said she would be here at 5:00 Saturday morning. Saturday morning, I woke up about 5:15 and washed up. She came and we began to build a small fire in the cooking arbor. She put four rocks in the four main directions around the fire. We waited until the fire got started. Then she put my hands in the flames and told me this was to keep me from being afraid of any kind of fire. That morning we waited until

Willetto Antonio, my medicine man, had come so she could dress me. He came and we went into the white tent. She laid my buckskin dress and boots and jewelry down on the rug. She blessed it all, and just before she put it on, she pushed it towards me four times. Then she put the dress on me. After I was all dressed, people came into the tent to be blessed. . . . They went outside so I could do my run. She told me to turn to the east. Some more people came to be blessed. As Willetto Antonio started to sing, she told me to lie down so she could rub me (massage me for strength). After she did that, they laid a buckskin down and Willetto put four half-moons on it, two of yellow pollen and two of red ochre outlined with black galena. Just before I was to run, I had to step on these moons. Then they told me I was to run my hardest so that I could run my babyhood out of me. I ran around the basket four times. But each time they would move it farther. After the ceremony outside, we went into the tipi so I could bless people. My sponsor showed me how to bless little kids and babies.

This initiate was well aware that she had undergone special teachings during the ceremony and that she had emerged somehow different. Analysis of the ceremonial procedures and their religious implications helps us to understand the transformative aspects of the ceremony. There is no single moment at which the transformation of girl to goddess, or of goddess to woman, occurs. It is the fusion of all the ceremony's elements, over the eight-day period, that produces the desired goals. During the ceremony, great attention is paid to the ritual details, and the meanings of the symbols are carefully explained to the girls. As the Singer and sponsor explain these teachings to the initiate, the girl begins to understand important elements of Apache culture that from now on she will be charged to maintain. After her ceremony, she will be a keeper of Apache

traditions and the pattern of everyday living in which they will continue to endure. Thus she is not only taught and protected by this ceremony; like Isanaklesh, who gave it, she will also teach and protect her tribe.

Sometimes it is not easy to convince young girls to participate in Isanaklesh Gotal. Many are intimidated by the prospect of becoming such a center of attention. Thus the mothers and grandmothers of the tribe's young girls try to prepare them psychologically for the ceremony long before the girls reach their menarche. The women try to convince the girls that they will change in a positive way if they participate fully—and that the ceremony will bring them a good and healthy life. Older women will often encourage pre-pubescent girls to observe the ceremonies of other initiates closely so they will know what to expect. I have heard mothers or other female kin say to a girl: "Go up toward the front of the Big Tipi where you can see and hear everything better."

The family begins preparations for the ceremony several years in advance of their daughter's menarche. They begin collecting the necessary ritual objects, including the sacred pollen which can only be gathered during the season when cattails are ripe. It is no less important to gather relatives' support, because the ceremony will be a tremendous burden on family resources. When the proud day of the girl's first menstruation arrives, her family celebrates with a small private dinner. Soon after, a male Singer and a woman sponsor are secured in the proper ritual manner: four gifts must be given, and the proper words must be exchanged.

Throughout the year following menarche, the girl's women kin and female sponsor then teach her the proper Apache ways. These include the use of medicinal herbs and healing skills. The women also prepare her deerskin dress, like Isanaklesh's dress, with elaborate symbolic beadwork; attached to the ends of the fringes are the tiny metal cones that now replace deer hoofs, which will gently jingle when she walks or dances. If the girl is to have a private ceremony, or "feast" as it is called today, her family and kin will usually host it at a carefully selected site well away from congested areas. The girl also has the option to join the several girls honored at the annual public Feast; in this case, her ritual will occur on the ceremonial grounds of the Mescalero tribal headquarters on whatever weekend falls closest to the Fourth of July. In either case, friends and family gather, supplies are stored, temporary tipis and cooking arbors are assembled; and preparations are made to feed all who come to the first four days of the ceremony.

Prior to dawn on the first day of the ceremony, the girl is placed in her own private tipi and carefully attended by female kin and her sponsor. The sponsor blesses the initiate with pollen, and ritually bathes and dresses her for the ceremony. She reminds the girl of how good it feels to be cared for, so that the girl will learn to care for others. The girl's hair is washed with *lzhee*, yucca suds; she is fitted with leggings and moccasins; she is ritually fed traditional Apache foods. She is given a special reed, or *uka*, through which she will sip water, since water is not allowed to touch her lips for fear that this will bring floods; she also receives a scratching stick, or *tsibeeichii*, for she is not to scratch with her fingernails.

Meanwhile, outside on the ceremonial grounds, the Singers and the girl's male kin begin to construct the sacred tipi. This will be the central structure where most of the rites take place. It is called the ceremonial home of Isanaklesh. According to Apache sacred songs, only when this tipi's four main poles are properly erected can the goddess reside there; then the power of the songs will go out from the tipi to carry the ceremony's benefit out to all of the people on earth. To raise these poles, first four rocks are used to mark the sacred place which was touched by the first rays of

the sun. Then, at this spot, the four poles are sung into place. A song is sung for each pole as it is placed into the earth and tied to the others at the top of the structure. Thus the Apache sacred number, four, is established musically as well as visually. Ideally, the first songs should be sung approximately at dawn, as the sun rises to the east, where the opening of the tipi must face. This way both song and sunrise mark the beginning of sacred time. Since the voice of the Singer can only carry so far in an outdoor setting, the songs also serve to mark off a sacred space for the circle of participants, who must move close enough to hear as well as to see.

The sacred tipi is now completed and readied for the goddess, who has been approaching from the east with the early dawn light. The tipi's upper portion is wrapped with a clean white canvas cloth, and its lower portion is filled in with branches. The eastward opening is built out to the sides, in order to let the sun's light inside. After the tipi is in place, the initiate in her ritual garment appears with her sponsor and family. She is freshly bathed and dressed and carries a blanket and white deerskin to be unfolded and placed in front of the tipi. The initiate, now taking on the role of the goddess, then blesses with pollen members of the tribe who come forward, and the people in turn bless the initiate. An essential component of this rite is the *tadadine*, the cattail pollen, which is the pollen that Isanaklesh used in the creation myth. The girl motions in the Apache way to the four directions and then applies the yellow life-giving substance over the bridge of the person's nose, moving from the right to the left side; she may also apply it to other parts of the person's body. This blessing assures the people of a good long life; it also prefigures the healing powers of this young goddess-to-be. Hence, to remind the girl of her role as healer, the sponsor now tells her:

When you become Isanaklesh in the ceremony, you will have her power to heal because it is Isanaklesh who handed this knowledge to us. There is a sacred story about this. Since you will be Isanaklesh, you will be asked to heal and bless people who come to see you. You must always remember how you felt during your ceremony, when you were the living goddess; then, later in life, you can call on her for help whenever you face problems; you will remember how you felt when you were her, when you became her.

The initiate's young, soft body is next "molded," that is, massaged and aligned by her sponsor to insure the transformation of girl to goddess as well as for continuing health and strength and a long, productive life. The Singer then draws four naturally paced footprints on the deerskin with pollen. While a sacred basket is put in place to the east of the tipi, the initiate steps on the pollen prints and is then gently "pushed off" to run around the basket and return to the tipi. This sequence symbolizes walking on the pollen path, again to bring the initiate a long, healthy life. The initiate runs around the basket four times, as four verses of the ritual song are sung. Before each run, the basket is moved a little closer to the tipi. Meanwhile, the girl's female sponsor makes the "ritual marker," a long high-pitched sound, to draw the attention of the supernaturals. For as she runs, the initiate meets the approaching Isanaklesh and escorts her back to the Apache people.

After the first morning's rituals, the initiate appears in public only during the next four nights. During the day, she may not have any ordinary social contact; only relatives, close friends, and those who wish to be blessed or healed may visit her in her private tipi.

When dusk arrives on the first night of the ceremony, male dancers appear to bless the young initiate and the central ceremonial fire. These dancers have been ritually transformed into *hastchin*, supernaturals who live inside the mountains near Mescalero. They wear buck-

skin kilts with long fringes finished with tin-cone jingles; above the waist, they are painted front and back with bold designs. Black cloth masks cover their faces and hide their human identities; yucca headdresses and ceremonial staffs complete their ritual dress. The *hastchin* dance in teams of four, each with its own drummer and group of singers. Trailed by one or more ritual clowns, or *libaye*, who are usually apprenticed *hastchin*, they also bless the ceremonial tipi. They bow toward it and back up four times from all four directions, making owl-like sounds. Then they return to the ceremonial grounds to dance around the central fire until the young initiate arrives.

At about 10 P.M., the initiate, her sponsor, and the Singer appear at the sacred tipi. The Singer leads the girl into the home of Isanaklesh by extending an eagle feather which he holds in his right hand. The girl takes hold of the other end of the feather and follows as he takes four steps into the tipi; each step is accompanied by the verse of a song that refers to the tipi as home of the goddess. Inside, facing the fire at the center of the tipi, the initiate and her sponsor sit on deerhides and blankets. The Singer kneels in front of the girl with his back to the fire and prays and blesses the initiate, whom he now calls by the goddess's name.

As other songs are sung in groups of four, the initiate dances back and forth across a deerhide, looking always just above the fire or at the Singer's rattle, as the ritual rules prescribe. Accompanied by the light, regular pulse of the Singer's deer-hoof rattles, each song and dance lasts for about four to six minutes. Between songs, the girl rests for three to four minutes; sometimes the Singer and sponsor will talk, but usually they are silent. As each group of four songs ends, a short formula is sung to mark its conclusion. Then the Singer lights hand-rolled cigarettes of ritual tobacco, and a longer break is taken, during which Isanaklesh is sometimes offered water through her drinking tube. During nights two and three, the same pattern occurs, with no morning or daytime activity. Only the content of the songs varies with each nightly performance.

A closer look shows that this seemingly endless repetition is a tightly structured and deliberate ritual form. The repetition establishes a stable place, quite literally when combined with the dancing, which is restricted to the area of a small deerhide. In the matrix of this stability, thoughts are free to wander. The young Isanaklesh appears to be in a trance-like state as she dances more vigorously each night. The Singer tells her to think in images about the tribe—to visualize troubles and illness and to send them over the mountain and away from the tribe. She is to set her mind and spirit in motion, even as her physical space is confined.

Similarly, the repetition also alters the sense of time. All necessary elements for a good life are said to be present in the ceremony; all the important symbols of Apache culture and of the world of women are contained in the songs that are sung each night. By calling on these symbols with the songs' powerful words, participants evoke images that are sometimes literally seen in the sacred space. The mind can travel between these images. When similar tunes are used it is as if no time has elapsed between one set of songs and the next—or between the present ceremony and the first ceremony ever sung. The goddess is *there*; and her *diye*, her healing power, is present, as it was during the first moments of the world's creation.

The ceremony lasts almost until dawn on the fourth day. Songs are counted by wooden markers that are driven into the ground around the fire. Many of these songs, both words and tunes, are repeated from the previous evenings. Then, on the fifth and final morning of the ceremony's public segment, the ceremonial circle is completed by actions which reverse the pattern of the first morning. The Goddess, the sponsor, and the Singer assemble in the tipi just as dawn is about to break. Isanaklesh

has again been freshly bathed. The sacred basket is beside them, holding pollen, the girl's eagle feather, tobacco, a gramma grass brush, several kinds of clay, and galena, a shiny black lead ore found in the mountains at Mescalero. Using the galena, the Singer paints an image of the sun on the palm of his hand. As he sings, he holds his hand up to the sun, so that the galena glitters as the early sun's rays hit it. When the song is finished, the Singer turns to the Goddess and touches his sunpainted hand to her shoulders and chest. Then he touches each side of her head and rubs the sun-image into her hair.

Singing another song, the Singer paints her with white earth clay, covering all the exposed skin on her arms and legs, as well as the lower half of her face. As this is happening, other participants remove the cloth and branches covering the sacred tipi, so that only the four main poles remain. Within this skeleton structure, the ritual blessing and healing of the tribe again take place. Taking red clay from a basket beside him, the Singer blesses every member of the community (and anyone else seeking blessing) by marking them with the clay, taking special care for young children, the elderly, and the sick. This period for blessing can last for over an hour.

The next and final ritual sequence occurs very quickly. The Goddess is led out of the tipi to the same tune which led her in; she walks on pollen footsteps which are again painted on the deerskin. The sacred basket is once again placed to the east of the tipi, at the same distance from the tipi as it had been during the final run of the ceremony's first morning. Once again, the initiate-Goddess takes the four ceremonial pollen footsteps and runs off, accompanied by the four verses of her running song. This time, after each run, the basket is moved further to the east. On the last run, she runs to the basket—now very far to the east. She picks up her eagle feather and begins to rub the white clay from her face while running on to her private tipi, where she will stay during the next four days. During the past four days she has symbolically left behind her childlike youth and has been ritually transformed into the goddess. Now the goddess, incorporated, has herself departed. After the next four days of quiet reflection, the initiate will emerge from her tipi as an adult Apache woman.

As the girl performs her last run, the Singer chants as the rope which tied together the tipi poles is loosened and undone. Now the tipi's last four poles fall to the ground with a great crash. During all of this excitement, the Singer has continued to sing, accompanied by his rattle. However, the crowd, which knows the traditions of this ceremony, has by now moved towards the cooking arbor. Here pick-up trucks have driven in, loaded with candy, fruit, and household goods. These are thrown to the crowd as gifts from the family sponsoring the feast. The effect of the final run, the dismantling of the sacred tipi, and the giveaway with all of its accompanying excitement are meant to decisively break the sense of sacred space and time. The music also ends at this point, appropriately, after the Singer has sung over 100 songs during the total five-day period. Except for the girl, the participants now return to normal tribal life. In a traditional ceremony of incomparable beauty and coherence, another girl has reached womanhood, guided by the women of her culture and reassured of both her female and her Apache identity.

Isanaklesh is a potent symbol for Apache women. This goddess whom the initiate has *been* for a while is also everything that a woman can hope to be. She is wise; she is powerful; she heals; she provides effective tools for living a life of harmony and balance. She is creative and fertile. As earth, she is the ultimate mother; but she also exemplifies ideal human motherhood by protecting and teaching her own child.

The ceremony of Isanaklesh Gotal constantly brings these female images to consciousness. All a woman has to do when she meets obstacles in her life is to remember how she felt during her ceremony when she was Isanaklesh. For the women who experience Isanaklesh, the goddess becomes a deeply engrained model and source of empowerment. For men, knowing that women's lives are closely entwined with such a being implies that women must therefore be treated with respect and esteem. Moreover, the shared reverence for Isanaklesh that is focused in this ceremony forges a strong sense of Apache community. Thus Isanaklesh indeed brings power to the Apache; she helps us to find balance in our lives, and knowledge of our identity.

Further Readings

Basso, Keith H. *The Gift of Changing Woman.* Bulletin of American Ethnology Anthropological Papers, No. 196. Washington D.C.: U.S. Government Printing Office, 1966.

Hoijer, Harry. *Chiricahua and Mescalero Apache Texts.* Chicago: University of Chicago Press, 1938.

——————. "The Apache Verb." *International Journal of American Linguistics*, Vols. XI, 13–23, 193–203; XII, 1–13; XIV, 247–259; XV, 12–22 (1945–1949).

Mescalero Apache Tribe. *Mescalero Apache Dictionary*, compiled by Evelyn Breuninger, Elbys Hugar, Ellen Ann Lathan, Scott Rushforth. Mescalero, New Mexico: 1982.

Nicholas, Dan. "Mescalero Apache Girl's Puberty Ceremony." *El Palacio* 46: 193–204. Originally published 1939.

Opler, Morris E. *An Apache Life-Way: The Economic, Social, and Religious Institutions of the Chiricahua Indians.* New York: Cooper Square Publishers, 1965. Originally published 1941.

——————. "Adolescence Rite of the Jicarilla," *El Palacio* 49: 25–38. Originally published 1942.

——————. *Childhood and Youth in Jicarilla Apache Society*, Publications of the Frederick Webb Hodge Anniversary Publication Fund, Vol. 5, Los Angeles: Southwest Museum. Originally published 1946.

Talamantez, Inés. "*Ethnopoetics: Theory and Method: A Study of 'Isánáklesdé Gotal with*

Analyses of Selected Songs, Prayer, Ritual Structure, and Contemporary Performance. Ph.D. Dissertation, University of California, San Diego.

——————. "Female Initiation: Introducing Mescalero Apache Girls into the World of Spiritual and Cultural Values," in *Working Papers of the Bunting Institute* (Cambridge, Mass.: Harvard University).

Turner, Victor W. *The Ritual Process: Structure and Anti-Structure*. Chicago: Aldine Publishing Co., 1969.

van Gennep, Arnold. *Les Rites du Passage*. Translated by Monika B. Vizedom and Gabrielle L. Caffee as *The Rites of Passage* (Chicago: University of Chicago Press, 1960). Originally published 1908.

24

Menstruation and Childbirth as Ritual and Religious Experience among Native Australians

RITA M. GROSS

The subjects of this chapter are menstruation and childbirth, as they figure in both Australian aboriginal women's and men's religious lives. In the religious lives of women these biological experiences are the occasion of significant rituals. In the religious lives of men, who, of course, cannot experience them directly, they are often ritually imitated. The significance of menstruation and childbirth in both women's and men's religious lives has not been especially noted or studied by most scholars of aboriginal traditions. I believe that this oversight is a result of the fact that aboriginal religions have usually been studied by male anthropologists from a strictly male point of view.

A few comments on Australian aboriginal culture and on scholarship about it are crucial preliminaries to our discussion. The aborigines are a hunting and gathering society whose material culture is exceedingly simple. Yet their social organization and world view are so complex that they have long fascinated anthropologists and historians of religion. Two noticeable

RITA M. GROSS received a Ph.D. in the History of Religions from the University of Chicago. Currently Associate Professor of Religious Studies at the University of Wisconsin—Eau Claire, she has published many works in the area of women and religion—among them, *Beyond Androcentrism: New Essays on Women and Religion* (Missoula: Scholars Press, Univerity of Montana, 1977).

Author's Note This paper was first read at the national convention of the American Academy of Religion in St. Louis in November 1976. A more complete version of the paper was published in *The Journal of the American Academy of Religion* (December 1977). Portions of that article are used here by permission of *JAAR*.

features of aboriginal religion have been the basis of all theories about the role of women in it. The first is the extreme sexual differentiation that characterizes religious life in aboriginal Australia. Women are almost completely excluded from the men's rituals; and—although this aspect has been much less noticed—men are completely excluded from women's rituals. Second, the most obvious, elaborate, and time-consuming dimension of aboriginal religion is represented by those men's rituals from which women are so rigidly excluded. These rituals alone are also the basis of most theories about aboriginal religion, because male anthropologists found them more interesting and easier to study than the women's rites. This situation led to the classic interpretation of sexual dichotomy in aboriginal religion:

> Masculinity is inextricably woven with ritual cleanness and femininity is equally intertwined with the concept of uncleanness, the former being the sacred principle and the latter the profane. This sexual dichotomy and its correlation with the Murngin beliefs of what are the sacred and profane elements of the group, are again connected with a further principle of human relations, namely, that of superordination and subordination.[1]

This idea of women's "profaneness" also led many scholars to downplay the religious significance of women's rituals. It has been argued that women's religious life is so different from men's as to be unworthy of the label "religious" and that menstrual taboos and childbirth seclusions are imposed on women by men who abhor and fear these physiological events. Women's ceremonies are said to be uninteresting and insignificant in comparison to men's rituals:

> Aboriginal women have ceremonies of their own, some commemorating their "femaleness," some with highly erotic content, but little is known of these except that they seem to be a pale imitation of masculine

ceremonies and they play little part in tribal life.[2]

In all these statements one theme predominates—the attempt to differentiate women's ceremonies from men's ceremonies and, in differentiating them, to indicate that women's ceremonies are inferior in scope, intensity, and religious significance. However, I would contend that, although women's ceremonies are indeed different from men's ceremonies, if we explore the differences rather than assume that the difference implies inferiority, other interpretations are possible. What is most significant about women's ceremonies is that, *by being different from men's ceremonies and by focusing on women's unique experience*, they perform the same function for women that the men's rituals perform for men. The women's unique experiences are ritual and religious experiences; they are symbols and metaphors through which women express and attain their adult status as sacred beings within the aboriginal community. Just as the men's ceremonies indicate the sacred status and potential of men, so the women's ceremonies indicate the sacred status and potential of women and not some opposite, "profane" condition.

The basic reason for my interpretation can be stated rather succinctly. The experiences and rituals of menstruation and childbirth are laden with clues and characteristics that, were they found in connection with anything else, would be automatically referred to as "sacred" or "religiously significant." *All* attitudes and behaviors that are correctly deemed clues to the sacredness of the male mode and of men's rituals are also found in connection with women's ceremonies; but, when observed in connection with women's ceremonies, their existence and significance have not been noted.

First, the exclusiveness and secrecy surrounding women's rituals are significant because, in aboriginal religion, both are indications of sacredness. Second, the ideological underpinnings of women's and men's ceremonies are identical. Both women's and men's ceremonies were instituted in mythic times by the totemic ancestors, and both confer great potency on those who perform them. The basic ritual patterns are identical, in general as well as in specific detail. Most important is the basic initiatory structure of withdrawal, seclusion, and return, thought of as death and rebirth, which is found in women's ceremonies to the same extent as it is found in men's ceremonies. Finally, neither men nor women achieve full initiation and sacred status until old age. All these parallel attitudes are important because they indicate a parallel (not identical) access to sacrality. The women's *different* religious life has the *same* outcome as the men's—membership in the sacred community, not exclusion from it.

Although girls undergo some prepuberty rituals, the first occurence of menstruation is the most significant event in a woman's ritual progression from the relatively insignificant status, religiously speaking, of being a child to the religiously significant status of being a woman. The reason for it lies in the significance of menstruation itself.

> Because menstruation was introduced by mythical characters—as, so to speak, a rite performed more or less automatically by women (although imitated artificially, in various regions, by men)—it has mythical sanction: it is . . . not a mundane or ordinary state of affairs. . . . Menstrual blood is "sacred," declared to be so by the mythical Sisters themselves.[3]

The details of first-menstruation rituals vary considerably, but the pattern is always the same. The girl is secluded by the other women of the group. During the seclusion men are avoided, and various ritual practices are followed. After the seclusion the girl's return to the group involves a celebration and recognition of new status.

The parallels between these rituals and male initiations are obvious. Not only the general pattern, but also innumerable details of ritual behavior are identical. Also, before contact with missionaries, the attainment of womanhood probably involved much more elaborate rituals.[4] If this is true, the parallels would be even stronger, since the relative simplicity of girls' initiations often results in the interpretation that they have less religious significance than the more elaborate boys' ceremonies.

If the *one* existing early account[5] of girls' initiations is accurate, it is clear that, indeed, girls' menstruation ceremonies were quite lengthy and elaborate in earlier times. According to that account, an old woman took the girl out of the camp into the bush. They made a shade, and the old woman built a fire and performed the smoking ritual for the girl. She made the girl sit over a hole in the ground and told her that she was now a woman. In two months "you go and claim your husband," she said. After a two-month seclusion, they moved their camp closer to the main group. The girl was decorated and painted. "To show that the occasion was a sacred one, a sprig of Dahl tree was placed through the hole in the septum of the nose," the account continues. Carrying smoking twigs, the girl walked toward the main camp, according to the old woman's instructions. When the women saw her coming, they sang to her. Her betrothed sat with his back to her. She walked up to him, shook him, and ran away, pelted with twigs and sticks by the women. For another month she camped with the old woman, moving even closer to the main camp. A few weeks later she camped just outside the main camp and then moved to the opposite side of her betrothed's fire. Finally, the couple slept on the same side of the fire.

Unfortunately, even this account cannot answer one of the most important questions that arise in connection with menstruation as an initiation into a woman's mode of sacred being. We know nothing of the spiritual teachings that may have been imparted during the seclusion, which, if this one early reporter was correct, was quite lengthy. It seems unimaginable that, during a three-month seclusion, secret instruction and initiation into women's modes of religious expression did not occur. Nor can anyone claim that, if such teaching had occurred, we would know about it. So far as I can tell, none of the early fieldworkers in Australia who produced the standard descriptions of men's ceremonies actually saw a woman's menstruation ceremony. The instruction in mythic and cultural knowledge, if it occurred, would strengthen even further the interpretation that men's and women's ceremonies are different but parallel ways of achieving the same results. Many of those who focus only on the differences between women's and men's ceremonies and see men's ceremonies as having deeper religious significance than women's ceremonies also contend that men's rituals are somehow concerned with cultural and spiritual matters, while women's rituals are merely biologically oriented ceremonies.

Because menstruation is so significant, subsequent monthly periods are also ritualized to some degree. These ritual practices usually include seclusion or avoidance of men as well as some dietary restrictions. Even today, when seclusion is impractical, some care is taken to ritualize menstrual periods. However, while menstrual blood is to be avoided by men, it is considered valuable to women so long as they observe the rituals correctly. For example,

> At each menstruation until she is fully developed a young girl receives some of her own menstrual blood, which is rubbed upon her shoulders by the older women. When she is mature, she may perform this duty for younger girls.[6]

Those who have tried to see women as "profane" vis-à-vis the "sacrality" of men have generally supposed that men have imposed menstrual taboos on women because they find this aspect of womanhood the most "profane" of all. However, this interpretation does not seem to point to the true reason why men avoid menstrual blood. Menstrual blood is powerful and magical, therefore, it must be handled carefully and circumspectly: but it is not shameful or unclean. A menstruating woman is taboo, but she is not impure. This realization is extremely important for an adequate interpretation of the role that menstruation plays in women's and men's religious lives.

Childbirth functions as a religious resource for women in much the same way. Pregnancy and childbirth are mythically grounded; female totemic ancestors underwent those experiences themselves, and provide the models for women today. In the relatively informal age-grading system that applies to native Australian women, pregnancy and childbirth mark another transition and another level of attainment. Childbirth ritual is secret. Children, younger women, and men are prohibited from the place where birth is occurring just as rigorously as the uninitiated are prohibited from the place where male sacred rituals are culminating. This prohibition is very widely reported. Even in those cases in which a medicine man attends some stages of labor, no man is permitted to see the actual birth.

Fortunately, the literature concerning childbirth rituals is richer than that dealing with menstruation. Phyllis Kaberry and Ursula McConnel have both provided extensive descriptions, based on their field experience, of aboriginal childbirth ceremonies.

Phyllis Kaberry's lengthy description is invaluable for its insights into the religious significance of these practices.

> The old women and those who had children went apart with a pregnant woman and danced around her . . . songs were sung. The old women examined her and then would sing. The women said it would make birth easier and charm the pelvis and the genital organs. . . .
>
> As the moment of birth approached the pregnant woman left the camp with her mother and an old female relative, one of whom would act as midwife. During labor, songs were sung to facilitate delivery and prevent haemorrhage, the umbilical cord

was cut and the placenta was buried secretly. . . . Mother and chld were secluded from the men for about five days.

This ritual is characterized by features which would seem to be typical of that associated with most of the physiological crises of the individual:

(1) The observance of food taboos—this time by the mother on behalf of the child; (2) the spells and rites to safeguard them both during parturition; (3) the remedial use of smoked conkaberry bushes; (4) the belief that the blood from the female genitals is dangerous to the men; hence the secret burial of the placenta and the refusal of the women to discuss it in the presence of the men. (5) Finally, the segregation of the woman—a prohibition that is paralleled by the seclusion of a girl at her first menstruation and introcision, and by isolation of a boy after circumcision and subincision. These two factors are so closely interlocked that they can scarcely be considered apart. On the one hand, the child itself may sicken if the placenta is found by the men or if the cord is lost; on the other hand, both mother *and* child, whether the latter is a boy or a girl, may be harmed if they have contact with the men until four or five days afterwards.

Now although the men know some of the details of childbirth, such as the severing of the umbilical cord by the female relative . . . still they are ignorant of those songs which are sacred . . . songs which for all their simplicity are fraught with the power that they possess by virtue of their supernatural origin . . . their efficacy is attributed to the fact that they are *narungani*; that they were first uttered by the female totemic ancestors. They have the same sanctions as the increase ceremonies, . . . subincision and circumcision. . . .

The whole of the ritual surrounding pregnancy, parturition, and lactation . . .

has its sacred and esoteric aspects, which are the most vital aspects to the women, and which are associated specifically with female functions. They are believed to be a spiritual or supernatural guarantee from the Totemic Ancestors that a woman will be able to surmount the dangers of childbirth.[7]

Ursula McConnel's materials are quite similar to Kaberry's. There are myths, known only to women, about the first birth. The myth that prescribes seclusion for the mother serves as a model that women still follow today. The women also have myths that establish the ritual method for extracting the placenta and naming the child. The two events occur simultaneously. The midwife tugs gently at the cord while reciting possible names for the baby. When she says the correct name, the placenta is expelled. It is then buried, and men are forbidden to go near that spot. The myths prescibe a seclusion of two weeks to a month following the birth, during which time no man, including the father, can see the mother or the baby. When the mother's afterbirth blood ceases, both mother and baby are painted for the presentation ritual, which also follows a mythic model. The painting takes place inside a shelter that is taboo to men. Then, followed by very old female relatives, the mother walks toward the father, who is seated on the ground waiting for her, and circles him twice. Then she kneels in front of him and hands him the baby.[8]

Finally, mythology also dictates certain ritual practices for the father. Among the Munkan he must observe dietary restrictions. In other groups he and other male relatives must remain silent from the time a woman enters her childbirth seclusion until the baby is born. Such rituals of support by men parallel some of the things women do for men during men's rituals. Women may observe dietary restrictions, silence, or other limitations for their male relatives while they are being initiated. Such parallel support rituals further strengthen the interpretation that native Australian men's and women's ceremonies are different but parallel ways of achieving the same "sacred" status and are not indications of men's "sacredness" and women's "profaneness."

Having demonstrated the religious significance of menstruation and childbirth for women, let us now discuss these events as symbols in the religious lives of men, for, as I said earlier, these events also play a central role in the men's ceremonies. Such a role indicates that not only do women have their parallel access to "sacred" status but men themselves see women as "sacred," in another complementary, although ambiguous, mode of sacrality.

The best-known fact about the role of women in aboriginal religion is their exclusion from the men's ceremonies. Many subtleties of that exclusion are not so well known. It is true that sexually mature women—those who menstruate and give birth—are rigorously excluded; however, in some rare cases *older* women past menopause are initiated into the men's rituals.[9] Furthermore, outside the men's ritual context, women are not generally avoided unless they are going through menstruation or childbirth. When these subtle aspects of women's exclusion have been noted at all, they have been interpreted as evidence that menstruation and childbirth are considered as negative symbols and as part of the justification for excluding women from men's ceremonies. However, the avoidance of women's blood in both menstruation and childbirth is part of a very complex ritual and mythical pattern in which these same events also serve as potent and important metaphors in the religious lives of men.

Let us consider the men's myths first. The northern Australian epic of the Djanggawul brother and his two sisters illustrates one kind of response to women's physiological events.[10] The sisters are perpetually pregnant and giving birth. During these childbearing activities the women are not kept separate from the man.

Instead, the brother often helps his two sisters as they deliver their children. Although this myth dwells extensively on childbirth, there is no implication of danger and no ambiguity. It is also interesting that menstruation is not mentioned at all. Equally important is the fact that at this mythical time the sisters still carry the sacred emblems and perform the tribal ceremonies. Later, things change. The brother steals the religious paraphernalia and rituals from the women as part of a series of events that mark the transition from mythic to postmythic conditions. Only when the women perform the tribal rituals do the men participate in childbirth. Thus it seems that what was mythically an undifferentiated complementarity became in postmythic times two mutually exclusive, but still complementary, spheres.

The mythology of the Wawalik sisters, also from the north, contains other themes that can help us understand the men's attitude toward women. Few statements illustrate more clearly the ambivalent fascination with childbirth, menstruation, and women's blood than the central parts of this narrative. The two sisters are traveling. The elder is pregnant, and, after she has her baby, they take to the road again while the afterbirth blood is still flowing. They camp near a sacred well, and the python dwelling in the well is attracted by the smell of the blood. The snake causes a great storm as it emerges from the well, intent on swallowing the sisters. The younger one dances and is able to keep the python away, but she tires and asks the older sister to dance. She, however, cannot keep the snake away because the odor of her blood attracts it. Finally the intense dancing causes the younger sister to begin menstruating. At this point she, too, cannot fight the snake, and they are all swallowed by it. The sisters later revealed these events to the men in dreams and such events represent the mythic basis of the men's ritual cycle.[11] Clearly the women and their blood are quite potent. Although the older sister's "mistake" of traveling too soon after delivery had "negative" results, since that "mistake" is a mythic model often ritually repeated by the men, one cannot say that the menstruation, childbirth, and the attendant blood are evil, profane, or unclean but only that they are potent, fascinating, and ambiguous in their potential.

The men's rituals are even more interesting than their myths. It seems that, in addition to the avoidance of women coupled with a sort of fascination with women and women's biological functions, the complex of men's religion also involves ritual duplication of childbirth and menstruation. The women serve as models for men and their rituals, a point that has been made by prominent anthropologists and students of aboriginal culture: "Many of the rites which men carry out themselves, away from women, imitate, symbolically, physiological functions peculiar to women. The idea is that these are natural to women, but where men are concerned, they must be reproduced in ritual form."[12]

It is difficult to imagine an initiation that does not involve rebirth symbolism. Therefore, in an abstract way, any initiation is a kind of duplication of birth. It should also be noted that duplication of birth occurs in almost every religiocultural context, and not just among the Australian aborigines. The ways in which birth is duplicated in ritual are quite varied; overall, however, the duplication of the birth process on the part of the Australian men is self-conscious and graphic.

A man's initiation, marked by circumcision, signifies death to the world of women and children and rebirth into the male world. But the circumcisers behave like male mothers, and the novices are thought of as their infants. Before the circumcision, but after the boys have been taken from their mothers, they are sometimes carried about by their fathers in the same way women carry babies. After the operation, the pattern continues. The initiators imitate women in childbirth to the extent that sometimes "the old men build a stone fire and the men inhale the smoke and squat over the fire

to allow the smoke to enter their anuses." The explanation given is that "'this is like the Wawalik women did when that baby was born.'"[13] (Women who have just given birth go through this same healing and purification rite today.)

Novices and initiators are both secluded from women—a practice that parallels women's seclusion from men at childbirth or menstruation. The newly circumcised boys learn from men how to behave in their new role, just as babies learn from women. The novices learn a totemic language unknown to women, which parallels their learning to talk when they were babies. Finally the boys are ceremonially exhibited as new beings by the men who have transformed them and seen them through rebirth, just as a baby is shown after its mother comes out of seclusion, or just as a girl is exhibited after her first menstrual seclusion. No wonder circumcision "is said to symbolize the severing of the novice's . . . umbilical cord."[14]

Although usually not so graphic and explicit as in aboriginal religion, the equation of birth and initiation is relatively common in religions around the world. However, male duplication of menstruation is much less common. In aboriginal Australia men's menstruation is less widespread than men's childbirth but still occurs over a wide enough area to be germane to this analysis. Two methods are used to produce male menstruation. Subincision is an operation in which the underside of the penis is repeatedly cut until it is grooved from root to tip. The initial operation is far less significant than the subsequent reopenings of the wound, which can be done periodically, yielding large quantities of blood. The large amounts of blood are used as body decoration and glue for attaching down and feathers to the body, thereby transforming the man into a totemic dream-time ancestor.

M. F. Ashley-Montague contends that subincision is considered valuable also because it allows men to menstruate, thereby getting rid of a collection of "bad blood" that results from sexual activity or dangerous tasks. Women lose this "bad blood" naturally, but men must take direct action to obtain the same result.[15]

Several authors who have written on the subject have made a further interesting observation concerning subincision. Not only does the male organ now produce blood periodically; the operation transforms the penis so that it looks much more like the vulva.[16] Thus the man can be said to possess symbolically the female, as well as the male, sex organs.

Other groups, which do not practice subincision, also imitate menstruation. Among some groups blood obtained from piercing the upper arm is used for the same purposes and interpreted in the same manner as subincision blood.

The blood that runs from an incision and with which the dancers paint themselves and their emblems is something more than a man's blood—it is the menses of the old Wawilak women. I was told during a ceremony: "that blood we put all over those men is all the same as the blood that came from that old woman's vagina. It isn't blood any more because it has been sung over and made strong. The hole in the man's arm isn't that hole any more. It is all the same as the vagina of that old woman that had blood coming out of it. . . . When a man has got blood on him, he is all the same as those two old women when they had blood."[17]

Thus, the men's secret ritual life has a kind of double-edged quality. Men are introduced to a world that is closed to women, but myth and ritual proclaim that, nevertheless, this world is the province of women in important ways. Achieving the sacred status of maleness occurs through mythic and ritual appropriation and imitation of the female mode of being— even though women themselves are avoided. Then, once men are inside the realm of male sacrality—having made the transition by ritual imitation of childbirth and menstruation—the secrets that are now revealed to them can include myths about female totemic ancestors, rituals reenacting their adventures, and designs and emblems representing them. At a certain point, in some groups the male initiate learns of mythic times when men knew nothing about the sacred. One day, he is told, the men reversed that situation and stole religion from the women. The men's myth states that, when the Djanggawul sisters discovered what had happened, they said, "We know everything. We have really lost nothing, for we remember it all, and we can let them have that small part. For aren't we still sacred, even if we have lost the bags? Haven't we still our uteri?"[18] Contemporary aborigines seem to agree with that mythic statement.

But we really have been stealing what belongs to them (the women), for it is mostly all women's business; and since it concerns them, it belongs to them. Men have nothing to do really, except copulate, it belongs to the women. All that belonging to those Wauwalek, the baby, the blood, the yelling, their dancing, all that concerns the women; but everytime we have to trick them. Women can't see what men are doing, although it really is their own business, but we can see their side. This is because all the Dreaming business came out of women— everything; only men take "picture" for that Julunggul. In the beginning we had nothing because men had nothing because men had been doing nothing; we took these things from the women.[19]

One could hardly find a more decisive statement that women's unique experiences are potent metaphors in the men's religious lives. Such a conclusion can be stated also in another form: it seems clear that women's experiences provide men as well as women with access to the sacred. By duplicating menstruation and childbirth and by identifying men's blood with women's blood, men transcend the ordinary and become "sacred." They become the mythic models themselves.

Thus I would argue that, when one carefully

analyzes all the relevant data—the myths and rituals of the secret male sacred life and not just men's ritual avoidance of women—a different interpretation of the relationship between the men's sacred life and the exclusion of women must emerge. Men's avoidance of women is only part of the total picture. It is one element of an ambiguous, ambivalent reaction to an incredibly potent and significant presence. Therefore, the exclusion of women is part of a typical avoidance/attraction pattern relating to that which is perceived as sacred and should not be interpreted as indicating religious irrelevance or lack of value. Insofar as the term "sacred" is relevant, there is every reason to use it in interpreting men's ritual responses to women.

It therefore seems clear that women, women's blood, menstruation, and childbirth are religiously significant for both female and male aborigines. For women, their biology is one of the major foci of their religious lives, providing them with a unique set of ceremonies, parallel to the men's, that allow them to express their "sacred" status. Menstruation and childbirth, rather than being disqualifiers for significant religious involvement (although they are disqualifiers for involvement in men's cults), are avenues to, and vehicles for, significant religious experience and expression. In the men's religious rituals and experiences, women's biological functions, far from being irrelevant or antireligious, are utilized as a root metaphor by men seeking to experience and express their own parallel and complementary "sacred" status.

What kind of conclusions can we draw from this chapter as well as those that precede it? First, we can suspect that most of the world's women have found some kind of significant religious expression, although the presuppositions of western scholarship have sometimes prevented it from seeing this. Second, we can also suspect that the relationship between men and women in religious life, as in everyday life, is far more complex than most scholars have

so far imagined. What becomes of classic patterns of male domination, for example, when they are counterbalanced by awe of women's sacral power? Third, just as we have found throughout this volume that women's religious lives cannot be understood without some reference to the religious worlds of men, so it now seems clear that the reverse is also true.

These conclusions result from the initial impulse to understand women's religious lives more accurately and fully. Thus, they underscore what is perhaps the most radical, and yet commonsensical, conclusion of all. If we seek to understand the whole of religious experience, we must study women as thoroughly and empathically as we have thus far studied men. This conclusion is radical because it involves a basic reorientation of scholarly vision. It is commonsensical and obvious because it is hard to imagine that people could actually have claimed to study something "human" without recognizing that women must be as much a focus of study as men.

Notes

1. W. Lloyd Warner, *A Black Civilization: A Study of an Australian Tribe*, Harper Torchbooks, rev. ed. (New York: Harper & Row, 1958), p. 384.

2. A. P. Abbie, *The Original Australians* (New York: American Elsevier, 1969), p. 125.

3. C. H. Berndt, "Women and the 'Secret Life,'" *Man in Aboriginal Australia* (Sydney: Angus & Robertson, 1964), p. 274.

4. R. M. Berndt and C. H. Berndt, *Sexual Behaviour in Arnhem Land*, Viking Ford Publications in Anthropology, No. 16 (New York: Viking, 1951), pp. 89–90.

5. K. Langloh Parker, *The Euahlayi Tribe: A Study of Aboriginal Life in Australia* (London: Archibald Constable, 1905), pp. 56–58.

6. R. Piddington, "Karadjeri Initiation," *Oceania*, 3, no. 1, (1932), p. 83.

7. Phyllis Kaberry, *Aboriginal Woman: Sacred and Profane* (Philadelphia: Blakiston Co., 1939) pp. 242–245.

8. Ursula McConnel, *Myths of the Munkan*

(Melbourne: Melbourne University Press, 1957), pp. 135–143.

9. R. M. Berndt and C. H. Berndt, *The World of the First Australians* (Chicago: University of Chicago Press, 1964), p. 237; *Man, Land and Myth: The Gunwinggu People* (East Lansing: Michigan State University Press, 1970), p. 116.

10. The fullest account of the Djanggawul myth cycle is found in R. M. Berndt, *Djanggawul: An Aboriginal Religious Cult of North-Eastern Arnhem Land* (London: Routledge & Kegan Paul, 1952).

11. R. M. Brendt, *Kunapipi: A Study of an Australian Aboriginal Religious Cult* (New York: International Universities Press, 1951).

12. R. M. and C. H. Berndt, *The World of the First Australians*, p. 221.

13. Warner, *A Black Civilization*, p. 318.

14. Berndt and Berndt, *World of the First Australians*, pp. 144–145.

15. M. F. Ashley-Montague, "The Origin of Sub-Incision in Australian," *Oceania*, 8, No. 2 (1937), pp. 204–7.

16. Berndt and Berndt, *The World of the First Australians*, p. 146.

17. Warner, *A Black Civilization*, p. 268.

18. R. M. Berndt, *Djanggawul*, p. 41.

19. R. M. Berndt, *Kunapipi, p. 55.*

Further Readings

Bell, Diane. *Daughters of the Dreaming.* Melbourne and North Sydney, Australia: McPhee Grible/George Allen and Unwin, 1983.

Berndt, Catherine H. "Women and the Secret Life." *Aboriginal Man in Australia*, ed. by Ronald M. Berndt and Catherine H. Berndt. Sydney, Australia: Angus and Robertson, 1965.

——————. "Interpretations and 'Facts' in Aboriginal Australia." *Woman the Gatherer*, ed. by Frances Dahlberg. New Haven, Conn.: Yale University Press, 1981.

Gale, Fay. *Women's Role in Aboriginal Society.* Canberra, Australia: Australian Institute of Aboriginal Studies, 1970.

Gross, Rita M. "Tribal Religions: Aboriginal Australia." *Women in World Religions*, ed. by Arvind Sharma. Albany, N.Y.: SUNY Press, 1987.

Kaberry, Phyllis Mary. *Aboriginal Woman: Sacred and Profane.* Philadelphia: Blakiston Co., 1939.

Roheim, Geza. "Women and Their Life in Central Australia." *Journal of the Royal Anthropological Institute of Great Britain and Ireland* 43 (1933): 207–65.

BIBLIOGRAPHY

To our readers: Three types of material are included in this bibliography. *Contextual* materials offer information about the various cultures within which women operate, and about the varied images and precepts that regulate their lives. Studies of *lives* parallel the selections offered in this book, offering biographical studies and/or materials about women's rites and women's religious movements. Samples of *voices* contain women's words and reflections on their own experience and/or traditions. For convenience of use, we have grouped these materials primarily by geographical location and/or tradition, using subcategories only in instances where lists are so long or complex that subdivision seems necessary. This bibliography does not pretend to be exhaustive, but it should contain enough helpful materials to launch students and new researchers into fruitful research projects.

GENERAL: CROSS-CULTURAL STUDIES

Contexts

Ardener, Shirley, ed. *Defining Females: The Nature of Women in Society.* New York: John Wiley & Sons, 1978.

——————. *Perceiving Women.* New York: John Wiley & Sons, 1975.

——————. *Women and Space: Ground rules and Social Maps.* New York: St. Martin's Press, 1981.

Dahlberg, Frances, ed. *Woman the Gatherer.* New Haven: Yale University Press, 1981.

Evans-Pritchard, E. E. "The Position of Women in Primitive Societies and Our Own." *Position of Women in Primitive Societies and Other Essays in Social Anthropology.* New York: Free Press, 1965.

Hays, H. R. *The Dangerous Sex: The Myth of Feminine Evil.* New York: Pocket Books, 1966. (First edition, Putnam, 1964.)

Matthiasson, Carolyn, ed. *Many Sisters; Women in Cross-Cultural Perspective.* New York: Free Press, 1974.

Reiter, Rayna R., ed. *Toward an Anthropology of Women.* New York Monthly Review Press, 1975.

Rosaldo, Michelle Zimbalist and Louise Lamphere. *Woman, Culture & Society.* Stanford, Calif.: Stanford University Press, 1974.

Women in Religion—General

Bynum, Carolyn Walker, et al., eds. *Gender and Religion: On the Complexity of Symbols.* Boston: Beacon Press, 1986.

Carmody, Denise Ladner. "Women and Religion." *The Study of Women: Enlarging Perspectives of Social Reality*, ed. by Eloise Snyder. New York: Harper and Row, 1979.

——————. *Women and World Religions.* Nashville, Tenn.: Abingdon Press, 1979.

Falk, Nancy. "Women: Status and Role in World Religions." *Abingdon Dictionary of Living Religions.* Nashville, Tenn.: Abingdon Press, 1981.

Gross, Rita M., ed. *Beyond Androcentrism: New Essays on Women and Religion.* Missoula, Mont.: Scholars Press, 1977.

Haddad, Yvonne Yazbeck and Ellison Banks Findly. *Women, Religion, and Social Change.* New York: State University of New York Press, 1985.

Heiler, Friedrich. *Die Frau in den Religionen der Menscheit.* Berlin, New York: Walther DeGruyter, 1977.

Journal of Feminist Studies in Religion. Ithaca, N.Y.: Scholars Press.

King, Ursula, ed. *Women in the World's Religions, Past and Present.* New York: Paragon House, 1987.

Parrinder, Edward Geoffrey. *Sex in the World's Religions.* New York: Oxford University Press, 1980.

Plaskow, Judith and Joan Arnold Romero, eds. *Women and Religion.* Missoula, Mont.: Scholars Press, 1974.

Sharma, Arvind, ed. *Women in World Religions.* New York: SUNY Press, 1987.

Women and Religion, Special Issue, *Signs* 2, no. 2 (Winter 1976).

Lives and Voices

Crapanzo, Vincent and Vivian Garrison. *Case Studies in Spirit Possession.* New York: John Wiley & Sons, 1977.

Eck, Diana L. and Devaki Jain. *Speaking of Faith: Global Perspectives on Women, Religion, and Social Change.* Philadelphia: New Society Publications, 1987.

Fried, Martha Nemes and Morton H. Fried. *Transitions: Four Rituals in Eight Cultures.* New York: W. W. Norton, 1980.

Goodman, Felicitas D. et al. *Trance, Healing and Hallucination: Three Field Studies in Religious Experience.* New York: John Wiley & Sons, 1974.

Halifax, Joan. *Shamanic Voices: A Survey of Visionary Narratives.* New York: Dutton, 1979.

Hoch-Smith, Judith and Anita Spring. *Women in Ritual and Symbolic Roles.* New York: Plenum Press, 1978.

Holden, Pat. *Women's Religious Experience.* Totowa, N.J.: Barnes and Noble Books, 1983.

Meltzer, David, ed. *Birth: An Anthology of Ancient Texts, Songs, Prayers, and Stories.* San Francisco: North Point Press, 1981.

Newton, N. "Birth Rituals in Cross-Cultural Perspective: Some Practical Applications." *Being Female: Reproduction, Power and Change,* ed. by Dana Raphael. The Hague: Mouton, 1975.

Women Saints East and West. Hollywood, Calif.: Vedanta Press, 1955.

AFRICA—SUB-SAHARAN

Krige, Eileen J. *The Realm of a Rain-Queen.* London, New York: Oxford University Press, 1943.

Lincoln, Bruce. *Emerging from the Chrysalis: Studies in Rituals of Women's Initiation.* Cambridge, Mass.: Harvard University Press, 1981.

Richards, Audrey A. *Chisungu: A Girl's Initiation Ceremony among the Bemba of Northern Rhodesia.* London: Faber & Faber, 1956.

Shostak, Marjorie. *Nisa: The Life and Words of a !Kung Woman.* Cambridge, Mass.: Harvard University Press, 1981.

Talbot, Mrs. D. Amaury, *Woman's Mysteries of a Primitive People, the Ibibos of Southern Nigeria.* London: Cassell and Co., 1915.

Turnbull, Colin M. *The Forest People.* New York: Simon & Schuster, 1961.

ANTIQUITY—MEDITERRANEAN

Heyob, Sharon Kelly. *The Cult of Isis among Women in the Graeco-Roman World.* Leiden, Netherlands: Brill, 1975.

Keuls, Eva C. *Reign of the Phallus: Sexual Politics in Ancient Athens.* San Francisco: Harper & Row, 1986.

Kraemer, Ross S. *Maenads, Martyrs, Matrons and Monastics: A Sourcebook on Women's Religions in the Greco-Roman World.* Philadelphia, Pa.: Fortress Press, 1988.

Lefkowitz, Mary R. and Maureen B. Fant, eds. *Women's Life in Greece and Rome.* Baltimore: Johns Hopkins University Press, 1982.

Paul-Zinserling, Verena. *Women in Greece and Rome.* New York: A. Schram, 1973.

Pomeroy, Sarah B. *Goddesses, Whores, Wives and Slaves: Women in Classical Antiquity.* New York: Schocken Books, 1975.

ASIAN RELIGION—REGIONAL

CHINA

Ahern, Emily. "The Power and Pollution of Chinese Woman." *Women in Chinese Society*, ed. by Margery Wolf and Roxane Witke. Stanford, Calif.: Stanford University Press, 1975.

Guisso, Richard W. and Stanley Johannesen, eds. *Women in China: Current Directions in Historical Scholarship*. Youngstown, N.Y.: Philo Press, 1981.

O'Hara, Albert Richard. *The Position of Women in Early China, According to the Lieh Nü Chuan, "The Biographies of Chinese Women."* Taipei, Taiwan: Mei Ya Publications, 1971.

Pruitt, Ida. *A Daughter of Han. The Autobiography of a Chinese Working Woman.* New Haven, Conn.: Yale University Press, 1945.

Schipper, Kristopher. "The Taoist Body." *History of Religions* 17, nos. 3 and 4 (February–May 1978): 355–86.

Shafer, Edward H. "The Capeline Cantos: Verses on the Divine Loves of Taoist Priestesses." *Asiatische Studien/Études Asiatiques* XXXII, no. 1 (1978): 5–64.

Van Gulik, Robert Hans. *Sexual Life in Ancient China: A Preliminary Survey of Chinese Sex and Society from ca. 1500 B.C. till 1644 A.D.* Leiden, Netherlands: E. J. Brill, 1961.

Young, Marilyn Blatt, ed. *Women in China: Studies in Social Change and Feminism.* Ann Arbor, Mich.: University of Michigan Center for Chinese Studies, 1973.

INDIA

General and Contextual

Allen, Michael, and S. N. Mukherjee. *Women in India and Nepal.* Canberra, Australia: Australian National University, Monographs on South Asia, No. 8, 1982.

Das, Ram Mohan. *Women in Manu and his Seven Commentators.* Varanasi: Kanchana Publications, 1962.

Gupta, A. R. *Women in Hindu Society: A Study of Tradition and Transition.* New Delhi: Jyotsna Prakashan, 1976.

Gupta, Giri Raj. *Marriage, Religion, and Society. Pattern of Change in an Indian Village.* London: Curzon Press, 1974.

Jacobson, Doranne. "The Chaste Wife." *American Studies in the Anthropology of India*, ed. by Sylvia Vatuk. Delhi: Manohar, 1978.

Jacobson, Doranne and Susan Wadley. *Women in India: Two Perspectives.* Columbia, Mo.: South Asia Books, 1977.

Jayal, Shakambari. *The Status of Women in the Epics.* Delhi: Motilal Banarsidass, 1966.

Meyer, J. J. *Sexual Life in Ancient India: A Study in the Comparative History of Indian Culture.* New York: G. P. Dutton, 1930.

Mitter, Dwarka Nath. *The Position of Women in Hindu Law.* New Delhi: Inter-India Publications, 1984.

O'Flaherty, Wendy Doniger. *Women, Androgynes and Other Mythical Beasts.* Chicago: University of Chicago Press, 1980.

Roy, Manisha. *Bengali Women.* Chicago: University of Chicago Press, 1975.

Sastri, Shakuntala Rao. *Women in the Sacred Laws.* Madras: Amalgamations, 1953.

——————. *Women in the Vedic Age.* Chaupatty, India: Bharatiya Vidya Bhavan, 1952.

SenGupta, Sankar. *Women in Indian Folklore: A Short Survey of Their Social Status and Position: Linguistic and Religious Study.* Calcutta: Indian Publications, 1969.

Thomas, Paul. *Indian Women Through the Ages.* Bombay, N.Y.: Asia Publishing House, 1964.

Wadley, Susan S., ed. *The Powers of Tamil Women.* Syracuse, N.Y.: Syracuse University, Foreign and Comparative Studies/South Asian Series, No. 6, 1980.

——————. "Women and the Hindu Tradition." *Signs* 3, no. 1 (1977): 13–25.

Lives and Voices

Abbott, Justin E., trans. *Bahiṇā Bai: a Translation of Her Autobiography and Verses.* The Poet-Saints of Maharashtra 5. Poona: Scottish Mission Industries, 1929.

Archer, William G. *Songs for the Bride: Wedding Rites of Rural India*, ed. by Barbara Stoller Miller and Mildred Archer. New York: Columbia University Press, 1985.

Athavale, Parvati. *My Story: The Autobiography of a Hindu Widow*, trans. by Rev. Justin E. Abbott. New York, London: G. P. Putnam's Sons, 1930.

Bhaiji. *Mother as Revealed to Me*, trans. by G. Das Gupta. Varanasi: Shree Shree Anandamayee Sangha, 1962.

Chatterjee, Chanchal Kumar. *Studies in the Rites and Rituals of Hindu Marriage in Ancient India.* Calcutta: Sanskrit Pustak Bhandar, 1978.

Cormack, Margaret Lawson. *The Hindu Woman.* New York: Columbia University Teachers College, 1953.

Falk, Nancy Auer. "Women In-Between: Conflicting Values in New Delhi." *Journal of Religion* 67, no. 2 (April 1987): 257–74.

Fruzetti, Lina. *The Gift of a Virgin: Women, Marriage, and Ritual in a Bengali Society.* New Brunswick, N.J.: Rutgers University Press, 1982.

Jeffrey, Patricia. *Frogs in a Well: Indian Women in Purdah.* London: Zed Press, 1979.

Kinsley, David. "Devotion as an Alternative to Marriage in the Lives of Some Hindu Women Devotees." *Journal of Asian and African Studies* 15, no. 1–2 (1980): 83–93.

Mazumdar, Shudha. *A Pattern of Life: The Memoirs of an Indian Woman*, ed. by Geraldine H. Forbes. New Delhi: Manohar, 1977.

Marglin, Frédérique. *Wives of the God-King: The Rituals of the Devadasis of Puri.* New York: Oxford University Press, 1985.

Swami Nikhilananda. *Holy Mother: Being the Life of Sri Sarada Devi, Wife of Sri Ramakrishna and Helpmate in His Mission.* New York: Ramakrishna-Vivekananda Center, 1962.

Ramabai Sarasvati, Pundita. *The High Caste Hindu Woman.* New Delhi: Inter-India Publications, 1984. (First published 1888.)

—————. *A Testimony.* Kedgaon, India: Ramabai Mukti Mission, n.d.

Ranade, Mrs. Ramabai. *Himself: the Autobiography of a Hindu Lady*, trans. and adapted by Katherine Van Akin Gates. New York: Longmans, Green & Co., 1938.

Rao, B. Sanjiva. *Mother as Seen by Her Devotees.* Bhadaini, India: Shree Shree Anandamayee Sangha, 1967.

Richard, Mira, "The Mother" of Pondicherry. *Mother's Agenda*, vols. 1–3. Conversations recorded by Satprem. New York: Institute for Evolutionary Research, n.d.

Swami Saradeshananda. *The Mother as I Saw Her: Being Reminiscences of Holy Mother Sri Sarada Devi*, trans. by J. N. Dey. Madras, India: Ramakrishna Math, 1982.

KOREA/JAPAN

Blacker, Carmen. *The Catalpa Bow: A Study of Shamanistic Practices in Japan.* London: Allen & Unwin, 1975.

Dalby, Liza Crihfield. *Geisha.* Berkeley, Calif.: University of California Press, 1983.

Davis, Winston. "Women and Their Sexual Karma." Chapter in *Dojo: Magic and Exorcism in Modern Japan.* Stanford, Calif.: Stanford University Press, 1980.

Hardacre, Helen. "Sex Role Norms and Values in Reiyukai." *Japanese Journal of Religious Studies* 6, no. 3 (September 1979): 445–59.

Harvey, Youngsook Kim. *Six Korean Women: The Socialization of Shamans.* St. Paul, Minn.: West Publishing Co., 1979.

Kendall, Laurel. *Shamans, Housewives, and Other Restless Spirits: Women in Korean Ritual Life.* Honolulu: University of Hawaii Press, 1985.

King, Sallie B., trans. *Passionate Journey: The Spiritual Autobiography of Satomi Myōdō.* Boston: Shambhala, 1987.

Koyama, Takashi. *The Changing Social Position of Women in Japan.* Paris: UNESCO, 1961.

Lebra, Joyce et al., eds. *Women in Changing Japan.* Stanford, Calif.: Stanford University Press, 1976.

Nakamura, Kyoko. "Revelatory Experience in the Female Life Cycle: A Bibliographical Study of Women Religionists in Modern Japan." *Japanese Journal of Religious Studies* 8, nos. 3 and 4 (September-December 1981): 187–206.

Nakayama, Shōzen. *Hitokoto Hanashi: Anecdotes on the Foundress and Her Disciples.* Tenri, Japan: Tenrikyo Dōyūsha, 1936.

Okano, Haruko. *Die Stellung der Frau im Shintō.* Weisbaden: Harrassowitz, 1976.

Omori, Annie Shepley and Kochi Doi, trans. *Diaries of Court Ladies of Old Japan.* London: Constable and Co., 1921.

The Prophet of Tabuse. Tabuse, Japan: Tenshō-kōtai-Jingu-kyō, 1954 (on Sayo Kitamura).

Sievers, Sharon L. *Flowers in Salt: The Beginnings of Feminist Consciousness in Modern Japan.* Stanford, Calif.: Stanford University Press, 1983.

Smith, Robert John and Ella Lury Wiswell. *The Women of Suye Mura.* Chicago: University of Chicago Press, 1982.

SOUTHEAST ASIA/INDONESIA

Hanks, Jane Richardson. *Maternity and Its Rituals in Bang Chan.* New York: Cornell University, Southeast Asia Program, 1963.

Hart, Donn V. et al. *Southeast Asian Birth Customs: Three Studies in Human Reproduction.* New Haven, Conn.: Human Relations Area Files Press, 1965.

Kartini, Raden Adjeng. *Letters of a Javanese Princess*, ed. by Hildred Geertz. New York: A. A. Knopf, 1920.

Potter, Sulamith Heins. *Family Life in a Northern Thai Village: A Study in the Structural Significance of Women.* Berkeley, Calif.: University of California Press, 1977.

AUSTRALIA/OCEANIA

Bell, Diane. *Daughters of the Dreaming.* Melbourne: McPhee Gribble, 1983.

Kaberry, Phyllis M. *Aboriginal Women: Sacred and Profane.* Philadelphia: Blakiston Company, 1939.

Gross, Rita M. *Exclusion and Participation: The Role of Women in Aboriginal Australian Religion.* University of Chicago dissertation, 1975.

Weiner, Anette B. *Women of Value, Men of Renown: New Perspectives in Trobriand Exchange.* Austin: University of Texas Press, 1976.

BAHÁ'Í

Caton, Peggy, ed. *Equal Circles: Women and Men in the Bahá'í Community.* Los Angeles: Kalimát Press, 1987.

Compilation on Women. Port Hope, Ontario, Canada: Bahá'í Distribution Center, n.d.

Freeman, Dorothy. *From Copper to Gold: The Life of Dorothy Baker.* Oxford, England: George Ronald, Publishers, 1984.

Garis, M. R. *Martha Root: Lioness at the Threshold.* Wilmette, Ill.: Bahá'í Publishing Trust, 1983.

Root, Martha L., ed. *Tahirih the Pure: Iran's Greatest Woman.* Los Angles: Kalimát Press, 1980.

Rutstein, Nathan. *Corrine True: Faithful Handmaid of 'Abdu'l-Bah'a.* Oxford, England: George Ronald, Publishers, 1987.

Thompson, Juliet. *The Diary of Juliet Thompson.* Los Angeles: Kalimát Press, 1983.

BUDDHISM

Contexts

Hirakawa, Akira. *Monastic Discipline for the Buddhist Nuns: An English Translation of the Chinese Text of the Mahāsāṃgika-Bhikṣuni Vinaya.* Patna, India: K. P. Jayaswal Research Institute, 1982.

Hopkinson, Deborah et al. *Not Mixing Up Buddhism: Essays on Women and Buddhist Practice.* Fredonia, N.Y.: White Pine Press, 1986.

Kabilsingh, Chatsumarn. *A Comparative Study of Bhikkhuni Patimokkha.* Varanasi: Chaukhambha Orientalia, 1984.

Law, Bimala Churn. *Women in Buddhist Literature.* Ceylon: W. E. Bastian, 1927.

Paul, Diana Y. *Women in Buddhism: Images of the Feminine in the Mahāyāna Tradition.* Berkeley, Calif.: Asian Humanities Press, 1979.

Talim, M. V. "Buddhist Nuns and Disciplinary Rules." *Journal of the University of Bombay* 34, no. 2 (September 1965): 98–137.

Lives and Voices

Allione, Tsultrim. *Women of Wisdom.* Boston: Routledge & Kegan Paul, 1984.

Bode, Mabel. "Women Leaders of the Buddhist Reformation." *Journal of the Royal Asiatic Society* (1893): 517–66, 763–98.

Boucher, Sandy. *Turning the Wheel: American Women Creating the New Buddhism.* San Francisco: Harper & Row, 1988.

Davids, C. A. F. Rhys. *Psalms of the Early Buddhists I: Psalms of the Sisters.* London: Henry Frowde, 1909.

Dowman, Keith. *Sky Dancer: The Secret Life and Songs of the Lady Yeshe Tsogyel.* London: Routledge & Kegan Paul, 1984.

Friedman, Lenore. *Meetings with Remarkable Women: Buddhist Teachers in America.* Boston: Shambhala, 1987.

Gross, Rita M. "Buddhism and Feminism: Toward Their Mutual Transformation." *Eastern Buddhist* 19, nos. 1 and 2 (1986–87).

Gross, Rita M. "Yeshe Tsogyel: Enlightened Consort, Great Teacher, Female Role Model." *Tibet Journal* (forthcoming).

Horner, I. B. *Women under Primitive Buddhism: Laywomen and Almswomen.* London: G. Routledge & Sons, 1930.

Li Jung-Hsi, trans. *Biographies of Buddhist Nuns: Pao-chang's Pi-chiu-ni-chuan.* Osaka: Tohokai, Inc., 1981.

Owens, Claire Myers. *Zen and the Lady: Memoirs—Personal and Transpersonal in a World in Transition.* New York: Baraka Books, 1979.

Shin, Nan (Nancy Amphoux). *Diary of a Zen Nun.* New York: Dutton, 1986.

Sidor, Ellen, ed. *A Gathering of Spirit: Women Teaching in American Buddhism.* Cumberland, R.I.: Primary Point Press, 1987.

Tsu, Y. Y., trans. "Diary of a Chinese Buddhist Nun: T'ze Kuang." *Journal of Religion* 7, no. 5–6 (October 1927): 612–18. Reprinted in Laurence G. Thompson, ed., *The Chinese Way in Religion* (Belmont, Calif.: Wadsworth, 1973), 120–24.

Weeratane, Amarasiri. "The Bhikkuni Order in Ceylon." *Maha Bodhi* 58, nos. 10 and 11 (October-November 1970): 333–37.

CHRISTIANITY

GENERAL

Comprehensive Studies

Clark, Elizabeth and Herbert Richardson. *Women and Religion: A Feminist Sourcebook of Christian Thought.* New York: Harper & Row, 1977.

Culver, Elsie Thomas. *Women in the World of Religion.* New York: Doubleday, 1967.

Faria, Stella et al., eds. *The Emerging Christian Woman: Church and Society Perspectives.* Indore, India: Satprakashan Sanchar Kendra, 1984.

Greaves, Richard L., ed. *Triumph over Silence: Women in Protestant History.* Westport, Conn.: Greenwood Press, 1985.

Harkness, Georgia. *Women in Church and Society: A Historical and Theological Inquiry.* Nashville, New York: Abingdon Press, 1972.

Herzel, Susannah. *A Voice for Women: The Women's Department of the World Council of Churches.* Geneva: World Council of Churches, 1981.

MacHaffie, Barbara J. *Her Story: Women in Christian Tradition.* Philadelphia: Fortress, 1986.

O'Faolain, Julia and Lauro Martines. *Not in God's Image.* New York: Harper & Row, 1973.

Ruether, Rosemary Radford. *Religion and Sexism: Images of Women in the Jewish and Christian Traditions.* New York: Simon & Schuster, 1974.

Ruether, Rosemary and Eleanor McLaughlin. *Women of Spirit: Female Leadership in the Jewish and Christian Traditions.* New York: Simon & Schuster, 1979.

Tavard, George. *Women in Christian Tradition.* South Bend, Ind.: University of Notre Dame Press, 1973.

Webster, John C. B. and Ellen Low Webster, eds. *The Church and Women in The Third World.* Philadelphia: Westminster Press, 1985.

Special Aspects

Bernstein, Marcelle. *The Nuns.* New York: J. B. Lippincott Co., 1976.

Eckenstein, Lina. *Women under Monasticism; Chapters on Saint Lore and Convent Life between A.D. 500 and A.D. 1500.* New York: Russell and Russell, 1963. (Orig. copyright 1896.)

Gardiner, Anne Marie, ed. *Women and Catholic Priesthood: An Expanded Vision. Proceedings of the Detroit Ordination Conference.* New York: Paulist Press, 1976.

Huber, Elaine C. *Women and the Authority of Inspiration: a Reexamination of Two Prophetic Movements from a Contemporary Feminist Perspective.* Lanham, Md.: University Press of America, 1985.

McKenna, Mary Lawrence. *Women of the Church: Role and Renewal.* New York: P. J. Kenedy & Sons, 1967.

Meer, Haye van der. *Women Priests in the Catholic Church? A Theological-Historical Investigation.* Philadelphia: Temple University Press, 1973.

Raming, Ida. *The Exclusion of Women from the Priesthood: Divine Law or Sex Discrimination?* trans. by Norman R. Adams. Metuchen, N.J.: Scarecrow Press, 1976.

Smith, Betsy Covington. *Breakthrough: Women in Religion.* New York: Walker, 1978.

Swidler, Arlene and Leonard Swidler, eds., *Women Priests: A Catholic Commentary on the Vatican Declaration.* New York: Paulist Press, 1977.

Ware, Kallistos et al. *Women and The Priesthood: Essays from the Orthodox Tradition.* Crestwood, N.Y.: St. Vladimir's Seminary Press, 1983.

Women in the Bible

Faxon, Alicia Craig. *Women and Jesus.* Philadelphia: United Church Press, 1973.

Lofts, Norah. *Women in the Old Testament: Twenty Psychological Portraits.* New York: Macmillan, 1949.

Otwell, John J. *And Sarah Laughed: The Status of Women in the Old Testament.* Philadelphia: Westminster Press, 1977.

Stagg, Evelyn and Frank Stagg. *Women in The World of Jesus.* Philadelphia: Westminster Press, 1978.

Swidler, Leonard. *Biblical Affirmations of Women.* Philadelphia: Westminster Press, 1979.

Tetlow, Elisabeth Meier. *Women and Ministry in the New Testament: Called to Serve.* New York: Paulist Press, 1980.

Teubal, Savina J. *Sarah the Priestess: The First Matriarch of Genesis.* Athens, Ohio: Swallow Press, 1984.

PRIMITIVE/CLASSICAL

Brock, Sebastian P. and Susan Ashbrook Harvey. *Holy Women of the Syrian Orient.* Berkeley, Calif.: University of California Press, 1987.

Clark, Elizabeth A. *Ascetic Piety and Women's Faith: Essays in Late Ancient Christianity.* Lewiston, N.Y.: Edwin Mellen Press, 1986.

————. "John Chrysostom and the Subintroductae," *Church History,* 46, no. 2 (1977): 171–85.

————, trans. and intro. *The Life of Melania the Younger.* Lewiston, N.Y.: Edwin Mellen Press, 1984.

————. *Women in the Early Church.* Wilmington, Del.: Michael Glazier, 1983.

Daniélou, Jean. *The Ministry of Women in the Early Church.* London: The Faith Press, 1961.

Gryson, Roger. *The Ministries of Women in the Early Church.* Collegeville, Minn.: Liturgical Press, 1976.

Kastner, Patricia Wilson. "Macrina: Virgin & Teacher." *Andrews University Seminar Studies* 17 (Spring 1979): 105–17.

LaPorte, Jean. *The Role of Women in Early Christianity.* Lewiston, N.Y.: Edwin Mellen Press, 1982.

Lefkowitz, Mary R. "The Motivations of St. Perpetua's Martyrdom." *Journal of the American Academy of Religion* 44 (1976): 417–21.

McNamara, Jo Ann. *New Song: Celibate Women in the First Three Christian Centuries.* New York: Haworth Press, 1983.

Pagels, Elaine H. *The Gnostic Gospels.* New York: Random House, 1979.

Rader, Rosemary. *Breaking Boundaries: Male/Female Friendship in Early Christian Communities.* New York: Paulist Press, 1983.

Ward, Sister Benedicta. *The Harlots of the Desert: A Study of Repentance in Early Monastic Sources.* Kalamazoo, Mich.: Cistercian Publications, 1987.

Wilson-Kastner, Patricia et al. *A Lost Tradition: Women Writers of the Early Church.* Lanham, Md.: University Press of America, 1981.

Witherington, Ben. *Women in the Earliest Churches.* New York: Cambridge University Press, 1988.

MEDIEVAL & COUNTER-REFORMATION

General and Contextual

Bolton, Brenda M. et al. *Women in Medieval Society,* ed. by Susan M. Stuard. Philadelphia, Penn.: University of Pennsylvania Press, 1976.

Drenke, Peter. *Women Writers of the Middle Ages.* New York: Cambridge University Press, 1983.

Gies, Frances and Joseph Gies. *Women in the Middle Ages.* New York: Crowell, 1978.

Labarge, Margaret Wade. *A Small Sound of the Trumpet: Women in Medieval Life.* Boston: Beacon Press, 1986.

Morton, James, trans. *Ancren Riwle: The Nun's Rule, Being the Ancren Riwle Modernised.* London: Alexander Moring, 1905.

Power, Eileen Edna. *Medieval English Nunneries, c. 1275 to 1535.* New York: Biblo and Tannen, 1964.

—————. *Medieval Women,* ed. by M. M. Postan. Cambridge, England: Cambridge University Press, 1975.

Shahar, Shulamith. *The Fourth Estate: A History of Women in the Middle Ages.* New York: Methuen, 1983.

Shank, Lillian Thomas and John A. Nichols. *Medieval Religious Women:* Vol. I, *Distant Echoes,* 1984; Vol. II, *Peaceweavers,* 1987. Kalamazoo, Mich.: Cistercian Publications.

Wemple, Susanne Fonay. *Women in Frankish Society: Marriage & the Cloister, 500 to 900.* Philadelphia: University of Pennsylvania Press, 1981.

Lives

Abels, Richard and Ellen Harrison. "The Position of Women in Laguedocian Catharism." *Medieval Studies* 41 (1979): 215–51.

Barstow, Anne Llewellyn. *Joan of Arc: Heretic, Mystic, Shaman.* Lewiston, N.Y.: Edwin Mellen Press, 1986.

Bell, Rudolph M. *Holy Anorexia.* Chicago: University of Chicago Press, 1985.

Brown, Judith C. *Immodest Acts: The Life of a Lesbian Nun in Renaissance Italy.* New York: Oxford University Press, 1986.

Bynum, Carolyn Walker. *Holy Feast and Holy Fast: The Religious Significance of Food to Medieval Women.* Berkeley, Calif.: University of California Press, 1987.

Collis, Louise, *Memoirs of a Medieval Woman: The Life and Times of Margery Kempe.* San Francisco: Harper & Row, 1964.

Furlong, Monica. *Thérèse of Lisieux.* New York: Pantheon, 1987.

Gaucher, Guy. *The Story of a Life: St. Thérèse of Lisieux.* San Francisco: Harper & Row, 1987.

Greven, Joseph. *Die Anfänge der Beginen: ein Beitrag zur Geschichte der Volksfrömmigkeit und des Ordenswesens im Hochmittelalter.* Vorreformationgeschichtliche Forschungen 8. Münster in Westphalia, 1912.

Grundmann, Herbert. *Religiose Bewegungen im Mittelalter.* Hildesheim: Olms, 1961. (For material on Beguines.)

Kieckhefer, Richard. *Unquiet Souls: Fourteenth Century Saints and Their Religious Milieu.* Chicago: University of Chicago Press, 1984.

King, Margaret L. "The Religious Retreat of Isotta Nogarola (1418–1466): Sexism and Its Consequences in the Fifteenth Century." *Signs* 3, no. 4 (Summer 1978): 807–22.

Koch, Gottfried. *Frauenfrage und Ketzertum im Mittelalter: die Frauenbewegung im Rahmen des Katharismus und des Waldensertums und ihre sozialen Wurzeln (12–14 Jahrhundert).* Forschungen zur mittelalterlichen Geschichte, Bd. 9. Berlin: Akademie-Verlag, 1962.

Lincoln, Victoria. *Teresa: A Woman. A Biography of Teresa of Avila.* New York: Paragon House, 1984.

McDonnell, Ernst W. *The Beguines and Beghards in Medieval Culture, with Special Emphasis on the Belgian Scene.* New Brunswick, N.J.: Rutgers University Press, 1954.

McLaughlin, Eleanor. "Women and Medieval Heresy." *Concilium* 111 (1976): 73—90.

Morris, Joan. *The Lady Was a Bishop: The Hidden History of Women with Clerical Ordination and the Jurisdiction of Bishops,* trans. by Paul Barrett. New York: Macmillan, 1973.

Parisse, Michel. *Les nonnes au Moyen Age.* Le Puy, France: Christine Bonneton, 1983.

Perrin, Joseph Marie. *Catherine of Siena.* Westminster, Md.: Newman Press, 1965.

Petroff, Elizabeth. "Medieval Women Visionaries: Seven Stages to Power." *Frontiers* 3, no. 1 (Spring 1978): 34–45.

Raymond of Capua. *The Life of St. Catherine of Siena,* trans. by George Lamb. New York: P. J. Kenedy, 1960.

Reynolds, Roger. "Virgines Subintroductae in Celtic Christianity." *Harvard Theological Review* 61 (1968): 547–66.

Szarmach, Paul E., ed. *An Introduction to the Medieval Mystics of Europe.* Albany, N.Y.: SUNY Press, 1984.

Taylor, H. O. "Mystic Visions of Ascetic Women." *The Mediaeval Mind; A History of the Develop-*

ment of Thought and Emotion in the Middle Ages. New York: Macmillan, 1919.

Undset, Sigrid. *Catherine of Siena*, trans. by Kate Austin-Lund. New York: Sheed & Ward, 1954.

Voices

Angela of Foligno. *Divine Consolation of the Blessed Angela of Foligno*, trans. by Mary G. Steegman. New York: Cooper Square Publishers, 1966.

Bynum, Caroline Walker. "Women Mystics in the Thirteenth Century." *Jesus as Mother: Studies in the Spirituality of the High Middle Ages.* Berkeley, Calif.: University of California Press, 1982.

Catherine of Genoa. *Purgation and Purgatory, the Spiritual Dialogue*, trans. by Serge Hughes. New York: Paulist Press, 1979.

Catherine of Siena. *The Dialogue*, trans. by Suzanne Noffke. New York: Paulist Press, 1980.

—————. *The Prayers of Catherine of Sienna.* New York: Paulist Press, 1983.

Hadewijch of Antwerp. *Hadewijch. The Complete Works*, trans. by Mother Columba Hart. New York: Paulist Press, 1980.

Harley, Marta Powell. *A Revelation of Purgatory by an Unknown Fifteenth Century Woman Visionary: Introduction, Critical Text and Translation.* Lewiston, N.Y.: Edwin Mellen Press, 1986.

Hildegard of Bingen. *Hildegard of Bingen's Book of Divine Works with Music and Letters*, ed. by Matthew Fox. Santa Fe: Bear & Co., 1987.

—————. *Scivias*, trans. by Bruce Hozeski. Santa Fe: Bear & Co., 1986.

Julian of Norwich. *Showings*, trans. by Edmund Colledge and James Walsh. New York: Paulist Press, 1978.

—————. *Revelations of Divine Love*, ed. by Roger L. Roberts. Wilton, Conn.: Morehouse-Barlow Co., 1982.

Kempe, Margery. *The Book of Margery Kempe*, ed. by Sanford Brown Meech. Oxford, England: Oxford University Press, 1940.

Llewelyn, Robert, ed. *Julian: Woman of Our Day.* Mystic, Conn.: Twenty-Third Publications, 1987.

Mechtild of Magdeburg. *The Revelations of Mechtild of Magdeburg (1210–1297)* or *The Flowing Light of the Godhead*, trans. by Lucy Menzies (a partial translation). London: Longmans, Green, 1953.

Newman, Barbara. *Sister of Wisdom: St. Hildegard's Theology of the Feminine.* Berkeley, Calif.: University of California Press, 1987.

Petroff, Elizabeth Alvilda. *Medieval Women's Visionary Literature.* New York: Oxford University Press, 1986.

Radice, Betty, ed. and trans. *The Letters of Abelard and Heloise.* Baltimore, Md.: Penguin Books, 1974.

Scudder, Vida Dutton, ed. and trans. *Saint Catherine of Siena as Seen in Her Letters.* New York: E. P. Dutton, 1905.

Teresa of Avila. *The Complete Works of St. Teresa of Jesus*, trans. and ed. by E. Allison Peers. London, New York: Sheed & Ward, 1957.

—————. *The Life of Teresa of Jesus: The Autobiography of St. Teresa of Avila*, trans. and ed. by E. Allison Peers. Garden City, N.Y.: Doubleday & Co., 1960.

—————. *The Letters of St. Teresa of Jesus*, trans. by E. Allison Peers. London: Sheed and Ward, 1980.

Thérèse of Liseux. *Autobiography of St. Thérèse of Liseux. The Story of a Soul*, trans. by John Beevers. Garden City, N.Y.: Doubleday & Co., 1957.

Thiébaux, Marcelle, trans. *The Writings of Medieval Women.* New York: Garland Publishing, 1987.

Wilson, Katharina, ed. *Medieval Women Writers.* Athens, Ga.: University of Georgia Press, 1984.

EUROPEAN REFORMATION TO MODERN EUROPE

Bainton, Roland H. *Women of the Reformation in Germany and Italy.* Minneapolis: Augsburg Publishing House, 1971.

—————. *Women of the Reformation in France and England.* Minneapolis: Augsburg Publishing House, 1973.

—————. *Women of the Reformation, from Spain to Scandinavia.* Minneapolis: Augsburg Publishing House, 1977.

Booth Tucker, Frederick. *The Life of Catherine Booth: The Mother of the Salvation Army.* London: Salvation Army Printing Works, 1893.

Corrigan, D. Felicitas. *The Nun, the Infidel and the Superman: The Remarkable Friendships of Dame Laurentia McLachlan with Sydney Cockerell, Bernard Shaw, and Others.* Chicago: University of Chicago Press, 1985.

Greaves, Richard L. "The Role of Women in Early English Nonconformity." *Church History* 52, no. 3 (September 1983): 299–311.

Irwin, Joyce L. *Womanhood in Radical Protestantism 1525–1675.* Lewiston, N.Y.: Edwin Mellen Press, 1979.

Johnson, Dale A., ed. *Women in English Religion, 1700–1925.* Lewiston, N.Y.: Edwin Mellen Press, 1983.

Malmgreen, Gail, ed. *Religion in the Lives of English Women, 1760–1930.* Bloomington, Ind.: Indiana University Press, 1986.

Maritain, Räissa. *Räissa's Journal.* Albany, N.Y.: Magi Books, 1974.

Prelinger, Catherine M. *Charity, Challenge, and Change: Religious Dimensions of the Mid-Nineteenth-Century Women's Movement in Germany.* Westport, Conn.: Greenwood Press, 1987.

Stendahl, Brita K. *The Force of Tradition: a Case Study of Women Priests in Sweden.* Philadelphia: Fortress Press, 1985.

Thomas, Keith. "Women & The Civil War Sects." *Past and Present* (April 1958): 43–62.

Warnicke, Retha M. *Women of the English Renaissance and Reformation.* Westport, Conn.: Greenwood Press, 1983.

Williams, Ethyn Morgan. "Women Preachers in the Civil War." *Journal of Modern History* 4 (1929): 561–69.

AMERICAN CHRISTIANITY

General

James, Janet Wilson. *Women in American Religion.* Philadelphia: University of Pennsylvania Press, 1980.

Porterfield, Amanda. *Feminine Spirituality in America: From Sarah Edwards to Martha Graham.* Temple University Press, 1980.

Ruether, Rosemary and Rosemary Keller. *Women and Religion in America.* Vol. I, *The Nineteenth Century* (San Francisco: Harper & Row, 1981); Vol. II, *The Colonial and Revolutionary Period* (San Francisco: Harper & Row, 1983); Vol. III, *Nineteen Hundred to Nineteen Sixty-Eight* (San Francisco: Harper & Row, 1986).

Special Aspects

Barfoot, Charles H. and Gerald T. Sheppard. "Prophetic vs. Priestly Religion: The Changing Role of Women Clergy in Classical Pentecostal Churches." *Review of Religious Research* XXII, no. 1 (September): 2–7.

Beaver, R. Pierce. *All Loves Excelling: American Protestant Women in World Missions.* Grand Rapids, Mich.: Eerdmans, 1968.

Brown, Alden V. *Women in the Lay Apostolate: The Grail Movement in the United States 1940–1962.* South Bend, Ind.: Charles and Margaret Hall Center for the Study of American Catholicism, 1984.

Brown, Earl Kent. *Women of Mr. Wesley's Methodism.* Lewiston, N.Y.: Edwin Mellen Press, 1983.

Campbell, Debra. "'I Can't Imagine Our Lady on an Outdoor Platform': Women in the Catholic Street Propaganda Movement." *U.S. Catholic Historian* (Spring-Summer, 1983): 103–14.

Donovan, Mary S. *A Different Call: Women's Ministries in the Episcopal Church, 1850–1920.* Wilton, Conn.: Morehouse-Barlow, 1986.

Douglas, Ann. *The Feminization of American Culture.* New York: Knopf, 1977.

Ewens, Mary. *The Role of the Nun in Nineteenth-Century America.* New York: Arno, 1978.

Friedman, Jean E. *Enclosed Garden: Women and Community in the Evangelical South, 1830–1900.* Chapel Hill, N.C.: University of North Carolina Press, 1985.

Gilkes, Cheryl Townsend. "Together and In Harness: Women's Traditions in the Sanctified Church." *Signs* 10, no. 4 (Summer 1985): 678–99.

Grimshaw, Patricia. "Christian Woman, Pious Wife, Faithful Mother, Devoted Missionary: Conflicts in Roles of American Missionary Women in 19th Century Hawaii." *Feminist Studies* 9, no. 3 (Fall 1983): 489–521.

Gundersen, Joan R. "The Local Parish as a Female Institution: The Experience of All Saints Episcopal Church in Frontier Minnesota." *Church History* 55, no. 3 (September 1986): 307–22.

Hardesty, Nancy A. *Women Called to Witness: Evangelical Feminism in the Nineteenth Century.* Nashville, Tenn.: Abingdon Press, 1984.

——————. *"Your Daughters Shall Prophesy": Revivalism and Feminism in the Age of Finney.* University of Chicago, Ph.D. dissertation, 1976.

Hill, Patricia R. *The World Their Household: The American Women's Foreign Mission Movement and Cultural Transformation, 1870–1920.* Ann Arbor, Mich.: University of Michigan Press, 1985.

Hunter, Jane. *The Gospel of Gentility: American Women Missionaries in Turn-of-the-Century China.* New Haven, Conn.: Yale University Press, 1984.

Hyatt, Irwin, Jr. *Our Ordered Lives Confess: Three Nineteenth Century American Missionaries in East Shantung.* Cambridge, Mass.: Harvard University Press, 1976.

Lee, Susan Earls. *Evangelical Domesticity: The Origins of the Woman's National Christian Temperance Union under Frances E. Willard.* Northwestern University, Ph.D. dissertation, 1980.

Montgomery, Helen Barrett. *Western Women in Eastern Lands: An Outline Study of Fifty Years of Woman's Work in Foreign Missions.* New York: Macmillan, 1911.

Myers, Grace Funk. *"Them Missionary Women": or Work in the Southern Mountains.* Hillsdale, Mich.: (s.n.), 1911.

Thomas, Hilah and Rosemary Skinner Keller. *Women in New Worlds. Historical Perspectives on the Wesleyan Tradition*, vols. 1 and 2. Nashville, Tenn.: Abingdon Press, 1981, 1982.

Lives and Voices

Allchin, A. M. *Songs to Her God: Spirituality of Ann Griffiths.* Cambridge, Mass.: Cowley Publications, 1987.

Andrews, William L. *Sisters of the Spirit: Three Black Women's Autobiographies of the Nineteenth Century.* Bloomington, Ind.: Indiana University Press, 1986.

Bozath-Campbell, Alla. *Womanpriest: A Personal Odyssey.* New York: Paulist Press, 1978.

Brown, Annie E. *Religious Works and Travels.* Chester, Pa.: Olin T. Pancost, 1909. (Autobiography of a black evangelist.)

Catherine Thomas of Divine Providence. *My Beloved: The Story of a Carmelite Nun.* New York: McGraw-Hill, 1955.

Coles, Robert. *Dorothy Day: A Radical Devotion.* Reading, Mass.: Addison-Wesley, Merloid Lawrence Book, 1987.

Cromwell, Otelia. *Lucretia Mott.* Cambridge, Mass.: Harvard University Press, 1958.

Curb, Rosemary and Nancy Manahan, eds. *Lesbian Nuns: Breaking Silence.* Tallahassee, Fla.: Naiad Press, 1985.

Dillon, Mary Earhart. *Frances Willard: From Prayers to Politics.* Chicago: University of Chicago Press, 1944.

Fauset, Arthur Huff. *Sojourner Truth: God's Faithful Pilgrim.* Chapel Hill, N.C.: University of North Carolina Press, 1938.

Hare, Lloyd Custer Mayhew. *The Greatest American Woman, Lucretia Mott.* Westport, Conn.: Greenwood Press, 1970. (First edition, American Historical Society, 1937.)

Harris, Sara. *The Sisters: The Changing World of the American Nun.* Indianapolis, New York: Bobbs-Merrill, 1970.

Heywood, Carter. *A Priest Forever: The Formation of a Woman and Priest.* New York: Harper & Row, 1976.

Isasi-Díaz, Ada María and Yolanda Tarango, eds. *Hispanic Women: Prophetic Voice in the Church.* San Francisco: Harper & Row, 1988.

Johnson, Clifton H. *God Struck Me Dead: Religious Conversion Experiences and Autobiographies of Ex-Slaves.* Philadelphia, Pa.: Pilgrim Press, 1969. (About half on women.)

Kimball, Gayle. *The Religious Ideas of Harriet Beecher Stowe. Her Gospels of Womanhood.* Lewiston, N.Y.: Edwin Mellen Press, 1982.

King, Coretta Scott. *My Life With Martin Luther King, Jr.* New York: Holt, Rinehart & Winston, 1969.

Lawless, Elaine J. *We are Peculiar People: Women's Voices and Folk Tradition in a Pentecostal Church.* Lexington, Ky.: University Press of Kentucky, 1987.

McPherson, Aimee Semple. *The Story of My Life.* Waco, Tex.: Word, 1973.

Milhaven, Annie Lally. *The Inside Stories: Thirteen Valiant Women Challenging the Church*. Mystic, Conn.: Twenty-Third Publications, 1987.

Mollenkott, Virginia Ramey, ed. *Women of Faith in Dialogue*. New York: Crossroad, 1987.

Mott, Lucretia. *Lucretia Mott: The Complete Speeches and Sermons*, ed. by Dana Greene. Lewiston, N.Y.: Edwin Mellen Press, 1980.

Numbers, Ronald L. *Prophetess of Health: A Study of Ellen G. White*. New York: Harper & Row, 1976.

Quiñonez, Lora, ed. *Starting Points: Six Essays Based on the Experience of U.S. Women Religious*. Washington, D.C.: Leadership Conference of Women Religious of the U.S.A., 1980.

Raser, Harold E. *Phoebe Palmer: Her Life and Thought*. Lewiston, N.Y.: Edwin Mellen Press, 1987.

Sexton, Lydia. *Autobiography of Lydia Sexton*. New York: Garland, 1987. (First edition, United Brethren Publishing House, 1882.)

Smedley, Katherine. *Martha Schofield and the Re-education of the South, 1839–1916*. Lewiston, N.Y.: Edwin Mellen Press, 1987.

Smith, Amanda. *An Autobiography: The Story of the Lord's Dealings with Mrs. Amanda Smith, the Colored Evangelist*. Chicago: Meyer & Bros., 1893. Reprinted Nobelsville, Ind.: Newby Book Room, 1972.

Sweet, Leonard I. *Minister's Wife: Her Role in Nineteenth Century Evangelicalism*. Philadelphia, Pa.: Temple University Press, 1982.

Truth, Sojourner. *The Narrative of Sojourner Truth, A Bondswoman of Olden Times Emancipated by the New York Legislature in the Early Part of the Present Century, with a History of Her Labors and Correspondence*. New York: Arno Press, 1968; originally published 1875.

Warner, Wayne E. *The Woman Evangelist: The Life and Times of Charismatic Evangelist Maria B. Woodworth-Etter*. Metuchen, N.J.: Scarecrow Press, 1986.

Wheatly, Richard. *The Life and Letters of Mrs. Phoebe Palmer*. New York: Garland, 1984. (First edition, W. C. Palmer, Jr., 1896.)

White, Alma. *The New Testament Church*. New Jersey: Pentecostal Union, 1912.

Wisbey, Herbert Andrew. *Pioneer Prophetess: Jemima Wilkinson, The Publick Universal Friend*. Ithaca, N.Y.: Cornell University Press, 1964.

Zanotti, Barbara, ed. *A Faith of One's Own: Explorations by Catholic Lesbians*. Freedom, Calif.: The Crossing Press, 1986.

American Sects and Utopias

General

Kern, Louis J. *An Ordered Love: Sex Roles and Sexuality in Victorian Utopias—the Shakers, the Mormons, and the Oneida Community*. Chapel Hill, N.C.: University of North Carolina Press, 1981.

Rohrlich, Ruby and Elaine Hoffman Baruch. *Women in Search of Utopia: Mavericks and Mythmakers*. New York: Schocken, 1984. (Mostly American—some cross-cultural.)

Adventists

Covington, Ava Marie. *They Also Served: Studies of Pioneer Women of the Advent Movement*. Washington, D.C.: Review & Herald, 1940.

Criss, Lillian M. *That Tent by the Sawdust Pile*. Mountain View, Calif.: Pacific Press Pub. Assoc., 1977.

Fahrner, Mary. *Way of the Cross—Where It Led Me: The Story of a Franciscan Nun*. Mountain View, Calif.: Pacific Press Pub. Assoc., 1977.

Fassett, O. R. *The Biography of Mrs. L. E. Fassett, a Devoted Christian, a Useful Life*. Boston: Advent Christian Publishing Society, 1885.

Graham, Roy E. *Ellen G. White, Co-founder of the Seventh-Day Adventist Church*. New York: P. Lang, 1985.

Noorbergen, Rene. *Ellen G. White, Prophet of Destiny*. New Canaan, Conn.: Keats Publishing, 1972.

Osmunson, Robert L. *Hannah: True Story of a Spirited Oklahoma Girl's Struggle for Life, Love and Peace with God*. Mountain View, Calif.: Pacific Press Pub. Assoc., 1976.

Zerne, Winnie. *Maria, Daughter of Shadow*. Mountain View, Calif.: Pacific Press Pub. Assoc., 1975.

Christian Science

Eddy, Mary Baker. *Miscellaneous Writings, 1883–1896*. Boston: A. V. Stuart, 1911.

Hansen, Penny. *Woman's Hour: Feminist Implications of Mary Baker Eddy's Christian Science*

Movement (1885–1910). University of California, Irvine, Ph.D. dissertation, 1981.

Peel, Robert. *Mary Baker Eddy: The Years of Authority.* New York: Holt, Rinehart & Winston, 1980.

——————. *Mary Baker Eddy: The Years of Discovery.* New York: Holt, Rinehart & Winston, 1966.

——————. *Mary Baker Eddy: The Years of Trial.* New York: Holt, Rinehart & Winston, 1971.

(Other biographies of Mary Baker Eddy are also available.)

Latter-Day Saints

Beecher, Maureen Ursenbach and Lavinia Fielding Anderson. *Sisters in Spirit: Mormon Women in Historical and Cultural Perspective.* Urbana, Chicago: University of Illinois Press, 1987.

Foster, Laurence. "From Frontier Activism to Neo-Victorian Domesticity: Mormon Women in the Nineteenth and Twentieth Centuries." *Journal of Mormon History* 6 (1979): 3–21.

Johnson, Sonia. *From Housewife to Heretic.* New York: Doubleday, 1981.

Warenski, Marilyn. *Patriarchs and Politics: The Plight of the Mormon Woman.* New York: McGraw-Hill, 1978.

Oneida

DeMaria, Richard. *Communal Love at Oneida: A Perfectionist Vision of Authority, Property and Sexual Order.* Lewiston, N.Y.: Edwin Mellen Press, 1978.

Kinsley, Jessie Catherine. *A Lasting Spring: Jessie Catherine Kinsley, Daughter of the Oneida Community.* Syracuse, N.Y.: Syracuse University Press, 1983.

Quakers: Europe and America

Brailsford, Mabel R. *Quaker Women, 1650–1690.* London Duckworth & Co., 1915.

Fell, Margaret. *A Brief Collection of Remarkable Passages and Occurrences Relating to the Birth, Education, Life, Conversion, Travels, Services and Deep Sufferings of that Ancient, Eminent, and Faithful Servant of the Lord, Margaret Fell.* London: J. Sowle, 1710.

Lutz, Howard T., ed. and trans. *Reality and Radiance: Selected Autobiographical Works of Emilia Fogelklou.* Richmond, Ind.: Friends United Press, 1987.

Manners, Emily. *Elizabeth Hooten: First Quaker Woman Preacher (1600–1672).* London: Headley Brothers, 1914.

Rogers, Horatio. *Mary Dyer of Rhode Island: The Quaker Martyr that was Hanged on Boston Common, June 1, 1660.* Providence, R.I.: Preston & Rounds, 1896.

Ross, Isabel. *Margaret Fell: Mother of Quakerism.* London, New York and Toronto: Longmans Green, 1949.

Stoneburner, John and Carol Stoneburner, eds. *The Influence of Quaker Women on American Society: Biographical Studies.* Lewiston, N.Y.: Edwin Mellen Press, 1986.

Shakers

Campion, Nardi Reeder. *Ann the Word: The Life of Mother Ann Lee, Founder of the Shakers.* Boston, Toronto: Little, Brown, 1976.

Proctor-Smith, Marjorie. *Women in Shaker Community and Worship: A Feminist Analysis of the Uses of Religious Symbolism.* Lewiston, N.Y.: Edwin Mellen Press, 1985.

Spiritualists

Farnell, Earl Wesley. *The Unhappy Medium: Spiritualism and the Life of Margaret Fox.* Austin, Tex.: University of Texas Press, 1964.

Green, Frances H. *Biography of Mrs. Semantha Mettler, The Clairvoyant, Beginning a History of Spiritual Development and Containing an Account of the Wonderful Cures Performed Through Her Agency.* New York: The Harmonial Association, 1853.

Kingsford, Anna Bonus. *The Perfect Way, or the Finding of Christ.* London: Field & Tuer, 1882.

Maitland, Edward. *Anna Kingsford: Her Life, Letters, Diary, and Work.* 2 vols. London: G. Redway, 1896.

WICCA/Western Pagan

Adler, Margot. *Drawing Down the Moon: Witches, Druids, Goddess-Worshippers, and Other Pagans in America Today.* Boston: Beacon, 1981.

Starhawk. *The Spiral Dance: A Rebirth of the Ancient Religion of the Great Goddess.* San Francisco: Harper & Row, 1979.

——————. *Dreaming the Dark: Magic, Sex, and Politics.* Boston: Beacon Press, 1982.

Feminist Critique of Religion (America) and Feminist Theology

Bushnell, Katherine C. *God's Word to Women: One Hundred Bible Studies on Women's Place in the Divine Economy.* Piedmont, Oakland, Calif.: published by author, n.d. Reprint North-Collins, N.Y.: Ray B. Munson, 1976.

Carr, Anne E. *Transforming Grace: Christian Tradition and Women's Experience.* San Francisco: Harper & Row, 1988.

Christ, Carol P. *Diving Deep and Surfacing: Women Writers on Spiritual Quest.* Boston: Beacon, 1980.

—————. *Laughter of Aphrodite: Reflections on a Journey to the Goddess.* San Francisco: Harper & Row, 1987.

Christ, Carol and Judith Plaskow, eds. *Womanspirit Rising: A Feminist Reader in Religion.* San Francisco: Harper & Row, 1979.

Daly, Mary. *Beyond God the Father: Toward a Philosophy of Woman's Liberation.* Boston: Beacon, 1973.

—————. *The Church and the Second Sex: With a New Post-Christian Introduction.* Rev. ed. San Francisco: Harper & Row, 1975.

—————. *Gyn/ecology: The Metaethics of Radical Feminism.* Boston: Beacon, 1979.

—————. *Pure Lust: Elemental Feminist Philosophy.* Boston: Beacon, 1984.

Fiorenza, Elisabeth Schüssler. *Bread Not Stone: The Challenge of Feminist Biblical Interpretation.* Boston: Beacon, 1984.

—————. *In Memory of Her: A Feminist Theological Reconstruction of Christian Origins.* New York: Crossroad, 1983.

Gage, Matilda Johnson. *Woman, Church and State: The Original Exposé of Male Collaboration Against the Female Sex.* Watertown, Me.: Persephone Press, 1980.

Goldenberg, Naomi R. *Changing of the Gods: Feminism and the End of Traditional Religions.* Boston: Beacon, 1979.

Heschel, Susannah, ed. *On Being a Jewish Feminist: A Reader.* New York: Schocken Books, 1983.

Meadow, Mary Jo and Carol A. Rayburn, eds. *A Time to Weep, A Time to Sing: Faith Journeys of Women Scholars in Religion.* Minneapolis: Winston Press, 1985.

Morton, Nelle. *The Journey is Home.* Boston: Beacon, 1985.

Ochshorn, Judith. *The Female Experience and the Nature of the Divine.* Bloomington, Ind.: Indiana University Press, 1981.

Plaskow, Judith. *Sex, Sin, and Grace: Women's Experience and the Theologies of Reinhold Niebuhr and Paul Tillich.* Washington, D.C.: University Press of America, 1980.

Rabuzzi, Kathryn. *The Sacred and the Feminine: Toward a Theology of Housework.* New York: Seabury Press, 1982.

Ruether, Rosemary Radford. "The Feminist Critique in Religious Studies." *A Feminist Perspective in the Academy: The Difference It Makes.* Special Issue of *Soundings: An Interdisciplinary Journal* 64, no. 4 (Winter 1981): 388–401.

—————. *New Woman—New Earth: Sexist Ideologies and Human Liberation.* New York: Seabury, 1975.

—————. *Sexism and God-Talk: Toward a Feminist Theology.* Boston: Beacon, 1983.

—————, ed. *Womanguides: Readings Toward a Feminist Theology.* Boston, Beacon: 1985.

Russell, Letty M., ed. *Feminist Interpretation of the Bible.* Philadelphia: Westminster, 1985.

Spretnak, Charlene, ed. *The Politics of Women's Spirituality: Essays on the Rise of Spiritual Power within the Feminist Movement.* Garden City, N.Y.: Anchor Books, 1982.

Stanton, Elizabeth Cady. *The Woman's Bible.* New York: Arno Press, 1972. (Original ed. in 2 vols., 1895–98.)

Trible, Phyllis. *God and the Rhetoric of Sexuality.* Philadelphia: Fortress Press, 1978.

—————. *Texts of Terror: Literary-Feminist Readings of Biblical Narratives.* Philadelphia: Fortress Press, 1984.

Walker, Barbara G. *The Skeptical Feminist: Discovering the Virgin, Mother, and Crone.* San Francisco: Harper & Row, 1987.

Washbourn, Penelope. *Becoming Woman: The Quest for Wholeness in Female Experience.* San Francisco: Harper & Row, 1979.

—————. *Seasons of Woman: Song, Poetry, Ritual, Prayer, Myth, Story.* New York: Harper & Row, 1979.

Weaver, Mary Jo. *New Catholic Women: A Contemporary Challenge to Traditional Religious Authority.* San Francisco: Harper & Row, 1985.

Weber, Christin Lore. *Womanchrist: A New Vision of Feminist Spirituality.* San Francisco: Harper & Row, 1987.

ISLAM

General and Contextual

Abbott, Nabia. "Pre-Islamic Arab Queens." *American Journal of Semitic Languages* 58 (1941): 1–22.

————. "Women and the State in Early Islam." *Journal of Near Eastern Studies* 1 (1942): 106–26, 341–68.

————. "Women and the State on the Eve of Islam." *The American Journal of Semitic Languages* 58 (1941): 259–84.

al-Hibri, Azizah, ed. *Women and Islam.* Elmsford, N.Y.: Pergamon Press, 1982.

Aït Sabbah, Fatna. *Woman in the Muslim Unconscious.* New York: Pergamon Press, 1984.

Beck, Lois and Nikki Keddie. *Women in the Muslim World.* Cambridge, Mass.: Harvard University Press, 1978.

Esposito, John L. *Women in Muslim Family Law.* Syracuse, N.Y.: Syracuse University Press, 1982.

Gibb, Sir Hamilton. "Women and the Law." *Correspondances d'Orient Colloque sur la Sociologie Musulmane.* Actes XI–XIV (September 1961): 233–47.

Ginat, J. *Women in Muslim Rural Society: Status and Role in Family and Community.* New Brunswick, N.J.: Transaction Books, 1982.

Jones, V. R. and L. Bevan. *Women in Islam. A Manual with Special Reference to Conditions in India.* Lucknow, India (now Pakistan): Lucknow Publishing House, 1941.

Khan, Mazhar-ul-Haq. *Purdah and Polygamy. A Study of the Social Pathology of the Muslim Society.* Pakistan: Imperial Press, 1972.

Levy, Reuben. *The Social Structure of Islam.* Cambridge, England: Cambridge University Press, 1957.

Minai, Naila. *Women in Islam: Tradition and Transition in the Middle East.* New York: Seaview Books, 1981.

Minces, Juliette. *The House of Obedience: Women in Arab Society.* London: Zed Books, 1982.

Siddiqi, Mohammad Mazheruddin. *Women in Islam.* Lahore: Institute of Islamic Culture, 1952, 1975.

Smith, Jane I., ed. *Women in Contemporary Muslim Societies.* Lewisburg, Pa: Bucknell University Press, 1980. (Two articles specifically addressed to religion; others on women under Muslim laws.)

————. "Women in Islam: Equity, Equality and the Search for the Natural Order." *Journal of the American Academy of Religion* 47, no. 4 (December 1979): 517–38.

Waddy, Charis. *Women in Muslim History.* London, New York: Longman, 1980.

Lives and Voices

Abbott, Nabia. *Aishah—The Beloved of Mohammed.* Chicago: University of Chicago Press, 1942.

Abu-Lugod, Lila. *Veiled Sentiments: Honor and Poetry in a Bedouin Society.* Berkeley, Calif.: University of California Press, 1986.

Brij Bhushan, Jamila. *Muslim Women, in Purdah and Out of It.* New Delhi: Vikas Publishing House, 1980.

Callaway, Barbara. *Muslim Hausa Women in Nigeria: Tradition and Change.* Syracuse, N.Y.: Syracuse University Press, 1987.

Davis, Susan Schaefer. *Patience and Power: Women's Lives in a Moroccan Village.* Cambridge, Mass.: Schenkman Press, 1983.

el Sa'dāwī, Nawāl. *The Hidden Face of Eve: Women in the Arab World,* trans. and ed. by Irene Gendzier. Boston: Beacon Press, 1982.

Fernea, Elizabeth Warnock. *Guests of the Sheik: An Ethnography of an Iraqi Village.* Garden City, N.Y.: Doubleday and Co., 1965.

————. *A Street in Marrakesh.* Garden City, N.Y.: Doubleday, 1975.

————. *Women and the Family in the Middle East: New Voices of Change.* Austin: University of Texas Press, 1985.

Fernea, Elizabeth Warnock and Basima Qattan Bezirgan. *Middle Eastern Muslim Women Speak.* Austin, London: University of Texas Press, 1977.

Fernea, R. and E. Fernea. "Variation in Religious Observance among Islamic Women." *Scholars, Saints and Sufis,* ed. by Nikki Keddie. Berkeley, Calif.: University of California Press, 1972.

Hansen, Henry Harald. *Daughters of Allah: among Moslem Women in Kurdistan (Iraq).* London: Allen & Unwin, 1960.

Jeffery, Patricia. *Frogs in a Well: Indian Women in Purdah.* London: Zed Press, 1979.

Maudoodi, Syed Abul 'Ala. *Purdah and the Status of Women in Islam.* Maulana, Pakistan: Islamic Publications, 1972.

Mernissi, Fatima. *Beyond the Veil: Male-Female Dynamics in a Modern Muslim Society.* New York: Schenkman Pub. Co., distrib. Halstead Press, 1975; 2d ed., Bloomington, Ind.: Indiana University Press, 1987.

Sanasarian, Eliz. *The Women's Rights Movement in Iran: Mutiny, Appeasement, and Repression from 1900 to Khomeini.* New York: Praeger, 1982.

Smith, Margaret. *Rabia the Mystic and Her Fellow Saints in Islam.* 2d ed. New York: Cambridge University Press, 1984.

Stern, Gertrude H. "The First Women Converts in Early Islam." *Islamic Culture* 13 (1939): 298.

Tabari, Azar and Nahid Yeganeh, eds. *In the Shadow of Islam: The Women's Movement in Iran.* London: Zed Press, 1982.

Tabari, Azar. "The Women's Movement in Iran: A Hopeful Prognosis," *Feminist Studies* 12, no. 2 (Summer 1986): 343–60.

Tweedie, Irina. *Chasm of Fire: A Woman's Experience of Liberation through the Teaching of a Sufi Master.* Wilshire, Great Britain: Element Books, 1979.

Vreede-de Stuers, Cora. *Parda. A Study of Muslim Women's Life in Northern India.* Assen, Netherlands: Van Gorcum, 1968.

Wikan, Unni. *Behind the Veil in Arabia: Women in Oman.* Baltimore, Md.: Johns Hopkins University Press, 1982.

JUDAISM

General and Contextual

Baum, Charlotte, et al. *The Jewish Woman in America.* New York: New American Library, 1977.

Biale, Rachel. *Women and Jewish Law: An Exploration of Women's Issues in Halakhic Sources.* New York: Schocken Books, 1984.

Brayer, Menachem M. *The Jewish Woman in Rabbinic Literature: A Psychosocial Perspective.* Hoboken, N.J.: Ktav Publishing House, 1986.

————. *The Jewish Woman in Rabbinic Literature: A Psychohistorical Perspective.* Hoboken, N.J.: Ktav Publishing House, 1986.

Falk, Marcia. *Jewish Wife.* Binghamton, N.Y.: Bellevue Press, 1975.

Falk, Ze'ev W. *Jewish Matrimonial Law in the Middle Ages.* London: Oxford University Press, 1966.

Fuchs, Stephen. *The Expansion of Women's Rights During the Period of the Misnah.* Hebrew Union College, Cincinnati, Ph.D. thesis, 1974.

Greenberg, Blu. *On Women and Judaism: A View from Tradition.* Philadelphia: The Jewish Publication Society of America, 1981.

Kahana, Kopel. *The Theory of Marriage in Jewish Law.* Leiden, Netherlands: E. J. Brill, 1966.

Lacks, Roslyn. *Women and Judaism: Myth, History and Struggle.* Garden City, N.Y.: Doubleday & Co., 1980.

Loewe, Raphael. *The Position of Women in Judaism.* London: S.P.C.K., 1966.

Meiselman, Moshe. *Jewish Woman in Jewish Law.* Library of Jewish Law and Ethics, No. 6. Hoboken, N.J.: Ktav Publishing House, 1975.

Neusner, Jacob. *A History of the Mishnaic Law of Women.* Studies in Judaism in Late Antiquity, vol. 33, Leiden, Netherlands: E. J. Brill, 1980.

Swidler, Leonard J. *Women in Judaism: The Status of Women in Formative Judaism.* Metuchen, N.J.: Scarecrow Press, 1976.

Trenchard, Warren C. *Ben Sira's View of Women: A Literary Analysis.* Chico, Calif.: Scholars Press, 1982.

See also Reuther, *Religion and Sexism*; Reuther and Keller, *Women and Religion in America*; and Reuther & McLaughlin, *Women of Spirit* in section of this listing titled *CHRISTIANITY* (General). Each of these volumes has a limited number of essays on Jewish women.

Lives and Voices

Arendt, Hannah. *Rahel Varnhagen: The Life of a Jewess.* London: East and West Library, 1957.

Brooten, Bernadette. *Women Leaders in the Ancient Synagogue: Inscriptional Evidence and Background Issues.* Chico, Calif.: Scholars Press, 1983.

Hazleton, Lesley. *Israeli Women: The Reality Behind the Myths.* New York: Simon and Schuster, 1977.

Henry, Sondra and Emily Tate, eds. *Written Out of History: A Hidden Legacy of Jewish Women Revealed Through Their Writings and Letters.* New York: Bloch Publishing Co., 1978.

Kaplan, Marion A. *The Jewish Feminist Movement in Germany: The Campaigns of the Jüdischer Frauenbund, 1904–1938.* Westport, Conn.: Greenwood Press, 1979.

Kaye/Kantrowitz, Melanie and Irena Klepfisz, eds. *The Tribe of Dina: A Jewish Women's Anthology.* Montpelier, Vt.: Sinister Wisdom Books, 1986.

Koltun, Elizabeth, ed. *The Jewish Woman: New Perspectives.* New York: Schocken Books, 1976.

Lerner, Anne Lapidus. *"Who Hast Not Made Me a Man": The Movement for Equal Rights for Women in American Jewry.* New York: American Jewish Committee, 1977.

Marcus, Jacob R. *The American Jewish Woman: A Documentary History.* Cincinnati: Ktav Publishing House, Inc., 1981.

——————. *The American Jewish Woman, 1654–1980.* Cincinnati: Ktav Publishing, 1981.

Morton, Leah. *I Am a Woman and a Jew.* New York: Arno Press, 1969.

Priesand, Sally. *Judaism and the New Woman.* New York: Behrman House, 1975.

Senesh, Hannah. *Hannah Senesh—Her Life and Diary*, trans. by Marta Cohn. New York: Schocken Books, 1973.

Sochen, June. *Consecrate Every Day: The Public Lives of Jewish American Women 1880–1980.* Albany, N.Y.: SUNY Press, 1981.

Umansky, Ellen M. *Lily Montagu and the Development of Liberal Judaism: From Vision to Vocation.* Lewiston, N.Y.: Edwin Mellen Press, 1983.

——————, ed. *Lily Montagu. Sermons, Addresses, Letters and Prayers.* Lewiston, N.Y.: Edwin Mellen Press, 1985.

Weiss, Avraham. *Women's Prayer Groups: A Halakhic Analysis.* Hoboken, N.J.: Ktav Publishing House, 1987.

NATIVE AMERICAN

Allen, Paula Gunn. *The Sacred Hoop: Recovering the Feminine in American Indian Traditions.* Boston: Beacon Press, 1986.

Bourque, Susan Carolyn and Kay Barbara Warren. *Women of the Andes: Patriarchy and Social Change in Two Peruvian Towns.* Ann Arbor, Mich.: University of Michigan Press, 1981.

Brant, Beth. *A Gathering of Spirit: Writing and Art by North American Indian Women.* Rockland, Me.: Sinister Wisdom Books, 1984.

Buss, Fran Leeper. *La Partera: Story of a Midwife.* Ann Arbor, Mich.: University of Michigan Press, 1980.

Frisbie, Charlotte Johnson. *Kinaald'a: A Study of the Navaho Girls' Puberty Ceremony.* Middletown, Conn.: Wesleyan University Press, 1967.

Hungry Wolf, Beverly. *The Ways of My Grandmothers.* New York: Morrow, 1980.

Jones, David E. *Sanapia: Comanche Medicine Woman.* New York: Holt, Rinehart & Winston, 1972; originally published in 1900.

Landes, Ruth. *The Ojibwa Woman: Male and Female Life Cycles among the Ojibwa Indians of Western Ontario.* New York: W. W. Norton and Co., 1971; originally published in 1938.

Linderman, Frank B. *Pretty-Shield: Medicine Woman of the Crows.* Lincoln, Neb.: University of Nebraska Press, 1972.

Lurie, Nancy O., ed. *Mountain Wolf Woman, Sister of Crashing Thunder: The Autobiography of a Winnebago Indian.* Ann Arbor, Mich.: University of Michigan Press, 1961.

Marcos, Sylvia. "Curing and Cosmology: The Challenge of Popular Medicines." *Development: Seeds of Change* (1987): 20–25. (On women healers in Mexico.)

Murphy, Yolanda, and Robert F. Murphy. *Women of the Forest.* New York: Columbia University Press, 1974.

Niethammer, Carolyn. *Daughters of the Earth: The Lives and Legends of American Indian Women.* New York: Macmillan, 1977.

Powers, Marla N. *Oglala Women: Myth, Ritual and Reality.* Chicago: University of Chicago Press, 1986.

Silverblatt, Irene. *Moon, Sun and Witches: Gender Ideologies and Class in Inca and Colonial Peru.* Princeton, N.J.: Princeton University Press, 1987.

Steiner, Stan, ed. *Spirit Woman: The Diaries of Bonita Wa Wa Calacaw Nuñez, an American Indian.* San Francisco: Harper & Row, 1980.

Taylor, Pat Ellis. *Border Healing Women: The Story of Jewel Babb.* Austin: University of Texas Press, 1981.

Underhill, Ruth M. *Papago Woman.* New York: Holt, Rinehart & Winston, 1979.

——————. "Woman Power." *Red Man's Religion: Beliefs and Practices of the Indians North of Mexico.* Chicago: University of Chicago Press, 1965.

Ywahoo, Dhyani. *Voices of Our Ancestors: Cherokee Teachings from the Wisdom Fire.* Boston: Shambhala, 1987.

THEOSOPHY

Blavatsky, Helen Petrovna Hahn-Hahn. *The Letters of H. P. Blavatsky to A. P. Sinnett, and Other Miscellaneous Letters*, ed. by A. T. Barker. Pasedena, Calif.: Theosophical University Press, 1973.

Despard, C. *Theosophy and the Women's Movement.* London: Theosophical Publishing Society, 1913.

Murphet, Howard. *When Daylight Comes: A Biography of Helena Petrovna Blavatsky.* Wheaton, Ill.: Theosophical Publishing House, 1975.

Nethercot, Arthur Hobart. *The First Five Lives of Annie Besant.* Chicago: University of Chicago Press, 1960.

—————. *The Last Four Lives of Annie Besant.* Chicago: University of Chicago Press, 1963.

Symonds, John. *The Lady with the Magic Eyes: Madame Blavatsky, Medium and Magician.* New York: T. Yoseloff, 1960.

Wessinger, Catherine Lowman. *Annie Besant and Progressive Messianism (1847–1933).* Lewiston, N.Y.: Edwin Mellen Press, 1988.

See also the works of Blavatsky and Besant.

BIBLIOGRAPHIES

Al-Qazzaz, Ayad. *Women in the Middle East and North Africa: An Annotated Bibliography.* Austin, Texas: University of Texas, Center for Middle Eastern Studies, 1977.

Bass, Dorothy C. and Sandra Hughes Boyd. *Women in American Religious History: An Annotated Bibliography and Guide to Sources.* Boston: G. K. Hall, 1986.

Cantor, Aviva. *A Bibliography on the Jewish Woman: A Comprehensive and Annotated Listing of Works Published 1900–1985.* Fresh Meadows, N.Y.: Biblio Press, 1987.

Carson, Anne. *Feminist Spirituality and the Feminine Divine: An Annotated Bibliography.* Trumansburg, N.Y.: The Crossing Press, 1986.

Fan, Kok-sim. *Women in Southeast Asia: A Bibliography.* Boston: G. K. Hall, 1982.

Fariens, Elizabeth. *Selected Bibliography on Women and Religion 1965–1972.* Cincinnati, Ohio: E. Fariens, 6125 Webbland Place, 1973.

Goodwater, Leanna. *Women in Antiquity: An Annotated Bibliography.* Metuchen, N.Y.: Scarecrow Press, 1975.

Hamelsdorf, Ora. *The Jewish Woman, 1900–1985: A Bibliography.* Sunnyside, N.Y.: Biblio Press, 1980.

Hamelsdorf, Ora and Sandra Adelsberg. *Jewish Women and Jewish Law: Bibliography.* Sunnyside, N.Y.: Biblio Press, 1980; supplement, 1987.

Kendall, Patricia. *Women and the Priesthood: A Selected and Annotated Bibliography.* Philadelphia: Episcopal Diocese of Pennsylvania, 1976.

Knaster, Meri. *Women in Spanish America: An Annotated Bibliogaphy from Pre-Conquest to Contemporary Times.* Boston: G. K. Hall, 1977.

Koh, Hesung Chun. *Korean and Japanese Women: An Analytic Bibliographical Guide.* Westport, Conn.: Greenwood Press, 1982.

Meghdessian, Samira Rafidi. *The Status of the Arab Woman: A Select Bibliography.* Westport, Conn.: Greenwood Press, 1980.

Pandit, Harshida. *Women of India: An Annotated Bibliography.* New York: Garland Publishing, 1985.

Raccagni, Michelle. *The Modern Arab Woman: A Bibliography.* Metuchen, N.J., and London: Scarecrow Press, 1978.

Richardson, Marilyn. *Black Women and Religion: A Bibliography.* Boston: G. K. Hall, 1980.

Ruud, Inger Marie. *Women and Judaism: A Selective Annotated Bibliography.* New York: Garland Publishing, 1988.

Sakala, Carol. *Women of South Asia: A Guide to Resources.* Millwood, N.Y.: Kraus International Publications, 1980.

Vaid, Jyotsna et al. *South Asian Women at Home and Abroad: A Guide to Resources.* Committee on Women in Asian Studies of the Association for Asian Studies, 1984.

Wei, Karen T. *Women in China: A Selected and Annotated Bibliography.* Westport, Conn.: Greenwood Press, 1984.

Young, Katherine K. and Arvind Sharma. *Images of the Feminine—Mythic, Philosophic and Human—in the Buddhist, Hindu and Islamic Traditions: A Bibliography of Women in India.* Chico, Calif.: New Horizons Press, 1974.

Zaretsky, Irving I. *Spirit Possession and Spirit Mediumship in Africa and Afro-America: An Annotated Bibliography.* New York: Garland Publishing, 1978.